Poverty & Race in America

Poverty & Race in America

The Emerging Agendas

Edited by Chester Hartman

LEXINGTON BOOKS

A division of
ROWMAN & LITTLEFIELD PUBLISHERS, INC.
Lanham • Boulder • New York • Toronto • Oxford

LEXINGTON BOOKS

A division of Rowman & Littlefield Publishers, Inc.
A wholly owned subsidiary of The Rowman & Littlefield Publishing Group, Inc.
4501 Forbes Boulevard, Suite 200
Lanham, MD 20706

PO Box 317
Oxford
OX2 9RU, UK

British Library Cataloguing in Publication Information Available

Library of Congress Cataloging-in-Publication Data

Library of Congress Control Number: 2005936905

ISBN-13: 978-0-7391-1418-6 (cloth : alk. paper)
ISBN-10: 0-7391-1418-2 (cloth : alk. paper)
ISBN-13: 978-0-7391-1419-3 (pbk : alk. paper)
ISBN-10: 0-7391-1419-0 (pbk : alk. paper)

Printed in the United States of America

™ The paper used in this publication meets the minimum requirements of American
National Standard for Information Sciences—Permanence of Paper for Printed Library
Materials, ANSI/NISO Z39.48–1992.

Contents

Foreword   xi
    Congressman Jesse L. Jackson, Jr.

Editor's Introduction   xv
    Chester Hartman

Race/Racism   1

Chapter 1: Whites Swim in Racial Preference   3
    Tim Wise

Chapter 2: Diversity Over Justice   7
    Eric Foner

Chapter 3: Remembrance and Change in Philadelphia, Mississippi   9
    James W. Loewen

Chapter 4: Sundown Towns   15
    James W. Loewen

Chapter 5: Minority Exclusion in Small Town America   20
    James H. Johnson, Jr., Ann Moss Joyner and Allan Parnell

Chapter 6: Skewing Democracy: Where the Census Counts Prisoners   25
    Peter Wagner

Chapter 7: Language as Oppression: The English-Only Movement
    in the United States   29
    Andrew Hartman

Chapter 8: Apologies/Reparations   38

Chapter 9: Organizing for Reparations: Lessons from the Holocaust   43
        Marc Masurovsky

Chapter 10: Race Literacy Quiz   49
        Califonia Newsreel

Chapter 11: Reverse Discrimination Quiz   52
        Fred L. Pincus

Poverty   55

Chapter 12: From Poverty to Social Exclusion: Lessons from Europe   57
        Hilary Silver and S.M. Miller

Chapter 13: The Ethno/Racial Context of Poverty in Rural
        and Small Town America   71
        Calvin L. Beale

Chapter 14: Concentration of Poverty Declined in the 1990s   79
        Paul Jargowsky

Chapter 15: The Living Wage: A Progressive Movement in Action   82
        Jared Bernstein and Jeff Chapman

Chapter 16: Children Get Social Security, Too   89
        William E. Spriggs

Chapter 17: The Benefit Bank   93
        Robert Brand

Chapter 18: Race, Poverty and Shared Wealth   96
        Andrew T. Lamas

Chapter 19: Race, Poverty and the Estate Tax   103
        *Gary Bass, Ellen Taylor, Catherine Paskoff Chang
        and Adam Hughes*

Chapter 20: Race, Poverty and "Economic Development" Gone Haywire   111
        Greg LeRoy

Chapter 21: Poverty Quiz   116
        Catholic Campaign for Human Development

Housing 119

Chapter 22: Why Housing Mobility? The Research Evidence Today 121
    Margery Austin Turner and Dolores Acevedo-Garcia

Chapter 23: Racial Disparities in Housing and Health 130
    Dolores Acevedo-Garcia and Theresa L. Osypuk

Chapter 24: A National Gautreaux Program: A Symposium 137
    Alexander Polikoff, Paul L. Wachtel, john a. powell,
    Sudhir Alladi Venkatesh, Sheryll Cashin, George Galster,
    Libby Perl, David Rusk

Chapter 25: The Power and Limits of Place: New Directions
    for Housing Mobility and Research on Neighborhoods 168
    Xavier de Souza Briggs

Chapter 26: Democracy's Unfinished Business: Federal Policy 173
    and the Search for Fair Housing, 1961-68
    David M.P. Freund

Chapter 27: Some Lessons from *Brown* for the Fair Housing Movement 178
    Philip Tegeler

Chapter 28: Race, Poverty and Homeowner Insurance 183
    Gregory D. Squires

Chapter 29: The CLT Model: A Tool for Permanently Affordable
    Housing and Wealth Generation 189
    Gus Newport

Chapter 30: Predatory Lending: Undermining Economic Progress 194
    in Communities of Color
    Mike Calhoun and Nikitra Bailey

Chapter 31: Housing Quiz 199
    California Newsreel

Education 201

Chapter 32: The O'Connor Project: Intervening Early to Eliminate
    the Need for Racial Preferences in Higher Education 203
    Lisbeth B. Schorr

Chapter 33: Why Is School Reform So Hard? 211
    Linda Christensen and Stan Karp

Chapter 34: Socioeconomic School Integration: A Symposium   215
    Richard D. Kahlenberg, Gary Orfield, Theodore M. Shaw,
    Makani Themba-Nixon, john a. powell, S.M. Miller,
    Thomas J. Henderson

Chapter 35: Schools and the Achievement Gap: A Symposium   241
    Richard Rothstein, Pedro A. Noguera, John H. Jackson,
    Jenice L. View, Stan Karp, Wendy Puriefoy, Mark Simon,
    Krista Kafer, Dianne M. Piché/Tamar Ruth

Chapter 36: High Classroom Turnover: How Some Children
    Get Left Behind   269
    Chester Hartman and Alison Leff

Chapter 37: Race, Poverty and Special Education: Apprenticeships
    for Prison Work   273
    Rosa Smith

Chapter 38: Race, Poverty and Virtual Learning   278
    Sharon Johnston and Michelle Kinley

Chapter 39: Race, Poverty and Residential Schools   282
    Heidi Goldsmith

Chapter 40: Race, Poverty and Community Schools   288
    Ira Harkavy and Martin J. Blank

Chapter 41: Education Quiz   296
    Derrick Z. Jackson

Health   299

Chapter 42: What Works: A Fifty-Year Retrospective   301
    David Barton Smith

Chapter 43: Why Is HHS Obscuring a Health Care Gap?   304
    H. Jack Geiger

Chapter 44: Race, Poverty and New Strategies to Control
    the Obesity Epidemic   307
    Anthony Robbins, Wendy E. Parmet and Richard Daynard

Chapter 45: The Contribution of Black-White Health   311
         Differences to the Academic Achievement Gap
         Richard Rothstein and Tamara Wilder

Chapter 46: Eliminating the Slave Health Deficit: Using Reparations
         to Repair Black Health   320
         Vernellia R. Randall

Chapter 47: Health Quiz I   331
         Health Policy Institute

Chapter 48: Health Quiz II   334
         David Barton Smith

Democracy   337

Chapter 49: From Slave Republic to Constitutional Democracy:
         The Continuing Struggle for the Right to Vote 339
         Jamin Raskin

Chapter 50: Voting Right for Immigrants   351
         Catherine Tactaquin

Chapter 51: Bringing American Democracy to America's Capital 357
         DC Vote

Chapter 52: The Birth of the White Corporation   362
         Jeffrey Kaplan

Chapter 53: Democracy Quiz   369
         Peter Kellman

Miscellaneous   371

Chapter 54: Race, Poverty and Hunger   373
         Alison Leff and Alexandra Cawthorne

Chapter 55: Race, Poverty and Youth Development   381
         Carla Roach, Hanh Cao Yu and Heather Lewis-Charp

Chapter 56: Race Poverty and LGBT Youth   387
         L. Michael Gipson

Quiz Answers   396

Contributors   407

PRRAC Board of Directors and Social Science Advisory Board   419

Index   423

Foreword

Congressman Jesse L. Jackson, Jr.

Where does the movement to end poverty and bring about racial justice go from here? Do we need new leadership, new faces or a new direction?

Whatever your conclusion with respect to those questions—whether we need new leaders or continue with the old, whether to project new faces or support the old, and whether to stay the course or move in a new direction—we ought to be able to agree on a common denominator: that we need to put *movement by the people* back into it. That's why *Poverty & Race* and this book are so valuable.

I'm from the school of thought that's saying, whatever the leadership, we need a change in direction. I'm arguing that the traditional civil rights and social justice movements must be honored for their past accomplishments and that they must fight to defend their gains—no doubt about that—but at the same time they must *transition* in a new direction.

We need to move from *civil rights* to *human rights,* and from fighting merely for *legislation* to fighting for *constitutional amendments*.

Clearly, we must continue the daily fight for incremental progressive legislation. But legislation, relatively speaking, is easier to reverse, de-fund, not enforce or otherwise circumvent than are constitutional amendments.

At the same time, constitutional amendments usually *take longer* to achieve, and the effect of Supreme Court interpretations of them *last longer,* which means the exact wording of new amendments is extremely important.

However, there is *never* absolute clear meaning in the broad language of constitutional amendments, and all Supreme Court interpretations are reflective of the political context in which they are decided—i.e., which people are active and moving politically. The exact same language in the Fourteenth Amendment, ratified in 1868, was interpreted one way in *Plessy v. Ferguson* (1896), as "separate but equal," and another way 58 years later in *Brown v. Board of Education* (1954), as "separate but equal is inherently unequal."

But where did I get this harebrained idea of fighting for constitutional amendments as the way of putting *movement* back into the broader coalition fighting for social, political and economic justice?

From the Republicans!

Republicans have a *theme*—less government, lower taxes, strong defense—and *whoever* the candidate is, he or she runs on the theme.

Republicans are on the *offensive*—they run *for* things, even if they're negative and discriminatory (e.g., an anti-gay rights or so-called marriage amendment).

Republicans have a *strategy*—they fight for constitutional rights and put us on the record "for" or "against" them by making us vote in Congress between elections. Then they make it an issue in the next election and run against us, using our vote as the criteria.

Republican *programs* flow from their fight for *rights* (e.g., their so-called partial birth abortion and the denial of federal funds to the poor and women in the military for abortions all come from their campaign for a right to life amendment).

And the Right Wing introduces a bunch of these constitutional amendments. They've introduced a:

- Right to life amendment
- Balanced budget amendment
- Tax limitation amendment
- Term limitation amendment
- Don't desecrate the flag amendment
- Prayer in school amendment
- Ten Commandments in public places amendment
- God in the Pledge of Allegiance amendment
- Religious freedom amendment
- Marriage or anti-gay rights amendment
- Establish English as the official language of the United States amendment
- And they campaign on the belief—and many Americans believe this, rightly or wrongly—that the Second Amendment gives then a right to a gun.

Democrats have elections, too—but every four years, *each presidential candidate provides the theme,* and it varies from election to election. Democrats are on the *defensive*—we run to protect our past gains (e.g., Social Security, 1965 Voting Rights Act), but we're mostly not on the offensive.

Democrats have *no long-term strategy*—we run on *programs*—and Republicans co-opt them, often just before an election (e.g., prescription drugs, homeland security, education, "Leave No Child Behind"—stolen and changed from Marian Wright Edelman's slogan and dream.)

It's highly unlikely that any of these Republican amendments will ever become part of the Constitution. They merely use them to keep their politically conservative base active *during* and *between elections* in their "culture war" over "values."

What *rights* do Democrats fight for? *None!* We fight for *programs!* Democrats have been made so defensive over these absurd proposed constitutional rights and these un-American amendments that we've developed a negative rationale and posture that the Constitution is good just the way it is and we shouldn't change it. Democrats don't seem to be able to distinguish between *good amendments* and *bad amendments*, between *real practical needs* that *should* be addressed with constitutional amendments and *conservative ideological wishes* that *shouldn't*.

Conservative Republicans argue that the Constitution is a *static* document. Yet they propose adding all these amendments to it. That really means they actually see it as a *living* document, even as they say they want judges who are "strict constructionists" who will "interpret" the Constitution as a "non-living document" and not "activist judges" who will "legislate from the bench."

Liberal Democrats *say* the Constitution is a living document, but they *act* like it's static.

The questions to those who believe the Constitution is static and shouldn't be changed are:
- If it's static, when did it become static?
- If it's no longer a living document, when did it die?
- Before or after the first ten Amendments?
- Before or after the Thirteenth, Fourteenth and Fifteenth Amendments?
- Before or after the Twenty-Seventh Amendment?

My suggestion to Democrats is that we need a *theme*—I suggest the idea of building "a more perfect Union"—and a *strategy* that will broaden our political appeal and base beyond our current "special interest" groups (e.g., labor, women, African Americans, Hispanics, Asians, environmentalists, gays and lesbians) to include *all* Americans. And human rights and constitutional amendments, by definition, include all Americans!

Democrats should fight for *human rights* that the American people already believe they have or already believe they should have; and fight to make them *American rights* by putting them in the US Constitution.

Fighting for human rights and constitutional amendments has other advantages as well. They are non-partisan (not Democratic, Republican or Independent), non-ideological (not conservative, liberal or moderate) and nonprogrammatic (they allow for a variety of approaches and programs to achieve the right).

Therefore, I've offered nine constitutional amendments as a *long-term* framework for what Democrats should be fighting for—*one at a time*—a sort of Second Bill of Rights:

The individual *right* to vote
The individual *right* to a public education of equal high quality
The individual *right* to health care of equal high quality
ERA—individual equal *rights* for women
The individual *right* to decent, safe, sanitary and affordable housing
The individual *right* to a clean, safe and sustainable environment
The individual *right* to fair and progressive taxes
The individual *right* to full employment
The individual *right* to elect our President and Vice President directly and do away with the Electoral College

All of my amendments take on "states' rights" and the Tenth Amendment directly—which gives some Democrats problems because, historically, Democrats are the ideological founders and the political party of states' rights, local control and voluntary solutions. That's what slavery was all about—using the Tenth Amendment's ideology of states' rights, local control and voluntary solutions over time to establish and maintain the institution of slavery. The Emancipation Proclamation didn't free the slaves. It took the Thirteenth Amendment to overcome the limitations of the Tenth Amendment.

We need the same thing in regard to overcoming the limitations of the Tenth Amendment with respect to voting, education, health care and the other issues, which my amendments address. It's the only foundation upon which we can build a more perfect Union.

And all of my amendments give Congress the *power* to implement the particular article with appropriate legislation.

A theme of building *A More Perfect Union*, combined with a human rights agenda and constitutional rights *movement,* will keep Democrats and progressives together, on track and busy for a very long time—between elections, as well as election after election.

So whether it's struggling for constitutional amendments, civil rights or racial justice, progress will only come if there's *movement by the people.*

Editor's Introduction

Chester Hartman

This is the third volume containing the best articles and symposia from *Poverty & Race*, the bimonthly newsletter journal of The Poverty & Race Research Action Council (PRRAC), a Washington, DC-based national public interest organization founded in 1990. The first two collections were *Double Exposure: Poverty & Race in America* (1997), Foreword/Preface by Bill Bradley and Julian Bond, and *Challenges to Equality: Poverty & Race in America* (2001), Foreword by Congressman John Lewis (both published by M.E. Sharpe, and both still in print; both under my editorship).

In this new book, we reprint over six dozen pieces (some in symposium form) originally published between mid-2001 and 2005 (many of the articles and commentaries have been updated and revised for this volume). The 91 contributing writers to this collection (whose short biosketches and contact information appear starting on page 407 represent the best of progressive thought and activism on America's two most salient, and seemingly intractable, domestic problems.

PRRAC's mission is to foster an active dialogue between the racial justice and economic justice worlds, and to disseminate and support research on the race*/poverty intersection that in turn supports and makes more effective advocacy work of any sort (community organizing, litigation, legislation, public education, etc.) Details about our mission and accomplishments can be found at www.prrac.org. And a list of our present and past Board of Directors and Social Science Advisory Board members appears starting on page 419.

---

* An orthographic note: With regard to terminology on race and racial categories, we opt to let each author use whatever is her or his word, punctuation, capitalization preference; such usage embodies issues that, for many, have levels of meaning well beyond mere style, and we choose not to impose any arbitrary single format or rule.

While we function in and across many substantive fields, housing and education, which we identify as the key areas where structural racism manifests itself, are our principal focus. But we work on health, criminal justice, immigration, economic development, food and family issues as well—especially the links between and among all of these areas, both for purposes of analysis and policy/programmatic prescriptions.

We very much hope this volume can be a vehicle for stimulating creative thought *and* action to bring about swift and meaningful amelioration of America's historical and continuing twin shames of racism and poverty. The fallout from the August/September 2005 Gulf Coast region hurricanes has forcefully brought race and class disparities and their consequences out into the public arena. Issues of housing, health, jobs and schools—as well as the role and responsibilities of government—are, as of this writing (Fall 2005), out there forcefully. Whether they will stay out there, and produce meaningful solutions, cannot be predicted. We very much hope the current volume can contribute to this awareness and to needed, in some cases radical, reforms.

We gratefully acknowledge the assistance provided by Frank Watkins, Philip Tegeler, Brenda Fleet, Rebekah Park and Angela Parker in assembling this volume. But most especially, we thank Teri Grimwood, who, over two decades, has done wonders to connect this technologically impaired editor/writer to the electronic world, and Alexandra Cawthorne, PRRAC's 2004-05 Bill Emerson National Hunger Fellow, whose high-level work at every step of the way made this book possible. Serena Krombach, Katie Funk and Catherine Forrest of Lexington Books have been a pleasure to work with.

Race/Racism

Chapter 1

Whites Swim in Racial Preference

Tim Wise

Ask a fish what water is and you'll get no answer, and not only because fish can't speak. Even if they were capable of vocalizing a reply, they wouldn't have one for such a question. When water surrounds you every minute of the day, explaining what it is becomes impossible. It simply is: It's taken for granted.

So too with this thing we hear so much about, called "racial preference." While many whites apparently are convinced that the notion originated with affirmative action programs, intended to expand opportunities for historically marginalized people of color, racial preference has actually had a long and very white history.

Affirmative action for whites was embodied in the abolition of European indentured servitude, which left black (and occasionally indigenous) slaves as the only unfree labor in the colonies that would become the US. Affirmative action for whites was the essence of the 1790 Naturalization Act, which allowed any European immigrant to become a full citizen, even while blacks, Asians and American Indians could not. Affirmative action for whites was the guiding principle of segregation, Asian exclusion and the theft of half of Mexico for the fulfillment of Manifest Destiny.

In recent history, affirmative action for whites motivated racially-restrictive housing policies that helped 15 million white families procure homes with FHA loans from the 1930s to the 1960s, while people of color were mostly excluded from the same programs. In other words, on balance, white America is the biggest collective recipient of racial preference in history. Such preference has skewed our laws, shaped our public policy and helped create the glaring inequalities with which we still live.

White racial preference explains why white families, on average, have a net worth eleven times that of black families—a gap that remains substantial even when only comparing families of like size, composition, education and income status. It also helps explain, at least in part, why a full-time black male worker in 2003 made less in real dollar terms than similar white men were earning in 1967. Such realities do not merely indicate the disadvantages faced by blacks, but indeed are evidence of the preferences afforded whites—the necessary flipside of discrimination.

Indeed, the value of preferences to whites over the years is so enormous that the baby-boomer generation of whites is currently in the process of inheriting between $7-10 trillion in assets from their parents and grandparents: property handed down by those who were able to accumulate assets at a time when people of color couldn't. To place this in perspective, we should note that this amount of money is more than all the outstanding mortgage debt, all the credit card debt, all the savings account assets, all the money in IRAs and 401(k) retirement plans, all the annual profits for US manufacturers, and our entire merchandise trade deficit combined.

Yet few whites think of our position as resulting from racial preference. Indeed, we pride ourselves on our hard work and ambition, as if we invented the concepts; as if we have worked harder than the folks who were forced to pick cotton and build levees for free; harder than the Latino immigrants who spend ten hours a day in fields picking strawberries or tomatoes; harder than the (mostly) women of color who clean up messy hotel rooms or change bedpans in hospitals, or the (mostly) men of color who collect our garbage—a crucial service without which we would face not only unpleasant smells but the spread of disease.

We strike the pose of self-sufficiency while ignoring the advantages we have been afforded in every realm of activity: housing, education, employment, criminal justice, politics and business. We ignore that, at every turn, our hard work has been met with access to an opportunity structure to which millions of others have been denied similar access. Privilege, to us, is like water to the fish: invisible precisely because we cannot imagine life without it.

It is that context that best explains the duplicity of the President's critique of affirmative action at the University of Michigan, during the court battle over so-called "racial preferences" at that institution.

President Bush, himself a lifelong recipient of affirmative action—the kind set aside for the rich and mediocre—proclaimed that the school's policies were unfair. Yet in doing so he not only showed a profound ignorance of the Michigan policy, but also made clear the inability of yet another white person to grasp the magnitude of white privilege still in operation—an inability sadly ratified by the Supreme Court when it ruled in favor of the plaintiffs in the Michigan case in June 2003.

To wit, the President, and ultimately the Supreme Court, attacked Michigan's policy of awarding 20 points (on a 150-point evaluation scale) to undergraduate applicants who were members of under-represented minorities, which at U of M means blacks, Latinos and American Indians. To many whites, such a "preference" was blatantly discriminatory. Yet what Bush and the Court failed to mention were the greater numbers of points awarded for other things, and which had the clear effect of preferencing whites to the exclusion of people of color.

For example, Michigan awarded 20 points to any student from a low-income background, regardless of race. Since those points could not be combined with those for minority status (in other words poor blacks don't get 40 points), in effect this was a preference for poor whites. Then Michigan awarded 16 points to students from the Upper Peninsula of the state—a rural and almost completely white area.

Of course, both preferences were fair, based as they were on the recognition that economic status and geography (as with race) can have a profound effect on the quality of schooling one receives, and that no one should be punished for such things that are beyond their control. But note that such preferences, though disproportionately awarded to whites, remained uncriticized throughout the litigation on this case, while preferences for people of color become the target for reactionary anger. Once again, white preference remained hidden because it wasn't called white preference, even if that was the effect.

But that's not all. Ten points were awarded under the Michigan plan to students who attended top high schools, and another eight points were given to students who took an especially demanding AP and Honors curriculum. As with points for those from the Upper Peninsula, these preferences may have been race-neutral in theory, but in practice they were anything but. Because of intense racial isolation (and Michigan's schools are the most segregated in America for blacks, according to research by the Harvard Civil Rights Project), students of color will rarely attend the "best" schools, and on average, schools serving mostly black and Latino students offer only a third as many AP and Honors courses as schools serving mostly whites. So even truly talented students of color would have been unable to access those extra points simply because of where they live, their economic status and ultimately their race, which is intertwined with both.

Then, up to 12 points were awarded for a student's SAT score, which is itself directly correlated with a student's socioeconomic status, which in turn is highly correlated with race in a way that favors whites and disadvantages most students of color.

Four more points were awarded to students with a parent who attended the University of Michigan: a kind of affirmative action with which the President is intimately familiar, and which almost exclusively goes to whites.

In other words, Michigan was offering 20 "extra" points to the typical black, Latino or indigenous applicant, while offering various combinations worth up to 70 extra points for students, almost all of whom would be white. But while the first of these were seen as examples of racial preferences, the second were not, hidden as they were behind the structure of social inequities that limit where people live, where they go to school and the kinds of opportunities they have been afforded.

White preferences, by being the result of the normal workings of a racist society, can remain out of sight and out of mind, while the power of the state is turned against the paltry preferences meant to offset them.

To recognize just how blind so many white Americans are to the workings of white privilege, one need only consider the oft-heard comment by whites that "if I had only been black I would have gotten into my first-choice college." Such a statement not only ignores the fact that whites are more likely than members of any group, even with affirmative action, to get into their first-choice school, but it also presumes, as anti-racist activist Paul Marcus explains, "that if these whites were black, everything else about their life would have remained the same: that it would have made no negative difference as to where they went to school, what their family income was, or anything else."

But this ability to believe that being black would have made no difference (other than a beneficial one when it came time for college), and that being white has made no positive difference, is rooted in privilege itself: the privilege of not having one's intelligence questioned by books like *The Bell Curve*, or one's culture attacked as dysfunctional by politicians and so-called scholars; the privilege of not having to worry about being viewed as "out of place" when driving, shopping, buying a home or attending the University of Michigan; the privilege of not being denied an interview for a job because your name sounds "too black," as a recent study discovered happens often to African-American job-seekers.

So long as those privileges remain firmly in place and the preferential treatment that flows from those privileges continues to work to the benefit of whites, all talk of ending affirmative action is not only premature but a slap in the face to those who have fought and died for equal opportunity.

Chapter 2

Diversity Over Justice

Eric Foner

The Supreme Court's 2003 decision upholding the University of Michigan's affirmative action program was rightly applauded by civil rights advocates. Yet it is important to understand the limitations of the decision. We reprinted, with permission and thanks, Columbia University historian Eric Foner's sober analysis of the decision, originally published in The Nation *(July 14, 2003).*

In the current political climate, the Supreme Court's decision upholding the right of colleges and universities to take race into account in admissions must be considered a victory for those committed to racial justice. Celebration, however, should be tempered by some unpleasant facts about American history and society, and the Court itself.

When first developed in the 1960s, affirmative action formed part of a far broader program for attacking both poverty and racial inequality, including a domestic Marshall Plan to reverse urban decay and create jobs, and government action to end housing segregation and drastically improve urban public education. This program has virtually vanished. Affirmative action, the one surviving element, must be defended, but with no illusions that it alone can adequately address the enduring legacy of 250 years of slavery and a century of Jim Crow. In the long run, the Court's decision will be cause for cheer only if it serves to reinvigorate a broader struggle for racial equality.

Among the Justices, only Ruth Bader Ginsburg seemed willing to face the extent of inequality in America. Her powerful dissent in the undergraduate case forthrightly stated what should be obvious—that race still matters enormously in housing, health care, income, schooling and other areas of American life. Ginsburg directly attacked the conservative sophistry that, under the rallying cry of "colorblindness," conflates affirmative action with past efforts to stigmatize minorities. Programs designed to create greater equality, she writes, cannot be equated with "policies of oppression." Her dissent marks Ginsburg's emergence as an uncompromising voice of liberalism on the Court, something absent since the departure of Thurgood Marshall and William Brennan.

Partly because they assumed, correctly, that Justice Sandra Day O'Connor, a strong critic of the idea of "societal racism," would turn out to be the swing vote in a 5-to-4 decision, Michigan's lawyers decided to emphasize not persistent racial inequality but the educational value of racial diversity. The diversity argument presents affirmative action not as a program that primarily aids minorities but as one that improves the educational environment, a more politically palatable case. But it runs the risk of suggesting that access for nonwhite students is desirable mainly because it enhances the educational experience of whites by exposing them to classmates from different backgrounds. Diversity is undoubtedly a worthy goal. But a single-minded focus on diversity deflects attention from the need to combat the numerous inequalities to which Ginsburg referred.

Most nonwhite students do not attend elite colleges and professional schools that feed the upper echelons of society but public two- and four-year ones. As a recent article in *The Chronicle of Higher Education* makes clear, the greatest threat to educational diversity today arises from the severe cutbacks in public funding imposed on these institutions by cash-strapped state governments. Tuition is rising rapidly, and scholarships are being reduced. A significant drop in minority enrollment will inevitably follow.

O'Connor's opinion suggests that she was strongly influenced by briefs on behalf of affirmative action filed by major corporate executives and retired military officers. They argued that the United States cannot compete in today's global economy, or maintain an effective military, without racially diverse business and military leaders. This argument has a historical precedent. Half a century ago, when *Brown v. Board of Education* was before the Court, the Eisenhower Administration urged the Justices to consider segregation's effect on the world standing of the United States in the Cold War. People of other nations, it declared, "cannot understand how such a practice can exist in a country which professes to be a staunch supporter of freedom, justice, and democracy."

Once again, the international interests of the United States have prompted steps toward greater racial equality at home. The result should be applauded. But we should not lose sight of the fact that corporate globalization has had a devastating impact on the black working class by hastening deindustrialization, and that military service offers many nonwhites the opportunity to advance socially only by taking part in wars abroad. It is a sign of the times that it required an appeal to the demands of globalization and an imperial foreign policy to persuade the Court to uphold affirmative action in higher education.

Chapter 3

Remembrance and Change in Philadelphia, Mississippi

James W. Loewen

June 2004 marked the 40th anniversary of Freedom Summer, which brought a thousand young Americans, mostly white college students, to Mississippi for the summer of 1964. They would instruct African Americans on how to register to vote, teach history and other subjects to black youngsters in "Freedom Schools," and assist the Civil Rights Movement in other ways. Most of all, leaders of the Mississippi movement like Robert Moses hoped that the presence of these volunteers would provide some safety for civil rights workers, who were being beaten and arrested across the state without protection from the federal government or attention from the media.

Four of five Americans alive today were unborn or younger than six in 1964, and since the event is not well taught in high school, where most US history courses dwindle to an end shortly after World War II, let me summarize the tragic beginning of the 1964 summer. Mickey Schwerner, white, Jewish, from New York City, had already been working for the Movement in Meridian, in east Mississippi. James Chaney, a young black Meridian resident, had signed on as a volunteer. On Memorial Day, 1964, they went to Mt. Zion Methodist Church in Neshoba County to talk about voter registration. A few days later, they drove to Oxford, Ohio, where training was going on for the volunteers about to come to Mississippi. On June 16, KKK terrorists, having heard of the earlier meeting, visited Mt. Zion, and beat and intimidated members of a church committee who happened to be meeting there that night. The next day, they burned the church to the ground.

On June 20, Schwerner and Chaney drove back to Mississippi with several summer volunteers, including Andrew Goodman. The next morning, the three drove to Mt. Zion and talked with parishioners about the violence. As they were driving back toward Philadelphia, the county seat, Deputy Sheriff Cecil Price arrested all three for an alleged traffic violation and threw them in jail. They were released at 10 pm, but as they drove out of Philadelphia they were stopped again and delivered into the hands of the KKK. They were never seen alive again.

A terrible Hollywood movie, *Mississippi Burning,* fictionalizes what happened next, making heroes of the FBI. In reality, the FBI had no black agents at all, no office in Mississippi and little enthusiasm to solve the crime. National outcry about the deaths, spurred by letters and telegrams from parents of the 1,000 volunteers, forced FBI Director J. Edgar Hoover to open a Mississippi office, however, and LBJ called out the Navy to search for the bodies. During the summer, while working in northern Wisconsin, I got a letter from my uncle telling me that, according to rumor, the sheriff and deputy sheriff took part, as well as Ku Klux Klansmen, and the bodies were buried in an earthen dam somewhere in Neshoba County. I realized that if my uncle—a Northern professor at Mississippi State University—knew, then everyone in Mississippi knew. Yet the FBI seemed stymied. At last, agents bribed one Klansman to inform on the others, and in December federal authorities charged 19 people with conspiring to interfere with the civil rights of the three victims. Eventually 7 of the 19 were convicted and received sentences of three to ten years but served less than that: Price did four years, for example. Murder is a state crime, of course, but Mississippi never charged anyone.

During the trials and appeals, lasting until 1970, Neshoba County exemplified a closed society. The State of Mississippi never charged anyone with a crime. Because the perpetrators still walked its streets, in a sense the entire white community was complicit in the decision not to prosecute them for murder. I remember doing research in the county one day in 1967. At noon, I broke for lunch, at the white cafe on the courthouse square. As I ate alone at a small table for two, a white man detached himself from a group that had been eyeing me, came over, sat in the chair opposite me, glared at me and asked what I was doing in Philadelphia. Luckily, my reason—learning about the social position of Mississippi's Choctaw Indians, who also live in Neshoba County, to contrast that of Chinese Mississippians in the Mississippi Delta, about whom I was writing a PhD dissertation—satisfied him, but the experience was unsettling. Those few whites who lived in Philadelphia and spoke out against the murders experienced more serious consequences. The principle of cognitive dissonance teaches us to expect that opinions will get twisted to harmonize with past acts, and that is what happened in Neshoba County.

Moving On

If we revisit later years in Neshoba County, we can see how far it—and the nation—has come since 1964, partly as a result of the events of that year. We may also find clues as to how we have also gone wrong.

Fast-forward to January, 1970, when Neshoba County finally began to turn around. School desegregation proved key. In that month, the Supreme Court's order in *Alexander v. Holmes* took effect, ending "freedom-of-choice" desegregation. No longer should blacks be free to choose white schools, or vice versa (which didn't happen anyway), because there should not *be* "white" or "black" schools—there should be "just schools." Neshoba whites found compliance easier than whites in many other districts did, because African Americans were in a minority in the county. Although most schools lost such amenities as social clubs and PTAs when they merged, most parents kept their children in the public schools. Now, suddenly, a car with both races riding in the front seat might not be an "integrated car" but just teachers on their way to school together.

Fast forward to 1980. On his first day of campaigning after winning the GOP Presidential nomination, Ronald Reagan spoke at the Neshoba County Fair. He said not a word about the event that had made Neshoba famous around the world. Instead, he declared his support for "states' rights," the code word that signalled that the federal government should not enforce laws mandating equal treatment for African Americans. Thirty-five thousand white supporters roared approval. Thus, Reagan furthered Nixon's "Southern strategy," which continues to bear fruit for Republicans today—not just in the South, but also in white suburbs and sundown towns in the North.

Fast forward to 1989. At the 25th anniversary remembrance on June 21, then-Secretary of State Dick Molpus, who grew up in Philadelphia, made a historic apology to the families of James Chaney, Andrew Goodman and Michael Schwerner at Mount Zion Methodist: "We deeply regret what happened here 25 years ago. We wish we could undo it. We are profoundly sorry that they are gone. We wish we could bring them back."

Unfortunately, when Molpus ran for governor in 1995, he lost to the incumbent Republican.

Fast forward to 1994. On the 30th anniversary of the murders, Jackson State University and Tougaloo College hosted an emotional reunion of Freedom Summer volunteers and local people that included an excursion to Neshoba, but almost no local whites attended the service at Mt. Zion or the rally at the courthouse in Philadelphia.

Fast forward to 2004. Four major events marked the 40th anniversary. Jackson State University, Tougaloo College and Tulane University mounted a four-day symposium, "Unsettling Memories." A pair of remembrance services was held in Neshoba County on June 20. And Ben Chaney, James Chaney's younger brother, led a busload of young people from Washington, DC, to Jackson, doing voter registration along the way.

I attended the Jackson State, Tougaloo and Neshoba events and found them both moving and disturbing. In Neshoba, this time local whites played a central role in hosting the larger remembrance—too central to some, including Chaney, who felt that this new event would upstage the traditional Mt. Zion service. About 1,800 people attended the happening organized by a newly formed "Philadelphia Coalition," held at the Neshoba County Coliseum and chaired by the young president of the Neshoba NAACP. At the rear of the spacious building, white Philadelphians, anxious to make a good impression, served a catfish dinner to all, at no charge.

Without a doubt, the motives of white Neshobans were mixed. In time for the occasion, the Philadelphia Chamber of Commerce produced a remarkable booklet, "African-American Heritage Driving Tour," that includes the jail, the murder site, the swamp where a Choctaw Indian found the burned station wagon, Mt. Zion of course, and even modest gathering places for the black community like the Busy Bee Cafe and Barber Shop. Business leaders knew that this tragedy was the most important event ever to take place in Neshoba County; one sponsor of the booklet was Philadelphia/Neshoba Tourism.

But what would we have them do? *Not* put out such a brochure? It also includes photos and vignettes of 19 residents, mostly African-American, who played positive roles in the Neshoba freedom struggle. Thirteen additional photos and vignettes, titled "Rewards of Sacrifice," highlight young African Americans from Neshoba who have become physicians, educational leaders or professional athletes. The booklet includes a useful bibliography on the tragedy and ends with a paragraph stating, "Neshoba County discovered that the cancer of racism infects each person it touches...."

Similarly, would we have them *not* hold a 40th remembrance? In preparation for the event, the County Board of Supervisors and the Philadelphia City Council drafted and signed a statement calling for "justice in this case." Excerpts follow:

> There is, for good and obvious reasons, no statute of limitations on murder.... We call on the Neshoba County District Attorney, the state Attorney General, and the FBI to make every effort to seek justice in this case. We deplore the possibility that history will record that the

state of Mississippi, and this community in particular, did not make a good faith effort to seek justice. We state candidly and with deep regret that some of our own citizens, including local and state law enforcement officers, were involved in the planning and execution of these murders.... Finally, we wish to say to the families of James Chaney, Andrew Goodman, and Michael Schwerner, that we are profoundly sorry for what was done in this community to your loved ones.

To be sure, there were false notes. One speaker called the three "Christian martyrs"—Goodman and Schwerner were Jewish. Mississippi's Republican governor Haley Barbour assured us, "Our state of Mississippi is a wonderful place and our nation the greatest ever," and then conflated the struggle for civil rights with the fight against "Islamic terror." He drew only tepid applause. But hypocrisy is a first step toward civilized behavior, and at least the governor's appearance meant he was exposed to Dick Molpus, who again provided the words that made the occasion memorable.

Molpus called the three "American patriots" and those who killed them "domestic terrorists." Addressing the locals, he noted that the perpetrators had "certainly told wives, children and buddies of their involvement," and he urged those persons to come forward to the authorities. Most importantly, he declared, "We Mississippians must announce to the world what we have learned in the last 40 years: our enemies are...," and he then provided a list including ignorance, racism and an inferior educational system that drew an ovation.

Some Justice, Finally

In the wake of the successful prosecution of other white supremacist murderers in Mississippi and Alabama and the reopening of the Emmett Till murder case, this anniversary and the statement bore fruit. Mississippi Attorney General Jim Hood announced he was seeking help from federal authorities, and US Attorney Dunn Lampton of Jackson said his office has been working on it. Eventually, the case was re-opened, and on the 41st anniversary of the murders, to the day, the man who orchestrated them, Edgar Ray Killen, was found guilty on three charges of manslaughter by a local jury of nine whites and three blacks, and sentenced to three consecutive 20-year terms. Already 80, he will spend the rest of his life in prison, kept in solitary confinement. Killen remains unrepentant.

Despite the verdict, not all is well in Neshoba County. Several other Klan members who participated in the three murders are still alive but have not been charged. A young white adult told me at the 2004 commemoration that he had never heard a word about the Civil Rights Movement in the Philadelphia public schools. The history page at the Chamber of Commerce website spends two paragraphs on Neshoba County's first 30 years, from 1833 to 1863, then "covers" the period from 1863 to 2004 in a single paragraph that never mentions civil rights or the events of 1964! Local libraries do not have the books that are listed in the bibliography of the Chamber of Commerce brochure. (One speaker at the 2004 Mt. Zion service announced she was remedying that forthwith and handed copies of each book to a church representative.) Only 34% of black students in the Philadelphia public schools read on grade level, compared to 90% of white students.

Similarly, not all is well in America. In 1980, Reagan helped to derail us from our work toward the "beloved community" called for by the Civil Rights Movement. Instead, he implied that resistance to justice across racial lines was appropriate and would be rewarded. Today, the educational and social disparities in Philadelphia, Mississippi, are mirrored in Philadelphia, Pennsylvania, and across our "greatest ever" nation.

Remembering Freedom Summer—which was much more than the Neshoba tragedy—can help us get back on track. I hope to have whetted your appetite to learn more—you who are in that four of five too young to have experienced it the first time. You can connect with this event and its continuing commemorations. You can call for the prosecution of all living perpetrators of the murders of Schwerner, Chaney and Goodman—and of other martyrs of the civil rights struggle. You can sing along: "Keep on a-walkin'. Keep on a-talkin'. Gonna build a brand new world." And you can help build the beloved community where *you* live—nationally and even internationally as well.

Chapter 4

Sundown Towns

James W. Loewen

Between 1890 and 1968, thousands of towns across the United States drove out their black populations or took steps to forbid African Americans from living in them. Thus were created "sundown towns," so named because many marked their city limits with signs typically reading, "Nigger, Don't Let The Sun Go Down On You In ___." Some towns in the West drove out or kept out Chinese Americans. A few excluded Native Americans or Mexican Americans. "Sundown suburbs" developed a little later, mostly between 1900 and 1968. Many suburbs kept out not only African Americans but also Jews.

I learned of these towns gradually, over many years. Back in the 1960s, when going to college in Minnesota, I heard residents of Edina, the most prestigious suburb of Minneapolis, boast that their community had, as they put it, "Not one Negro and not one Jew." The Academy Award-winning movie of 1947, *Gentleman's Agreement*, taught me about the method by which Darien, Connecticut, one of the most prestigious suburbs of New York City, kept out Jews. Later I learned of the acronym that residents of Anna, Illinois, applied to their town: "Ain't No Niggers Allowed."

Each of these stories seemed outrageous. I resolved to write a book about the phenomenon. Initially, I imagined I would find maybe ten of these communities in Illinois (my home state, where I planned to do more research than in any other single state), and perhaps 50 across the country.

To my astonishment, I found 472 sundown towns in Illinois, a clear majority of all of the 621 incorporated places of more than 1,000 population. (I made no systematic study of towns smaller than that.) I found hundreds more across the United States and now estimate that probably 10,000 such towns exist. By 1970, *more than half* of all incorporated communities outside the traditional South probably excluded African Americans. (Whites in the traditional South were appalled by the practice—why would you make your maid leave?) Similar proportions obtained in Indiana, Missouri, Oregon and probably many other states. Sundown towns ranged from hamlets like DeLand, Illinois, population 500, to large cities like Appleton, Wisconsin, with 57,000 residents in 1970. Sometimes entire counties went sundown, usually when their county seats did. Independent sundown towns were soon joined by "sundown suburbs," often even larger, such as Glendale, a suburb of Los Angeles, with more than 60,000; Levittown, on Long Island, more than 80,000; and Warren, a Detroit suburb with 180,000.

The History

These towns and these practices do not date back to the Civil War. On the contrary, between about 1863 and 1890, African Americans went everywhere in America. During this "springtime of freedom," many communities, especially those with large Quaker, Unitarian or Republican populations, welcomed them. Then, between 1890 and 1940, blacks commenced a "Great Retreat." This period is becoming known as the "nadir of race relations," when lynchings peaked, white owners expelled black baseball players from the major (and minor) leagues, and flourishing unions drove African Americans from such occupations as railroad fireman and meat processor.

During this era, whites in many communities indulged in little race riots that until now have been lost to history. Whites in Liberty, Oregon, for example, now part of Salem, ordered their blacks to leave in 1893. Pana, Illinois, drove out its African Americans in 1899, killing five in the process. Anna, Illinois, followed suit in 1909, Pinckneyville probably in 1928. Harrison, Arkansas, took two riots by whites before the job was done—in 1905 and 1909. Decatur, Indiana, expelled its black population in 1902. White workers in Austin, Minnesota, repeatedly drove out African Americans in the 1920s and 1930s. Other towns that drove out their black populations violently include Myakka City, Florida; Spruce Pine, North Carolina; Wehrum, Pennsylvania; Ravenna, Kentucky; Greensburg, Indiana; St. Genevieve, Missouri; North Platte, Nebraska; Oregon City, Oregon; and many others. Some of these mini-riots in turn spurred whites in nearby smaller towns to have their own, thus provoking little waves of expulsions. White residents of Vienna, Illinois, set fire to the homes in its black neighborhood as late as 1954!

Many towns that had no African-American residents maintain strong oral traditions of having passed ordinances forbidding blacks from remaining after dark. In California, for example, the Civilian Conservation Corps in the 1930s tried to locate a company of African-American workers in a large park that bordered Burbank and Glendale. Both cities refused, each citing an old ordinance that prohibited African Americans within their city limits after sundown. Other towns passed ordinances in Arizona, Oklahoma, Kansas, Nebraska, Iowa, Missouri, Wisconsin, Illinois, Indiana, Tennessee, Ohio, Maryland and probably many other states. Some towns believed their ordinances remained in effect long after the 1954 *Brown* decision and 1964 Civil Rights Act. The city council of New Market, Iowa, for example, suspended its sundown ordinance *for one night* in the mid-1980s to allow an interracial band to play at a town festival, but it went back into effect the next day. Other towns kept out African Americans by less formal measures, such as cutting off city water, having police call hourly all night with reports of threats, or assaulting African-American children as they tried to go to school.

Some sundown towns allowed one exception. When whites drove African Americans from Hamilton County, Texas, for example, they allowed the elderly "Uncle Alec" and "Aunt Mourn" Gentry to remain. In about 1950, whites in Marshall, Illinois, even christened their exception, "Squab" Wilson, the barber, an "honorary white man." Meanwhile, Marshall posted the traditional sundown signs. Other permitted exceptions included live-in servants in white households and inmates of mental and penal institutions.

Maintaining Sundown-ness

How have these towns maintained themselves all-white? By a variety of means, public and private. DWB, for example—"driving while black"—is no new phenomenon in sundown towns; as far back as the 1920s, police officers routinely followed and stopped black motorists or questioned them when they stopped. Suburbs used zoning and eminent domain to keep out black would-be residents and to take their property if they did manage to acquire it. Some towns required all residential areas to be covered by restrictive covenants—clauses in deeds that stated, typically:

> No lot shall ever be sold, conveyed, leased, or rented to any person other than one of the white or Caucasian race, nor shall any lot ever be used or occupied by any person other than one of the white or Caucasian race, except such as may be serving as domestics for the owner or tenant of said lot, while said owner or tenant is residing thereon. [from Edina]

Always, lurking under the surface, was the threat of violence or such milder white misbehavior as refusing to sell groceries or gasoline to black newcomers.

The Civil Rights Movement left these towns largely untouched. Indeed, some locales in the Border States forced out their black populations in response to *Brown v. Board of Education.* Sheridan, Arkansas, for example, compelled its African Americans to move to neighboring Malvern in 1954 after the school board's initial decision to comply with *Brown* prompted a firestorm of protest. Having no black populations, these towns and counties then had no African Americans to test their public accommodations. For 15 years after the 1964 Civil Rights Act, motels and restaurants in some sundown towns continued to exclude African Americans, thus forcing black travelers to avoid them or endure humiliating and even dangerous conditions. Today, public accommodations in sundown towns are generally open. Many towns—probably more than half—have given up their exclusionary residential policies, while others still make it uncomfortable or impossible for African Americans to live in them.

Adverse Impacts

These towns also have an adverse impact on their own residents. When kids ask parents why they live in a given town, especially if it is a suburb, parents are apt to reply that it is a good environment for raising children. The children know full well that their town is overwhelmingly white, making it logical to infer that an environment without blacks is "good." While anti-racist whites *can* emerge from such settings, and some have, it is far easier to conclude that African Americans are bad and to be avoided. Young people from sundown towns often feel a sense of dread when they find themselves in racially mixed situations beyond their hometowns.

Still worse is the impact of sundown suburbs on the social system. The prestige enjoyed by many elite sundown suburbs—such as Edina, Darien or Kenilworth, the richest suburb of Chicago—makes it harder for neighboring suburbs to become and stay interracial. When a white family makes even more money than average for the interracial suburb of Oak Park, Illinois, say, they may want to express their success by moving to an even more prestigious (and more expensive) suburb, like Kenilworth. Such a family may not choose Kenilworth *because* it has no black families (as of the 2000 Census), but because of its prestige—but the two have been intertwined for a century.

What to Do?

What is to be done about sundown towns? Governmental action does help. Until 1968, new all-white suburbs were forming much more rapidly than old sundown towns and suburbs were caving in. In that year, Title VIII of the Civil Rights Act, along with the *Jones v. Mayer* decision, barring discrimination in the rental and sale of property, caused the federal government to change sides and oppose sundown towns. Since then, city-wide residential prohibitions against Jews, Asians, Native Americans and Hispanics have mostly disappeared. Even vis-à-vis African Americans, many towns and suburbs relaxed their exclusionary policies in the 1980s and 1990s. As of 2005, however, exclusion of blacks is still all too common.

At a minimum, any former sundown town should now be asked to make three statements: admit it ("We did this."), apologize for it ("We did this, and it was wrong.") and proclaim they now welcome residents of all races ("We did this; it was wrong; and we don't do it any more.") Even George Wallace managed these statements before he died, after all!

The last chapter of my 2005 book *Sundown Towns* is titled "Remedies." It suggests things that individual families can do, policies that local governments should put into effect, acts that corporations can take, and a new law that states or the federal government should pass. The last, titled "Residents Rights Act," is modeled to a degree on the very successful 1965 Voting Rights Act. If a community has a provable sundown past (and this can be done, as my research shows), continuing overwhelmingly white demographics, and two or more complaints from recent black would-be renters or homebuyers, then the act would kick in. Among its provisions, residents would lose the ability to exempt mortgage interest and local property tax payments from their incomes at tax time. After all, by this exemption the federal government, seconded by state governments, means to encourage homeownership in America, a fine aim. However, homeownership by whites in sundown towns is *not* so fine an objective and does not deserve encouragement in the tax code. The day after this act is applied to a given sundown town or suburb, its residents will be up in arms, requesting that their government and realtors *recruit* African Americans as residents so they can recover this important tax break.

Even if no government enacts the Residents Rights Act, individuals can do the research to "out" sundown towns. Especially elite sundown suburbs, but even isolated independent sundown towns, rely upon deniability for their policy to work. I call this the "paradox of exclusivity." Residents of towns like Darien, for instance, *want* Darien to be known as an "exclusive" community. That says good things about them—that they have the money, status and social savvy to be accepted in such a locale. They do *not* want to be known as "excluding"—especially on racial or religious grounds—for that would say *bad* things about them. So long as towns like Darien, Kenilworth, Edina and La Jolla, California, can appear "accidentally" all-white, they can avoid this difficulty. At the very least, then, making plain the conscious and often horrific decisions that underlie almost every all-white town and neighborhood in America is a first step toward ending what surely remains as the last bastion of racial segregation in America.

Chapter 5

Minority Exclusion
in Small Town America

James H. Johnson, Jr., Ann Moss Joyner
and Allan Parnell

Using GIS-based spatial analysis and mapping techniques, we are documenting several pernicious forms of contemporary racial discrimination that are sapping the lifeblood from African-American and other minority communities in towns across the United States. Documentation of this type of minority exclusion is typically done by superimposing racial and ethnic composition data onto geo-coded public records pertaining to city boundaries, zoning, water and sewer services, infrastructure, and land-use development plans.

This technique shows a contemporary pattern of discrimination which builds upon a common historical pattern of racial residential segregation and involves the intentional manipulation of boundaries, zoning and land-use regulations—most often by local White elites. Resembling the apartheid-like conditions that have contributed to the growth of an underclass in US cities, African Americans and other minorities in these towns are denied political involvement in economic development decision-making and access to critical infrastructure resources like sewer services, while their neighborhoods are typically targeted simultaneously for locally unwanted land-uses such as highways, landfills and sewage treatment facilities. These discriminatory actions expose minorities to major public health risks, heighten the incidence of poverty in their neighbor-hoods and are a heretofore unrecognized contributor to Black land loss.

We highlight how two specific, related mechanisms—annexation and extraterritorial zoning—are being used to create racial apartheid-like conditions in towns throughout the US. We conclude with a call for additional research on this topic.

Annexation

Annexation is the process by which municipalities expand their borders. Proponents argue that annexation is an effective tool to facilitate business and employment growth, stabilize tax rates and improve the overall quality of life, especially in fiscally- and financially-strapped communities. But annexation can produce exclusionary segregation.

In North Carolina, for example, the state's annexation and planning laws give towns the discretion to annex only properties with high tax values (even non-contiguous properties), which often results in a confusing maze of boundaries that skip over poor and Black neighborhoods. This appears to be more common in smaller cities and towns. Municipalities in North Carolina must extend all major municipal services performed within the jurisdiction (police protection, fire protection, solid waste collection, street maintenance, etc.) to the area to be annexed on substantially the same basis and in the same manner as such services are provided within the rest of the municipality prior to annexation. Such services must be completed within two years of the effective date of annexation.

While this requirement for provision of services appears to be equitable, it acts as a disincentive for local officials to annex older areas which lack city services, as is frequently the case with minority neighborhoods adjacent to town borders. In new neighborhoods, developers usually provide essential services and incorporate the associated costs into the price of the properties. In older neighborhoods, however, residents must finance such improvements themselves (a near impossibility) or request the municipality to provide the funds to pay for the services. Since most towns need their limited tax proceeds or Community Development Block Grant funds for neighborhoods already within their borders, the requirement that service extension parallel annexation in a timely manner acts as a disincentive to annex older neighborhoods without services.

State law requires documentation of how the proposed annexation will affect the city's finances and services, including estimates of city revenue changes. Because most minority neighborhoods consist of lower-valued housing and few commercial establishments, the costs associated with such annexations often conflict with the overarching goal of annexation, which is to enhance the local revenue base.

Annexations also can potentially affect voting because they can change the electorate who can participate in elections. In reviewing annexations under Section 5 of the Voting Rights Act, the Justice Department stipulates that a jurisdiction must demonstrate that the revision of municipal boundaries to "include certain voters within the city [while] leaving others outside" may not be based, even in part, on race. Local jurisdictions must also demonstrate that the annexation policies and standards applied to minority areas are the same as those applied to White areas. If the standards are not the same or have been applied inconsistently, there is a strong likelihood that the decision not to annex the minority area had a discriminatory purpose.

Extraterritorial Zoning

Extraterritorial zoning, or Extraterritorial Jurisdiction (ETJ) as it is popularly known, is another exclusionary tool that local power elites employ in small towns. ETJ is a zoning "overlay" that allows a town to zone areas outside of but contiguous to its limits in order to plan for future growth.

Fifteen states have some form of extraterritorial zoning authority for some or all municipalities. At least eleven states have some form of extraterritorial subdivision control.

In North Carolina, state law grants municipalities broad powers to control planning and growth for up to three miles beyond their borders (up to one mile for smaller towns). The area chosen must be based on "existing or projected urban development and areas of critical concern to the city, as evidenced by officially-adopted plans for its development." A 1995 North Carolina League of Municipalities survey revealed that 89% of state's larger towns and 68% of its smaller municipalities (1,000-2,500 residents) have adopted extraterritorial zoning.

While small towns often show little inclination to annex minority neighborhoods, they still take such neighborhoods into their ETJ, establishing the right to zone parcels. Minority neighborhoods are left in ETJ status longer (in perpetuity in some cases) than White neighborhoods or newly-developed areas that most likely will be predominantly White.

Residents of a municipality's ETJ cannot vote for the town council, but that administrative body has the authority to change land-use policies that can significantly reduce home values in the ETJ. For example, the local jurisdiction can rezone African-American residential neighborhoods within the ETJ as commercial/industrial (often against the wishes of the residents), resulting in a drastic reduction in home values, an inability to leave their children land for residential use, and eventual African-American land loss and destruction of the minority neighborhood.

Further, ETJ residents have to request permits from the town council for division of land, building and other uses of their property. Anecdotal evidence suggests racial disparities in the granting of such permits. For example, there are reports that African-American property owners in the ETJ of one North Carolina town are only given building permits for single-wide mobile. homes, never for stick-built houses on permanent foundations.

African-American property owners in ETJs may be more at risk of eminent domain condemnation than their White counterparts. Governments often target minority-owned land in a town's ETJ for highway construction and other major infrastructure projects.

Summary

Little systematic research attention has been devoted to race relations and patterns of racial residential segregation in small cities and towns over the past 40 years. Many of these towns are still dominated by the local White elite. Their political and business interests are inextricably intertwined, and they control the boundaries of the town, often excluding minority neighborhoods.

City council members, town managers and even foundation board members have defended this form of exclusion on the grounds that it is not motivated by racism but by economics, and that "towns are not charitable institutions." Recently, a town in North Carolina went so far as to refuse to annex a church, citing a concern that the town "not overburden our resources," according to the town manager. This maximization of revenue at the expense of community corrodes civic life and ignores humane values.

Whether the result of *unintentional* fiscal annexation and ETJ processes or of *intentional* institutionalized, discriminatory actions of local governments, minorities are excluded from towns and their associated political and material benefits. With lower levels of service, minority-owned property values are reduced, and, in states with ETJs, the residents are without the basic democratic right of representative government.

We have identified a number of towns in which these exclusionary tactics are being used, especially in North Carolina. They range from wealthy towns like Pinehurst, the site of the 2005 U.S. Open, which continues to deny local African-American neighborhoods access to sewer service, to many small farm-market towns across eastern North Carolina.

However, the use of these tactics is not limited to North Carolina or even the South. A complaint filed recently in federal court in California alleges that the city of Modesto has refused to annex Latino neighborhoods and denied the minority residents access to needed public infrastructure, including sewers, street lights and storm water drainage facilities. Similar discrimination in annexation and withholding of public services has been an issue in Zanesville, Ohio.

Considerable work remains to determine the causes, the geographic scope and the material consequences of these insidious forms of racial discrimination in small-town America. Both the analytical tools (GIS) and the requisite geocoded data are available to conduct this type of research. We invite other scholars and community activists to join us in not only documenting the extent of these discriminatory practices but also in developing strategies to ensure that minorities have equal access to the local resources that constitute the lifeblood of healthy and sustainable communities.

Chapter 6

Skewing Democracy: Where the Census Counts Prisoners

Peter Wagner

New York's conservative State Senator Dale Volker is glad prisoners can't vote, because if they did, he told Newhouse News Service, "They would never vote for me." Given Volker's role as the leading defender of the draconian Rockefeller drug laws, prisoner opposition to Volker might not be surprising. But that Volker, who represents a mostly white rural part of the state, would care who the state's mostly Black, Latino and urban prisoners might vote for is, on the surface, surprising. The explanation is that Volker owes his seat to a once-obscure Census Bureau glitch that credits the prison location with the population of prisoners involuntarily incarcerated there. Without credit for the 8,951 prisoners in his district, Volker's sparsely populated rural district would need to be redrawn.

Our modern conception of democracy—based on the One Person, One Vote rule that requires legislative districts to be redrawn each decade to contain roughly equal numbers of people—is now skewed by the Census Bureau's outdated method of counting incarcerated people. The Bureau developed the "usual residence rule" for determining where people are counted for the first Census in 1790. While the rule for other special populations like students and military have evolved over time, the method of counting prisoners remains mired in the past. In 1790, this rule might have made sense, because the Census Bureau had a far simpler purpose: to count the number of people in each state, in order to determine their relative populations for purposes of Congressional reapportionment. It did not matter—for purposes of comparing New York's population to

New Jersey's—whether an incarcerated person was counted at home in New York City or in the remote Attica Prison, as long as they were counted in the right state. Although our society and our uses for Census data have changed radically since 1790, the Census' method of counting prisoners has unfortunately remained the same.

Some State Impacts

The Census Bureau developed its methods for its own purposes and admits, right in its residence rules, that where it counts some populations "is not necessarily the same as the person's voting residence or legal residence." But that is precisely the type of count the states require for internal redistricting. While all states currently rely on Census Bureau data for drawing legislative districts, most states have state constitutional clauses or election law statutes that explicitly define a prisoner's residence to be the place where she or he lived prior to incarceration. Simply put, states that rely on federal Census data to draw state legislative districts violate not only federal One Person, One Vote requirements but their own state constitutions. Census Bureau data as currently collected are inappropriate for use within states because they do not reflect how these states define residence for election purposes.

The impact of the Census Bureau's outdated counting method on the fair distribution of political power is aggravated by the radical changes in incarceration patterns since the mid-1970s. From 1980 to 2000, the number of people in prison quadrupled. Alongside a large and growing racial disparity in who gets sent to prison has been a growing trend to locate prisons in rural areas far from the urban communities that most prisoners originate from. In New York, for example, 66% of the state's prisoners come from New York City, but all of the 43 new prisons built in New York since 1976 have been built upstate. Ninety-one percent of New York's prisoners are incarcerated in the upstate region. This geographic disparity translates into a clear racial disparity as well: Although the New York State prison population is 82% Black or Latino, 98% of the prison cells are located in state senate districts that are disproportionately White. Because of these trends, what might have once been a matter of little consequence has developed into a crisis that violates state and federal constitutional protections.

Impact on Home Communities

So while politicians like Dale Volker benefit, the people who pay the highest price for this policy are the Black, Latino and urban communities from which most prisoners come. This counting practice intersects with other punitive electoral policies to great negative effect. Forty-eight states (all but Maine and Vermont) and DC bar prisoners from voting, and 33 states, including New York, ban parolees from the polls. The burden for this disenfranchisement falls most heavily on minority communities. In New York, 62% of the state population is White, but 82% of the prison population is Black or Latino. Disenfranchisement disproportionately denies these minority voters a voice in government.

As argued by the National Voting Rights Institute and the Prison Policy Initiative in a friend of the court brief challenging New York's disenfranchisement policies, this counting practice illustrates how the effects of disenfranchisement extend beyond those convicted of crimes to affect entire communities not under criminal justice control. Disenfranchisement may be nominally aimed at the "guilty," but its effects are felt as well by the innocent families and communities from which the prison population is taken, because their legislative representation is diminished by the interplay of felon disenfranchisement laws and the method of counting prisoners for redistricting purposes.

While not all states have yet received the same level of detailed study as New York, the Census counting method creates problems for democracy in virtually every state. Sixty percent of Illinois' prisoners call Cook County (Chicago) home, yet 99% of the state's prison cells are outside the County. Los Angeles County supplies 34% of California's prisoners, yet only 3% of the state's prisoners are incarcerated there. Philadelphia is the legal residence for 40% of Pennsylvania's prisoners, but Philadelphia County contains no state prisons.

My "Importing Constituents: Prisoners and Political Clout" report series has applied this regional analysis down to the district level in eight states. In Texas, one rural district's population is almost 12% prisoners. Every group of 88 residents in that district are represented in the State House as if they were 100 residents from urban Houston or Dallas. Even states with lower incarceration rates see serious distortions in their democratic processes. In one Montana district, 15% of the population is disenfranchised prisoners from other parts of the state.

Some Hopeful Signs of Change

Until recently, this was an unrecognized issue. Researcher Tracy Huling discovered the prisoner counting issue shortly before Census 2000 while preparing her ground-breaking 1999 documentary about rural prisons, *Yes In My Backyard*. While this was far too late to make a change in that Census, her work sparked interest in measuring these effects. The first "Importing Constituents..." report quantified the distortions in each New York legislative district, but was not completed until shortly before the new district lines were finalized. Since then, the national Prisoners of the Census project at the Prison Policy Initiative has worked to extend this analysis to other states.

The growing interest in this issue suggests that a change in Census counting policy may be possible by the time of the 2010 Census. Historically, the Census Bureau has proven very responsive to the needs of its data users, provided such issues are presented early in the Census planning process. The method of counting other special populations has changed numerous times, in each case responding to the country's changing demographics and needs. When evolving demographics meant more college students studying far from home and more Americans living overseas, Census policy changed in order to more accurately reflect how many Americans were living where.

Also encouraging is the work of many state-based advocates who are proposing legislation in New York, Illinois and other states to correct how the Census Bureau counts prisoners. If the Census Bureau fails to correct this serious flaw in its data, state officials are discovering that they can take matters in to their own hands to preserve the fairness of their election districts.

Chapter 7

Language as Oppression: The English-Only Movement in the United States

Andrew Hartman

An expanded, fully footnoted version of this article appeared in Socialism and Democracy *(Winter/Spring 2003) and is available from the author (ae.Hartman @verizon.net).*

Within the United States resides the largest population of native English-speakers of any country. Despite the huge influx of non-English-speakers from the global South and East since the 1965 Immigration Act (which relaxed earlier restrictions), the domination of English in the United States is not threatened; according to the 1990 Census, 97% of US residents speak English "well" or "very well." The 2000 Census revealed that, while there has been a growing percentage of non-English-speaking immigration, rates of English fluency are on the rise. Nonetheless, the English-only movement gained momentum in the 1990s and, according to some opinion studies, is currently supported by over 80% of the body politic in the United States.

So widely popular a movement is bound to enjoy legislative successes. Recently, Iowa became the 24th state to mandate English as its official language. Citizens in English-only states must interact with their local and state governments using only English (this includes voting)—a startling development. However, the movement has more far-reaching implications. The structure of education for non-English-speakers is being dramatically altered across the country due to the English-only movement and the resulting backlash against bilingualism and bilingual education. The pedagogical implications of such a trend are dangerous; most serious research supports bilingual instruction as the best means to advance language skills, thus enhancing long-term English acquisition.

The Racist Roots of the English-Only Movement

The English-only movement has its roots in the historical racism and white supremacy of the United States. This does not mean, however, that it can be understood in the same way as overtly racist movements. Those who support the English-only movement, including many liberals, do not understand it to be racist. But that does not discount racism as a root of the movement; rather, it demands a more complex analysis of US racism. Such an analysis should account for the racism of American liberalism, historically rooted in Enlightenment ideology, and should also take into account two other Enlightenment legacies: colonialism and capitalism and their continued roles in American society.

First, a working definition of racism is in order. Colonial theorist Albert Memmi's study of racism and his concluding definition will serve this purpose: "Racism is the generalized and final assigning of values to real or imaginary differences, to the accuser's benefit and at his victim's expense, in order to justify the former's own privileges or aggression."

English-only supporters claim that English-only legislation and pedagogy will empower rather than victimize non-English-speakers. If they highlight language differences, it is in a spirit of benevolence. To them, English is a "common bond" that allows people of diverse backgrounds to overcome differences and reach mutual understanding—a theory particularly seductive to liberals. Unfortunately, the English-only movement's non-racist claims are seriously undermined by their systematic attacks on bilingual education. If English acquisition were indeed their mission, the English-only movement would not partake in these attacks.

The ideology of the English-only movement is constructed upon a well-worn national mythology. In 1995, the US House of Representatives passed the Language of Government Act (later defeated in the Senate), intended to mandate English as the only language of the federal government. During the Senate hearings, American nationalist diatribe was prominently on display. Former House Speaker Newt Gingrich decried bilingualism as a "menace to American civilization," and Senator Richard Shelby (Dem., AL) denounced opponents of English-only legislation as threatening the "sovereignty and integrity of this nation."

In the historical formation of nations, the construction of a common language has been one of the essential tricks the elites have played on the masses to forge "commonalities." A classic Winston Churchill quote epitomizes the myth of language and its importance in regard to nation: "The gift of a common language is a nation's most priceless inheritance." This myth is especially important to those who benefit from an American nation.

For many Americans, the symbolism of the English language has become a form of civic religiosity in much the same vein as the flag. Similarly, US English—the largest and oldest organization supporting the English-only movement—proclaims in its mission statement: "The eloquence [of the English language] shines in our Declaration of Independence and Constitution. It is the living carrier of our democratic ideals."

While proponents of the English-only movement commonly invoke the original institutions of the American nation and its surrounding mythology, opponents of the movement have fertile grounds for a historical rebuttal. The Constitution makes no mention of language. The new American elite of the revolution— distrustful of monarchical forces that regularly sought monolingual policies—did not seek a national policy on language. Jefferson viewed language as a pragmatic tool rather than an ideological symbol; the standardization of English became a cultural hegemonic process—comparable to the current global process—rather than a specific political agenda. The new nation welcomed hundreds of thousands of refugees from the French Revolution and did not try to force English upon them. An English-only nation was not the original nationalist goal.

The framers' views on language, however, are less important than their doctrines of freedom. Before a citizenry comes to identify the English language with freedom, it must embrace freedom itself as something more than an abstract myth. A population sold on this myth is one of the primary achievements of the American nationalist program; freedom is assumed as self-evident in the United States. The English-only rhetoric in relation to the immigrant experience underlies these assumptions, for it is assumed that immigrants who learn English and assimilate to American mainstream culture will share in the mythical freedom enjoyed by all US citizens.

There are countless instances of immigrants who discovered that freedom was an empty promise. Among the more damning cases was the experience of the Chinese in the 19th Century. Hundreds of thousands of them, brought in to build the railroads, endured back-breaking labor at gunpoint, pitiful wages and continuous attacks, including many cases of mob violence. American history is full of horror stories such as this; the life of the immigrant was rife with dangerous conditions, restrictive of their freedom.

Underlying the message of immigrant opportunity following language acquisition is the long-standing myth of the melting pot cultivated by generations of historians who portrayed the American narrative as the saga of a single people. Although scholars who recognized the distinct, and often conflicting, experiences that constitute American immigrant history have largely discredited this absurd image, the English-only movement testifies to its continuing influence. Through the lens of this fraudulent ideology, the downside of the American melting pot (loss of language and culture) is more than made up for by the upside (social mobility). Economist Lowell Galloway, testifying before the Senate, argued for English-only legislation by citing higher poverty rates among those who don't speak English. But his argument does not measure other factors that might account for higher poverty in these populations, including higher poverty rates for all Latinos in the US, regardless of what language or languages they speak. In fact, mastery of English is not an accurate predictor of social mobility among the Latino population. Surprisingly, Latinos who speak only English fare worse economically than those who speak no English. Spanish language skills offer Latinos a cultural, social and economic community. Latinos who lose the benefits of the Spanish-speaking community do not gain reciprocal rewards from the American English-speaking community.

Immigrant opportunity is an American national myth that, despite a great deal of contrary evidence, is alive and well. Integral to this myth are the assimilative qualities of the English language. But if English acquisition and resulting assimilation do not necessarily produce social mobility, why does this mythology persist? How can it justify the English-only movement? If it is true that English is not threatened in the United States, why does the English-only movement garner huge support and continue to push for legislative change? In order to answer these important questions, it is necessary to delve beyond the rhetoric of the English-only movement and examine its racist roots. Such an examination might reveal a level of complicity most Americans are unwilling to recognize.

Unz and Co.

Ron Unz, the foremost anti-bilingual advocate, chairman of English for the Children, states that bilingual education "destroyed the lives of millions upon millions of students." In an October 2001 debate with bilingual theorist and Harvard professor Catherine Snow, Unz opportunistically continued his attack on bilingual education and bilingual educators:

> A few weeks ago, Americans witnessed the enormous devastation that a small handful of fanatically committed individuals can wreak upon society. Perhaps it is now time for ordinary Americans to be willing to take a stand against those similarly tiny groups of educational terrorists in our midst, whose disastrous policies are enforced upon us not by bombs or even knives, but simply by their high-pitched voices. Americans must remain silent no longer.

Unz and his organization have been instrumental in dismantling bilingual education programs. California's 1998 Anti-Bilingual Education Initiative (Proposition 227)—passed by 61% to 39%—placed over 500,000 students lacking English proficiency in mainstream, English-only classrooms to fend for themselves. Unz and other anti-bilingual proponents claim English skills are improving among California's Limited English Proficient (LEP) students thanks to Proposition 227, and use faulty scholarship to justify this claim. Unz argues—and a *New York Times* editorial parroted his line of argument—that the increase

New York Times editorial parroted his line of argument—that the increase in state-mandated standardized test scores among LEPs is due to Proposition 227. Stanford researcher Kenji Hakuta countered Unz and the *Times* piece by attributing the increase in test scores to other factors. Hakuta reasoned that all groups of students improved their test scores due to the increased standardization of instruction. In other words, more time is spent "teaching to the test." He argued that the test itself is a poor measure of English development because the test is geared to gauge native English speakers, not LEPs.

Serious pedagogical research supports bilingual education as the best means to learn English. A long-term national study has documented higher student achievement in bilingual classrooms than in transitional English as second language (ESL) classrooms or immersion (English-only) classrooms. In her debate with Unz, Prof. Snow cited research showing that "learning English faster does not equal learning English better." The level of a person's language skills will only be as advanced as the level of his or her first language. According to researcher Stephen Krashen: "The knowledge that children get through their first language helps make the English they hear and read more comprehensible. Literacy developed in the primary language transfers to the second language." Abstract thinking skills, such as those ideally practiced in social science classrooms, must first be nurtured in a student's native language. Children who are immersed and mainstreamed in English-only classrooms prior to developing abstract language skills will only learn functional English. Functional English may be all that is required to enable them, as adults, to work the monotonous semi-skilled jobs that the market demands, but it hinders these future citizens from learning how to think abstractly, which in turn limits their ability to address societal problems.

In order to understand the racism of the elite English speakers, it is helpful to understand the so-called "Ebonics" debate. In December 1996, the Oakland, California school board passed a resolution in order to, as it determined, "change the racist schooling of African-Americans." Teachers in Oakland were being prepared to understand the linguistic differences between themselves and their students, most of whom were African-American. The measure considered African-American patterns of speech to be more than a dialect; it recognized that many African Americans speak differently because of a long history of cultural and political segregation. A national consensus against the measure erupted, a backlash spurred by the mainstream media. The *New York Times* editorialized that Ebonics was "black slang," the "patois of many low-income blacks," and denounced the Oakland school board. The media dismissed Ebonics by assuming that it is nothing more than an accent and also theorizing that the Oakland school board was merely looking to acquire extra federal funding earmarked for bilingual education.

But who defines standard English? MIT linguist Noam Chomsky understands the debate to transcend linguistics: "If the distribution of power and wealth were to shift from southern Manhattan to East Oakland, 'Ebonics' would be the prestige variety of English and [those on Wall Street] would be denounced by the language police." Not allowing African-American speech patterns into social discourse maintains white supremacy. The African-American language termed Ebonics is a Creole-based language originating in American slave society, the result of Africans being intentionally separated from tribe-members with linguistic similarities, making it impossible to foster commonalities. African slaves were forced to communicate via a hybrid version of English. Like any language, Ebonics has evolved, and it now more closely resembles so-called "standard" English than during the time of slavery. But for many young African Americans, their language is labeled a "linguistic deviance," and these students are forced into "Educable Mentally Handicapped" (EMH) programs. A diploma from an EMH program is rarely even adequate to gain entry to a community college.

This is the crux of the issue: Who is being affected by the language debates? Like the English-only movement, the Ebonics backlash sought to immobilize nonwhites. And like the English-only movement, it enjoyed widespread support. Although this dynamic is controversial, and language acquisition does not guarantee upward mobility, in many cases those whose language is determined to be "standard" within their society enjoy an unfair advantage. Although race is hardly the sole determinant in the standardization of English, white Americans are much more likely than nonwhite Americans to read, write and speak an approximation of "standard" English. The standardization of language is an oppressive and racist agenda that limits social mobility for people of color. Whether through the belittlement of a distinct African-American dialect, or by the dismantling of bilingual education programs, the oppression of language successfully defends a society constructed according to the supremacy of whites.

US English

The English-only movement is not on the margins of American society; it is a mainstream operation. The first order in understanding the English-only movement is to understand the organization known as "US English." US English claims it does not maintain a racist, anti-immigrant agenda. Many of its original supporters were people of color or immigrants, including former Reagan Administration official Linda Chavez, former US Senator S.I. Hayakawa and California Governor Arnold Schwarzenegger. However, according to federal records, US English has had close ties to the anti-immigrant organization Federation for American Immigration Reform (FAIR) and has been financed by the Pioneer Fund, a racist organization that promotes the use of eugenics and also funded Richard J. Herrnstein and Charles Murray's infamously racist work, *The Bell Curve*. John Tanton, the founder and original chairman of US English, states that "the question of bilingualism grows out of U.S. immigration policy."

To Tanton, the huge influx of non-English-speaking immigrants overwhelms the "assimilative capacity of the country."

Colonial U.S.A.

Jefferson, Franklin and their ilk were interested in extending their humanism to those they considered the civilized few, not those defined as "inferior in body and mind." Manifest Destiny was the maxim of the American Enlightenment; all who stood in the way of progress were doomed to extinction. American Indians represented the savage, who by definition obstructed the path of civilization and progress. The democratic ideals of the United States, derived from the Enlightenment and further expounded by American liberalism, forced the Indians to either assimilate or die. The path of death was born out of a monopoly of force established by the white colonists. The path of assimilation required the American colonial power to embark on a program of linguistic oppression.

In the United States, as in other imperial and colonial societies, the language of the powerful is the language sought by those wishing to ascend into "civilization." The better one speaks "standard" English in the United States, the more likely one is to be elevated in American society. The speaker of "standard" English is then able to assume the role of a "civilized" being and is entitled the accoutrements of the civilized. The colonial model of language as oppression follows: The colonizer uses language to assimilate and control the colonized; the colonized strive to speak the language of the colonizer and develop an inferiority complex to the extent that they fall short. The English-only movement embodies the colonial model of language as oppression. Albert Memmi argues that elitism desires a seal of approval. The English-only movement offers just this for English-speakers. With English granted elite status, native speakers of other tongues are assigned both real and imaginary differences—a necessary feature of racist ideology. This is merely the beginning of the aggression that racist ideology justifies—aggression that manifests itself in a variety of ways.

The American colonial process includes the oppression of language model. An 1868 commission on Indian affairs concluded:

> Now, by educating [Indian] children in the English language …differences [will] disappear, and civilization [will] follow at once….Through sameness of language is produced sameness of sentiment and thought…Schools should be established, which children should be required to attend; their barbarous dialects should be blotted out and the English language substituted.

The psychological inferiority of nonwhites in a colonial society—the US included—is reinforced by the standardization of language, as recognized by Franz Fanon: "The Negro who wants to be white will be the whiter as he gains greater mastery of the cultural tool that language is." For the English-only movement, representative of American civilization, Spanish is no longer a Western language but has instead become the language of the savage, of the "wetback" illegally crossing the Rio Grande hoping to steal American jobs. It is the language of brown-skinned and hungry children growing up along a militarized border—militarized in order to block the paths of these millions of needy seeking to "sponge" off American civilization.

The Role of Capitalism

The English-only movement enjoys popular support in the US because American society is constructed upon the racist ideology of colonialism. But something is missing from this analysis—the role of capitalism. The English-only movement operates within a capitalist framework; capitalism is vital to its propagation.

An important feature consistent with a capitalist economic structure is fear and insecurity. Even in times of rapid growth and perceived prosperity, capitalism subjects human beings to the whims of an impersonal market. Globalization has extended this process as never before. The successes are enormous; the failures, apocalyptic. The long and tumultuous struggle to create labor security in the United States is being overwhelmed. Jobs in manufacturing and textiles are fleeing the US in search of cheaper labor. American workers no longer enjoy the economic security they have come to expect—even if this security was more perceived than real.

The statistics are startling: One in four children in America lives in poverty; workers' average inflation-adjusted wages are 16% less than 20 years ago; even college-educated workers earn 7% less than 20 years ago. Full-time jobs are becoming a scarcity, replaced by a nation of temporary workers. Union levels are the lowest since the pre-World War II labor movement. Predictably, this social insecurity has created a surplus segment of the population engulfed by a prison-industrial complex. Over two million people are imprisoned in the US, the highest per-capita level in the world. These developments have created a population searching for answers—and an atmosphere ripe for scapegoating. The English-only movement is one example of this process.

Targeting the Hispanic population, the English-only movement reinforces the divisive effects of capitalist stratification, thereby diverting the resentments of those who are on the bottom rung of the ladder. For example, the English-only movement places first-generation Latino immigrants at odds with those Latinos who have been in the US for more than one generation, and who are thus further along the process of assimilation and English language acquisition. The victims are diverted from the economic causes of their insecurity. The victims are then blamed and blame others who are being victimized by the economic structure.

Racial divisions were the most effective method to undermine labor solidarity. According to W.E.B. DuBois, low-paid white workers in the US "were compensated in part by a psychological wage." White workers' struggle with capital was made more livable through what historian David Roediger refers to as the "wages of whiteness." White workers, while not enjoying the riches of the capitalist class, at least had the benefits of being white, which included access to most, if not all, public facilities: restaurants, theaters, hospitals, parks. This was a benefit not shared by people of color. Roediger writes:

> White working-class racism was underpinned by a complex series of psychological and ideological mechanisms which reinforce racial stereotypes and thus help to forge the identities of white workers in opposition to blacks.

While *de jure* segregation has been abolished in the US, *de facto* segregation continues through new and innovative wages of whiteness, of which one of the more important current versions is the English language.

Most white Americans can operate from an advantageous social position granted them by their "standard" English language skills. White Americans learn to enjoy this advantage and seek to maintain it. The English-only movement recognizes the disadvantages of those who do not speak "standard" English. This rift in the population creates a fertile breeding ground for the English-only movement.

Sometimes such stratification is intentionally fostered by the powerful. Other times, it is an invisible hegemonic process arising from life in the capitalist system—a system structured to reward the few. Groups perceived to be different from one another are left to fight for scraps, thus forming harmful divisions. The English-only movement, although supported by many government officials and other representatives of American capitalism, is not an intentional stratification program. But its end result is the formation of harmful divisions. The English-only movement is, in this respect, a form of social control.

The hegemony of capitalism is increasing the standardization of American society. Sometimes this process is the result of direct decision-making, such as orders for every young person in America to be judged according to a single set of standardized tests. Sometimes the process is less the result of design and more the product of a capitalist culture that posits technocratic values as primordial. In either case (and the difference between chance and design may be difficult to determine), we must resist the English-only movement, which reflects both the visible and the invisible hegemony of capitalism. The English-only movement needs to be denounced as racist. We must recognize the purpose of this movement as the immobilization of immigrants—particularly nonwhite immigrants —through harmful divisions and damaging policies. A concern for social justice requires us to reject it.

Chapter 8

Apologies/Reparations

As this book goes to press (late 2005), two extraordinary events have been in the headlines: 1) the US Senate's resolution formally apologizing for that body's failure, on three separate occasions—via use of the filibuster by Southern segregationist Senators—to pass federal anti-lynching legislation that the House had passed; and 2) the conviction, by a Mississippi jury consisting of nine whites and three blacks, of Edgar Ray Killen for his role as a Ku Klux Klan leader in the brutal 1964 murders of civil rights workers James Chaney, Andrew Goodman and Michael Schwerner in Philadelphia (Neshoba County), Mississippi—a town and county subsequently in the news when Ronald Reagan, in one of the more disgraceful and opportunistic symbolic political acts, spoke at the Neshoba County Fair, on his first day of campaigning after winning the 1980 GOP Presidential nomination—saying not a word about the 1964 crime and declaring his support for "states' rights," the well-known code word for exactly the political stance beloved by white segregationist Southerners.

Periodically, we publish in Poverty & Race *a compendium of recent items illustrating formal apologies and reparations steps for past racial and ethnic crimes and misdeeds. Below is a selection from the five such columns published since mid-2001, illustrating the range of issues and forms—both here in the US and internationally—that such actions take*

Our nation has a long way to go in the area of apologies and reparations. There are precedents to build on if and when we seriously want to undertake an honest look at our history in order to remedy the continuing effects of two-and-a-half centuries of slavery and nearly 100 years of Jim Crow laws.

- Princeton's graduating class of 2001 made Justice Bruce M. Wright (since deceased) an honorary member of the class, as symbolic apology for the university having turned Wright away in 1936 when he arrived to register. (Three years later, in response to Wright's request for an explanation of this indignity, the university's director of admissions wrote that Princeton "does not discriminate against any race, color or creed," but that there were a number of Southern students at the college, "and as you know, there is still a feeling in the South quite different from that existing in New England. My personal experience would enforce my advice to any colored student that he would be happier in an environment of others of his race.") Not until a decade after they rejected Wright did Princeton admit black students.

- The Tulsa Metropolitan Ministry Reparations Gift Fund, an interfaith coalition, has mailed reparations checks to 131 survivors of the 1921 race riot. Although the amounts were not large (ca. $200 per survivor—all were small children at the time of riot), it was regarded as a matter of honor, as Tulsa leaders in 1921 promised victims compensation for their losses but never made full restitution.

- The Belgian government issued its profound and sincere regrets and its apologies for its role in the 1961 assassination of Patrice Lumumba, the man elected (socialist) prime minister of Congo seven months earlier, as the culmination of its independence movement from Belgium. A Belgian parliamentary commission, following a two-year inquiry, concluded that Belgium was morally responsible for the assassination, which could not have been carried out without the complicity of Belgian officers backed by the CIA (which consistently has denied responsibility for the killing). The Belgian government also has created a $3.25 million fund in Lumumba's name to promote democracy in the Congo.

- The Foundry United Methodist Church, Washington, DC, in 2002 apologized to its sister church, Asbury United Methodist Church, for acting dishonorably 166 years earlier, when it required African Americans to sit in the balcony and refused to give them equal opportunity to be church leaders. In response, in 1836, 75 free blacks and slaves, a third of Foundry's congregation, left to form a church where they could participate in the Sacraments and sit where they wanted. Pastor J. Philip Wogaman of Foundry described it as an act of institutional repentance, and Rev. Eugene Matthew, Asbury's pastor, responded, "We accept your repentance, your apology."

- The City of Vienna, in a ceremony of remembrance and public apology in April 2002, buried the last remains of handicapped or mentally ill children experimented upon and then killed by the Nazis. From 1940-45, when Austria was part of Hitler's Third Reich, at least 789 such children (few of whom were Jewish) were killed at an Austrian children's clinic. At the ceremony, Austria's President, Thomas Klestil, called the formal burial service "very late for our country" and promised, "this dark time of our history must constantly remain in the present."

- In May 2002, Virginia Governor Mark Warner formally apologized for the state's embrace of eugenics and denounced a practice under which some 8,000 people were involuntarily sterilized, starting in 1927 and continuing as late as 1979. The practice was embraced by 30 states and victimized an estimated 65,000 Americans. Virginia is the first state to express official regret over its role. The US Supreme Court's 1927 *Buck v. Bell* decision (8-1) upheld the practice. Justice Oliver Wendell Holmes, Jr. wrote in his opinion: "It is better for the world, if instead of waiting to execute degenerate offspring for crime, or to let them starve for their imbecility, society can prevent those who are manifestly unfit from continuing their kind." Along with Warner's apology, the state placed a historical marker honoring Carrie Buck, who brought a legal challenge to Virginia's law.

- The California Dept. of Insurance issued its May 2002 report to the California Legislature, as called for under a state law passed in 2000 (introduced by then-Sen. Tom Hayden) requiring all insurance companies doing business in the state to publicly release information about policies they or their predecessor companies wrote insuring slave owners for losses if slaves ran away or died.

- The Virginia Senate in 2003 gave final passage to a resolution that expresses "official regret" for the shutdown of the Prince Edward County public schools from 1959-64 to avoid desegregation orders. In June 2004, the Virginia legislature approved $1 million (matched by $1 million from a private philanthropist) in scholarships for African Americans who had suffered gaps in their education decades ago when their local public schools closed rather than enroll blacks. Implementation has been slow, however.

- The International Day for the Remembrance of the Slave Trade and Its Abolition is held every August 23. The date was proclaimed in 2002 by the United Nations Educational, Scientific & Cultural Organization to be observed each year, in commemoration of the uprising that took place on the night of Aug. 22-23, 1791, on the island of Santo Domingo (present-day Haiti and The Dominican Republic).

- Australia's 2003 Sorry Day—referring to historic treatment of Aboriginal people and the stolen generations—was commemorated in Parliament House with the theme, "Healing the Past, Shaping the Future." Across Australia, cities and towns held community events, and Journey of Healing marches took place in several cities.

- Columnist Earl Ofari Hutchinson, commenting on President Bush's July 2003 trip to Africa, noted that, although the President visited Gorée Island off Africa's west coast and called slavery "one of the greatest crimes in history," he failed to express either any personal sense of shame and disgust or formally apologize for slavery. A similar point was made by Adam Goodheart, a fellow at Washington College in Chestertown, MD: "Though it might have seemed perplexing, not least to the Senegalese—that America's leaders need to go to another continent in order to address an issue rooted so deeply in own history—that geographic awkwardness speaks volumes about the odd place that slavery currently occupies in American culture and memory. Despite the frequent attention given to the subject, slavery is still somehow held at arm's length, or even an ocean's breadth, away. There are any number of sites in this country far more intimately connected to America's slave past than Gorée Island is."

- Chief Leschi of the Nisqually Indian tribe, hanged in 1858 for the death of a white militia soldier in what is now Washington State, was exonerated by a special Historical Court of Inquiry and Justice, led by the Chief Justice of the State Supreme Court, at the request of the state legislature. The unanimous, but not legally binding, ruling (by seven active and recently retired Washington judges) held that if Chief Leschi, a revered icon of the tribe and a celebrated Indian martyr, did in fact kill the soldier (the evidence is by no means convincing), a murder charge was not justified, as they were lawful combatants in a time of war.

- The Jackson, Mississippi International Airport has been renamed Jackson-Evers International Airport, honoring the memory of assassinated NAACP Field Director Medgar Evers. The Jackson Municipal Airport Authority plans to create an exhibit in the terminal honoring Evers.

- On Nov. 3, 1979, in Greensboro, North Carolina, five community activists protesting Ku Klux Klan racism, in a legally scheduled march, were shot and killed, ten others wounded, in broad daylight—an action caught on film by cameramen from four TV stations. The killers, members of the KKK and American Nazi Party, were exonerated by an all-white jury in state court in 1981, by reasons of "self-defense"; a second federal civil rights trial ended in 1984 with acquittal by another all-white jury. Later, the widows and other survivors successfully sued the Klan, Nazis and Greensboro police (who were complicit in the violence) for wrongful deaths, and the City of Greensboro (not the KKK or Nazis) paid the small judgement, funds that formed the basis for The Greensboro Justice Fund. In 2004, the Greensboro

Truth and Reconciliation Commission (modeled after what post-apartheid South Africa and other countries have put in place) was created and will issue a report and recommendations for community reconciliation (www.greensborotrc.org).

- *Ray*, the Jamie Foxx film portrait of Ray Charles, contains a scene wherein Charles, arriving in Augusta, Georgia in 1961 for a concert, is repeatedly harangued by a fan for playing before a segregated audience. Charles blows him off, then at the last minute reconsiders and gets back on the bus with his entire entourage. In retaliation, Charles is banned from performing in the state. Then, in 1979, the Georgia Legislature passed a formal proclamation and apology, in the process making "Georgia on My Mind" the state song. In a nice contemporary touch, the movie has none other than NAACP Chair Julian Bond, a former Georgia legislator himself expelled from that body for his opposition to the Vietnam War, portraying the legislator who read the proclamation.

- In June 2005, the United States Senate passed a bi-partisan Resolution (S.39), apologizing for never having passed federal anti-lynching legislation. The House had done so three times, but each time Southern segregationist Senators, using the filibuster and parliamentary maneuvers, prevented the resolution from coming to a floor vote. Eighty of the Senate's 100 members co-sponsored the measure; 12 more added their names after taking heat for their absence. The 8 remaining hold-outs, all Republicans, included both Senators from Mississippi, Wyoming and New Hampshire, plus one each from Texas and Tennessee. The action was inspired by publication of James Allen's book of photographs—of the victims as well as the celebrating crowds of onlookers, *Without Sanctuary: Lynching Photography in America*.

Chapter 9

Organizing for Reparations: Lessons from the Holocaust

Marc Masurovsky

Reparations for slavery (and Jim Crow laws) are a hotly debated topic, related to, and an extension of, the issue of apologies for past crimes and misdeeds. Many precedents exist, including payments made to Japanese-American citizens interned during World War II and payments made to Holocaust victims. In this article, Marc Masurovsky describes his work for the Conference on Jewish Material Claims Against Germany and the Presidential Advisory Commission on Holocaust-Era Assets in the United States. That part of his project showing the ways in which Jewish groups organized to research and implement a reparations program of vast proportions—a program that has found wide acceptance among the nations as well as the public—provides some useful lessons for those advocating a reparations program for African Americans.

The issue is reparations (financial compensation for loss of objects or property), as opposed to restitution (material recovery of lost objects or property). The difference between the two notions is important because there has been a tendency to confuse them and substitute one for the other. Reparations can never constitute an exact reimbursement for actual losses suffered by a victim of an act of persecution. It is a symbolic gesture aimed at recognizing that something terribly wrong occurred which inflicted irreparable harm to this individual on account of his/her identity—be it ethnic, racial, religious, sexual, and/or political. For our purposes, the emphasis is on ethnic, racial and religious identity. I speak here about Nazi persecutions aimed at the Jewish population of continental Europe and North Africa. The acts of persecution were deliberate, state-sponsored and part of a general program aimed at enslaving and exterminating the vast majority, if not the totality, of members of the Jewish faith living and working in Europe in the 1930s and 1940s. Had the Nazis achieved their heinous mission, eight to ten million Jews would have perished in the Holocaust. The fact that only six million died is no consolation.

Why reparations? By 1944, Jewish leaders, lay religious figures, political and intellectual figures in the United States, Switzerland and Great Britain had awakened to the immensity of the crimes being committed in Europe in the name of racial supremacy and National Socialism. Government officials in Washington, DC, and London, both civilian and military, grappled with the preparations for administering war-torn Europe after an Allied military victory over the Third Reich, and especially with the inevitable, unfathomable humanitarian catastrophe that lay ahead of them. Part of this unprecedented societal crisis was the fact that millions of men, women and children had been dispossessed, reduced to slavery and subjected to the cruelest forms of punishment in specially-built compounds called "concentration camps," and forced to work for the German war machine over a six-year period—between 1939 and 1945. An average of 10% of the enslaved Jewish population survived Nazi atrocities. The question facing the Western Powers—the United States, Great Britain and France—was: How to right the wrong that they suffered.

The idea of reparations had first been used in the aftermath of World War I as a form of punishment to make Germany pay for the damage it caused during four years of trench warfare. Here, the accused nation was forced to pay the aggrieved nations it had attacked and fought against. Thirty-five years later, the Allied Powers (absent the Soviets, who had agreed at the July 1945 Potsdam Conference to relinquish any title to enemy property seized in Western Europe by the Allies) insisted that Germany pay reparations as well, but this time, owing to the complexity of the crimes for which its leaders were being held accountable—genocide, slavery, plunder, as well as military aggression— reparations included compensation to individuals for losses they had suffered. Hence, the unprecedented nature of the Allied reparations program in the wake of the Second World War.

Creating a Reparations Program

How would the Jewish victims of Nazism be compensated for what they had suffered? The governments of the Allied Powers realized that administration and enforcement of a program aimed at assessing the needs of each persecuted and surviving individual would overwhelm their resources and paralyze their program to rehabilitate European nations and rebuild their infrastructure, while overseeing the military occupation of Germany and Austria. An international treaty was ratified in the spring of 1946—the Paris Reparations Conference—which designated two organizations to oversee relief and rehabilitation efforts for surviving Jews who had been persecuted by the Nazis: the American Jewish Joint Distribution Committee (AJDC) and the Jewish Restitution Successor Organization (JRSO). Eight American and European Jewish groups had chartered the JRSO for the purpose of seeking reparations for Jewish victims of the Holocaust after gaining title to Jewish properties left unclaimed by their persecuted owners. The AJDC and the Jewish Agency for Palestine shared the leadership functions of the JRSO. (Details of these arrangements are found in Benjamin Ferencz, *Two Generations in Perspective*, H. Schneiderman, Ed., Monde Publishers, New York, 1957; website www.benferencz.org/restitut.htm.)

The post-war campaign for Jewish reparations received an added impetus from Nahum Goldmann, the charismatic post-war leader of the World Jewish Congress (WJC). Jewish delegates from 32 countries had assembled in Geneva in 1936 to coordinate their efforts aimed at combating Nazism and anti-Semitism, defending Jewish rights world-wide and advocating for the establishment of a Jewish homeland in Palestine. Through its Institute of Jewish Affairs (co-sponsored by the American Jewish Congress), the WJC had authored a number of pioneering studies in 1943 and 1944 that argued in favor of a massive reparations program to cover damages inflicted by the Nazis on the Jewish communities of Europe.

In 1949, the Federal Republic of Germany was born, and with it, the US occupation of Germany ended. A new regime of compensation was therefore mandated to ensure that those who had been persecuted by the Nazis would still receive some form of reparations from the Germans. The JRSO and the WJC coalesced in 1951 to found the Conference on Jewish Material Claims Against Germany (Claims Conference). Representatives of 23 national and international Jewish groups chartered this new organization to enter into negotiations with the German government for the purpose of obtaining reparations for Jewish survivors. The Chancellor of the newly-established Federal Republic of Germany (FRG), Konrad Adenauer, accepted the fact that Germany had to make some form of payment for the crimes it had committed against the Jews. Although opposed at the time by many Israelis (including the late prime minister of Israel, Menachem Begin) as "blood money," the FRG signed a series of landmark agreements with Israel and the Claims Conference which have since cost the German government upwards of $60 billion in reparations payments to hundreds of thousands of survivors. Some of those monies were initially earmarked for relief and reconstruction projects in Israel (less than $1 billion), housing thousands of refugees in temporary tent cities. The Claims Conference administered the rest of these funds on behalf of Holocaust survivors and needy Jews living in destitution in Eastern Europe. The German government also provided direct aid to individual survivors through its *Wiedergutmachung* program (literally, "making good," or reparations).

The success of the Jewish organizations in obtaining multi-billion dollar reparations settlements over the past four decades stems in part from their collective agreement that, in principle, the Germans were morally responsible for compensating the Jewish people for their irreparable losses, knowing full well that no amount of money could ever make up for the loss of six million lives and untold masses of individual and communal properties. International reparations agreements between the former Allied Powers and the German state facilitated these negotiations because they established some of the legal frameworks by which claims for reparations could be made on behalf of individual victims. Furthermore, the leadership of these organizations (Nahum Goldmann from the WJC, Saul Kagan from the Claims Conference) infused the negotiations with their charisma and well-established credentials as respected leaders of the Jewish community.

To summarize: a successful reparations strategy for Jewish victims of the Holocaust combined strong leadership, consensus on minimalist positions—reparations at all cost—that brought to the table very different, rival groups and a favorable legal and political climate.

Individual Claims

How does a survivor get compensated for his or her time spent as a slave laborer during Nazi rule? One way is to go to court. To illustrate: In 1953, a Jewish survivor from Auschwitz sued the German chemical combine, IG Farben, in a *Land* (District) Court in Frankfurt—the corporate seat of the company—for "back pay" and "reparation" of the "material prejudice" he had suffered while working for Farben against his will. The court ruled in his favor. Farben appealed, and the equivalent of the State Supreme Court was asked to rule on this landmark case. The Court asked Farben to reach a compromise for the purpose of settling all claims that would arise as a result of their use of slave labor at Auschwitz. The company, upon request of the German court, contacted the Claims Conference, the official spokesperson for 23 Jewish organizations seeking reparations from the German government.

Farben and the Claims Conference reached an agreement whereby the German firm would set aside 30 million Deutsch Marks (DM)—roughly $8 million, or about $1,250 to each of more than 5,000 Farben claimants—to "alleviate the suffering endured" by the former slave laborers. It specified, however, that this gesture was precisely that—a gesture aimed at showing its goodwill towards the former Auschwitz inmates. The Claims Conference acted as the designated disbursing agency for the former Jewish inmates. Each claimant had to demonstrate that he/she had spent at least six months at Farben's Auschwitz facility in order to receive a modicum amount of 3,000 DM. As a condition for receiving the settlement, each claimant signed a waiver by which he/she agreed not to seek any further damages from Farben. For those survivors who refused to adhere to the settlement with Farben, their only recourse to obtain compensation was to take on Farben as individual petitioners through the German courts—a costly and lengthy process. Moreover, the dearth of publicly available records at the time of the settlement made it close to impossible for these survivors to prove they had ever been "employed" at Farben. Their names were present on captured German lists of deportees, but that was not sufficient to prove their presence at the Farben rubber-making facility near Auschwitz.

After 50 years, millions of pages of previously unavailable documents are now accessible in American and European archives to any and all who are interested in the issue of slave labor. The petitioners are in a better position now than ever before to obtain some form of compensation for as many as five years and as little as six months of slave labor. But the process of obtaining compensation has not changed. Two avenues are available: the global settlement reached by institutions that act as the claimant's representative or the individual course of action through the courts of the country where the company is based. The former is cheaper and less satisfying because the "reparation" is definitely symbolic at best. The latter is very expensive, and the chances of winning in a court of law are perhaps greater today than they were in the 1950s. To wit, a Jewish survivor won a $100,000 settlement in 2002 in a suit filed against the Swiss Bank Corporation (SBC) for its role in misappropriating her family's assets on deposit at the SBC's main branch in Bern during and after World War II. That action succeeded after more than six years through the federal courts of the United States (the SBC has assets in the US which a federal judge could attach, as long as the judge was convinced that jurisdiction existed to justify such a seizure).

The Role of American Companies

American companies have still not been sued for their use of slave labor in Nazi-occupied Europe. A 1943 US government census of American corporations overseas revealed the existence of more than 300 American subsidiaries operating in Germany alone, in violation of the numerous American laws aimed at ceasing American private-sector activity that might benefit the Nazis. Some of those subsidiaries were wholly owned ventures, while others were German-American joint ventures. A number of them manufactured goods for the German government and used laborers drawn from concentration camps throughout Europe. Evidence surfaced in recent years proving that American automobile manufacturers like Ford used slave labor, and that American banks like JP Morgan and Chase recorded millions of dollars in profits during the war years, especially in occupied France. For domestic political reasons, the American government never punished any of these companies for wartime wrongdoing at the service of the Reich, although a number of American firms were prosecuted and fined during the war for continuing to consult with their German and Italian colleagues on price-fixing and market-regulating matters governing the sale and distribution of products overseas.

Any legal action by the descendants of African Americans who were held in conditions of servitude that succeeds against American companies which profited from their slave labor will serve as a reminder to Holocaust survivors that they too can take on these companies in American courts for the crimes they committed over 60 years ago in Nazi-occupied Europe. A two-pronged strategy —collective action against these firms as well as individual cases—might become the Trojan Horse that releases the floodgates of reparations.

Chapter 10

Race Literacy Quiz

California Newsreel

The Race Literacy Quiz was developed by California Newsreel, in association with the Association of American Colleges and Universities. The myths and misconceptions it raises are explored in the 3-part documentary series, *RACE— The Power of an Illusion*, available on video and DVD from California Newsreel at www.newsreel.org. For more information and background, visit the companion website at www.pbs.org/race. *Answers are on page 396.*

1. Humans have approximately 30,000 genes. On average, how many genes separate all members of one race from all members of another race?
    A. None
    B. 1
    C. 23
    D. 142
    E. 1,008
    F. We don't know

2. Which characteristic did the ancient Greeks believe most distinguished them from "barbarians"?
    A. Religion
    B. Skin color
    C. Language
    D. Dress
    E. Hairiness

3. Members of a race can be identified by their:
    A. Blood group
    B. Skin color
    C. Ancestry
    D. Genes
    E. None of the above
    F. All of the above

4. Skin color correlates most closely with:
    A. Hair form
    B. IQ
    C. Risk for sickle cell, Tay-Sachs and other genetic diseases
    D. Geographic latitude
    E. Continent of ancestral origin
    F. Jumping and sprinting ability

5. Which group has the most genetic variation?
    A. Humans
    B. Chimpanzees
    C. Penguins
    D. Fruit flies
    E. Elephants

6. Which two populations are most likely, on average, to be genetically similar?
    A. Italians and Ethiopians
    B. Senegalese and Kenyans
    C. Italians and Swedes
    D. Chinese and Lakota (Sioux)
    E. Saudi Arabians and Ethiopians

7. Most human genetic variation can be found:
    A. Within any local population—for example, among Zulus or among the Hmong
    B. Between two populations on the same continent—for example, between Irish and Poles
    C. Between two populations on different continents—for example, between Koreans and Zulus
    D. Between tall people and short people
    E. Between the darkest- and the lightest-skinned people

8. Which continent has the greatest human genetic diversity?
    A. Europe
    B. Asia
    C. Africa
    D. North America
    E. South America

9. Which of the following was NOT an important reason why African slavery first took root in North America:
    A. As non-Christians, they had no legal protections
    B. They were skilled semi-tropical farmers
    C. The supply of indentured servants from Europe was becoming unreliable
    D. They were deemed innately inferior
    E. Unlike Native Americans, they were resistant to European diseases
    F. They couldn't easily run away

Chapter 11

Reverse Discrimination Quiz

Fred L. Pincus

Answers are on page 398.

1. In public opinion polls, what proportion of White respondents say that they have personally been discriminated against on the job because of their race?
    A. Less than one-eighth
    B. About one-third
    C. About one-half
    D. More than two-thirds

Questions 2 and 3 are based on a study of 183,445 employment-related race and sex discrimination complaints that were resolved by the US Equal Employment Opportunity Commission between 1995 and 2000.

2. An analysis of these complaints shows that:
    A. The number of Black and White complaints was approximately the same.
    B. Women filed about five times more complaints than men.
    C. There were more *race* discrimination cases filed by *Whites* than *sex* discrimination cases filed by *men.*
    D. All of the above.

3. In an EEOC study of race discrimination complaints filed by Whites (female as well as male) and sex discrimination complaints filed by all men, what was the most common type of discrimination alleged?

A. Hiring
B. Promotion
C. Firing
D. Harassment and intimidation

Questions 4-6 are based on a study of all 48 decisions made by the US Courts of Appeals between 1998 and 2001 involving allegations by Whites that they were discriminated against on the job because of their race and allegations by men that they were discriminated against because of their sex.

4. In these Appeals Court decisions:
   A. Most involved allegations that affirmative action policies were used illegally.
   B. The plaintiff won most of these cases.
   C. Both A and B are correct.
   D. Neither A nor B is correct.

5. The plaintiffs in these decisions are most likely to come from which of the following occupational categories:
   A. Professional/manager
   B. Blue-collar
   C. Police officer/firefighter
   D. Lower-level white-collar

6. The defendant (i.e., the employer being sued) in these decisions is most likely to be:
   A. A state or local government
   B. The federal government
   C. A for-profit corporation
   D. A not-for-profit organization

7. Hiring and promotion quotas, where a certain percentage of positions are set aside for women and minorities, are extremely controversial. According to the legal guidelines that were in effect on December 31, 2002:
   A. Quotas are the same thing as the hiring and promotion "goals."
   B. Any employer can voluntarily adopt a quota without the approval of a court.
   C. It is generally illegal for an employer to have a quota where no White men could be hired or promoted.
   D. All of the above.

Questions 8-10 are based on statistics collected by various agencies of the federal government.

8. Looking at the 2001 national unemployment rates for college graduates 25 years of age or older:
    A. Blacks and Hispanics are more likely than Whites to be unemployed.
    B. Men are more likely than women to be unemployed.
    C. Both A and B are correct.
    D. Neither A nor B is correct.

9. Looking at the median income of year-round, full-time workers with bachelors degrees but no advanced degree:
    A. White males earn over $10,000 more than any other race/gender group.
    B. Black and Hispanic women earn more than White women.
    C. Black and Hispanic men earn less than White women.
    D. All of the above.

10. According to a 2001 Small Business Administration study:
    A. Minorities account for 30% of the population and 15% of the business owners but had only 6% of federal contracts.
    B. Women account for more than half of the population and 38% of the business owners but had only 2% of federal contracts.
    C. Both A and B are correct.
    D. Neither A nor B is correct.

Poverty

Chapter 12

From Poverty to Social Exclusion: Lessons from Europe

Hilary Silver and S.M. Miller

The United States has been slow in updating its conceptualization of poverty and its understanding of those living at the margins of society. The US government considers poverty to be strictly a deficiency of income for basic necessities. In contrast, the European Union has continually revised its thinking about social deprivation, adopting a view of poverty relative to rising average living standards and, more recently, as encompassing non-monetary aspects of deprivation. Further, Europeans are now committed to include the "excluded," the outsiders, the people left out of mainstream society and left behind in a globalizing economy. The EU has adopted resolutions and issued directives to actualize this goal. As American experts debate changes to the nation's poverty statistics, they would do well to consider the European approach to "social exclusion."

Ironically, Europeans, such as the Englishman B. Seebohm Rowntree, pioneered the American method of counting the poor. The US Census Bureau uses an absolute monetary threshold based upon bare subsistence requirements. This "poverty line" reflects a convenient rule of thumb that a government economist, Mollie Orshansky, devised in 1964 and has since become a policy and social science fixture. It multiplies the value of an "economy food plan" times three (since families then spent about one-third of their after-tax earnings on food). This narrow approach persists, even though today, food, including restaurant meals, occupies a mere 15% of American budgets on average. The extant poverty threshold for families of different sizes and compositions, adjusted over

time only for inflation, identifies those living in the direst material circumstances, not those living below what John Kenneth Galbraith termed "the grades
and standards" of society.

In 1995, the National Research Council recommended limited changes to
the poverty line to reflect real consumption relative to income from all money
and non-monetary sources, including government taxes and transfers, minus
basic and medical needs, child support and work-related expenses. After a decade of research and over 50 scientific articles examining close to two dozen experimental poverty measures, there has not yet been an official redefinition. A
consensus is emerging, however, that a new "quasi-relative" measure of "low
income" is needed, and should be periodically updated to reflect actual American expenditure data, although not relative to changes in overall median income.

The European Commission considers poverty to be an inadequacy of resources that precludes people "from having a standard of living considered acceptable in the society in which they live." Therefore, the EU adopted as the
official poverty line a *relative* indicator: one-half of the nationally-equivalent
median disposable household income. It rises when societies grow richer. EU
statistical reports also provide data on 60% of median income in order to count
people "at risk of poverty." Furthermore, concern about rising income inequality, a problem much worse in the US than in Europe, motivated the development
of comparative income distribution measures, most notably with the Luxembourg Income Study, established in 1983. As the European Community Household Panel Survey (ECHP) and the longitudinal EU Statistics on Income and
Living Conditions (SILC) study build up data over the years, Europe will also
have dynamic indicators of poverty, tracking those who enter, leave and stay
mired in destitution.

The European approach to poverty grew out of the first three EU Poverty
Programmes, launched in the mid-1970s and ending in the mid-1990s. But the
real European innovation is the development of non-monetary indicators of "social exclusion," transcending economists' focus on money. Since the 1980s,
mention of "social exclusion" in European public and academic discourse has
increased much faster than references to "poverty" or "the underclass," although
these terms are commonly used synonymously. Cognizant that deprivation is a
multi-dimensional condition, Eurostat (the EU Statistical Office), national statistical agencies and European social scientists have developed social and political
benchmarks to track progress not only against poverty, but also social exclusion.

The Origins of "Social Exclusion"

Europeans conceive of social exclusion as distinct from income poverty. Poverty
is a distributional outcome, whereas exclusion is a relational process of declining sociability, participation, solidarity and access to social rights and resources.
To some, exclusion is the broader term encompassing poverty; to others, it is a

cause or a consequence of poverty. Most research finds they are empirically inter-related, but independent, social phenomena. Disrespect, discrimination and degradation are as much at work as monetary poverty and physical need.

Social exclusion is: (1) multi-dimensional or socioeconomic, and encompasses collective as well as individual resources; (2) dynamic or processual, along a trajectory between full integration and multiple exclusions; (3) relational, in that exclusion entails social distance or isolation, rejection, humiliation, lack of social support networks and denial of participation; (4) active, in that there is clear agency doing the excluding; and (5) relative to context.

There may be consensus that exclusion is multi-dimensional, but that does not mean agreement on which dimensions are operative. There is also disagreement over whether multi-dimensionality refers to "cumulative" disadvantage or to any one of a wide range of deprivations that need not be material or economic. Multiple disadvantages obviously characterize fewer individuals and neighborhoods than those suffering from one of a number of disadvantages. Similarly, many more people suffer disadvantage at some point in their lives than those who remain disadvantaged for long periods.

The meaning of social exclusion also varies across countries. The term originated in France, where they rejected the "Anglo-Saxon" idea of "poverty" as patronizing or denigrating equal citizens. French Republican thinkers refer to social exclusion as a "rupture of the social bond" or "solidarity." In the social contract, society owes its citizens the means to a livelihood, and citizens in turn have obligations to the larger society. As an expression of solidarity, the welfare state should do away with "charity" for "the poor," providing basic social assistance, hence eliminating absolute material deprivation as a right of citizenship.

Many sociological theories adumbrated the concept of exclusion, but French advocates for destitute groups, especially Social Catholics such as the ATD-Fourth World Movement, were among the first to employ the term in its contemporary sense. By the 1970s, references to "the excluded" became more frequent. The coining of the term in policy circles is frequently ascribed to René Lenoir who, in 1974, estimated the excluded, such as the handicapped, delinquents and substance abusers, at one-tenth of the French population. After the oil shocks, as unemployment began to mount, especially among youth, older workers and immigrants, the problem groups "excluded" from economic growth multiplied. In the 1980s, "exclusion" discourse helped cement a national coalition of diverse associations, ALERTE, urging France to launch a comprehensive war on exclusion. Among the leaders was Father Joseph Wresinski, founder of the ATD-Fourth World Movement and author of an influential report on severe poverty.

Unlike the US, where a guaranteed income was proposed but rejected in the Nixon years, and where the Earned Income Tax Credit, Food Stamps and other social transfers have eligibility restrictions, France enacted in 1988 a universal (adult) minimum "insertion" income (RMI). The program won support from both the Right and the Left. Conforming to Republican thinking, the RMI entails signing an "insertion" contract specifying a trajectory to become a productive member of society, whether through work, volunteering, studying, family reunification or the like. Social workers and nonprofits provide multi-faceted, comprehensive and personally tailored assistance, from health care to subsidized jobs, to help the excluded re-enter social life in all its spheres. Thus, in France, social bonds are reknit in families and communities as well as in the workplace.

Most policies promoting social inclusion emphasize: (1) multi-pronged interventions crossing traditional bureaucratic domains and tailored to the multidimensional problems of excluded individuals and groups; (2) a long-term process of insertion and integration moving through transitional stages; and (3) participation of the excluded in their own inclusion into economic and social life. The latter is especially important because targeted and means-tested programs may unintentionally stigmatize their intended beneficiaries.

From France, the "exclusion" approach dispersed throughout Europe. Between 1989 and 1997, when it became part of the Amsterdam Treaty, the term was increasingly used in a wide range of EU documents. During this period, the third EU "poverty programme" was gradually transformed into a fight against social exclusion. The program supported over two dozen local Model Actions and 12 Innovatory Initiatives "to foster the economic and social integration of the least privileged groups."

The transition from poverty to exclusion thinking was not an easy one. Academics argued that "social exclusion" transcends the idea of "poverty" because (as noted above) it is a multi-dimensional, relational, dynamic process, encompassing individual and community resources and political and social participation. Robert Castel, Serge Paugam and other French sociologists emphasized the social dynamics and duration of exclusion, tracing a trajectory of "disaffiliation" and "disqualification" from a condition of economic and social integration through vulnerability or fragility to a breakdown of social ties.

In 1997, once Britain's New Labour government accepted the Social Protocol of the 1992 Maastricht Treaty and created a "Social Exclusion Unit" in Prime Minister Blair's office, the EU's fight against social exclusion could begin in earnest. Committed to "basic principles of solidarity which should remain the trademark of Europe" and drawing upon lessons from building monetary union, the "Luxembourg Process" set in motion a European Employment Strategy intended to mutually reinforce economic and social policies. This comprehensive approach was reaffirmed at the March 2000 Lisbon meeting of the European Council of Ministers, consisting of heads of state. In order for Europe to become the "most competitive and dynamic knowledge-based economy" over the next decade, the Council declared, it must combine "sustainable economic growth with more and better jobs and greater social cohesion."

Yet the Employment Strategy was "soft law"—that is, it integrated European, national and local level efforts through peer pressure and without recourse to regulations with formal sanctions. This "open method of coordination" makes use of multi-level iterative monitoring to promote learning from national best practices and from modifications of targets and procedures over time. Though lacking legal force, these tools of target-setting, peer review and benchmarking are viewed by scholars as a means to "name and shame" countries that lag behind the others.

In December 2000 at Nice, the EU Council applied the open method of coordination to the social dimension of EU strategy, separating the fight against poverty and exclusion from the more general Employment Strategy. Every two years beginning in June 2001, nation-states were to produce "National Action Plans" on social inclusion, laying out their progress towards agreed-upon goals on a variety of social indicators. A Community Action Programme running from 2002-06 would provide funds to coordinate the fight against exclusion among local associations.

Between 2001 and 2003, Tony Atkinson and other experts in the Indicators Sub-Group of the Social Protection Committee worked on developing common indicators for the National Action Plans on social inclusion. They used a "shorthand" or working definition of social exclusion, because it is so difficult to define, and drew upon available data. Although most of the indicators covered material and labor market deprivation better than social, political or cultural dimensions, they provided an initial framework for the national comparisons in the first two Joint Reports on Social Inclusion in 2001 and 2003.

In late 2001, the European Commission and Council of Ministers adopted the first *Joint Inclusion Report*. It specified four objectives:
1. Facilitating participation in employment and access to resources and rights, goods and services for all citizens
2. Preventing the risks of exclusion
3. Helping the most vulnerable
4. Mobilizing participation of all relevant actors, including the excluded.

After reviewing national action plans, the second Joint Report on Social Protection and Social Inclusion laid out new, more detailed policy priorities to tackle poverty and social exclusion in a coordinated, participative manner at the national, regional and local levels:
1. Increasing labor market participation
2. Modernizing social protection systems
3. Tackling disadvantages in education and training
4. Eliminating child poverty, especially intergenerational inheritance of poverty
5. Ensuring decent accommodations and integrating approaches to homelessness
6. Improving access to quality services
7. Overcoming discrimination and increasing the integration of people with disabilities, ethnic minorities and immigrants.

Since May 2003, the fight against social exclusion has become just one strand in a larger "streamlined" open method of coordination of social protection. The Commission's attempt to strengthen the "social dimension" of the Lis-

bon Strategy for growth and employment joined social inclusion efforts to reforms, first, of pensions, and subsequently, of health care. Streamlining also
included a reduction in strategic reports to a single one every three years from
2006 on.

The European approach to social exclusion has recently extended beyond
the EU's original 15 members. As of 2004, the ten Central and Eastern European "accession countries" joining the European Union adopted the goal of social inclusion. During the 1990s, the Council of Europe had already developed a
program that encompassed Central and Eastern Europe. But social exclusion
discourse has further diffused. After an initial comparative study for the 1995
Copenhagen Social Summit, the International Labour Office established the
STEP program (Strategies and Tools against Social Exclusion and Poverty) and
the CIARIS (Center for Informatic Apprenticeship and Resources in Social Inclusion) network to exchange good practices among local community groups
throughout the world. The World Bank, Asian Development Bank and Inter-
American Development Bank have all devoted resources to promoting social
inclusion. Indeed, former World Bank President James Wolfensohn made a major speech in 1997 on "The Challenge of Inclusion." The United Nations Development Program and the UNESCO MOST Program (Management of Social
Transformations) also published reports on exclusion.

Racial/Ethnic Exclusion

Social exclusion takes on different meanings, depending upon context. When
Americans speak of "exclusion," racial connotations often spring to mind: There
are "exclusionary" institutions, like clubs or zoning, or "exclusive" prestigious
resources, like neighborhoods or prep schools. President Bill Clinton made frequent use of exclusion discourse. His 1995 Affirmative Action Report, calling to
"mend it, don't end it," is full of calls for inclusion. His 1998 race relations
speech maintained that affirmative action "has given us a whole generation of
professionals in fields that used to be exclusive clubs." In Clinton's 1993 remarks on inner-city problems, he declared, "It's not an underclass anymore, it's
an outer class." Clearly, American race relations are central in defining the significance and common understanding of the term "integration" in the US.

Other countries have different ideas about what belonging, membership and
full participation mean and about the benefits they bestow. Different histories,
cultures and social compositions shape national identities and criteria for citizenship and the salient types of inclusion. On the Continent, access to social
rights traditionally came through class representation by the "social partners"
(e.g., union federations and employers' organizations). "Solidarity" entailed
both recognition and redistribution.

Since the end of World War II, Europeans, unlike Americans, have felt uncomfortable with the word "race." Until recently, Europe had few affirmative

action policies and avoided specific diversity targets. Equal opportunity policies, such as the 1975 Equal Pay Directive and later directives on equal treatment, part-time working rights and parental leave, applied mainly to women. Yet the vastly higher rates of unemployment, poverty and other disadvantages among immigrants and ethnic foreigners were difficult to address with existing welfare state policies. Belatedly, on June 20, 2000, the European Council adopted Directive 2000/43/EC, "Implementing the Principle of Equal Treatment between Persons Irrespective of Racial or Ethnic Origin." This "racial directive" went into effect in 2003, requiring member states to bring national legislation into conformity with this law. The EU also initiated a well-funded Community Action Programme to combat discrimination, partly through the EQUAL program to fight labor market discrimination. After the second Open Method of Coordination round on social inclusion, the 2005 Joint Report on Social Protection and Social Inclusion called for more attention to the social "integration" of minorities, including the Roma (gypsies) in the Central and Eastern European countries. In the next few years, the EU will also attack age and disability discrimination, as well as health and environmental dimensions.

Most agree that the excluded should participate in their own inclusion. This means policies must provide them access, status and "voice," rather than making them passive recipients of material assistance. Following the practices of the "social partners," Europeans associations, NGOs, professionals and other interest groups have mobilized and demanded to participate in designing, executing, monitoring and evaluating social inclusion policies. However, this has proved easier at the local than the national level. In some countries, there is a fear that official state recognition of racial, religious and other groups may institutionalize minority identities and impede integration in the long run. France, in particular, resists "multi-culturalism," while the United Kingdom embraces it.

Measuring Social Exclusion

The complexity and relativity of social exclusion, its sensitivity to context and time, and its variation across salient dimensions, processes and domains of social relations have made it extremely difficult to define and measure "scientifically." Yet, driven by EU policy mandates, efforts to operationalize the concept separately from poverty have outpaced theoretical work.

The dominant approach to measurement is clearly British-inspired. In line with the "results-oriented government" of Prime Minister Tony Blair, the 1999 White Paper, *Opportunity for All*, and the Social Exclusion Unit enumerated dozens of indicators and targets to monitor progress, especially towards the promise to eradicate child poverty by 2020. Elsewhere in Europe, all approaches attempt to capture exclusion's multi-dimensionality, but aside from low income and unemployment, they do not agree upon which dimensions are salient or causal. Tony Atkinson's influential measurement scheme was adopted for the

National Action Plans. It proposed three levels of social exclusion indicators. Level 1 has a small number of leading or primary indicators to be reported in all National Action Plans. Nine Level 2 secondary indicators elaborate these. Level 3 refers to nationally specific indicators. The revised list of primary indicators used in the second 2003 Open Method of Coordination round appears in the accompanying box.

EU Common Indicators of Poverty and Social Exclusion

Primary Indicators
(broken down by age and gender)

- At Risk of Poverty (household size and composition-adjusted disposable income relative to 60% of nationally equivalent median income with OECD equivalence scales, before and after social transfers) by economic activity; household type; housing tenure
- Income inequality (top-20%-to-bottom-20% quintile share ratio)
- Persistent at-risk-of-poverty (share of the population below the poverty line for current year and at least two of three preceding years
- Relative median poverty risk gap (ratio of median income of those at-risk-of-poverty and the at-risk-of-poverty threshold)
- Regional cohesion (coefficient of variation of employment rates among territorial regions)
- Long-term unemployment rate (share of 15-64-year-olds in active population who were unemployed by ILO definition for 12 months or more)
- Share of children and working-age adults living in households with no member employed
- Early school leavers not in education or training (proportion of 18-24-year-olds with only lower secondary education and not in education or training in the prior four weeks)
- Life expectancy at birth
- Self-defined health status (as bad or very bad) by bottom and top of income distribution

Source: European Commission, Joint Report on Social Inclusion. Brussels, July 2003, Appendix.

Although this official list stresses consumption and production, work is under way to measure more social and political dimensions of exclusion. The 2005 Joint Report underlined "the need to better capture the multi-dimensional nature of social exclusion" and "adapting to the diversity of challenges in the Member States." European researchers are examining less tangible aspects like non-participation in civic life, poor future prospects, financial precariousness, inability to participate in customary family and community activities, multiply-deprived areas in depressed regions and large cities, education, literacy/numeracy, access to the Internet, housing and homelessness. Events increasing exclusion, such as prior delinquency or a prison record, are considered. Some studies examine exclusion from public and private services, from social relations and sociable activities, from social support, even from leisure and culture. Insofar as social exclusion is a relational concept associated with social isolation or civic participation, one might employ indicators of "social capital," such as associational membership, social network involvement, and democratic inclusion or voting rights. Regional disparities aside from unemployment also exist, including exposure to crime and dangerous environmental conditions. The duration, accumulation and spatial concentration of any of these "ruptures" can be measured, too. The list can go on and on, as NGOs and the "social partners" participate in the statistical process, giving a voice to the excluded in devising benchmarks that hold governments accountable for social inclusion.

The latest innovation in measuring social inclusion addresses the growing numbers of non-naturalized immigrants, composing over 13 million people, or 3½% of the population living in the 15 older member states of the European Union. Immigrant unemployment is double or more that of the native-born in most European countries. Recognizing that social cohesion rests on the peaceful incorporation of newcomers through a process of mutual acceptance and tolerance, the British Council, Foreign Policy Center and Migration Policy Group initiated the development of a "European Civic Citizenship and Inclusion Index." It gauges the extent to which immigrants have rights and obligations comparable to EU citizens. Although an international team was involved, British institutions and scholars again took the lead in developing this measure.

The index is based upon almost 100 indicators, grouped into five policy areas ordered by immigrants' progressive stages towards full citizenship. It assumes the immigrant inclusion process requires: 1) Labor market inclusion, 2) Family reunion, 3) Long-term residence, 4) Naturalization, and 5) Anti-discrimination measures. The first annual report provides the initial 2003 benchmarks for each country, and reveals that countries implement their common commitment to inclusion very differently, although they tend to rank consistently across the five areas. So far, member states have not systematically enforced EU Directives and national laws forbidding discrimination against immigrants.

The report states that: "Inclusion requires more than just access to the labour market. Work is not enough—for immigrants to be included successfully into society, they need to feel secure, and to feel that their contribution over time is valued." Yet, the index only looks at inclusion from the perspective of the labor market and civic citizenship, and neglects cultural integration and political participation. Furthermore, the index measures a "thin" definition of citizenship (legal formalities like the existence of laws and policies) more than a "thick" or substantive conception, assessing whether those policies are effective in prodding communities to actually include and accept immigrants. Work on European racial and ethnic inclusion indicators has just begun. In sum, reviewing the existing indicators and confronting the challenges of measurement suggest that no single "exclusion line" is likely in the near future.

Empirical Research

Despite the measurement challenges, researchers throughout the EU have conducted empirical studies of social exclusion itself, its causes and consequences. Most of the research has analyzed survey data or relied on local field work. Consequently, individual characteristics that increase the risks of various kinds of social exclusion and face-to-face relations in the family and local community have received most attention as "causes" of exclusion. Policy evaluations focus more on clients than on the professionals and bureaucrats who run the programs or employers who might hire them.

Reflecting the long British tradition of poverty studies, empirical research on social exclusion in that country burgeoned after the establishment of the Social Exclusion Unit in 1997. Aside from the government's research, two other important groups have produced studies of social exclusion in Britain. The Centre for the Analysis of Social Exclusion operationalizes exclusion with the British Household Panel Survey in terms of four inter-related dimensions of participation in "normal" activities of society: (1) consumption (less than half the mean net household income) and savings; (2) production (those still economically active who are not engaged in socially valued activity); (3) political engagement (those who do not vote or belong to political organizations); and, most important for our purposes, (4) social interaction (social isolation as a lack of social support in five different situations). While inter-related, the associations among dimensions were moderate to weak. Very few British people are excluded on all these dimensions, especially over a five-year period.Second, the Bristol group conducted a new Poverty and Social Exclusion survey that examined four "themes" of social exclusion: (1) income poverty and material deprivation; (2) exclusion from the labor market; (3) exclusion from public services; and (4) exclusion from social relations. Four aspects of the latter received attention. First, on indicators of participation in "common social activities," respondents indicated whether they considered an activity essential, whether they actually engaged in it, and if not, what prevented them. For some essential social activities, sizable minorities did not enjoy an evening out once a fortnight, a meal out once a month, a week's holiday away from home, a hobby or leisure activity, and having friends round for a meal, snack or drink. Second, indicators of "social isolation" and living alone included marital status and household composition. Third, isolation and non-participation implied the lack of emotional and material "social support." Fourth, "civic disengagement" tapped more than just "thick" formal citizenship but also active involvement in public affairs.

Another Bristol innovation was that, rather than define inclusion arbitrarily, the researchers did something similar to those constructing "subjective" poverty measures: They asked a representative sample of Britons what *they* considered "normal" social activities. The Poverty and Social Exclusion survey also examined constraints on individual choice. Respondents indicated whether their unwanted exclusion was due to lack of affordability or to non-financial obstacles, such as poor transport, fear of crime, child care needs, time stress, physical barriers or cultural inappropriateness. Perhaps more comprehensively than any other study to date, the Bristol group examined the specifically *social* aspects of exclusion.

National-level studies following the coping strategies of long-term unemployed individuals have also been conducted in the Netherlands and Germany. They reveal a variety of adaptations to multiple disadvantage and joblessness, some more positive than others.

There are also several cross-national studies of social exclusion, most using the European Community Household Panel survey. Target groups at high risk of exclusion—youth, lone parents, the disabled, the elderly—are compared across countries in different regions and with different welfare regimes. The national welfare mix of support from family, market and state helps account for the extent and demographics of material disadvantage. Most studies show that income poverty is not closely correlated with social relations, participation or isolation. For example, the unemployed in the Southern European countries score higher than the employed on indicators of sociability in the primary sphere of family relations, the secondary sphere of neighbors, friends and extended kin, and the tertiary sphere of organizational and associative life. In fact, some studies find that poverty and exclusion are unrelated. Research also shows that social exclusion can increase the risk of individual material deprivation as well as the reverse. These findings appear to support the autonomous existence of social exclusion as a problem distinct from poverty, and to reinforce the assertion that cumulative disadvantage in all aspects of life is exceedingly rare.

Implications for the United States

Poverty-line thinking pervades American social policy. For example, "welfare" in the US has narrowed its meaning to means-tested income transfers to lone parents. Yet welfare "reform" in many states has in fact gone beyond mere income transfers to mobilizing multi-dimensional social support that enables these parents to enter the paid labor force. In this context, the rhetoric of "inclusion"

—the demand for access to jobs, respect and a place at the table—may not be as foreign as it sounds.

How many working Americans are excluded from good jobs because of inadequate family support or child care or transportation or inferior public schools? How many are excluded from health, unemployment or disability insurance? How many are shut out of the housing market by unaffordable rents? Isn't segregation about exclusion from white middle-class neighborhoods, schools, suburbs? Has the Americans with Disabilities Act really eliminated physical exclusion from all public facilities? Are not formally equal citizens denied a say, while politicians listen only to campaign contributors, and school officials listen only to English speakers?

Social exclusion and inclusion could become important ideas in the American public discourse alongside concerns with absolute poverty. Currently, groups concerned about neighborhoods (crime, services, education), the labor market (low wages, insecure employment, long-term unemployment, contingent work, unemployment insurance), social programs and services (Medicaid, Temporary Assistance for Needy Families, Food Stamps, child care), school performance, immigration and many other issues are fragmented and even competitive. A social exclusion/inclusion approach could serve as the rhetorical umbrella that cements a coalition among these groups.

The role of symbolic discourse in building political alliances should not be underestimated. Talking about "exclusion" connects people at all levels of the society through a common emotional experience found in social relations everywhere. No one can get through life without some rejection, humiliation or unfair treatment. We have all been subjected to sanctions like gossip, or felt unwanted, left out, stigmatized or "dissed." The goal of inclusion appeals to our democratic impulses and common humanity, promoting solidarity with the excluded. Emma Lazarus's poem still strikes a deep chord with Americans whose ancestors were welcomed into our nation of immigrants. We are ashamed today of our history of nativist exclusion laws. Similarly, Americans demand equal opportunity, even if they do tolerate unequal rewards. Hard times can befall anyone, and everyone deserves a second chance. This thought too can help us empathize with the excluded.

Just as "social exclusion" highlights the complex multi-dimensionality and sometimes cumulative character of social disadvantage, so must inclusionary policies transcend traditional bureaucratic domains. Discrete programs and single-focus policies that now administer to people in need are, to put it euphemistically, disjointed. Service providers in different agencies have little contact with one another. Families with multiple problems must make the rounds among many bureaucracies operating in different ways, each with scant understanding of families' overall situation, nor attention to improving their overall situation. Americans need more comprehensive, "transversal," or what the British call "joined-up policies for joined-up problems" across social policy domains. Britain's Social Exclusion Unit or France's "inter-ministerial" commissions coordinate national policy areas across ministries. Regional and local public-private partnerships collectively administer social assistance and service programs. One-stop service centers and casework that tailors entire packages of support and assistance to individual needs are back in vogue. In the US, more progressive states now pursue similar strategies in their welfare-to-work policies, but integrating TANF with the Workforce Improvement Act and social services should become national policy.

Social inclusion policies in Europe also point to the importance of expanding the American notion of "work" in welfare reform. To participate in society does not have to mean simply taking a low-paid job. Work should encompass further education and training, engaging in community service and contributing to a sustainable environment.

The great divides of American society are not only economic but are also based on racial-ethnic, gender, cultural, educational and political status lines. Discrimination and disrespect have material consequences, denying access to information, contacts and resources, consigning minorities to low-quality schools, dangerous neighborhoods, poorly paid jobs and even joblessness. Americanizing the social exclusion perspective could put new wind in the sails of affirmative action. Calling for full inclusion would show how poverty, racism and other forms of domination are integral to the functioning of American society, rather than accidental or unintended consequences easily addressed with an ameliorative program or financial adjustment here or there.

As the critics warn, there is a danger of ghettoization and stigmatization whenever we introduce new labels for social problems. Calling attention to spectacular forms of cumulative disadvantage may distract attention from other problems and undermine support for other social programs. Any discourse can serve a variety of political purposes, but insuring widespread participation may overcome these downsides. While experts honestly argue about the precise nature and measures of exclusion and cohesion, these ideas do provide a flexible and popular framework for discussing the new, complex forms of disadvantage. If appropriate, easily understood indicators could be found for these notions, benchmarking our progress as a society could go beyond the simple, intuitive and familiar poverty line to track multiple forms of disadvantage. The British Social Exclusion Unit is already doing this.

Skeptics may find it useful to recall FDR's 1944 State of the Union address in which he called for "a second Bill of Rights under which a new basis of security and prosperity can be established for all, regardless of station, race, or creed." He enumerated many dimensions of social inclusion, such as a right to "a useful and remunerative job," a right "to earn enough to provide adequate food and clothing and recreation" and a "right to a decent home." The discourse of this great American President can continue to inspire us today. His goal was nothing less than "to make a country in which no one is left out." A more recent President, in his 1996 acceptance speech to the Democratic Party, proclaimed, "I want to build a bridge to the twenty-first century that ends the permanent underclass, that lifts up the poor, and ends their isolation, their exile." With the right leadership, Americans cannot fail to resonate with the discourse of social exclusion.

Resources on Social Exclusion

EAPN (European Network of Associations of the Fight Against Poverty and Social Exclusion), rue Belliard 205 – Box 13, B-1040, Brussels, telephone (32) 2230 44 55

UNIOPPS (Inter-federal national institution of social and medical private works and organisms of France), 122, rue Saint-Maur 75541, Paris cedex, telephone (33) 1 53 36 35 00

ATD-Quart Monde (Fourth World Movement, US National Center, 7600 Willow Hill Drive, Landover, MD 20785-4658, telephone (301) 336-9489

* * *

Atkinson, Tony, Bea Cantillon, Eric Marlier & Brian Nolan. *Social Indicators: The EU and Social Inclusion* (Oxford University Press, 2002).

Castel, Robert. *From Manual Workers to Wage Workers* (Transaction, 2002).

Commission of the European Communities. *Joint Report on Social Protection and Social Inclusion.* (Brussels, 2005).

Commission of the European Communities, *Joint Report on Social Inclusion* (Brussels, 2003).

Gordon, David & Peter Townsend, eds. *Breadline Europe: The Measurement of Poverty* (Policy Press, 2000).

Iceland, John. *Experimental Poverty Measures: Summary of a Workshop* (National Academies Press, 2005).

Gallie, Duncan & Serge Paugam, eds. *Welfare Regimes and the Experience of Unemployment in Europe* (Oxford University Press, 2000).

Rosenfeld, Jona & Bruno Tardieu. *Artisans of Democracy: How Ordinary People, Families in Extreme Poverty, and Social Institutions Become Allies to Overcome Social Exclusion* (University Press of America, 2000).

Silver, Hilary. "Social Exclusion and Social Solidarity: Three Paradigms" (*International Labour Review*, 1994).

Chapter 13

The Ethno/Racial Context of Poverty in Rural and Small Town America

Calvin L. Beale

Everyone with an interest in rural and small town poverty in the United States is aware that it frequently occurs in an ethno/racial context, just as in cities. This article is intended primarily to look at nonmetropolitan (nonmetro) areas having high incidence of poverty, as revealed by the 2000 Census, and: (1) to determine the extent to which such poverty is that of minority populations; and (2) to identify ways in which these areas vary by their ethno/racial makeup in poverty-relevant characteristics of education, health, dependency per worker, steadiness of work, family structure, transportation and language proficiency. It will also review trends in poverty levels from 1990-2000.

The standard used to denote a high-poverty incidence is 20% or more of the population. This is better than a third higher than the nonmetro average of 14.7% and, by representing a fifth or more of all residents of an area, is surely a conservative indicator of the presence of serious income problems. (Poverty income thresholds vary by number and age of persons in households and families. For a family of two adults and two children, the Census poverty measure was annual income less than $16,895 in the preceding year, 1999.) Nonmetro counties are those not in metro areas, which contain urbanized cores of 50,000 or more people, with boundaries generalized out to county lines and including any fringe counties that meet certain tests of metro character and job commuting into the core counties.

Of all nonmetro counties, 444 (a fifth) had poverty rates of 20% or higher in the 2000 Census, based on income received in the prior year (Table 1). In three-fourths of this group, the high poverty proves to be primarily that of racial or ethnic minorities. In such counties, either: (1) a majority of the poor are Black, Native American or Hispanic; or (2) it is only the high incidence of poverty among these minority groups that brings the overall county rate above 20%. In the remaining fourth of the high-poverty counties, the problem is predominantly among non-Hispanic Whites, with most such areas being in the Southern Highlands—centered on Eastern Kentucky, West Virginia and parts of Missouri and Oklahoma.

Black High-Poverty Areas

Two hundred and ten of the high-poverty counties were characterized by poverty among Blacks. They lie in the old plantation belt of the Southern coastal plain, especially from Southern North Carolina through Louisiana. Here, 39% of the Black population lived with poverty-level income (Table 1), a proportion well above that of Blacks in other nonmetro counties (28.1%) or in metro areas (23.7%). Among measures relevant to poverty that can be identified from the Census, the counties of high Black poverty stand out most prominently in the fact that 32.7% of all children under 18 lived in female-headed households with no husband present. This is a much higher proportion than that found in other types of high-poverty areas, and double that in nonmetro counties that have less than 20% poverty. Poverty in female-headed families with children, but no husband present, is dramatically higher everywhere than is true of other household types. In nonmetro America as a whole, persons in such families had a poverty rate of 41.6%, whereas in all other families with minor children the rate was just 9.6%.

The Black high-poverty counties also have the highest rate of households without a motor vehicle (12.5%), thus inhibiting access to employment and essential services. In addition, they have the highest self-reported incidence of disability (27% of the population 21-64 years of age) of any of the minority high-poverty county blocs. In this respect, though, the high-poverty areas of the Southern Highlands—where the population is overwhelmingly non-Hispanic White—report a higher disability rate (31%) than any of the minority groups, a pattern consistent with earlier censuses.

Hispanic High-Poverty Areas

In 74 counties, high poverty derived from conditions among Hispanics. Although these counties are still concentrated in the Southwest, especially in Texas and New Mexico, they have begun to appear elsewhere, with examples now in Florida, Georgia, Missouri and Washington as Hispanics have both dispersed and grown rapidly from immigration. Within the 74 counties, Hispanic poverty averaged 32.3%, a lower incidence than that of Blacks in Black poverty areas, and a major decline from the 41% level in the 1990 Census. This drop was achieved despite the fact that Hispanics rose as a percentage of the entire population in these areas (from 52.8% to 58.5%), while the higher-income non-Hispanic Whites became a smaller proportion and often decreased in absolute numbers as well from outmigration. Despite this rising dominance of Hispanics in high-poverty areas where the poor are mostly Hispanic, a declining proportion of all nonmetro Hispanics live in such areas. Their growth in other areas was so rapid in the 1990s that the percentage of all nonmetro Hispanics living in the Hispanic high-poverty counties fell from 34.1% to 25.6%. This contrasts with nonmetro Blacks and Native Americans, who showed little shift away from high-poverty areas beyond their 1990 level.

The Hispanic high-poverty counties are very different from others in one social measure—the percentage of people who reported they do not speak English "very well" (21.7%). The lack of English proficiency is especially prevalent in areas where recent immigration has been large, such as along the Mexican border, but also is far above average in longer-settled areas. Hispanic poverty counties have a large minority of adults who have not completed high school (36.8%), a condition partly derived from the frequency of recent immigration. This is well above the corresponding figure of 21.3% for Hispanics in nonmetro counties that do not have high poverty, although it is no worse than is found in the non-Hispanic Southern Highlands poverty areas. Both the Hispanic and Black high-poverty county groups have more than double the ratio of high school dropouts to persons with a four-year college degree than is found in nonmetro counties that do not have high-poverty.

Native American High-Poverty Areas

Forty nonmetro counties with high poverty incidence reflected low income among Native Americans, including Alaskan natives. They are all in areas of either historic tribal presence or 19th Century Indian removal, especially in the Northern Plains, coastal Alaska, the Southwest and Oklahoma. The poverty level of Native Americans within these counties was 40.7%, a level greater than that of the dominant minorities in other high-poverty county groups. Furthermore, the Native American counties did not simply have a higher incidence of poverty, they had the highest occurrence of severe poverty. A full fifth (20.5%) of the total population in these areas lived in households with income less than three-fourths the poverty standard. Thus, substantial increases in income—whether from earnings, retirement or assistance—would be required to lift this segment of the population to a minimally sufficient level of living.

The Native American high-poverty counties also had the highest ratio of total population to employed people of all county groups, with 288 persons of all ages for every 100 with jobs. By comparison, in nonmetro counties with poverty lower than 20%, there were just 214 persons for each 100 workers. The high dependency ratio in Native American counties stems partly from the age composition of the population, but its impact on income adequacy is worsened by the fact that only 36% of all males 16 years old and over had full-time, year-round work, compared with 47.5% in nonmetro counties without high poverty. Low labor force participation, high unemployment within the labor force and lack of steady work for those employed all contribute to the situation.

Children and the elderly are typically regarded as the most vulnerable classes in society. With a comparatively young population, Native American persons in poverty consist much more of children (and, perforce, the parent or parents with whom they live) than of elderly people, in comparison with other minorities or the general population. In the Native American high-poverty counties, there were 5.9 poor children (under age 18) for each poor person 65 and over. This compares with ratios of 4.2:1 in Hispanic counties, 3.2:1 in the Black counties and only 2.6:1 in nonmetro counties with poverty incidence below 20%. Thus, alleviation of the conditions produced by poverty has to be more focused on children and their parents than it does in most other areas.

In many of the Native American high-poverty areas, especially in the Northern Plains, the non-Hispanic White proportion of the population has been dwindling steadily as the Native American population has grown and the number of local White farmers and ranchers has fallen. The non-Hispanic White share of population in these areas fell from 44.5% in 1990 to 39.8% in 2000. Thus, the overall 1990-2000 reduction in poverty rate in the Native American areas, from 34.0% to 28.3%, was achieved despite the diminished presence of the racial group with the highest income.

Asian and Pacific Islander High-Poverty Areas

The Asian and Pacific Islander population is comparatively small in nonmetro locations and is the main component of the poor in only two high-poverty counties. One is Aleutians East Borough, Alaska, where in 2000 a large group of Filipino men lived who worked in seafood processing but lacked good income. The other instance was Kalawao County, Hawaii, where most residents are elderly Hawaiian and Asian survivors of the former colony for persons with Hansen's disease (leprosy). Nationally, Asian and Pacific Islander nonmetro poverty stood at 15.6%, well below that of other ethno/racial minorities.

Table 1 – Characteristics of nonmetro counties by high-poverty status, 2000

Item	Total	Black	Hispanic	Native American	Other	All Other nonmetro
Number of counties	444	210	74	40	120	1,861
Population (1,000s)	8,919	4,809	1,361	770	1,978	47,240
			percent			
Poverty rate, 2000						
Total	25.3	24.6	25.6	28.3	25.5	12.6
Black	38.9	39.0	35.0	32.6	38.6	28.1
Hispanic	32.2	35.0	32.3	25.6	35.5	24.9
Native American	37.5	25.0	35.1	40.7	27.7	25.3
Non-Hispanic White	17.6	13.3	14.0	13.8	25.1	10.8
Adults without a high-school diploma	33.9	33.1	36.8	27.1	36.3	21.3
			ratio			
Ratio of HS dropouts to 4-year college (or more) grads	2.8	2.7	2.9	2.0	3.3	1.3
			number			
Population per 100 workers	262	254	270	288	266	214
			percent			
Males with full-time, full-year work	38.8	40.9	37.3	36.0	36.0	47.5
Persons reporting disability	27.3	27.2	24.4	24.1	30.3	20.2
Children in female-headed, no husband present households	26.7	32.7	19.9	23.7	18.3	16.8
Households with income below 75% of poverty level	18.1	17.8	17.4	20.5	18.2	8.4
Persons who do not speak English "very well"	5.5	1.9	21.7	11.0	1.1	2.7

Source: Calculated by ERS using Census 2000 data, US Census Bureau.
Note: High-poverty counties are those with 20% or higher rates of poverty, 2000.

Non-Hispanic White Poverty in Minority Areas

In all three types of minority high-poverty areas, the poverty rates of non-Hispanic Whites are somewhat higher than they are in nonmetro counties without 20% poverty. They range from 13.3% in the Black counties to 14% in Hispanic areas, compared with a 10.8% incidence in counties with overall poverty of less than 20%. Thus, non-Hispanic Whites are not altogether immune from the forces that lead to high poverty in minority areas. However, the difference in these areas between White poverty and minority poverty is still stark. Black and Native American poverty rates run nearly three times that of the non-Hispanic White population in the respective Black and Native American poverty areas and better than double that of non-Hispanic Whites in Hispanic areas.

Trends from 1990-2000

Minority nonmetro poverty rates declined from 1990-2000, as did those in the nation as a whole. In the South, poverty among nonmetro Blacks dropped from 40.8% to 33.4%, a reduction of better than a sixth. All states saw declines. In the Deep South states of Arkansas, Louisiana, Mississippi and Texas, with the highest prior rates of nonmetro Black poverty (45% to 53%), the incidence fell by more than a fifth. The relative amount of decline was more limited (about one-ninth) in states that had already achieved levels below 30% by 1990 (Delaware, Maryland, Virginia). Thus, some leveling of differences within the South has occurred, but the total nonmetro Black poverty rate is still so high that at the recent pace of change it would take 2½ decades to bring it below 20%, much less to a more acceptable level. The worst conditions now remaining are in Louisiana, where there are still 11 high-poverty parishes in which over half of the Black population was still in poverty in 2000. This is a level rarely seen elsewhere now, even in Mississippi.

Nonmetro Hispanic poverty nationwide fell from 33.4% to 27.2% in the 1990-2000 decade (Table 2). This was very similar to the rate of decline among Blacks, but is notable given the fact that the Hispanic group—alone among the three major minorities—was substantially enlarged by rapid infusion of immigrants of below-average education and immediate earning capacity, whose presence would be expected to retard a lowering of the poverty rate in the short term.

Areas of high non-Hispanic White poverty are not discussed here. It is worth noting, though, that in such areas of the Southern Highlands, the pace of White poverty decline in the 1990s (12.8%) was distinctly below that of the principal minorities in each of the high-poverty county groups where minority poverty predominates. In part, this may stem from the fact that Southern Highlands poverty levels are lower than those of minorities—even though high by national standards—and high-poverty levels generally fell at a faster rate than lower levels in the 1990s.

Although poverty-level income is more common in the nonmetro population than in metro areas, most of the progress made in the United States between 1990 and 2000 in reducing national poverty occurred in nonmetro areas. This was true both among minority populations and among non-Hispanic Whites.

In nonmetro counties, there was a strong correspondence between the 1990 poverty rate and the relative change by 2000—that is, the greater the poverty, the greater the rate of decline. Thus, there is now a good bit less disparity in poverty rate between nonmetro areas than was the case earlier, both for minorities and non-Hispanic Whites. There was a modest convergence among metro counties as well, but in part this resulted from counties that had below-average poverty in 1990 reverting to slightly higher levels in 2000, rather than from strong reductions in higher-poverty areas.

Table 2 – Incidence of poverty in the United States by race and Hispanic status and metro-nonmetro residence, 1990 and 2000

	Total		Nonmetro		Metro	
	2000	*1990*	*2000*	*1990*	*2000*	*1990*
	percent in poverty					
Total	12.4	13.1	14.6	17.1	11.8	12.1
Black	24.9	29.5	33.0	40.2	23.7	27.7
Native American and Alaskan	25.7	30.9	31.0	38.8	21.4	24.1
Asian and Pacific Islander	12.8	14.1	15.6	16.0	12.6	14.0
Non-Hispanic White	8.1	9.0	11.6	13.7	7.1	7.6
Hispanic	22.6	25.3	27.2	33.4	22.2	24.5

Source: Calculated by ERS using Census 2000 data, U.S. Census Bureau.
Note: Metro-nonmetro boundaries are those based on the 1990 Census.
Hispanics may be of any race.

Summary

The year 1999, for which the 2000 Census income data were collected, was a banner year for earnings—with the lowest unemployment rate in 30 years—and also a prime period for non-earnings income, such as capital gains. Two findings would appear to deserve equal emphasis in this context. The first is that while nonmetro areas more than shared in the reduction of poverty rates reported for that year in comparison with the 1990 Census, this was particularly true of Blacks, Native Americans and Hispanics of any race. Secondly, however, de-

spite this improvement, the nonmetro population is still more subject to low income and high poverty than are metro residents. And within nonmetro areas,
minorities have poverty rates that are more than double those of non-Hispanic
Whites.

Although the minority high-poverty counties vary in the kinds of poverty-
related measures by which they are most affected, without exception they show
multiple types of social and economic characteristics on which they differ in a
problem context from the mass of nonmetro counties that have less poverty.

Where high rural and small town poverty characterizes entire counties, it
reflects historic geographic concentrations of minority populations in three cases
of every four. It limits the tax base and, where chronic, as it typically is, imposes
a poverty of services. It is usually in such concentrations that conditions among
minorities are the worst. But each of the major minorities has its unique history
and its own signature characteristics that are poverty-related and essential to
recognize if income problems are to be addressed successfully.

Chapter 14

Concentration of Poverty Declined in the 1990s

Paul Jargowsky

The strong economy of the 1990s had many beneficial effects, including falling unemployment, rising wages and declining poverty rates. Further analysis of the 2000 Census data reveals another important trend, driven at least in part by the economy. The geographic concentration of poverty, which had been increasing for decades, was sharply reduced during the 1990s. In other words, poor people were far less likely to live in isolated high-poverty ghettos and barrios.

Poverty, especially as experienced by African Americans, means more than just struggling with a low family income. For many of the poor, the experience of poverty also means living in a blighted, segregated, inner-city neighborhood. The conditions in such neighborhoods exacerbate the problems of poverty in a multitude of ways, and ultimately make it more difficult to break the cycle of poverty.

Concentration of poor people leads to a concentration of the social ills that cause or are caused by poverty. Poor children in these neighborhoods not only lack basic necessities in their own homes, but they also must contend with a hostile environment that holds many temptations and few positive role models. Equally important, school districts and attendance zones are generally organized geographically, so that the residential concentration of poor families frequently results in low-performing schools. The concentration of poverty in central cities also may exacerbate the flight of middle-income and higher-income families to

the suburbs, driving a wedge between social needs of poor communities and the
fiscal base needed to address them.

For all these reasons, researchers and policymakers were concerned when
poverty became more concentrated between 1970 and 1990. Over that period,
there was a near doubling in the number of persons living in high-poverty census tracts—small geographic areas that approximate neighborhoods—in which
at least 40% of the residents had poverty-level incomes. Of the 10 million persons living in high-poverty neighborhoods in 1990, about half were African-
American, and about one-fourth were Hispanic.

The 2000 Census, however, revealed a very different trend. Between 1990
and 2000, the number of people living in high-poverty neighborhoods declined
by 2.5 million (24%). The decline was even steeper for African Americans. In
1990, 4.9 million blacks lived in high-poverty census tracts; by 2000, the figure
declined 36% to 3.1 million. Poverty per se—based on family income alone—
also declined for blacks, but not nearly as rapidly. As a result, the probability
that a black poor person lived in a high-poverty zone dropped from 30.4% to
18.6%. This rapid decline signals a fundamental change in the spatial organization of poverty.

A number of different factors may have played a role in this historic
change. The strong economy was clearly a factor. The 2000 Census was taken in
April of that year, which in some ways was the peak of the boom. The economy
has slumped badly since then, so that much of the improvement documented by
the 2000 Census may have already been lost. The economy was not the only
factor at work, however. There have also been large shifts in the public policy
environment. First, we no longer build large-scale high-rise public housing projects, which are the surest way to geographically concentrate poverty. In fact,
such projects are increasingly being torn down. In their place, we have substituted scattered site housing, Section 8 vouchers and HOPE VI programs. While
these programs have their problems, each has as an explicit goal the deconcentration of poverty. Although more research needs to be conducted in order to
understand how much of the change was driven by the economy and how much
by the change in public policies, it seems likely that both played a role.

The deconcentration of poverty is an unambiguously positive development.
However, one cause for concern is that in many of the nation's large metropolitan areas, there were increases in the poverty rates of neighborhoods located in
the inner ring of suburbs, which is quite astonishing given that the economy in
the late 1990s was as strong as it is ever going to be.

It would be very unfortunate if gentrification in the central cities and the
continued out-migration of non-poor people to the outer ring of suburbs lead to
the re-creation of high-poverty zones in the inner ring of suburbs.

In the final analysis, these findings demonstrate that urban blight and the
decay of central cities' neighborhoods are not inevitable, as many had believed.
In the context of a strong economy with low unemployment, and with sensible
public policies, central city neighborhoods can indeed be revived. More impor-

tantly, the possibility exists for low-income people to improve their geographic access to educational and labor market opportunities, a necessary condition to make the American ideal of equality of opportunity a reality.

Chapter 15

The Living Wage: A Progressive Movement in Action

Jared Bernstein and Jeff Chapman

In these times of dominant conservative politics, it's particularly interesting to reflect on the marked success of a progressive policy, one that directly intervenes in the wage-setting function of the private market. We're talking, of course, about the living-wage movement.

A living-wage ordinance is local legislation—typically at the city or county level—that establishes, for workers covered by the ordinance, a wage floor above that of the prevailing minimum wage. There are over 120 living-wage ordinances in place, plus over 70 ongoing campaigns to pass such measures. No two ordinances are the same; they differ in terms of what types of firms or employers are covered, which workers are covered and the nature of the coverage.

When the contemporary living-wage movement began in the mid-1990s, the "contract model" dominated. Under these ordinances, private firms under contract with the city to provide a service—cleaning streets, maintaining public areas, etc.—are mandated to pay the wage level specified in the ordinance, typically a few dollars above the minimum wage. Many ordinances allow employers to take a dollar or more off the mandated living-wage level if they provide health insurance. As the movement evolved, ordinances began to extend coverage to firms that receive a subsidy from the locality. The idea was that if you're an employer who's benefiting from doing business with the city, then you ought not to be creating poverty-level jobs. The way one organizer put it: "It's our money, and as taxpayers, we'd prefer not to subsidize low-wage employers creating lousy jobs in our city."

Thus, from the perspective of advocates, the movement is seen as a way to accomplish a variety of goals. Foremost, to raise the pay of affected workers. Also, by raising the pay in firms with which the city does business, living wages lower the wage differential between public- and private-sector workers. This then can dampen the motivation of city councils to outsource services provided by public-sector workers, whose jobs are usually of higher quality than the privatized version. Historically, the public sector has been an important source of employment opportunities for African Americans. Higher rates of unionization and affirmative action laws within government employment have ensured higher wages and better mobility than in the private sector. Living-wage ordinances also recoup some of financial assistance cities provide to firms that demand such subsidies, and do so in the form of higher compensation to workers. Finally, many living-wage campaigns involve broad coalitions including labor, religious groups and low-wage workers themselves, giving rise to the possibility of an economic justice coalition that outlasts the wage campaign.

Variations in Coverage

Why have living wages appeared on the scene, and why have they been so successful? What impact have they had? What is their relevance for minority populations? To what extent are the goals of the movement being realized?

To begin with, we describe a typical living-wage ordinance, just in case one hasn't yet come to your town. Since one of us lives in Alexandria, Virginia, where an active ordinance is in place, let's describe that one. The ordinance applies to all non-construction contracts for over $50,000. In 2004, firms that win such contracts with the City had to pay their workers no less than $11.36 an hour, going up to $11.80 in 2005. This equals the poverty line for a family of four—$19,484 in 2004—divided by full-time, full-year work, or 2,080 hours. The result is an hourly wage that would lift a family with a full-year worker to the poverty threshold. About $2.50 per hour—the average hourly cost of providing health insurance coverage—is added to the base wage. Since the poverty line is indexed to inflation, the Alexandria living wage is also adjusted for price changes.

As noted, ordinance frameworks are extremely flexible, allowing living-wage campaigners and city councils to inject their particular preferences into the legislation. One flexible parameter is the contract value beyond which firms have to pay the living wage. In Arlington County, Virginia, contracts for less than $100,000 are exempted; in Cincinnati, the threshold is $20,000. In Boston, the original law stated that direct service contracts with the city must be for over $100,000 (for subcontractors, the limit was $25,000), but advocates later successfully campaigned to lower the direct contractors' cutoff to $25,000. The

Oakland, California law requires coverage for workers on service contracts of at least $25,000 and development assistance of $100,000 or more (the tenants and leaseholders of the subsidy recipient are covered). In Chicago and other cities, nonprofits that contract with the city are exempted; in other cities, they are included, though there often exists a threshold here as well in order to exempt smaller providers.

One relatively new application of the living-wage model is in the university setting. A renowned recent example is Harvard University, where student supporters staged an aggressive campaign on behalf of low-wage workers employed by the University directly or indirectly (through subcontractors). The agreement covers security guards, custodians and dining service workers. Along with the initial pay raises, the agreement includes a "wages and benefits parity policy" requiring that outsourced jobs provide wages and benefits comparable to in-house unionized workers performing the same job.

A recent trend in the movement is to push for laws closer in both coverage and spirit to the minimum wage. Currently, policies of this type are active in Santa Fe, San Francisco and Madison, Wisconsin. Santa Fe and San Francisco both passed their laws in 2003 and require a minimum wage of $8.50 from many of the cities' employers, and the Madison City Council passed an ordinance in 2004 that phases in a minimum wage that will reach $7.75 by 2008. New Orleans also passed a city-wide minimum wage, but implementation was prohibited by the state's Supreme Court, based on jurisdictional issues.

Pragmatic political concerns often generate compromises regarding coverage. This flexibility avoids the "one size fits all" model of, for example, the federal minimum wage, where regional differences are not taken into account. For example, the San Jose, California living wage is relatively high compared to other ordinances around the nation, but community organizers there pushed for this level based on the very high cost of housing in the Silicon Valley area and the fact that, due to those costs, many of the covered workers had to travel long distances to get to work. In other cases, workers in certain occupations, such as those who work in the school system (as in Milwaukee) might be seen as particularly deserving by influential parties and thus might be strategically highlighted in the campaign and ultimately in the ordinance.

A further motivation for the living-wage movement lies in the negative economic trends that have beset low-wage workers and the lack of federal response. Prior to the late 1990s, this led to falling living standards as incomes stagnated or fell due to a series of forces—deindustrialization, fewer unions, lower minimum wages, high unemployment—that reduced the quality of jobs available to non-college-educated workers. The tight labor market of the late 1990s reversed these trends for a few years, but as the unemployment rate has crept up over the past couple of years, despite the alleged economic recovery, real wage growth is once again stagnant for all workers. Since African Americans tend to earn lower wages and rely more heavily on those wages to make ends meet, stagnating wage growth is of particular concern to black workers. They are also more likely to benefit from a living-wage ordinance—16% of the workers directly assisted by the most recent (1996) increase in the federal minimum wage are black, despite making up only 11.3% of the total workforce.

Over the long run, the economy has not provided much of a lift for many earning low wages. At the same time, other than the 1996 minimum wage increase, which brought the federal minimum up to $5.15 in 1997, there has been little to no action regarding policies to raise pre-tax wages (a large increase in the federal Earned Income Tax Credit in 1993 and the addition of various state EITCs have, however, made important contribution to raising incomes in families with low-wage workers). To the contrary, what changes have occurred, such as the passage of international trading agreements in the 1990s and highly regressive tax cuts more recently, can be seen as evidence of a more deregulatory approach to economic policy, changes that tend to further reduce the bargaining power of low-wage workers.

In this environment, the living-wage movement offers local organizers a simple, straightforward policy which they can pursue, one with the demonstrable result of raising wages for some of those workers facing these challenging trends.

Impact of Living-Wage Ordinances

But have the ordinances delivered? Those who opposed the introduction of living wages argue that instead of helping the least advantaged, the wage mandates will lead employers to lay workers off or firms to avoid seeking contracts in cities with living wages (or, in the case of business subsidies, to avoid locating there). What does the evidence show?

A few years ago, this would have been a very tough question to answer. But since then, there has been a great deal of research evaluating living-wage outcomes (see Bernstein 2005 in the accompanying Box).

The best way to learn about living-wage outcomes is to do a before/after study in a city that has adopted the policy. There are two such studies, one for Los Angeles, the other for Boston. Both find that the ordinance lifted wages of affected workers significantly. Regarding job losses, there is some evidence that employers reduced hiring in response to the mandated wage hike, but a closer look at the Boston study suggests that affected firms tended to use fewer part-time workers and more full-time workers compared to unaffected firms—that is, total hours worked didn't change.

Another useful strand of research is by city administrators called upon to report the impact of the ordinance in their city. These reports have the advantage of reflecting information by people who are "closest to the ground" regarding the implementation and impact of the laws.

The city/county studies are summarized in a review paper by Andrew Elmore of the Legal Aid Society of NYC, who tells us that the reports

"...suggest that localities after implementation of a living-wage law tend to experience modest contract price increases for a small proportion of contracts," leading to overall increases in contract costs to the city that were usually less than 1%. He does, however, note a few larger increases in individual contracts due to the ordinances, including a 31% increase in a security contract in Hartford (the only contract covered there), a 22% increase in a janitorial contract in Warren, Michigan, and increases of 10% in about 5% of the city contracts in Berkeley, California.

How do contractors respond to these increases? According to the same study, they appear to absorb at least some portion (in some cases, all) of the increase, and there was little evidence of any diminution of competitiveness in the bidding process. One Ypsilanti, Michigan town supervisor found that the cost of the ordinance there was held down by an increase in the numbers of bidders. Her explanation was that "now that the wage standard is equal, the ability to compete is based on factors other than wages, so you've got to be tighter and provide less of a profit margin." Other research reports that affected firms take lower profits as the primary means by which they absorb the wage increase.

While the above relates to service contracts, Elmore also reviews the impact of living-wage ordinances as they affect private-sector businesses receiving public subsidies, and here the results are more mixed. He reviews nine cities with subsidy-based living-wage ordinances and reports that only one—Oakland—reported a decline in the number and size of economic development projects. However, the Oakland example may reveal an important impact of this dimension of the policy. This is a city with a relative large proportion of underemployed minorities, and while the attraction of low-wage retailers (think Wal-Mart) is surely a double-edged sword, those jobs might still be viewed by local residents as valuable opportunities. We don't mean to imply that retailers will necessarily respond this way when making location choices. Probably, most won't. But some of these retailers—again, we're thinking of Wal-Mart—will go to great lengths to avoid anything that smacks of local regulation, such as wage mandates or union presence. Whether localities want to pursue such "low-road" employers is an open question—there are obvious reasons to avoid engaging in their bargaining strategy—but living-wage advocates should be aware of the possible trade-off.

Are Goals Being Reached?

So if wages are up, with few of the economic distortions critics worry about, is it clear that the movement is realizing its goals? Yes and no. Living-wage campaigns have been tremendously successful at passing ordinances, and that of course is a first-order goal of the movement. Along the way, they've created a juggernaut, wherein opponents are hard-pressed to fight back against the logic of the ordinance. Any forecast of where this movement is headed would have to predict continued success.

On the other hand, there is a paradox here: The movement's strength is also a weakness in terms of making a serious dent in working peoples' poverty. The primary reason underlying the favorable results from the impact studies, and thus an explanation of why opponents are often unsuccessful in their crusade against these ordinances, is that coverage is very narrow. By remaining limited in the coverage provided by these ordinances, advocates have been able to convince city officials and, by proxy, taxpayers, that they will accomplish their stated goals of raising the economic fortunes of affected workers without leading to economic distortions in the form of significant layoffs, tax hikes or reduced competition for contracts.

But the marginal coverage of the policy limits its effectiveness to raise the living standards of more than a few thousand workers per ordinance. While no national total of affected workers (those who have received wage hikes due to the policy) is available and is a quickly moving target, a rough count would unlikely surpass 200,000 and may be closer to half that level. In a low-wage labor market of roughly 30 million, this gives a sense of the limitations of the movement and the nature of the paradox it faces.

As with any new policy, especially one as diverse as this, important questions remain. First, to what extent can coverage be expanded without generating unacceptable inefficiencies? Taken together, much—not all—of the literature on minimum and living wages suggests that given the indeterminacy of wages and the myriad other factors that determine hiring, quite modest wage increases with broad coverage (as in minimum wage increases) and much less modest increases with very limited coverage (living wages) can be absorbed without significant displacements or distortions. If, in fact, the next stage of the living-wage movement is towards expanding coverage, as in minimum wages for all employees in the city, research will be needed to gauge the impact on the relevant outcomes.

Second, even if coverage remains limited, there is the question of spillovers from the living-wage movement, specifically to the labor movement. There is some evidence that living wages successfully diminish the outsourcing of publicly-provided services (by unionized workers), and such effects should continue to be monitored. But a larger question is the extent to which living-wage campaigns can serve as organizing tools for unions. There's not much evidence that the movement has gained much ground in that regard thus far, but there is almost no systematic research on this important question.

At this point, the living wage is one of the better known and more successful policies designed to address the difficulties faced by low-wage workers in the new economy. And, as we have stressed, unless the landscape changes dramatically, the number of ordinances is only likely to grow, perhaps at an even faster rate. The low levels of coverage constrain the policy's reach, but it is a successful political strategy, and one that's targeted at a deserving group of workers. The next step in the movement should be thinking about ways to take it to scale, increasing coverage and reaching greater numbers of the working poor. At the same time, researchers can monitor the impacts, to see if expanding living wages continue to provide higher living standards to low-wage workers without leading to layoffs or other distortions.

Resources on Living Wage

Jen Kern at ACORN's Living Wage Resource Center—natacorncam@ acorn.org

Stephanie Luce at Political Economy Research Institute— sluce@econs.umass.edu

Paul Sonn at Brennan Center for Justice—paul.sonn@nyu.edu

* * *

Bernstein, Jared. "The Living Wage Movement: What Is It, Why Is It, and What's Known About Its Impact?, *Emerging Labor Market Institutions for the Twenty-First Century*, eds. Richard B. Freeman, Joni Hersch and Lawrence Mishel (University of Chicago Press, 2005).

Brenner, Mark & Stephanie Luce. "Living Wage Laws in Practice: The Boston, New Haven and Hartford Experiences" (Political Economy Research Inst., 2005).

Elmore, Andrew. "Contract Costs and Economic Development in Living Wage Localities: A Report from Cities and Counties on the Impact of Living Wage Laws on Local Programs (NYU Brennan Center for Economic Justice, 2003).

Elmore, Andrew. "Living Wage Laws & Communities: Smarter Economic Development, Lower Than Expected Costs," (NYU Brennan Center for Economic Justice, 2004).

Fairris, David et al. "Examining the Evidence: The Impact of the Los Angeles Living Wage Ordinance on Workers and Businesses" (Los Angeles Alliance for a New Economy, 2005).

Mishel, Lawrence, Jared Bernstein & Heather Boushey. *The State of Working America, 2002-03* (Cornell University Press, 2002).

Chapter 16

Children Get Social Security, Too

William E. Spriggs

In 2002, some 3.1 million children 18 and under were getting Social Security benefits (roughly one in twelve of all Social Security beneficiaries)—a number virtually equal to the 3.8 million children getting TANF benefits that year. One in sixteen African-American children receive a Social Security benefit. That makes Social Security very important to child advocates. And so, changes in the Social Security system could have a drastic impact on children, and disproportionately on children in minority families.

When Social Security came into being in 1935, it originally emphasized individual workers and focused on retirement. But the Act was amended in 1939, changing the program from insuring that individual workers got back money they had paid in payroll taxes, to protecting the worker's family. Widows and other of the worker's dependents became beneficiaries. The basis for calculating benefits was shifted from lifetime earnings to replacing a worker's average monthly earnings. In this way, the family's lifestyle was protected from the loss of a wage earner.

The Risk of Dying/Becoming Disabled

Today, the typical 20-year-old faces a 3-in-10 risk of becoming disabled before reaching retirement, and an almost 2-in-10 risk of dying before reaching retirement. While Social Security Administration actuaries do not report those data by race (only by gender), it is known that the odds of becoming disabled or dying younger are higher for African Americans, who make up 11.5% of workers paying into the system but constitute 13.2% of those getting survivors' benefits and 17.8% of those getting disability benefits. These actuaries also estimate that, for the average worker who becomes disabled, the disability insurance is equivalent to a $353,000 disability policy; and for the worker who dies young, the survivors' benefits are equivalent to a $403,000 life insurance policy. When signing the Social Security legislation in August 1935, President Franklin Roosevelt reflected: "We can never insure one hundred percent of the population against one hundred percent of the hazards and vicissitudes of life, but we have tried to frame a law which will give some measure of protection to the average citizen and to his family."

So, far from Social Security being a fight of the young versus the old, the program is really about family security—young and old. Today, about the same share (46%) of children get survivor benefits, through the loss of a working parent, as receive benefits because their parent is a disabled worker. Another 7% get benefits because their adult guardian (parent or grandparent) is getting retirement benefits. As dependents of a working adult, children get a check designated for them. The average family of widowed parent with children got an average monthly check of $1,614 in 2002, and in families where only the children were dependent survivors (for instance, if the wife remarried) the average check was $785 a month. In 2002, for families of disabled workers, the typical benefit for the worker with spouse and children was about $1,280 a month, and for a disabled parent with children the average monthly benefit was about $1,130 a month.

The National Urban League Institute for Opportunity and Equality estimates that Social Security benefits lift one million children out of poverty each year, and that another one million are spared the depths of extreme poverty (falling below half the poverty line). African-American children make up 20% of children getting benefits, and Valerie Rawlston of the University of North Carolina estimates that, coupled with their low income from other sources, Social Security lifts four times more African-American than white children out of poverty.

Privatization's Impact on Children

So how might changes in the program affect children? When American workers pay their FICA (Federal Insurance Contribution Act) tax each paycheck, they are buying insurance for their immediate family members to protect those dependents from crushed lifestyles because of the loss of income if the worker becomes disabled, dies early leaving children behind or becomes too old to work full-time. The program's benefit, based on the primary insurance amount, uses the same formula to calculate benefits across the risks of disability, death and old age. So, the family receives the same benefit regardless of why they are filing a claim. That means that efforts to reduce benefits can easily lead to cuts for children. For instance, Plan II of the President's Commission to Strengthen Social Security recommended changing the primary insurance amount formula to set benefits to reflect a fixed lifestyle—this is called "price indexing." Currently, benefits are set to replace a share of a workers' typical earnings, with low-wage workers having a higher share replaced than high-wage workers— this is called "wage indexing." Because wages have risen faster than prices, our real living standards have gone up over time. The Congressional Research Service estimated that if price indexing of benefits began with the first monthly checks mailed in 1940, then today's benefits based on a 1940s lifestyle would result in a cut of 60%.

The second key issue is that the program operates as a family insurance policy, where the family is defined as a spouse (or divorced spouse) and children, plus dependent parents. Each member of the family is given a specific claim amount, so long as he or she is economically dependent on the primary worker.

Eligibility for survivors' benefits is made relatively easy for young workers, so about 98% of children under age 18 would get a benefit if one of their working parents died. Biological and adopted children are automatically covered. In most cases, a stepchild would be covered, and children who have other legal guardians—such as grandparents—would also be covered.

President Bush has suggested that workers would be free to designate beneficiaries. This suggests that the private accounts will act more like Individual Retirement Accounts that are governed by state law property rights than like 401(k) plans, which are governed by federal pension laws. In either case, the rights of children are normally subsumed secondary to that of the surviving spouse. Both state and federal pension law are less clear with regard to a divorced spouse, and with regard to children spread across different parents. Thus, it is unclear under what conditions children would receive a benefit.

Even less clear are the rights of children who become disabled before age 22. Those children are beneficiaries of their parents' work efforts as adults, designated as adult disabled children. In 2002, roughly 748,000 adult disabled children received benefits. Under private accounts, the fate of these beneficiaries is totally unclear.

Further, under the Bush plan, the private accounts are a loan against the worker's retirement benefit, which must be paid out of the Social Security retirement benefit with interest, calculated at 3% above inflation—in 2004, 6.2% interest. It is unclear whether the loan would have to be repaid out of survivor or disability benefits. It is also unclear how those benefits would be distributed. President Bush requires retirees to buy an annuity to insure that, coupled with their traditional Social Security benefits, they would not drop below the poverty level. Valerie Rawlston showed that the typical account of a survivor could only absorb a very small cut in the traditional Social Security benefit level. And, given the short horizon over which the portfolio of a worker who dies or becomes disabled would have to accumulate, there is a very real risk that the market could be in a downturn, with money then lost. This risk is not avoided, even if the parent chose the President's proposed safe investment of a life-cycle fund that would slowly shift out of risky stock investments and toward more stable bonds as the parent got closer to retirement age.

A Radical Departure

President Bush's proposal to privatize Social Security is a radical departure for the program. The benefits for children are greatly threatened by changing the focus of the program—from assuring American parents that their children will be protected from economic calamity if the parent becomes disabled, dies or lives long enough to avoid being a burden on their children—to being solely an individual savings vehicle for retirement. President Bush promised in his 2005 State of the Union Address that he would not cut the benefits of anyone under 55. His speech mentioned the 49.6% of Social Security beneficiaries who get a retirement check based on their own work history. He never mentioned the 12% of disabled workers, whose average age is less than 55, or the 38% of beneficiaries who were family members being protected by their parent or spouse. For the millions of children whose parents worked hard to insure their children's future, and most of whom were under 18, President Bush's silence says a lot.

Chapter 17

The Benefit Bank

Robert Brand

The Benefit Bank (TBB) is an Internet-based, counselor-assisted service that enables moderate- and low-income working families to increase their income dramatically by researching, finding and automatically applying for benefits to which they may be entitled. TBB is designed to work at a fourth-grade reading level, with counselor training at a ninth-grade reading level. Extensive health screens are provided online, and there is a Help Desk which responds to counselor calls on a toll-free number.

Current Census data show that 34.8 million people in the United States— 12.2 million of them children—are living below the federal poverty level. Slightly more than half of the jobs in the US pay $12 per hour or less, contributing to the poverty of working people. In virtually all affluent nations, between 20% and 40% of jobs pay a wage that will keep workers in poverty. Where social policy in the US falls apart, compared to all of our economic peers, is the lack of social wage payments: wage supplements, health care, pensions, housing allowances, nutritional supports, energy assistance and other programs to compensate for low wages.

There are programs in the US that help, although most income enhancement programs serve far fewer people than those eligible and needing assistance. Indeed, more than $35 billion in public funds go unclaimed each year by low-income people in the US. This situation keeps people in poverty and undercuts the potential of policies to "make work pay."

Tax and public benefit income enhancement programs are under-enrolled, in large part because nearly all of them have cumbersome enrollment procedures, sometimes combined with discretionary policies designed to screen out those deemed unworthy of public support. These procedures challenge public bureaucracies in times of scarcity while placing individuals and families who are eligible for public benefits at a disadvantage.

TBB centralizes and simplifies tax forms and benefits that exist at every level of government, as well as those available through private initiatives. Use of this program can increase the incomes of low- and moderate-income families by as much as $10,000 per year, although income enhancements in the $3,000-$4,000 per year range are more common.

TBB will eventually track more than 70 federal, state, local and private benefits, with the goal of making these benefits accessible. The Benefit Bank helps build an ongoing service relationship with users so they can find ways to work and to organize their way out of poverty. In the future, we will link The Benefit Bank to homeownership education, mortgage and financial literacy, and counseling. The Benefit Bank serves as a portal to a range of services that build communities and help individuals and families achieve self-sufficiency.

The Benefit Bank can be part of a community-wide response to poverty. It can help millions overcome poverty, and it can help millions more understand the importance of sound public policies that recognize the dignity of all of us. It lets families learn what income-enhancing benefits they qualify for, helps them apply for those benefits, and has advocates who will stand by them until the benefit is successfully received.

Community-based counselors are available to assist. Basic computer skills, mastery of simple training materials, and an interest in helping neighbors work their way out of poverty are all that is necessary. In addition, The Benefit Bank is multi-lingual, in Spanish and Creole, with additional languages planned. TBB software supports counselors through comprehensive help screens and messages to assist with even the most basic aspects of the program. Counselors have toll-free access to a team of technical support experts who know the software and the benefit programs the system offers.

We are developing The Benefit Bank to be on hundreds of thousands of computers—in faith communities, social service agencies, government offices, schools, libraries, union halls, employers' offices—anywhere people want to work together to overcome poverty.

We are piloting The Benefit Bank in a group of early-adopter sites that include: congregations, community development corporations, social service agencies and job-training programs.

The Benefit Bank currently covers: federal taxes, including the Earned Income Tax Credit; the Child and Dependent Care Credit; the Additional Child Tax Credit; the Hope and Lifetime Learning Education Credits; amended taxes for up to three years; state taxes, including the state Earned Income Tax Credit; state Children's Health Insurance Plan (including coverage for parents); Medicaid; Low-Income Heating and Energy Assistance; Food Stamps; Child Care Subsidy; pharmaceutical coverage for the elderly; and voter registration. We are also preparing to program four uniform federal benefits: Department of Veterans Affairs programs, Free Application for Federal Student Aid (FAFSA), Supplemental Security Income/Disability Income, and Free and Reduced Cost School Breakfast and Lunch.

In late 2005, we will launch The Benefit Bank in Pennsylvania, Florida, Ohio, Mississippi and the District of Columbia. We have a plan to expand to all 50 states over the next five years. TBB is free to all users and free to all sites offering the services, and we have developed a sustainable model to cover the extensive cost of system improvements, updates and user support.

As TBB grows in service and in campaigns to end poverty, we will develop a rich, longitudinal set of data (collected with attention to privacy and confidentiality) about the economic lives of people forced to live in poverty. We will work in an environment of repeated voluntary use in a trusted environment, and we will be able to look at data and ask questions that policy research has not had the tools to address. We are in the process of forming an open roundtable to help guide us to make TBB more useful in assisting low- and moderate-income people while building campaigns against poverty.

Chapter 18

Race, Poverty and Shared Wealth

Andrew T. Lamas

What is the central fact of slavery? Is it the degrading work, the objectification of human life, the denial of basic liberties guaranteed to others, the failure to exchange wages for work, the poverty of living conditions, the destruction of family and culture? What *distinguishes* slavery is something else, and it is deeply embedded in our own economy today.

The eminent historian Ira Berlin chronicles a meeting in Savannah, Georgia, in January 1865, of former slaves and free blacks queried by none other than General William Tecumseh Sherman and US Secretary of War Edwin M. Stanton. In response to the most serious question of the day, George Frazier, an elderly Baptist minister and spokesperson of the group, arose and replied:

> Slavery is receiving by the *irresistible power* the work of another man, and not by his *consent*, [while freedom] is taking us from the yoke of bondage, and placing us where we could reap the fruits of our own labor, take care of ourselves and assist the Government in maintaining our freedom.

The central fact of slavery—*the theft of another's labor*—has long been the basis of production and unjust economic arrangements. This usurpation has long been understood as a threat to democracy. Oppression and inequality are inextricably linked. Modern oppressive systems—such as those historically informed by institutionalized *racism* and *patriarchy*—arise amidst and reproduce *class hierarchies*.

96

Most popular considerations of inequality, including poverty definitions utilized by the US Census, stress that *inequality is all about income, not wealth.* Recall the most influential book about poverty in the latter half of the 20th Century—Michael Harrington's *The Other America*; or turn to the recent bestseller about the working poor—Barbara Ehrenreich's *Nickel and Dimed.* The first generated federal support for *income security*, while the second sought *living wages* for the working poor. When the right ignores wealth inequality, it is understandable. When the left does so, it is tragic—as wealth is not only a fundamental source of livelihood and equality but also of power.

Let's review in more depth two other sources of evidence—from the classroom and the media—regarding the preoccupation with income inequality to the exclusion of wealth distribution.

Students on Inequality

Ask the following questions to your colleagues or students and listen for the responses:

Q: "What comes to mind when you think about inequality?"

A: "Race"…"Class"…"Education"…"Gender"…"Globalization and Comparative Standards of Development."

Q: "How would you explain this inequality to someone else?"

A: "Blacks labored as slaves for generations, and even today they earn less on the job than whites." … "The rich are high-earners who can afford good neighborhoods and good educations for their children, who prepare for high-paying careers, while the poor—with low-paying jobs and inadequate public support—lack the means to meet basic needs." … "Women's work has not been historically valued; in the domestic realm, women have worked without pay; for work outside the home, they are paid less than men even in similar positions." … "A large percentage of the world's population labors for less than \$2 per day."

Q: "How will you know if progress is being made?"

A: "Inequality is about the inequality of income from work. Absolute poverty will be addressed, and improvements in relative equality of compensation will be achieved over time through private sector bargaining and governmental redistribution through taxation and transfers."

Media on Inequality

In 2003, I entered a variety of terms into the Google search engine and into the Lexis-Nexis database of more than 50 newspapers in the US and world-wide. By linking these search terms (e.g., poverty, inequality, ownership, race, property, wealth, assets, capital, income, rich, poor) in all possible combinations, I was able to generate some rough evidence about popular conceptions.

Popular information sources generally frame issues of inequality and poverty by focusing on *income* rather than on wealth, property, capital, ownership or assets. For example, the overwhelming majority of charts, tables and graphs that depict inequality focus on income and not on wealth distribution. Moreover, analysis of selected text samples—including from the *New York Times* (during the previous six months, five years, and ten years)—indicates that income, when discussed in connection with inequality or poverty, typically refers to two kinds of income, *viz.*, wages (primarily) and government transfer payments (secondarily). (For a rare and interesting counter-example, see the series on "Class in America" in the *New York Times*, May and June, 2005.) Journalistic accounts of poverty and race are much more often about income than about wealth, property, capital, ownership or assets.

In any given society, income inequality may reach a point where injustice arises and remedies are required. But from Thomas Paine's *Agrarian Justice* (1797) to Melvin Oliver and Thomas Shapiro's *Black Wealth/White Wealth*, we have been called to task for ignoring ownership and asset development.

At the present moment, opportunities for wealth creation by poor and working people are again endangered, with the rise of predatory lending, weakening enforcement of key federal laws (e.g., Community Reinvestment Act), the defunding of governmental programs (e.g., CDFI Fund for community development financial institutions, affordable housing programs) and waning foundation support for the asset-building initiatives of the past decade.

Strategies for Addressing Inequality

Under the banner of economic democracy, four broad strategies for addressing inequality are suggested by critical historical inquiry and progressive practice.

The first two strategies are: *Labor-Based Claims for Increases in Employment-Related Compensation* and *Citizen-Based Claims for Increases in Publicly Funded Transfer Payments*. No doubt, labor and community organizing campaigns will continue the important work of asserting these claims.

The two other strategies, reviewed below, significantly focus on reducing wealth inequality: *Labor-Based Claims for Shared Ownership of Capital* and *Citizen-Based Claims for Shared Ownership of Common Wealth.*

Share the Wealth: Labor Owning Capital

Labor is prior to and independent of capital. Capital is only the fruit of labor, and could never have existed if labor had not first existed. Labor is the superior of capital, and deserves much the higher consideration. (Abraham Lincoln, "Annual Message of the U.S. President," 37th Congress, Second Session, December 3, 1861)

The cooperative and employee ownership movements are many, varied and global. The long-standing, transformative models in Italy and Spain are particularly noteworthy. In the United States, one of the many current streams of significance was initiated in Depression-era deprivations and the populist tradition of social reform.

Huey Long, the infamous Governor and US Senator from Louisiana, developed a comprehensive reform agenda that combined: (a) substantial government support for public works, education and health; (b) highly progressive taxation on income and inheritance; and (c) egalitarianism regarding income and wealth distribution.

Explaining his "Share the Wealth" platform in a national radio address in April 1935 (and using dollar amounts relevant for the time), Long said:

> Here is what we stand for in a nutshell:
>
> Number one, we propose that every family in America should at least own a homestead equal in value to not less than one-third the average family wealth. The average family wealth of America, at normal values, is approximately $16,000. So our first proposition means that every family will have a home and the comforts of a home up to a value of not less than around $5,000 or a little more than that.
>
> Number two, we propose that no family shall own more than three hundred times the average family wealth, which means that no family shall possess more than a wealth of approximately $5 million—none to own less than $5,000, none to own more than $5 million. We think that's too much to allow them to own, but at least it's extremely conservative.
>
> Number three, we propose that every family shall have an income equal to at least one-third of the average family income in America. If all were allowed to work, there'd be an income of from $5,000 to $10,000 per family. We propose that one-third would be the minimum. We propose that no family will have an earning of less than around $2,000 to $2,500 and that none will have more than three hundred times the average, less the ordinary income taxes, which means that a million dollars would be the limit on the highest income.
>
> We also propose to give the old-age pensions to the old people, not by taxing them or their children, but by levying the taxes upon the excess fortunes to whittle them down, and on the excess incomes and excess inheritances, so that the people who reach the age of sixty can be retired from the active labor of life and given an opportunity to have surcease and ease for the balance of the life that they have on earth.
>
> We also propose the care for the veterans, including the cash payment of the soldiers' bonus. We likewise propose that there should be an education for every youth in this land and that no youth

would be dependent upon the financial means of his parents in order
to have a college education.

Note two points: (1) While entirely compatible with and fully embracing of
an agenda reducing income inequality, Long's commitments reveal a more fundamental analysis about the source of inequality; hence, the focus on property,
ownership and asset development. (2) That he and the New Dealers eventually
secured significant, enduring, income-related programs suggests that the focus
on *wealth inequality* created space for addressing *income security*.

Long's son, Russell (who became the powerful Chairman of the US Senate
Finance Committee), extended aspects of this agenda further into the 20th Century, in no small part due to the influence of Louis Kelso and Mortimer Adler's
The Capitalist Manifesto, which promoted broadly held stock ownership. Russell Long's crowning legislative achievement, in 1978, provided federal tax incentives for the establishment of employee stock ownership plans (ESOPs) in
the country's corporations, more than 10,000 of which have instituted a measure
of employee stock ownership, though often as an additional worker benefit and
not also as a transformative framework for democratizing corporate governance
and broader social reform. Today, more than 10% of these companies are committed to using their ownership structures as the foundation for generating participation and ownership cultures on the shop floors and in board rooms.
Productivity, profitability, quality of life and global competitiveness are
enhanced while asset development for working people is generated.

Share the Wealth:
Iraqi Citizens Owning Oil Resources

The privilege to claim the common wealth of humanity—water, airwaves, oil—
issues from the same power and hubris that claims the fruits of others' labor
without consent; however, an extraordinary opportunity recently arose to promote wealth equality among an impoverished people.

The plan was to hold President George Bush to his words: "The oil in Iraq
belongs to the Iraqi people." How? Establish a permanent fund, capitalized by
oil revenues and paying annual dividends to each Iraqi citizen.

This plan was (and remains) practical and immune to red-baiting, as the
model has been operating successfully, with Republican and Democrat support,
for more than 20 years in the United States, albeit in only one state. It is called
the Iraqi Permanent Fund and is modeled on the Alaska Permanent Fund (APF).
Every autumn since 1982, *dividends*—derived from trust investments financed
by oil revenues—*are paid to every Alaskan*. In 2002, approximately 600,000
citizens *split equally* approximately $900 million, yielding $1,540 for each
woman, man and child. In recent years, these payments have generated an aver-

age of $6,000-$8,000 per Alaskan family. An additional portion of the trust's proceeds are dedicated for state infrastructure projects.

While wealth accounts also exist in Norway, Chad, Kuwait and Alberta, the unique Alaska-style program was raised by US Senator George Allen (Rep., VA) with US Secretary of State Colin Powell in the US Senate's Foreign Relations Committee hearings on April 29, 2003:

> *Senator Allen:* I would like to hear any comments or thoughts you may have on the constitution in Iraq of creating something like the Alaska Permanent Fund so that the people of Iraq indeed are the owners of not only their government but also of that key resource [oil].
> *Secretary Powell:* The [Iraqi] people, if they had access to that money directly, as is the case in Alaska, to some of the money that has been generated by Alaskan oil, then they can make choices in their own lives with respect to how to use that money.

Later, according to the *Los Angeles Times,* Powell said: "[Alaska's lawmakers have] educated me over the years as to the merit of this approach to the use of oil...to compensate the people in a way that they can make a choice as to how the wealth of the state is being used. And I think that's a concept that applies in the case of Iraq as well."

Not surprisingly, but unfortunately for the citizens of Iraq, the Bush Administration did not pursue this proposal. Instead, officials have worked to privatize Iraq's economic institutions and resources in the conventional manner; as in Russia in the 1990s, Iraq's wealth will become highly concentrated overnight.

Privatization need not result in gross inequality; in fact, if implemented pursuant to democratic norms, it can facilitate the egalitarian project. The Permanent Fund is the best simple measure for leaving Iraq with a progressive legacy. But for now, in Iraq, this opportunity appears lost. What an irony it would be if an initiative to stem inequality in Iraq re-awakened the American consciousness about its own common wealth.

The democratic, egalitarian mission can proceed against the logic of the market and through it as well.

Conclusion

Contemporary discourse about inequality nearly always focuses on income, and we are all the poorer for it. Inequality may be experienced, on a daily basis, as a lack of income. So, understandably, most people conceptualize inequality as income-based. This confusion results, in part, from the consumption-oriented nature of contemporary capitalist economy—where consumption, not production, is what we see when we look around.

Inequality, which most definitely is income-related, is not income-based.

Fundamentally, *inequality is wealth-based.* An engaged scholarship and a progressive politics must recognize the difference. The way in which wealth is produced, and the claims of ownership that are established at the points of production, are the defining determinants of wealth and income distribution.

With production out of view, and wealth out of mind, we have an impoverished theory and practice regarding inequality.

Wealth has two ultimate sources. The first is human labor, and the second is the environment of natural resources. Wealth can be plundered or wisely, sustainably and justly employed. As Lincoln acknowledged, in an economy like ours, "[c]apital has its rights." But rights evolve over time on a contested terrain.

The fight about income needs to continue, employing the two strategies for addressing income inequality noted above: Labor-Based Claims for Increases in Employment-Related Compensation and Citizen-Based Claims for Increases in Publicly Funded Transfer Payments.

The fight about wealth needs to be engaged. To repeat: The two strategies for addressing wealth inequality are Labor-Based Claims for Shared Ownership of Capital and Citizen-Based Claims for Shared Ownership of Common Wealth.

What a tragic irony that contemporary racial inequality—whose source is undeniably rooted in an unjust system of wealth accumulation—is largely understood today as a matter of income. Emancipation awaits.

Resources on Shared Wealth

Alaska Permanent Fund Corporation/APF Dividend Program— www.pfd.state.ak.us

Corporation for Enterprise Development/IDA Network— www.idanetwork.org

International Co-operative Alliance—www.coop.org

Iraqi Permanent Fund—www.iraqipermanentfund.com

National Center for Employee Ownership—www.nceo.org

* * *

Berlin, Ira. *Generations of Captivity: A History of African-American Slaves* (Harvard University Press/Belknap Press, 2003).

Kelso, Louis O. & Mortimer J. Adler. *The Capitalist Manifesto* (Greenwood Publishing Group, 1975).

Shapiro, Thomas M. *The Hidden Cost of Being African American: How Wealth Pepetuates Inequality* (Oxford University Press, 2004).

Chapter 19

Race, Poverty and the Estate Tax

Gary Bass, Ellen Taylor, Catherine Paskoff Chang and Adam Hughes

In April 2001, Black Entertainment Television (BET) founder and billionaire CEO Robert Johnson and 48 other African-American business leaders placed a full-page advertisement in the *Washington Post* and *New York Times* supporting repeal of the estate tax. Using many of the inaccurate arguments often made by conservatives and business lobbyists, Johnson and his co-signers incorrectly claimed the estate tax is particularly unfair to African Americans.

The facts belie Johnson's claim. The estate tax is not harmful to black prosperity: In fact, the tax actually helps to mitigate increasing income and wealth inequality in the United States, particularly between different races, and provides essential revenue for the federal government to fund programs supporting economic advancement and self-sufficiency for blacks.

An Estate Tax Primer

The estate tax is a one-time tax on the transfer of enormous amounts of wealth to heirs. It has been part of the US tax code in one form or another since the early part of the 20th Century and is an integral part of the attempt to establish a meritocratic American society in which inherited status matters less than one's actual contributions to society. Preserving this ideal in the tax code should be particularly important to blacks and other historically oppressed populations.

The estate tax is a consistent and logical extension of the principles underlying our progressive tax code. Just as any other transfer of assets results in taxes—for instance, the income or capital gains tax—so too should transferring assets as an inheritance.

As the most progressive aspect of the US tax system, the estate tax impacts only the richest 1.25% of Americans and does not tax low-, middle- or even upper-income people. In 2005, all estates of $1.5 million or less ($3 million or less for a couple) are exempt from taxation, and by 2009 the exemption levels are scheduled to rise gradually to $3.5 million for an individual ($7 million for a couple). In addition to these exemptions, an estate bequeathed to a spouse is totally exempt from tax. In 2009, only 3 out of every 1,000 Americans will ever pay any estate taxes.

The estate tax plays three vital roles in our society:

1)   Helps reduce concentrations of wealth and power.

The estate tax is the epitome of our progressive tax system. It helps prevent the concentration of wealth in the hands of a few. Many of the founding fathers, including Hamilton, Madison and Jay, considered such concentrations of wealth a threat to democracy because it would create an all-powerful aristocratic elite. This build-up of wealth is unhealthy for democracies.

2)   Encourages charitable giving.

The estate tax provides incentives encouraging charitable giving by including an unlimited deduction for transfers of wealth from an estate to charities (or to create foundations that fund charities). This policy ensures a way for the wealthy to reduce their estate tax liability and, at the same time, promote the good works that contribute to a rich and diverse civil society. Experts at the Brookings Institution estimate US charities would lose $10 billion in donations *per year* if the estate tax is repealed. The Congressional Budget Office (CBO) found a similar, but more drastic, trend. In a recent study, the CBO estimated if the estate tax had not existed in 2000, charitable donations would have dropped somewhere from $13-$25 billion in that year. This represents a substantial amount of resources that nonprofits, charities and direct service providers rely upon. This revenue cannot be replaced, and the effect of such losses on organizations—an enormous variety of groups, from soup kitchens to universities—will be debilitating.

3)   Provides substantial revenues to the federal and state government.

The estate tax is an important source of federal revenue. The CBO estimates a permanent estate tax repeal would cost $290 billion (2006 to 2015), and $745 billion during the first decade of full repeal (2012 to 2021). Since the federal government is facing budget deficits for years into the future and federal revenues are at the lowest levels since the 1950s, this revenue is especially vital. Repeal would cost state budgets an additional $9 billion per year.

The estate tax fills an important niche in the tax code that otherwise would result in a huge loophole allowing the tax-free accumulation of incredible sums of wealth across many generations. Repealing the estate tax would slowly exacerbate the economic and wealth inequalities already in existence in the US and threaten the underlying principles of democracy that are central to the American political system. In spite of the fairness of the tax and the many benefits it provides to society, an intense campaign of misinformation and demagoguery has been carried out to eliminate the estate tax.

The Role of Government in the Creation of Wealth

Both individual achievement and hard work play an important part in the creation of wealth, but they are certainly not the only aspects. It is equally important to recognize the role the US government and its laws and protections play in establishing the conditions necessary for wealth creation and accumulation. The US system of property rights and protections, patent and trade laws and regulations, as well as investments made in research, industrial, commercial and civic infrastructure (education, roads and railroads, electrical grids and power lines, etc.) also play a vital role in fostering and protecting the accumulation of wealth.

Many wealthy people recognize the important role a strong government plays in fostering a thriving capitalist society. Over 2,000 wealthy Americans who are part of the Responsible Wealth Project of the organization United for a Fair Economy have amassed enough wealth to owe estate taxes, yet have signed a petition urging Congress to reform, but not repeal, the estate tax. The Responsible Wealth Project, a national network of businesspeople, investors and affluent Americans concerned about deepening economic inequality, recognizes the role of government in allowing them to prosper economically, and believes the estate tax is a proper social claim of society for those benefits. Bill Gates, Sr., a leader of the Project, has said, "[The estate tax] is a very legitimate claim of society on an accumulation of wealth which would not have occurred without an orderly market, free education and incredible dollars spent on research."

Is the Estate Tax Racially Discriminatory?

The Estate Tax and Poverty

The BET advertisement argues the estate tax is particularly unfair to blacks because of America's legacy of racial discrimination and inherent bias against blacks that has restricted their social, educational and economic advancement. Ironically, repeal of the estate tax would weaken the ability of the government to level the playing field between minorities and whites through such means as enforcing civil rights protections, promoting small business loans for minorities,

enforcing FCC minority ownership rules or providing public subsidies to historically black colleges. These are only a few ways in which government uses
collective revenues to promote equality and increased opportunities for blacks
and other minorities.

In addition, the money brought in through the estate tax supports government programs providing resources for poor and disadvantaged families and
children, such as decent child care, pre-school health and nutrition, Medicaid,
job training, housing assistance, and drug and alcohol treatment programs. In
2003, almost one in four blacks lived below the national poverty line—over
three times the rate for whites (24.4% of blacks vs. 7.8% of whites). These governmental social programs overwhelmingly benefit African Americans and other
minorities in their mission to increase economic opportunity and equality.

The signers of the BET advertisement are throwing the baby out with the
bathwater; as economist Dr. Julianne Malveaux wrote shortly after the advertisement ran in the April 12, 2001 *Sun Reporter*, "[s]ome of the very programs
that African American business executives used to climb their ladder will be
jeopardized by budget cuts" that will likely result from repeal of the estate tax.

The Estate Tax and the Wealth Gap

Another consequence of repealing the estate tax would be an exacerbated
wealth gap in the US, which has grown at a disturbing rate over the last 20
years. From 1976 to 1999, the top 1% of America's wealthiest people increased
their ownership from 20% to more than 40% of the nation's wealth. During that
time, the percentage of families with no net worth has doubled.

The wealth gap is a persistent and troubling aspect of American society.
The founding fathers had many reservations and concerns about the concentration of power in the hands of a few. The entire US political system was designed
to balance and check the power of factions or what currently are called special
interests. The increasing wealth gap creates a small, but very powerful group of
people with shared interests. The wealth gap is contrary to the ideals of a democratic society and dangerous to the conditions necessary for it to thrive
—namely equality of opportunity.

The BET ad states: "Elimination of the estate tax will help close the wealth
gap in this nation between African-American families and white families [and]
permit wealth to grow in the black community through investment in minority
businesses that will...allow African-American families to participate fully in the
American dream." This claim is simply incorrect. The 48 signers of the advertisement represent approximately 22% of the 223 black Americans who have
sufficient net worth to have to pay the estate tax in 2002. It is those families, and
not the black community as a whole, who will benefit from the repeal of the
estate tax.

As disturbing as the general trend of an increasing wealth gap is, the country's widening racial wealth gap is even more pronounced. New York University

sociologist Dalton Conley believes wealth is, among others, the "one statistic captur[ing] the persistence of racial inequity in the U.S." While the racial income gap has narrowed, the racial wealth gap remains wide and is growing. According to 2000 Census data, median income of blacks is about 66% that of whites. Yet there are even greater differences in the net worth of whites as compared to blacks across all income brackets. In the lower income brackets, black households have just 15% of the wealth of their white counterparts. Even in the top two income brackets, black households have only between half and a third of the wealth of comparable white households.

The implications of the wealth gap on those on the bottom of the income scale are varied—from poor health care to a lack of educational opportunities to delayed retirement or the ability of a family to weather an economic "slowdown." Moreover, such gaps have enormous negative consequences on the long-term welfare of a country that is supposed to value the well-being of all of its individuals and not just the wealthiest 1.4%.

As Conley explains, this "inequity is, in part, the result of the head start whites have enjoyed in accumulating and passing on assets." Though there are many factors, including different savings rates and investment choices contributing to the racial wealth gap, sociologists Melvin Oliver and Thomas Shapiro have estimated that at least one-half of most wealth is inherited—and the majority of these inheritances go to well-educated, white professionals. Further, economist Edward Wolff cites data showing white households are more than three times more likely to receive inheritances than are black households, and the mean value of inheritances for whites is more than twice that for blacks.

These statistics highlight the importance of the estate tax in leveling the playing field over time between whites and blacks. Repealing the estate tax will further exacerbate the racial wealth gap while at the same time reducing the ability of the government to address fundamental racial inequality and bias in society. It will clearly harm the African-American community.

Recent Public Opinion and Action on the Estate Tax

The importance of the estate tax is something most African Americans already understand. Despite all the misinformation about the estate tax promoted by repeal advocates, the tax enjoys broad support among the public, particularly blacks. Many Americans support reforming the estate tax to make sure it continues to affect only the very wealthy and allows for the preservation of family farms and businesses, as opposed to repeal. In a May 2002 survey among 1,000 registered likely-voters, a solid majority indicated reforming the estate tax was a higher priority than repealing it. Sixty percent of voters said they strongly or somewhat supported reform, whereas only 35% said they strongly or somewhat supported repeal.

Perceptions of the estate tax were more positive among blacks. Only 24% of blacks support elimination of the estate tax, whereas 36% of whites do. Interest-

ingly, the poll revealed that even though less than one-third of 1% of estates that
pay any estate tax are paid by black decedents, 34% of black voters thought
someone in their household would have to pay the estate tax. The BET advertisement attempts to portray its signatories as representatives of the African-
American community as a whole, but its message and intent are contrary to the
preference of most black Americans.

The Estate Tax and Minority-Owned Businesses and Farms

One of the most commonly used arguments for repeal of the estate tax is it
causes the destruction of small family farms and businesses. There is little evidence to support this idea. According to the Tax Policy Center, only 30 family
farms or small businesses in the entire country will be impacted by the estate tax
in 2009. In addition, closely-held family farms and small businesses are given
more favorable treatment in the estate tax code, including a higher exemption
and a provision allowing the tax to be paid in yearly installments over 14 years.

Extensive data show the family-owned small business or farm is actually
left largely untouched by the estate tax. In their analysis "Rhetoric and Economics in the Estate Tax Debate," economists William Gale and Joel Slemrod find
"the vast majority of family businesses are not subject to the estate tax, either
because they fail well before the death of the owner or because their value is
well below the estate tax exemption."

Likewise, *New York Times* investigative reporter David Cay Johnston concluded in an April 2001 article, "Even one of the leading advocates for repeal of
estate taxes, the American Farm Bureau Federation, said it could not cite a single example of a farm lost because of estate taxes."

We have no information on how many black-owned businesses, if any, actually failed because of the estate tax. John Havens and Paul Schervish of Boston College in their recent study of wealth in African-American households
found the proportion of business ownership among African-American households to be about one-fourth the ownership rate among other racial demographic
groups. It is fair to surmise from the minute percentage of all businesses paying
the estate tax and the even smaller number of black-owned businesses, the estate
tax is not harming the development or continuation of businesses within the
black community. As noted above, it is far more likely that the lost revenue from
repealing the estate tax would force budget cuts in the very programs aiding and
encouraging African Americans in starting and continuing successful small
businesses in the first place.

Conclusion

To the highly emotional and often rhetorical debate already surrounding the estate tax, the BET advertisement attempted to up the ante—to the point of implying that the estate tax has an inherent racial bias and its elimination could be a form of partial reparations to the entire black community. The estate tax and the nation's growing racial wealth disparity, as well as the issue of slavery reparations, are complicated issues that demand and deserve sincere debate. The points made in the BET advertisement and in many other pro-repeal arguments, however, only distract the debate from the real issues. The country's growing racial wealth gap, as well as persistent economic inequality, must be confronted, but repeal of the estate tax will only exacerbate the problem, not improve it.

Repeal of the estate tax will benefit significantly more rich whites than the 223 rich blacks in this country who are currently subject to the tax. According to economist Edward Wolff, cited in the June 4, 2001 *American Prospect*, less than one-third of 1% of all heirs having to pay estate taxes are black. Repeal will be a windfall for the wealthiest whites in America and, because of the disproportionally small number of rich black Americans, will only exacerbate the racial wealth gap.

Repeal will not only disproportionally benefit super-rich whites, it will almost surely worsen conditions for the 36 million Americans living in poverty, 9 million of whom are black. It will force spending cuts, not only to programs that seek to alleviate the scourges of poverty but also to those fostering economic opportunity and development in poor, urban neighborhoods and among underserved populations.

The priorities of the BET advertisement are woefully misplaced. The government needs to dedicate time and resources to the goal of truly changing society on multiple levels to allow for the economic emancipation of millions of African Americans, not just the few hundred lucky and smart enough to amass a substantial amount of wealth. Unfortunately, the effects of repeal (substantial loss of federal revenue, decrease in charitable giving and growth of the wealth gap) will move us away from this goal.

Nearly 25% of all African Americans live in poverty. America needs to increase, not decrease, investments in our communities and neighborhoods to support and empower all Americans, especially blacks. Repeal of the estate tax will not lift blacks from economic dependency and poverty. It will not increase black savings. It will not increase the number of black-owned businesses. The estate tax itself provides the revenue to more effectively support black economic self-sufficiency and independence through economic, social and community investments over the long term.

The money saved by retaining the estate tax will help to ensure, in a time of growing budget deficits, the existence of a social safety net. Repeal of the estate tax will have negative effects on efforts to alleviate poverty and on those who suffer from it, especially the most disadvantaged who are still struggling to make it out of the net and onto the first rung of economic self-sufficiency.

Further, repeal of the estate tax will do nothing for those who are working hard to climb the ladder, like the majority of black Americans; it will only benefit those already at the top, such as Mr. Johnson and the co-signers of the BET advertisement. The way to address racial economic disparity is not to cut the taxes of the wealthy, of whatever race, but to continue to put federal resources towards ensuring that every American is allowed the basic opportunities necessary to succeed.

Chapter 20

Race, Poverty and "Economic Development" Gone Haywire

Greg LeRoy

States and cities spend an estimated $50 billion a year in the name of economic development. Yet a growing body of evidence indicates this massive spending—often justified with anti-poverty rhetoric—is at best ineffective and at worst unconcerned when it comes to reducing poverty and racial disparities in income.

The number and value of development subsidies has climbed sharply in the last 20 years, so that the average state now has more than 30 such subsidies of various sorts on the books, and deals providing more than $100,000 per job are old news. Subsidies typically include corporate income tax credits; utility, sales and excise tax breaks; property tax abatements; loans and loan guarantees; enterprise zones; tax increment financing districts; training grants; and land and infrastructure subsidies.

Despite lofty rhetoric about reducing poverty that has been used to justify this proliferation, it is increasingly clear that the programs are not really benefiting those workers who need help the most. Programs that were targeted to pockets of poverty but have strayed from their original mission are glaring examples; however, the problem is hardly limited to such subsidies.

Early Evidence of Straying Subsidies

Beginning two decades ago, a small but disturbing body of evidence began to appear that suggested development subsidies were being used by employers with discriminatory employment practices or by industries that were moving good jobs away from communities of color, or that affluent areas were getting most of the money.

For example, a 1984 analysis of industrial revenue bonds (IRBs, or low-interest loans) in the Chicago area found an adverse effect upon workers and minority entrepreneurs. The Illinois Advisory Committee to the US Commission on Civil Rights examined 104 deals. In fully one-fifth, either the recipient company or the bank that bought the bond had recently violated the Equal Employment Opportunity Commission's federal fair employment rules.

The same study also found that only 3 of the 104 IRBs went to African-American-owned firms, one to an Asian-owned firm and none to Hispanic-owned firms. At one-third of the companies, workforces had a much smaller share of black employees than the region's labor market. Two-thirds of the companies also had disproportionately small Hispanic employment, and more than half had disproportionately small female workforces.

A 1998 study by the Woodstock Institute examined the geographic distribution of loans made under the Small Business Administration's 504 loan guarantee program in the Chicago metro area and found that higher-income and outlying zip codes received more loans than lower-income and closer-in areas.

Several other studies found that incentive programs such as IRBs, intended to benefit distressed areas, more often go to prosperous jurisdictions. For example, a survey by the New York State Comptroller of 12 years of IRBs during the 1970s and 1980s found that just one county in affluent Long Island received 25% of the entire state's supply of the low-interest loans.

Lack of Concern for Race and Poverty

Several newer studies, including two national surveys, have made it clear that the earlier findings were not isolated cases or statistical flukes. Collectively, they suggest that the rules governing development subsidies have grown so loose as to moot out any positive effects they may ever have had towards reducing poverty or racial disparities.

Perhaps the most egregious official hypocrisy in economic development concerns public transit. In speeches, statutory intent language or official findings they use to justify subsidies, legislators often cite the reduction of poverty as a specific purpose. Families who depend on public transit to get to work because they cannot afford a car would meet most people's definition of impoverished. So among the 1,500-plus state subsidy programs, one would expect that at least a few would be structured to help transit-dependent workers gain new job opportunities. However, a 2003 study by Good Jobs First, *Missing the Bus*, finds that not one of those state subsidies requires—or even encourages—that a company in an urban area getting a subsidy locate the jobs at a site served by public transportation. (The standard definition of transit-accessible is a quarter-mile or less from a regularly served transit stop.)

In other words, despite the anti-poverty rhetoric, states are in fact completely indifferent to whether they are creating jobs accessible to people who cannot afford a car. Given that African-American households are about three-and-a-half times more likely than white families not to own a car, and Latino households are about two-and-a-half times more likely, the discriminatory bias of economic development in the US today could not be clearer.

It's a huge efficiency issue as well. States and cities spend about five times more a year on economic development than states spend on public transit. So if states adopted "location-efficient subsidies" requiring companies to locate jobs at transit-accessible sites, many good things would happen: More jobs would be created along transit routes, so that low-wage workers would gain new job opportunities; all workers would gain more commuting options; and exclusionary suburbs would be prodded to open up and allow more transit routes.

Another 2003 Good Jobs First study, *Straying from Good Intentions*, looks at how states have weakened the rules governing two geographically targeted anti-poverty programs: enterprise zones and tax increment financing (TIF). Both were originally restricted to areas with high rates of poverty, unemployment, and/or physical blight. However, the study found that over the past 20 years, 16 states have weakened their TIF laws and 11 have weakened their enterprise zone laws. That is, states weakened the geographic targeting rules, enabling TIF districts and enterprise zones to expand or migrate into affluent areas that were not originally intended to benefit from the programs.

For example, New York State permitted "Empire Zones" to double in size and then gerrymander into places that are not even contiguous to the originally designated high-poverty areas. Non-contiguous areas can be added to a zone if they are found to have potential for development, an extremely loose criterion. That has led to the creation of zones in areas that have low unemployment. Companies have also "gamed" the rules by creating a new entity within a zone, transferring jobs into it, and then getting tax credits for the "new" jobs in the zone. The *Buffalo News* found that many lawfirms and banks in the Central Business District were enjoying zone tax breaks, while jobs and investment were lagging in distressed neighborhoods.

A few states have so gutted their rules that they no longer make any anti-poverty pretense. For example, Arkansas, Kansas and South Carolina have declared *their entire states* to be enterprise zones. Louisiana no longer requires a company to locate in a depressed area in order to get zone credits, although some employees must live in zones.

Ohio no longer claims its huge zone program is for helping depressed areas; instead, its official purpose is to reduce business taxes and protect Ohio against subsidy competition from other states. The results of abandoning its anti-poverty intentions are already evident: A 2003 study by Policy Matters Ohio found that enterprise zones in high-income school districts receive five times more capital investment and twice as many jobs as those in low-income districts. It concluded that the "very areas [zones were] initially designed to help are now disadvantaged by the program....Ohio's [zone program] has succeeded in making the playing field even more tilted against urban areas by extending to wealthier suburbs an additional fiscal tool with which to compete for firms."

The same trends are evident in many states for tax increment financing, a device by which property taxes are diverted for long periods of time to subsidize redevelopment of small TIF districts. Originally targeted in narrow ways to reverse blight and abandonment, TIF has been watered down to a generic economic development tool in Alaska, Georgia, Indiana, Iowa, Minnesota, Mississippi, North Dakota, Utah and Virginia.

For example, Minnesota has more than 2,100 TIF districts—diverting more than 8% of the state's entire property tax base—yet less than a fourth of the districts have blight. The wealthy Chicago suburb of Lake Forest has a TIF district—and a Ferrari dealership!

Taxpayer-Subsidized Corporate Relocations

Multi-state competitions for high-profile projects such as auto assembly plants receive lots of media attention. But far more common are companies simply relocating within a metro area—relocating in a sprawling way that exacerbates concentrated poverty and racial disparities by moving jobs away from neighborhoods of color and pockets of poverty. Many studies have shown that the dispersion of jobs from central city to suburbs has disproportionately harmed minority and low-income workers because they face barriers finding housing in the suburbs. One case study examined a company's relocation from downtown Detroit to suburban Dearborn. After the relocation, the center of employee residence locations shifted, mirroring the company's move. Some employees moved closer to the new workplace; others quit. Black workers were more likely to quit, in part because of barriers to residential relocation.

Another study examined the distant Minneapolis suburb of Anoka. In the mid-late 1990s, it used TIF to fund a 300-acre industrial park and offer free land to light manufacturing companies that would relocate there. The lucrative offer landed 29 companies and about 1,600 jobs. All of the companies relocated to Anoka from within the Twin Cities region, mostly from Minneapolis and old, inner-ring northern suburbs. Overall, the relocations moved jobs and opportunity away from the region's poorest neighborhoods and away from people of color. They also moved jobs away from the region's largest pockets of welfare dependency—even as "welfare reform" was pushing many people into "work first," take-any-job routines. Low-wage workers without a car also lost opportunity: Before the relocations, 70% of the jobs had been accessible by public transit, but in Anoka they are not. Only 40% of African-American households in the Twin Cities region owned a vehicle in 1990.

A few journalists have also begun to make the subsidy-sprawl link. A 1995 *Kansas City Star* series cited several cases of prosperous suburbs giving tax breaks to companies leaving depressed core areas. The paper found the deals particularly galling because the tools being used by the wealthy suburbs were originally intended to help central cities. "Created to combat sprawl, tax breaks now subsidize it," the *Star* concluded. A 1999 series in the *Milwaukee Journal Sentinel* cited a mutual fund company in suburban Menomenee Falls that received a $3 million tax credit. The deal was justified because it is "close to Milwaukee County, which continues to have higher unemployment than the state average." A state senator commented: "[i]t's essentially a government subsidy to promote sprawl."

These many cases beg the broader regional equity issue: Since suburban sprawl already gives newer areas so many advantages, why should any development subsidies be allowed in them? As one Twin Cities civic wag put it: "Subsidizing economic development in the suburbs is like paying teenagers to think about sex."

With many states and cities facing chronic budget pressures—and more lean years ahead if the Bush Administration's proposed domestic budget cuts are enacted and its federal tax cuts continue to flow down to the states—there may be a chance to win greater scrutiny of corporate tax breaks. Reforming them so that they really reduce poverty and racial disparities—getting back to basics—is a winning argument.

Resources on Economic Development

Cassell, Mark. *Zoned Out: Distribution and Benefits in Ohio's Enterprise Program* (Policy Matters Ohio at www.policymattersohio.org/enterprise _zones.htm, 2003).

LeRoy, Greg, *The Giant American Jobs Scam: Corporate Tax Dodging and the Myth of Job Creation* (Berrett-Koehler, 2005).

LeRoy, Greg & Sara Hinkley. *Another Way Sprawl Happens: Economic Development Subsidies in a Twin Cities Suburb* (Good Jobs First at www. goodjobsfirst.org/anoka.htm, 2003).

Talanker, Alyssa. *Straying from Good Intentions: How States are Weakening Enterprise Zone and Tax Increment Financing Programs* (Good Jobs First at www.goodjobsfirst.org/pdf/straying.pdf, 2003).

Chapter 21

Poverty Quiz

Catholic Campaign for Human Development

The Poverty Quiz is updated annually (we are reprinting—with permission and thanks—the most recent version). Future updated versions are available at www.usccb.org/cchd/povertyusa/povquiz.shtml. *Answers are on page 399.*

1. The number of people living in poverty in the US decreased in 2003.
   True or False?

2. Most Americans could get out of poverty if they only had a job.
   True or False?

3. Asian Americans experienced the greatest increase in poverty.
   True or False?

4. The government says that a family of four is poor if it earns less than $35,000 annually.
   True or False?

5. The "working poor" in America are growing even poorer.
   True or False?

6. While the number of people in poverty is increasing, the number of people in extreme poverty is decreasing.
   True or False?

7. The rate of child poverty in America is higher than it is in most of the world's industrialized countries.
    True or False?

8. The federal minimum wage is now $5.15 per hour.
    True or False?

9. The elderly poverty rate is higher than for any other age group.
    True or False?

10. Most Americans believe that the federal government should play less of a role in helping the poor.
    True or False?

Housing

Chapter 22

Why Housing Mobility?
The Research Evidence Today

Margery Austin Turner and Dolores Acevedo-Garcia

For too much of the last century, federal housing programs helped create and sustain patterns of racial segregation and concentrated poverty. But beginning in the mid-1990s, housing mobility emerged as an explicit goal of federal housing policy, and efforts were launched in as many as 33 metro areas to help low-income families move from poor and predominantly minority neighborhoods to more affluent and racially integrated communities. Many of these efforts were inspired by research on the Gautreaux demonstration, part of the remedy achieved by a landmark desegregation lawsuit in Chicago. The Gautreaux research showed that children whose families moved from predominantly black neighborhoods of Chicago to integrated neighborhoods in the suburbs were substantially more likely to succeed in school and to go on to college or jobs.

Since then, considerably more research has explored both the consequences of living in a distressed community and the potential benefits of moving. Overall, the research evidence provides strong support for policies that promote housing mobility. But some findings raise questions or doubts about who is likely to benefit and how. And, not surprisingly, the research record remains inconclusive or incomplete in some respects.

How Neighborhoods Affect Our Lives

What is it about neighborhoods that affect the well-being and life chances of their residents? Social science suggests six important causal mechanisms—channels through which neighborhoods can shape or constrain opportunities. These six mechanisms make intuitive sense when we think about our own families and about the kinds of neighborhoods in which we want to live:

- *Local service quality.* Many essential public and private services are delivered at the neighborhood level. Most of us think about the quality of public schools as an important factor in choosing a neighborhood, but distressed neighborhoods often lack decent grocery stores, reliable child care, engaging after-school activities and healthy recreational facilities as well.

- *Shared norms and social control.* In healthy neighborhoods, shared norms and values help control everybody's behavior and teach children what is expected of them as they mature. Most of us would rather live in a neighborhood where other parents let us know when our children misbehave than one in which dealing drugs, dropping out of school, getting pregnant as a teenager or going to jail are seen as unexceptional or "normal."

- *Peer influences.* Young people are profoundly influenced by their immediate peer groups, which are often composed primarily of neighbors and schoolmates. And peers become especially important during the teen years, when they have the potential to fuel healthy competition over grades and athletics or to humiliate kids who do well in school and pressure them to join in on risky adventures.

- *Social networks.* Adults often get help and support from the networks of people they know, including neighbors. Who we know (and who we get to know because of where we live) can be an important source of job leads, parenting support, or health advice and referrals.

- *Crime and violence.* Living in a high-crime area increases risks for both adults and children, including the risk of being a victim of burglary or assault. But research increasingly suggests that exposure to crime and violence has more far-reaching consequences, including persistent anxiety and emotional trauma.

- *Job access.* As jobs become increasingly decentralized in most metropolitan areas, some inner-city neighborhoods have become physically isolated from economic opportunity. Although few of us work in the same neighborhoods where we live, people who rely on public transportation may have real difficulty finding jobs that are accessible to poor, inner-city neighborhoods.

Consequences of Neighborhood Distress

A considerable body of social science research finds evidence that living in profoundly poor or distressed neighborhoods can have a significant impact on people's well-being and longer-term life chances. These impacts—and the extent to which they have been rigorously studied—vary across different age groups.

Relatively little research has focused on how neighborhood distress affects infants and young children. But studies have found that having more affluent neighbors is associated with higher IQ for preschool kids; that preschool children living in low-income neighborhoods exhibit more aggressive behavior when interacting with others; and that elementary school performance is linked to neighborhood social and economic status.

Many more studies have focused on links between neighborhood environment and the social and economic well-being of adolescents. Young people from high-poverty and distressed neighborhoods are less successful in school than their counterparts from more affluent communities; they earn lower grades, are more likely to drop out and less likely to go on to college. Kids from poor neighborhoods are also less likely to get jobs during and immediately after high school. Studies have also documented that neighborhood environment influences teens' sexual activity and the likelihood that girls will become pregnant during their teen years. And finally, young people who live in high-crime areas have been found to be more likely to commit crimes themselves.

Adults may be influenced more by the neighborhood environments in which they grew up than by those in which they currently live. Nonetheless, some research has found evidence that distance from jobs reduces employment rates, particularly among lower-skilled adults.

Influence of Neighborhoods on Health

Since the 1980s, public health researchers and practitioners have been increasingly interested in the influence of neighborhood conditions on the health of residents. Individuals in lower socioeconomic positions (i.e., those with lower education, income and occupational status) tend to have higher rates of mortality and disease than individuals in higher socioeconomic positions. Additionally, research suggests that living in disadvantaged neighborhoods increases the risk of mortality and disease. This means that a poor person living in a disadvantaged neighborhood would tend to have worse health than a poor person living in a more prosperous neighborhood. Thus, improving neighborhood conditions might significantly improve population health. An article published in the June 2003 *Journal of Epidemiology and Community Health* showed that deaths would hypothetically be reduced by about 20% among white, black and Mexican-

American men and women if everyone had the same death rates as those people living in the neighborhoods with the most favorable socioeconomic conditions.

Possible mechanisms through which neighborhoods influence health may range from direct physical influences, such as exposure to toxic waste, to the cumulative stress associated with living in unsafe neighborhoods with limited resources. Additionally, since disadvantaged neighborhoods may limit opportunities for upward social mobility, neighborhoods may also influence health status by shaping socioeconomic attainment throughout the life course. In turn, the distribution of good health in society is strongly related to socioeconomic position, with those at the top of the socioeconomic ladder having better health than those at the middle and those at the bottom.

Living in disadvantaged neighborhoods may increase stress, which is associated with health problems such as cardiovascular disease. Stress may result, for example, from high exposure to violence. As landmark research by Arlene Geronimus has indicated, cumulative stress may in turn result in "weathering" or premature health deterioration. For example, the risk of hypertension and the risk of having a low birthweight baby may increase more rapidly with age among African-American women than among white women, because the former are more likely to be systematically and chronically exposed to stressors such as poor neighborhoods and discrimination.

There is also increasing evidence that residents of poor and minority neighborhoods find it much harder to sustain healthy behaviors, not only because those neighborhoods have more limited opportunities (e.g., there are fewer open spaces where one can exercise and fewer grocery stores with a variety of healthy food choices), but also because they are the target of companies that promote unhealthy lifestyles. Tobacco, alcohol and fast food are disproportionately advertised and placed in primarily minority and low-income neighborhoods. In the October 2004 *American Journal of Preventive Medicine*, Block and colleagues reported that in New Orleans, the number of fast food restaurants per square mile was higher in neighborhoods with lower household median income and in neighborhoods with a larger proportion of African-American residents. Thus, such disparities in neighborhood environment may contribute to the disparities we observe in health conditions, such as obesity, that are largely dependent on health behaviors—e.g., diet and physical activity.

A Note of Caution

Although a substantial (and growing) body of both theory and evidence points to the critical role of neighborhood in people's lives, it would be a mistake to overstate these conclusions. More specifically, there are two important caveats to keep in mind in thinking about the evidence of neighborhood effects.

First, individual and family characteristics interact with neighborhood environment and play a hugely important role in shaping outcomes. Some people can withstand the disadvantages of even the most distressed environment; and some families can help their children succeed despite their surroundings. Other individuals and families, however, may be particularly vulnerable to neighborhood influences. And still others are likely to encounter serious problems regardless of the neighborhoods in which they live. It would be a mistake, therefore, to assume that neighborhood environment is the only important factor in a family's life—or even the most important factor.

In addition, just because we observe a high incidence of a problem in high-poverty, distressed neighborhoods does not necessarily mean that the neighborhood environment actually *caused* the problem. It may simply mean that many families with problems ended up living in the same neighborhood, perhaps because housing is more affordable there or discrimination closed the door to other neighborhoods. This is the most common criticism raised by researchers who are skeptical about the evidence of neighborhood impacts. Consequently, the studies summarized here all use statistical techniques to control for individual and family characteristics, so as to measure the independent effect of neighborhood conditions on outcomes.

Benefits of Mobility

Now we turn to what research to date has found about the benefits of moving from a high-poverty, distressed neighborhood to a lower-poverty, more opportunity-rich neighborhood. Evidence on this issue is drawn from three primary sources:

- *Gautreaux demonstration*—research conducted over many years (primarily by researchers at Northwestern University) on families who moved from poor, predominantly black neighborhoods in Chicago to racially integrated suburban communities.
- *Moving to Opportunity (MTO) demonstration*—research conducted by researchers from a number of different institutions on a carefully controlled experiment to test the impacts of helping families move from high-poverty assisted housing projects (in Baltimore, Boston, Chicago, New York and Los Angeles) to low-poverty neighborhoods.
- *HOPE VI program*—research conducted by The Urban Institute on what is happening to the original residents of five distressed public housing projects that are being demolished and replaced under HUD's HOPE VI initiative.

The first key lesson from all three of these initiatives is that assisted housing mobility is feasible. Low-income families will apply for the opportunity to move to a better neighborhood. And many—though not all—succeed in using the combination of a voucher and some search assistance to find housing in lower-poverty and less racially segregated communities. For example, the share of MTO families who were successful in moving ranged from a low of 34% in Chicago to a high of 61% in Los Angeles.

Research to date clearly establishes that assisted housing mobility yields dramatic improvements in safety and security. Escape from crime and disorder is a primary motivation for families to participate in assisted housing mobility programs. For example, 53% of MTO applicants said that their most important reason for moving was to get away from drugs and gangs; another 29% gave this as their second most important reason.

Those who move end up in much safer neighborhoods. MTO research finds that moving with a regular Section 8 voucher (which supplements what low-income families can afford to pay for rental homes and apartments in the private market but requires recipients to conduct their own housing search)—generally to intermediate-poverty neighborhoods—increased families' perceptions of safety by 15.6 percentage points, while moving with an MTO voucher (to low-poverty neighborhoods) produced a 30.3 percentage point increase. We see similar gains among HOPE VI relocatees; in The Urban Institute's sample, eight out of ten families who moved with vouchers see their new neighborhood as safer. And families place tremendous value on these improvements, telling interviewers what a relief it is not to worry every day about possible violence and to have the freedom to let children play outside.

We have mixed evidence on how moving to a better neighborhood may affect children's educational achievement. Gautreaux research found dramatic benefits for children whose families moved to suburban neighborhoods. They were substantially more likely to complete high school, take college-track courses, attend college and enter the work force than children from similar families who moved to neighborhoods within Chicago.

So far, the MTO evidence is not as strong. Families have moved to neighborhoods with better schools, but—unlike Gautreaux movers—relatively few have left central city school districts. Moreover, some MTO children continue to attend the same schools, despite the fact that their families have moved. To date, there is no evidence that MTO moves have led to better educational outcomes, possibly because so few children are attending significantly better schools, or because it may be too soon to see benefits.

HOPE VI relocatees who have moved with vouchers report improvements in the schools their children attend. They see the schools as safer and better quality, and they also report that their kids are having fewer problems at schools, including trouble with teachers, disobedience at school and at home, and problems getting along with other children.

Some of the early research on MTO families in individual sites suggested that young people whose families moved to low-poverty neighborhoods were engaging in less risky behavior and committing fewer crimes. In Baltimore, for example, moving to a low-poverty neighborhood was found to cut violent crime arrests among juveniles roughly in half. More recent and comprehensive data for all sites suggests that moving to a lower-poverty environment is indeed improving the behavior of teen-aged girls, but not boys.

Specifically, for girls aged 15 to 19 in MTO families there were significant reductions in risky behavior, especially in marijuana use and smoking, as well as a reduction in the share of girls working rather than attending school. MTO boys in this age range, however, exhibit significant increases in smoking and arrests for property crime. Research is currently under way to better understand what is happening to the boys, and why they do not seem to be enjoying the same benefits from mobility as girls. One possible explanation is that black and Hispanic boys moving to integrated or predominantly white neighborhoods are not engaging in any more criminal behavior, but are being arrested more due to racial profiling. Another possibility is that girls and boys respond differently to the loneliness and fears of relocation.

The current evidence on how mobility affects adult employment and earnings is mixed and still somewhat inconclusive. It is important to note that mobility assistance does not directly address employment problems, although it may remove barriers standing in the way of employment. As a consequence, employment effects may take more time to materialize than other outcomes. Long-term research on Gautreaux families has found significant increases in employment and reductions in welfare recipiency. To date, we see no statistically significant employment or earnings effects across the total sample of MTO families. When we look at the sites individually, we do see significant impacts on employment and earnings among MTO families in New York and Los Angeles, but it is not clear why there would be an impact in these sites and not in others.

Housing Mobility and Health

The MTO demonstration has shown improvements in the health of the MTO group, and in some instances also in the health of the regular Section 8 voucher group. The most recent follow-up study indicated a reduction in adult obesity among the MTO group. This effect is noteworthy because the prevention of obesity has emerged as a national public health priority. The United States is facing an epidemic of overweight and obesity, which disproportionately affects African Americans and Hispanics, as well as those with lower socioeconomic status. The prevalence of obesity among US adults is 30.5% and has increased markedly over the past decade. Obesity increases the risk of illness from some 30 serious medical conditions, results in approximately 300,000 premature deaths each year and is associated with $117 billion in costs. In the MTO demonstration, reduction in obesity in adults may be partly due to healthier diets, as the MTO group showed increased consumption of fruits and vegetables.

MTO adults also showed significant improvements in mental health, including reductions in psychological distress and depression, and increasing feelings of calm and peacefulness. Improved mental health was also shown in the first

MTO follow-up study in New York and Boston, as well as in the Yonkers study of scattered-site public housing. The consistency of these results across three different studies is encouraging. Improvements in mental health are not surprising given that fear of crime was the main reason why MTO participants wanted to move out of their neighborhoods. As discussed above, adults and children moving to low-poverty neighborhoods reported increases in their perception of safety and reductions in the likelihood of observing and being victims of crime. Considerable stress in the neighborhoods of origin may have also resulted from chronic exposure to poor-quality housing and schools, two additional reasons why participants looked forward to moving out of those neighborhoods.

In addition to improvements in adult mental health, girls in the MTO group, and in some instances also girls in the regular voucher group, reported improvements in their mental health, including reductions in psychological distress, depression and generalized anxiety disorder. As discussed above, girls aged 15-19 in the MTO group also had better health behaviors than their counterparts in public housing—e.g., lower rates of smoking and marijuana use.

Although the reductions in obesity and mental health problems are promising, we should also note that at the latest follow-up, the MTO demonstration did not find significant improvements in other health outcomes such as asthma, blood pressure, smoking and alcohol use, all of which could also be influenced by neighborhood conditions. Additionally, evidence from the Gautreaux mobility program indicated that suburban movers may be less satisfied with medical care, possibly because in those neighborhoods there may be fewer health care providers, or former residents of public housing may be less familiar with them. In MTO, among those eligible to move, some did not want to because they were afraid of losing access to health care in their neighborhood. Also, families with a disabled member were less successful in moving to low-poverty neighborhoods. This suggests that although more prosperous neighborhoods may offer some better opportunities to maintain good health, residents' attachment to health care providers in disadvantaged neighborhoods may be a barrier to moving. Therefore, comprehensive mobility programs may need to address access to health care in their housing search counseling.

How Does It All Add Up?

Rigorous social science research convincingly shows that living in a severely distressed neighborhood undermines the health and well-being of both adults and children, and that moving to low-poverty areas is both feasible and beneficial. This evidence provides strong support for policies that help families move out of distressed neighborhoods and into lower-poverty communities. Ironically, although health improvements were not among the stated goals of MTO, they are currently among the most apparent gains realized by participating families, and MTO has provided some of the most compelling evidence to date that neighborhoods matter for health. In the long run, the positive effects of housing mobility on health may lead to improvements in other areas over the life course. For instance, healthier children may do better in school, and healthier adults may be able to hold better and more stable jobs. Additionally, the promise of housing mobility, if implemented at a large scale, may enhance population health, including contributing to reducing racial and ethnic disparities in health.

But research to date also highlights some limitations of assisted housing mobility. Not every family will be able to take advantage of mobility assistance, and not everyone who moves will necessarily benefit. It seems likely that the impact of mobility on educational achievement may depend on whether children actually change to significantly better schools (perhaps even better school districts), and that impacts on employment and earnings may occur indirectly and over a relatively long time horizon. Finally, as we learn more about how residential mobility works—and for whom—we should be looking for strategies to link mobility programs with other forms of assistance and support that families need in order to be stable and successful—including counseling for teens, job-training and placement services, treatment for mental or physical health problems, and assistance with budgeting and financial management.

Chapter 23

Racial Disparities in Housing and Health

Dolores Acevedo-Garcia and Theresa L. Osypuk

"The connection between the health of the nation and the dwellings of the population is one of the most important that exists." The words of Florence Nightingale, 19th Century nursing pioneer and housing advocate, seem relevant as America tries to address the vast disparities in health status that prevail between African Americans and whites. By any measure of access to good housing, African Americans are at a clear disadvantage. Given the well-recognized effect of housing conditions on health, it is relevant to outline the racial disparities in housing and ponder whether they may underlie the racial disparities in health.

African-American (i.e., non-Hispanic black) babies are more than twice as likely as non-Hispanic white babies to be low birthweight. In turn, low birthweight may lead to infant mortality, problems in child development and health conditions throughout the life course. Thus, as Dalton Conley and colleagues have eloquently argued, racial disparities in low birthweight are implicated in racial inequalities in life chances and across generations, as low birthweight affects people's potential for educational success, upward mobility and wealth accumulation.

African-American babies are about 2.5 times more likely than white babies to die before they reach their first birthday. Even when maternal socioeconomic status is taken into account, there are substantial racial disparities. Black infants whose mothers have college education or higher are 2.7 times more likely to die before they turn 1 than comparable white babies. These and many other disparities have led renowned social epidemiologist David Williams to conclude that "race still matters" in relation to one's chances for achieving a healthy life.

Racial stratification is expressed in multiple housing outcomes. The housing market and housing policies may be some of the most important vehicles for maintaining racial stratification. There are pronounced racial disparities in net worth. Roughly, the average white family has assets worth seven times the assets of the average black family. Racial/ethnic disparities in homeownership contribute substantially to racial disparities in wealth. Nationally, the homeownership rate is 75.1% for whites, but only 48.4% for African Americans. There are also sharp differences in the average quality of neighborhoods experienced by whites and African Americans. As reported by the Lewis Mumford Center, in many metro areas, blacks with incomes over $60,000 live in less advantaged neighborhoods than whites earning under $30,000.

Clearly, racial disparities in housing are a matter of concern in their own right. Their effect on health makes them even more unjustifiable, and the need to address them even more urgent. The magnitude and persistence of racial/ethnic disparities in health outcomes, even after taking into account differences in socioeconomic well-being among individuals, has led public health practitioners and researchers to seek explanations for these inequalities in the contexts where individuals live their daily lives, including their homes, their neighborhoods and their cities.

Housing and Health Disparities

Housing conditions impact health because they define our immediate living environment. Our homes are a refuge but may also be a source of dangerous exposures. Individuals who live in homes with structural problems, such as poorly designed stairs or windows, may face a higher risk of injury. Housing units may also be the source of hazardous chemical exposures, such as lead and radon. Lead poisoning in children may result in serious developmental problems, including cognitive deficits, and in adult behavioral problems. The risks at home also include biological exposures, such as cockroach and dust mite allergens, which may trigger asthma.

The quality of housing varies considerably by race. African-American kids are more likely than white kids to live in houses with dangerous lead levels. Not surprisingly, African-American children are more likely to have dangerous lead levels in their blood than is true for white children. According to the Centers for Disease Control and Prevention, 22% of black children living in housing built before 1946 have elevated blood lead levels, as opposed to 6% of white children living in comparable housing.

In addition to the impact of housing conditions on health, there is evidence that, on average, homeowners have better health than renters. Research found that children living in houses owned by their parents experienced lower rates of behavioral, emotional and cognitive problems. This may be because owned homes tend to be of higher quality and tend to be located in better neighborhoods, and also because homeownership may confer a sense of psychological well-being. Regardless of the reasons why homeownership promotes good health, given that whites are over 1.5 times more likely than African Americans to own their homes, it is clear that they and their children may have a better chance of being healthy.

Neighborhood Quality and Health Disparities

Health is influenced not only by the quality of individual housing units, but also by the quality of the neighborhoods where they are located, including neighborhood physical and socioeconomic environment, infrastructure, amenities and services. Even after taking into account individuals' socioeconomic status, better neighborhood environments may have a positive influence on health. For example, poor individuals experience better health in low-poverty neighborhoods than in high-poverty neighborhoods.

As a consequence of racial residential segregation operating at the metropolitan level, there are sharp racial disparities in neighborhood environment. According to Census data analyzed by the Mumford Center, in the Washington, DC metropolitan area, the average poor white household lives in a neighborhood where the median household income is $59,753, while the average poor black household lives in a neighborhood where the median household income is $41,412, a disparity of more than $18,000. Even middle- and high-income African Americans live in more disadvantaged neighborhoods than whites with comparable incomes. These differences are pervasive across all metropolitan areas.

Since neighborhoods influence health, and neighborhood quality varies sharply by race, differences in neighborhood environment are also likely to underlie racial disparities in health.

What is it about neighborhoods that affects health? Ingrid Ellen proposed that neighborhoods may influence health through access to services and resources, exposure to physical (e.g., pollution) and social (e.g., crime) stresses, and social networks, which may help people obtain health information and reinforce norms about healthy behaviors. For instance, although healthy eating habits are ultimately an individual choice, the ability to have a healthy diet may be constrained by limited access to healthy foods at the neighborhood level. Predominantly poor and African-American neighborhoods have a higher prevalence of alcohol and fast food outlets compared to wealthy and predominantly white neighborhoods, while the opposite is true for access to supermarkets that stock a variety of fresh produce. Residents of minority neighborhoods may also have fewer opportunities to be physically active, due to higher crime rates and limited availability of green space, sidewalks and bike paths.

In addition to the effects of material problems in highly segregated neighborhoods, less tangible neighborhood characteristics may also influence health. Recent evidence from the Project on Human Development in Chicago Neighborhoods found that higher social capital (membership in civic groups, trust, reciprocity) at the neighborhood level correlated with lower cardiovascular mortality. Segregation expert Douglas Massey recently proposed that African Americans suffer from high chronic stress, which leads to health and cognitive problems, due to their chronic exposure to social disorder and violence in neighborhoods characterized by concentrated poverty. High prevalence of crime in a neighborhood may also negatively affect residents' mental health status.

Racial Residential Segregation, Opportunity and Health Disparities

Although, on average, racial residential segregation between African Americans and whites has decreased in the last two decades, segregation levels are still very high. On average, African Americans live in neighborhoods that are over 50% black, and whites live in neighborhoods that are over 80% white. The separation between blacks and whites has serious ramifications. In metropolitan areas with higher levels of residential segregation, African Americans have fewer education and employment opportunities, and are more likely to live in neighborhoods characterized by concentrated disadvantage.

The extent to which opportunities available to African Americans in metropolitan areas are more limited than the opportunities available to whites cannot be overemphasized. For instance, in 50 of the largest 100 metro areas, the homeownership rate for blacks is between 40% and 49%, while only in three of these metro areas is the homeownership rate for whites that low. These disparities persist after taking income into account. Home loan rejection rates (the proportion of mortgage loan applications for financing purchase of a home which are rejected by banks) are another indicator of housing opportunities. In the largest 100 metro areas, the average home loan rejection rate for blacks with incomes above 120% of their metro area median income was 21%, well above the 8% average for whites. In 89 of these metro areas, banks rejected blacks for home loan applications more than twice as often as they did for whites.

Many health indicators across metropolitan areas are distinctly worse for African Americans than for whites. The mean rate of low birthweight across the 100 largest metro areas is only 4.8% for whites, but 11.3% for blacks. In the majority of metropolitan areas, the low birthweight rate is between 3% and 6% for white babies, but between 9% and 13% for black babies. In no metropolitan area do blacks have a lower rate of low birthweight babies than whites. On average, blacks experience over twice the rate of low birthweight as whites, and in five metro areas blacks experience over three times the rate of whites.

Residential segregation negatively affects the health of African Americans, possibly through its detrimental effects on individual (e.g., employment, education) and neighborhood level (e.g., concentrated poverty) factors. In metropolitan areas where racial residential segregation is higher, black adult and infant mortality rates are higher. As shown by Ingrid Ellen, African-American women are more likely to have low birthweight babies in metropolitan areas where segregation is higher, especially in those where blacks are more disproportionately concentrated in the central city, which tends to be more dilapidated and socioeconomically disadvantaged than the suburbs. The Mumford Center reported that in 2000, suburbs in the majority of metropolitan areas outpaced cities on eight indicators of prosperity.

In our research, we have seen that African Americans are more likely to report that their health is poor or fair (as opposed to good or excellent) in metropolitan areas where they are more likely to be isolated in predominantly black neighborhoods.

The Role of Housing Policies in Reducing Health Disparities

Government policies address many aspects of housing, from safety standards for individual housing units, to housing discrimination, to housing assistance for low-income households. Therefore, it seems reasonable to ask whether housing policies may contribute to correcting racial disparities in housing and thus racial disparities in health. There is evidence on the positive effects on health of interventions that address hazardous physical, chemical and biological exposures at the level of the housing unit. In the case of childhood lead exposure, research has documented the positive impact that various methods of lead hazard control have on dust and blood lead levels. We know considerably less about the possible effects on health of interventions and policies that address the socioeconomic (e.g., homeownership promotion) and locational (e.g., desegregation) aspects of housing.

A wide range of policies is available to reduce residential segregation across neighborhoods and along the central city-suburban divide, including restricting the power of local governments to enact exclusionary zoning regulations; limiting suburban growth (i.e., sprawl) through direct or indirect controls; and deconcentrating public housing. Of these policies, only the last mentioned—specifically, variants of the Section 8 housing voucher program—has been evaluated for its effects on health.

Housing mobility policies involve the geographic deconcentration of recipients of government housing assistance. Generally, their aim is to achieve racial desegregation and to offer individuals the opportunity to move from highly disadvantaged to middle-income neighborhoods. Improving health has not been an explicit objective of housing mobility policies, but given what is known about the link between neighborhoods, segregation and health, these policies may contribute to better health outcomes.

A compelling indication of the potentially beneficial impact of housing mobility policy on health has emerged from the Moving to Opportunity (MTO) policy demonstration. The participants in MTO were very-low-income families with children who lived in public housing or Section 8 project-based housing located in central city, high-poverty neighborhoods in five large cities (Baltimore, Boston, Chicago, Los Angeles, New York). Eligible participants were randomly assigned to one of three groups. The experimental group was offered Section 8 housing vouchers good only in low-poverty neighborhoods, as well as housing search counseling. The Section 8 group was offered an unrestricted Section 8 voucher. The control group stayed in traditional public housing. Researchers have followed the three groups since 1994, documenting their educational and employment outcomes, receipt of public assistance and several health indicators. The latest evaluation report by HUD showed that girls in the experimental group—i.e., those who moved to low-poverty neighborhoods—had improved mental health and a lower risk of using marijuana and smoking than girls who stayed in public housing. Adults in the experimental group experienced significantly lower obesity than those in public housing, and lower prevalence of mental health problems (psychological distress and depression). These findings suggest that housing mobility policies may contribute to improving health for children and parents. However, little is known about the mechanisms through which housing mobility may improve health. Is it because homes in low-poverty neighborhoods are of better quality? Is it because in those neighborhoods people are less likely to suffer from the stress associated with fearing and witnessing crime? Or is it because those neighborhoods offer more institutional resources, such as better schools and child care?

Housing mobility may also have unintended negative health consequences that housing and public health advocates should not overlook. During the 1990s, under the HOPE VI program, the federal government changed its housing policy towards low-income households, moving away from project-based assistance towards an increased use of housing vouchers and mixed-income housing developments. The nature and scale of such policy changes warrants an examination of its possible health effects, especially on families who have been displaced and are unable to find affordable housing. In a tracking study of HOPE VI, The Urban Institute has identified health problems as a major issue for former residents of distressed public housing.

Summary

The public health field is trying to address wide racial disparities in health. Sharp racial disparities also exist in housing at multiple levels, including access to safe homes and neighborhoods, and to opportunity in metropolitan areas. Given the effects of housing, neighborhood quality and segregation on health, the field is embarking upon a more systematic understanding of how addressing housing disparities at multiple levels may contribute to correcting health disparities. The links seem clear. Can we make them actionable?

Resources on Housing and Health

Acevedo-Garcia, Dolores & Kimberly A. Lochner. "Residential Segregation and Health," in *Neighborhoods and Health,* Ichiro Kawachi and Lisa F. Berkman, eds. (Oxford University Press, 2003).

Acevedo-Garcia, Dolores et al. "Future Directions in Residential Segregation and Health Research: A Multilevel Approach" (*American Journal of Public Health*, 2003).

Acevedo-Garcia, Dolores et al. "Does Housing Mobility Policy Improve Health?" (*Housing Policy Debate*, 2004).

Conley, Dalton. *Being Black, Living in the Red: Race, Wealth, and Social Policy in America* (University of California Press, 1999).

Conley, Dalton, Kate W. Strully & Neil G. Bennett, *The Starting Gate: Birth Weight and Life Chances* (University of California Press, 2003).

Massey, Douglas. "Segregation and Stratification: A Biosocial Perspective" (*Du Bois Review*, 2004).

Pettit, Kathryn L.S., G. Thomas Kingsley & Claudia J. Coulton. *Neighborhoods and Health: Building Evidence for Local Policy* (The Urban Institute, 2003).

U.S. Department of Housing & Urban Development, Office of Policy Development and Research. *Moving to Opportunity for Fair Housing Demonstration Program, Interim Impacts Evaluation* (2003).

Williams, David R. & Chiquita C. Collins. "Racial Residential Segregation: A Fundamental Cause of Racial Disparities in Health" (*Public Health Reports*, 2001).

Williams, David R., Harold W. Neighbors & James S. Jackson. "Racial/ethnic Discrimination and Health: Findings from Community Studies" (*American Journal of Public Health*, 2003).

Chapter 24

A National Gautreaux Program: A Symposium

Racial Inequality and the Black Ghetto

Alexander Polikoff

Reading Jason DeParle's 2004 book, *American Dream*, one is struck (for the thousandth time?) by the unremitting, inter-generational persistence of ghetto poverty. From W.E.B. DuBois through James Baldwin and Kenneth Clark; in compelling reportage by Nicholas Lemann, Alex Kotlowitz and DeParle; in numerous statistical analyses, ethnographic studies and academic research papers, the point is made over and over again: The concentrated poverty of urban ghettos condemns generation after generation of black Americans to what Clark called lives of impotence and despair.

Yet, some may object, only 2.8 million black Americans live in concentrated urban poverty—metropolitan census tracts with poor populations of 40% or more. That's only 1% of Americans. Sad to be sure, but not a big enough deal in terrorism times to get worked up about unless you're some bleeding heart liberal. The country has more pressing matters to attend to.

Query: Some 170 years ago, Alexis de Tocqueville called racial inequality "the most formidable evil threatening the future of the United States." Tocqueville went on to prophesy that the racial inequality evil would not be resolved—indeed, that it would eventually bring America to disaster. How could that be? How could

1% of Americans, confined to ghettos, be a nation-threatening matter? Bear with me, and I'll try to explain.

First, take small comfort from small numbers. In an earlier *New York Times* piece, DeParle makes this point about the small ghetto population:

> The poverty and disorder of the inner cities lacerate a larger civic fabric, drawing people from shared institutions like subways, buses, parks, schools and even cities themselves....Perhaps most damaging of all is the effect that urban poverty has on race relations. It is like a poison in the national groundwater that is producing a thousand deformed fruits...

What deformed fruits? Among them is nothing less than breaking up the coalition that birthed the New Deal and the Civil Rights Movement, a political sea-change that began in the World War II years, gathered strength over the next two decades, then led to Richard Nixon's election in 1968, followed in 1980 by the triumph of Ronald Reagan and the final dissolution of the New Deal coalition with its reigning creed of consensus liberalism.

Powered by the trauma of the Great Depression, America was becoming a nation concerned with social justice. New Deal measures were driven by social justice ideals. In 1944, FDR called on Congress to enact a "second" Bill of Rights, this one to be devoted to social and economic, rather than civil and political, "rights." He even vetoed a revenue bill because it failed to tax "unreasonable" wartime profits and provided relief "not for the needy but for the greedy." To be sure, the veto was overridden. Yet the Fair Deal moved "fairness" to center stage, and Truman initiated desegregation of the armed forces in its name. Johnson's Great Society was to be great precisely because it elevated social and economic justice to explicit national policy. Though far from having carried the day, social justice was clearly "in play" in the American psyche for the three decades from the onset of the New Deal through the cresting of the Civil Rights Movement in 1965.

In November 1968, that psyche underwent fundamental change. From a nation concerned with fairness we became a nation that under Richard Nixon slammed the doors on school and housing desegregation. After a brief interlude of "trusting" Jimmy Carter, our changed character re-emerged with traits deepened and intensified. Under Reagan, we became a thoroughly uncaring nation, obsessed with the "free" market and with crafting rules to foster still more personal acquisition by the most favored. The animating visions of the New Deal, the Fair Deal and the Great Society—"Government by organized money is just as dangerous as Government by organized mob," FDR once said—had become as irrelevant as ancient relics.

There is no single explanation for America's character change. But a major factor was disaffection by the blue-collar workers and white ethnics who had been core elements of the New Deal coalition. Disaffection over what? The answer is over blacks trapped in ghettos trying to penetrate white neighborhoods. Hubert Humphrey, champion of civil rights, not Richard Nixon, with his coded anti-black speeches and shameless pandering to Southern segregationists, suffered the consequences. There were other 1968 election issues, to be sure, but a number of historians make a powerful case that it was fear of ghetto blacks "invading" white neighborhoods that finally sundered the coalition that had given America its consensus liberalism creed.

Another example of a deformed fruit is the War on Drugs, targeted on black ghettos. Since Reagan assumed office, we have built over 1,000 new prisons and jails, many crowded beyond capacity. Crowded with whom? The answer is ghetto blacks. By 1990, nearly one of every four young black males in the United States was under the control of the criminal justice system, more in major cities (over 40% in Washington, over 50% in Baltimore). In his book, *Malign Neglect*, Michael Tonry observes that the rising levels of black incarceration were the foreseeable effect of deliberate policies: "Anyone with knowledge of drug-trafficking patterns and of police arrest policies and incentives could have foreseen that the enemy troops in the War on Drugs would consist largely of young, inner-city minority males." Part and parcel of our mass incarceration policy are "three strikes" laws that mandate long prison terms for third convictions. California has meted out a 25-year sentence for the third-strike theft of a slice of pizza, another for pilfering some chocolate chip cookies. Thirteen-year-olds have received mandatory, life-without-parole sentences.

Heartless sentencing may not be the worst of it. Like alcohol prohibition, the War on Drugs is directly responsible for the black market and the crime it spawns, fueling some of the very ills that are among the root causes of crime, diverting money from education and social initiatives. Between 1980 and 1995, the proportion of California's budget devoted to prisons grew from 2% to 9.7%, while the proportion for higher education dropped from over 12% to 9.5%. In 1980, there were over three times as many black men in college and university as in prison and jail, 463,000 as against 143,000. Twenty years later, there were *fewer* black men in college and university than in prison and jail—603,000 compared to 791,000.

In short, as a nation we are doggedly pursuing a ghetto-targeted mass incarceration policy that is both mindless and destructive of traditional American values. It is mindless because at enormous cost we insist on sticking with a policy that is having no demonstrable effect on drug availability, drug crime rates or crime rates generally. It is destructive of values because it has driven us to extremities that no fair-minded person can defend.

A final example of disfigured produce is the demise of welfare. The tangled skein of Americans' negative views about welfare is not easily unraveled. Yet racial hostility, mostly toward blacks, appears in the literature as a "major," even "decisive," factor. In the understated language of one study, racial animosity makes welfare for the poor, who are disproportionately black, "unappealing to many voters."

But rarely have high public officials matched the explicitness of Newt Gingrich. At the heart of Gingrich's successful dump-welfare campaign, linear successor to Ronald Reagan's Welfare Queen and George Bush's Willie Horton, was a stick-figure caricature of the ghetto: "You can't maintain civilization with twelve-year-olds having babies and fifteen-year-olds killing each other and seventeen-year-olds dying of AIDS." The image of the black ghetto was thus instrumental not only in ending decades-old welfare entitlement, but also in dropping the jobs, training and child care originally supposed to have been part of the deal. We don't yet know for sure what effect welfare reform is having on children, although DeParle's *American Dream* offers no cause for optimism. But the concern for maintaining civilization has not led to measures to help the ghetto children—American children, let us remember—who inhabit Gingrich's caricature.

Can these deformed fruits be blamed solely on black ghettos? No, they cannot. Ending black ghettos wouldn't end anti-black attitudes any more than ending Jewish ghettos ended anti-semitism. But it would be difficult to find many features of American society that match the black ghetto's poisoning effect on attitudes, values and conduct.

Sixty years ago, Gunnar Myrdal wrote: "White prejudice and discrimination keep the Negro low in standards of living, health, education, manners and morals. This, in its turn, gives support to white prejudice." Decades later, sociologist Elijah Anderson's studies of a ghetto and an adjacent non-ghetto neighborhood led him to conclude: "The public awareness is color-coded. White skin denotes civility, law-abidingness, and trustworthiness, while black skin is strongly associated with poverty, crime, incivility, and distrust."

In American society at large, most whites act like the ones Anderson studied—their public awareness is also color-coded, and they therefore steer clear of poor blacks and keep them in their ghettos. Predictable ghetto behavior then intensifies whites' sense of danger, validates their color-coding and drives their conduct.

Urban economist George Galster describes a self-reinforcing "ghettoizing cycle." First, ghettoization induces "behavioral adaptations" by ghetto-dwellers. Widely reported by the media, ghetto behavior is then seen as validating and legitimizing whites' prejudicial attitudes toward blacks. The prejudices translate into withdrawal from blacks, and into discriminatory conduct in housing, zoning, employment and institutional arrangements of all sorts, which in turn lead to more ghettoization.

Ghettoization is growing, in spite of many reasons to have expected the contrary (the Kerner Commission's admonition; passage of anti-discrimination laws; the substantial growth of the black middle class; the unprecedented good times of the 1990s). From 1970 to 2000, the number of metropolitan ghetto census tracts (40% or more poverty population) doubled, from around 1,100 to over 2,200, and the number of blacks in metropolitan ghettos increased from under 2.5 million to over 2.8 million. And there's every reason to believe the problem has grown since the 2000 Census.

In a nutshell, that is why I think we'd be well advised to play it safe with respect to Tocqueville's prophecy. Color-coded poison continues to flow into our groundwater, with disfiguring results that are plain to see. Disaster may not come in the form of riots and race wars, as Carl Rowan predicts in his book, *The Coming Race War in America*. But it will be disaster no less if American values are sufficiently deformed.

A National Gautreaux Program

So what can we do about it? One answer is the Gautreaux lawsuit's housing mobility program writ large: high-quality pre- and post-move counseling, coupled with housing search assistance and unit identification, to enable inner-city families to move with housing vouchers into middle-class neighborhoods far from the ghetto. Let me lay out the elements of what I believe would be a workable program, and respond to some of the multiple objections that will probably flood your minds. A sketch only, of course; the full rendition would take more than the allotted space.

Suppose 50,000 housing choice vouchers were made available annually, were earmarked for use by black families living in urban ghettos, and could be used only in non-ghetto locations—say, census tracts with less than 10% poverty and not minority-impacted. Suppose that the vouchers were allocated to our 125 largest metropolitan areas. Suppose, that to avoid "threatening" any community, no more than a specified number of families (an arbitrary number—say, ten, or a small fraction of occupied housing units) could move into any city, town or village in a year.

If an average of 40 municipalities in each metropolitan area served as "receiving communities," the result would be—using ten as the hypothetical annual move-in ceiling—that 50,000 families each year, or 500,000 in a decade, would move "in Gautreaux fashion." Notably, based on average family size, the 500,000 moves would equal almost half the black families living in metropolitan ghetto tracts.

We cannot, of course, assume that half of all black families in metropolitan ghettos would choose to participate (though they might). But neither would it require the departure of every other black household in order to change radically the black ghetto as we know it. With enough participants, radical change would be inevitable. Whatever the time frame, we would at last be treating a disease that has festered untreated in the body politic for over a century.

The hypothetical is plainly intended only to show that a national Gautreaux program could operate at a meaningful scale; it is not a real-life working model. Metropolitan areas vary in the size—in 2000, the 35 largest of the 331 metropolitan areas contained over half the metropolitan ghetto tracts. An actual program would be tailored to these variations, operating at greater scale in big ghetto areas and at lesser scale (or not at all) in metropolitan areas with small black ghettos.

(The hypothetical is also limited to census tracts with 40% or more poverty. Neighborhoods with 39% poverty can be pretty bad places too. Some of the literature even suggests that many neighborhoods in the 30-39% range are likely to be on their way to higher poverty. The response is that we must begin somewhere; once extreme poverty neighborhoods are dealt with, the mobility program could be expanded into lower-poverty areas.)

Several Questions

The hypothetical raises several questions. Would 50,000 vouchers a year be feasible? Could such an enlarged mobility program be administered responsibly? Would enough families volunteer to participate? Could 50,000 private homes and apartments be found each year?

The answers are speculative because mobility on such a scale has never been tried, but answers there are. The 50,000 annual vouchers, an arbitrary figure chosen for purposes of the hypothetical, really contemplates 100,000 new vouchers each year, with 50,000 of them earmarked for the Gautreaux-type program. The point would be to leave 50,000 new "regular" vouchers for other entering families who were ineligible for the mobility program or who, for a multitude of perfectly understandable reasons, were unable or unwilling to participate in it. Fairness to non-participants, and the need to deal with the charge that whites were telling blacks where they had to live, would make the "extra" 50,000 vouchers a necessity. However, 100,000 new vouchers per year is not a fanciful figure: Congress authorized more than that number as recently as the year 2000.

Yet the hypothetical program could be run without issuing any new vouchers at all. Currently, about 2.1 million vouchers are in circulation. The annual "turnover rate" is about 11%, meaning that for various reasons (for example, a family's income rises above the eligibility ceiling) some 230,000 vouchers are turned back to housing authorities each year for re-issuance to other families. A Congressional enactment could direct 50,000 of these turnover vouchers to the hypothetical program.

The cost of assisting mobility moves must of course be included in the calculus. But at an average of $4,000 per family—a reasonable, even generous, figure based on the Gautreaux experience—we are talking about $200 million a year, $2 billion total over ten years (excluding inflation). To put that figure in perspective and address the question of whether we could "afford" it, consider that for a single year (FY2004), the Bush Administration proposed a military budget of some $400 billion, which (also excluding inflation) would amount to $4,000 billion over ten years.

It is true that almost any program can be viewed as affordable by comparison with our military budget. But we aren't talking about "any" program. We are talking about a program to end the successor to slavery and Jim Crow that is perpetuating a caste structure in the United States and threatening incalculable harm to

American society. Achieving that, for a negligible fraction—.0005—of our military budget, would be our best bargain since the Louisiana Purchase.

That negligible fraction is the price tag for mobility assistance only; it does not include the cost of the vouchers themselves. At the current cost of about $6,500 per voucher, the ten-year voucher tab for 100,000 new vouchers each year would be just under $36 billion (again excluding inflation). Adding roughly 7% for the administrative fees HUD pays to housing authorities brings the total to about $38.5 billion, less than 1% of the $4,000 billion military figure. Our affordable housing crisis is so severe that, entirely apart from mobility and ghetto-dismantling, we should be—and politics will some day so dictate—making affordable housing expenditures of this magnitude. Housing expenditures "the Gautreaux way" would give us the double payback of ameliorating both our affordable housing and our black ghetto crises.

Suppose, however, that the country isn't ready to spend $38.5 billion over ten years for new "double payback" vouchers. Running the hypothetical program with turnover vouchers instead would eliminate entirely the $38.5 billion cost of new vouchers. This would mean that the only additional tab for the hypothetical program—beyond the costs we are today already incurring for our "regular" voucher program—would be about $200 million a year, taking us back to that .0005 fraction of our military budget. It is mind-boggling to think that, for an infinitesimal expenditure in budgetary terms, we could mount a program that could—to use a storied locution—end the ghetto as we know it.

What about administration? Under a consent decree in a housing desegregation case, the Dallas Housing Authority in a little over two years assisted some 2,200 families, most of them black, to move to "non-impacted" areas (census tracts in which few Section 8 vouchers were already in use, but in practice the receiving areas turned out to be predominantly non-black). Dallas was a case of direct administration by a housing authority. The Gautreaux Program was administered by a nonprofit organization. Moving to Opportunity, HUD's five-city Gautreaux-like demonstration program (using poverty, however, not race, as the measure), involves partnerships between housing authorities and nonprofits. These varied and largely positive experiences suggest that we could handle the administrative challenge of a nationwide Gautreaux-type program.

One often expressed administrative concern is that moving families will cluster in specific, perhaps "fragile," areas and lead to new poverty enclaves, even suburban ghettos. My proposal that program families move to very-low-poverty, non-racially-impacted communities, distant from high-poverty areas, and the low annual ceiling on the number of mobility families entering any city, town or village, makes that unlikely. But this potential problem was easily resolved by the direction included in the Gautreaux Program contract to place families in a dispersed fashion. In practice, this provision gave the Council authority—which it exercised (consistently, indeed, with an "anti-concentration of voucher families" provision in the underlying Section 8 statute)—to avoid clustering of moving families.

Would enough families volunteer to participate? We will not know until we try, but the Gautreaux experience suggests that they may. An average of 400 families moving each year in each participating metropolitan area would be required to reach the hypothetical goal (a smaller average number if more metropolitan areas were used). The 400-per-year number was surpassed more than once by the Gautreaux Program even though the number of entering families was artificially limited, not by market factors but by the funding and staff that could be extracted from HUD in the Gautreaux consent decree bargaining process.

Finally, could 50,000 homes and apartments be found each year? The Gautreaux Program placed families in over 100 cities, towns and villages in the Chicago area, while the hypothetical assumes an average of only 40. The Census Bureau counts 331 metropolitan areas in the country, while the hypothetical assumes that the mobility program would operate in only 125. Each assumption is conservative with respect to unit supply.

Most importantly, the potential supply of units is not a fixed sum. More fine-tuning of Fair Market Rents (increasing them in low-vacancy times and places, reducing them where they exceed market rents) and more creativity about responding to landlord concerns (for example, paying rent for the several weeks it sometimes takes a housing authority to "clear" a family for an apartment being held off the market) can make a big difference. For areas in which low Fair Market Rents remained a serious problem, the law creating the mobility program should direct HUD to approve whatever rents were demonstrated to be reasonable (based on comparable community rents) for participating families. If the 50,000 annual goal were made a bureaucratic imperative, and if local administrators were given the right tools, it is possible—indeed, likely—that the 50,000 goal would be achieved.

A Legal Issue

A different kind of question is prompted by the notion of setting aside 50,000 vouchers each year for black families. How can one justify denying poor whites, poor Latinos and poor Asians, many also living in high-poverty neighborhoods, an opportunity to participate in the mobility program? Would it even be legal?

A dual justification can be offered. The first is that the proposal is designed to help the nation confront its "most formidable evil," an evil that results in significant degree from fears and conduct generated by confining black Americans, not others, to ghettos.

The second is that the country is responsible for the confinement of blacks to ghettos in a manner and degree that is not the case with other groups. This is obviously so as to poor whites, who already live mostly among the non-poor. Latinos and Asians do not have slavery or Jim Crow in their histories. Nor have they been confined among their own to a comparable degree. Devoting 50,000 vouchers exclusively to blacks in ghettos can thus be justified both by the purpose of the proposal and by the unique history and current situation of black Americans.

As for legality, no one can be certain in a time when 5-4 Supreme Court decisions are routine. But when in 1988 Congress authorized compensation to Japanese citizens who had been herded into World War II detention camps, no serious legal question was even raised. Though the analogy is obviously imperfect, housing choice vouchers as "compensation" for confining blacks to ghettos is not a bad rationale. It is unlikely that even today's Supreme Court would upset an express Congressional determination to make partial amends in this way for a history of slavery, Jim Crow and ghettoization.

(One can imagine that, for reasons of policy or politics, Congress would choose to offer the mobility program to all residents of metropolitan ghettos. This would require a reworking of my numbers, and possibly prioritizing poverty families. In the New York City area, for example, almost half the population of extreme poverty areas is Hispanic, and in the Los Angeles area the number is over two-thirds—for the most part, of course, in different census tracts than blacks. Although such an expansion would blunt the programmatic thrust and rationale of ending the *black* ghetto, would increase cost and administrative complexity, and would probably extend the time frame, it should not affect the basic structure or feasibility of the proposed program.)

Those Who Remain

Even if a national Gautreaux-type program were doable and legal, objections remain to be addressed. One is that the program would be harmful to the moving families, severing them from family, friends and institutional support systems, and subjecting them to hostility and racial discrimination. One answer is to ask who are "we" to withhold a purely voluntary, escape-the-ghetto opportunity from "them" on the ground that we know better than they what is in their interest. I am reminded of what *New York Times* columnist Brent Staples once wrote about "butchery" in ghetto streets:

> Remember how Britons shipped their children out of London during the blitzkrieg? What American cities need are evacuation plans to spirit at least some black boys out of harm's way before it's too late. Inner-city parents who can afford it ship their children to safety in the homes of relatives. Those who are without that resource deserve the same option extended to parents in London during World War II.

Moreover, studies of the Gautreaux Program show that "evacuation" works well for many participating families.

A variation on the bad-for-them argument is that dismantling the ghetto will undermine black institutions, political power and ghetto communities that have values deserving preservation. As for black institutional and political strength, Italians, Irish, Jews and others have survived far more mobility than black Americans are likely to experience; it is absurd to contend that the strong, resilient black American culture has anything to fear from a Gautreaux-type program. As for values in ghetto communities, even apart from the butchery of which Staples writes, it is plain to any objective observer that the bad far outweighs the good.

A further variation on the bad-for-them argument is that non-movers will be worse off once some of the ablest and most motivated among ghetto residents leave. Even if true, this is not a sufficient reason to reject the approach. Should we not have passed the Fair Housing Act because the departure of better-off ghetto residents may have left those who remained worse off? Moreover, the likelihood that deconcentration will foster redevelopment means that even many of those who choose to remain will be benefited over time.

The latter point may raise eyebrows. Why will redevelopment be fostered? And if it is, won't gentrification simply drive out remaining ghetto residents? The answer to the first question is a matter of pressure: When, like a balloon being filled, migrants poured in, the ghetto expanded outward; as deconcentration lets out some of the air, the pressure will be reversed.

When ghettos are located near prime areas, redevelopment pressures will be strong. When they are not, the redevelopment pump may need to be primed with government assistance of one sort or another. In both circumstances, the concern that gentrification will drive out the remaining poor can be addressed. Where government assists the redevelopment process, the assistance should be conditioned on housing for the poor as part of the mix. Where is does not (although usually some form of assistance will be involved), inclusionary zoning can mandate that some low-income housing be included in all new residential development above a threshold number of units. Other techniques—for example, property tax caps—are also available.

Revitalization as an Alternative?

Others reject the Gautreaux approach in favor of preferred alternatives. A major one is "revitalization," but analysis discloses that, absent poverty deconcentration, this is an inadequate alternative. A rudimentary form of revitalization is simply to go in—without worrying about poverty deconcentration through housing mobility —and improve shelter and services for present residents. But with the suburbs having become the locus of metropolitan employment growth, with the opportunity engine the ghetto once was now a destructive, jobless environment, it is hubris to think we could reverse decades-old economic forces through improved shelter and services alone. William Julius Wilson concludes, correctly I think, that without increasing economic opportunities for poor blacks and reducing their segregation, programs that target ghettos are unlikely to have much success.

A more sophisticated revitalization approach is community redevelopment. With a nonprofit community development corporation generally leading the way, the idea is to attack all of a depressed community's needs comprehensively and simultaneously—not just housing, but commercial development, job creation, school improvement, health facilities, public and social services, credit supply, crime and drug control. This form of revitalization is almost always aided by government funding of one sort or another.

The attraction of community revitalization is considerable. Residents of depressed neighborhoods need hope; the revitalizing possibility may supply it. Cities need redevelopment; the prospect of revitalizing offers it. Democracy requires a strong citizenry; community-based revitalizing builds strong citizens. No wonder community revitalization is the darling of philanthropy, supported by a growing national movement.

But cautions are in order. First, community redevelopment does not generally focus on ghettos, for few black ghettos boast the key instrument -- a strong community development corporation. Second, even in the neighborhoods in which most revitalization has been attempted, the record is distinctly mixed. Revitalization is a difficult, multi-faceted, long-term undertaking. Numerous studies make it clear that even after decades of stupendously hard work and much achievement, jobs may still be scarce, neighborhood schools still problematic, poverty still widespread, crime and drugs still unvanquished. Two of revitalization's most enthusiastic supporters (Paul Grogan and Tony Proscio, in their book *Comeback Cities*), writing about one of its most notable successes—the South Bronx—acknowledge that the poverty rate there did not decline, that employment was mostly unchanged, and that "substantial racial segregation and isolation will continue."

The reason has to do with six decades of metropolitan development patterns which David Rusk examines in his 1999 book, *Inside Game/Outside Game*. The "inside game" is being played in many large cities and—increasingly—in many older, inner-ring suburbs as well. Relative to their metropolitan regions, these "inside" places face declining employment, middle-class populations, buying power, relative incomes and tax bases, along with increasing disproportionately poor minority populations. The "outside game" is of course the reverse of these patterns, with most of the suburbs, particularly the newer, farther-out ones, garnering a steadily growing share of the region's jobs, as well as middle-class families with their incomes, buying power and tax-paying capacities, while housing a disproportionately low fraction of the region's poor.

Inside Game/Outside Game analyzes the powerful social and economic forces that generate these metropolitan development patterns, and the institutional—including governmental—arrangements that foster them. The result is what Rusk calls the "tragic dilemma" of community-based redevelopment programs. "It is like helping a crowd of people run up a down escalator." No matter how hard they run, Rusk writes, the escalator keeps coming down. A few run so fast they reach the top, but most are weary and are carried back down.

To be sure, no effort to improve housing and services for poor families should be gainsaid. Some revitalizing activity may actually prevent marginal neighborhoods from becoming ghettos. Yet there is a danger that the appeal of community revitalizing will lead to plans that leave ghettos intact by focusing exclusively on improving conditions within them for their impoverished populations. We should not be about the business of fostering self-contained ghetto communities apart from the mainstream. We should instead be trying to bring the ghetto poor into the mainstream. The critical point is that only by enabling the poor to live among the non-poor will significant, long-term improvements be made possible in the life circumstances of most impoverished families trapped in ghettos.

Experience demonstrates that community revitalizing can best be achieved through a mixed-income approach that attracts higher-income families to (formerly) poverty neighborhoods, thereby creating an incentive for private profit and investment. Like housing mobility, mixed-income development also brings with it the crucial benefit of enabling the poor to live among the non-poor. Community revitalization should thus be seen not as an opposing or alternate strategy but as a follow-on, mixed-income complement to housing mobility.

The Politics

A final objection is that my entire proposal looks like an indulgent fantasy. Don't we clearly lack the political stomach for allowing large numbers of black families to move from inner-city ghettos to white neighborhoods? What on earth makes me think that a nation that has treated blacks the way America has through most of its history—the way it still treats the black poor—would give a moment's consideration to the course I am proposing? This very black ghetto issue was instrumental in shifting the political alignment of the entire country just a few decades ago, changing American character in the bargain. We remain today the uncaring nation we then became. Indeed, as this is being written, the Bush Administration is proposing to cut back radically on housing choice vouchers. A Gautreaux-type program would certainly be portrayed as liberal social engineering. Should it ever be seriously considered, wouldn't some modern-day George Wallace whip up the country's hardly dormant Negrophobia, perhaps especially easy to do at a time when working- and even middle-class Americans are having a hard time?

Maybe. Still, history is full of close calls and surprises. England might have succumbed to the Nazis if Roosevelt had not dreamed up lend-lease and persuaded a reluctant, America First Congress to go along. In 1941, selective service survived by a 203 to 202 vote in the House of Representatives. Truman beat Dewey. Nixon went to China. The Soviet Union collapsed. In one decade, the Civil Rights Movement ended generations of seemingly impregnable Jim Crow. In a single fair housing enactment, Congress stripped historically sacred private property rights from American landowners. Even with respect to black Americans, history tells us that we can sometimes manage forward steps. Leadership is key, but we will not have a Bush in the White House forever.

If my analysis is correct, it is ghetto fear—anxiety about inundation and anti-social conduct—that explains a good deal (though not all) of today's white attitudes toward blacks in general, and white rejection of in-moving blacks in particular. If the ghetto were replaced, over time those fears and anxieties would be ameliorated. Gautreaux teaches that the threshold fear of "them" can be overcome by effective pre- and post-move counseling; by certification from a credible agency that the moving families will be good tenants; and, most importantly, by keeping the numbers down. No more than a handful of families a year entering any receiving community makes a different ball game.

Two Courses

America confronts two courses. The first is to continue to co-exist with black ghettos. The second is to dismantle and transform them. The prospect along the first course, as Tocqueville prophesied, is that the evil of racial inequality will not be solved. Integration of some middle-class and affluent blacks will not change the prospect. Until the vast proportion of black Americans is securely middle-class, says the noted sociologist Herbert Gans, so long will whites continue to treat middle-class blacks as surrogates for the poor who might move in behind them. So long as black ghettos exist, threatening inundation should there be a break in any neighborhood's dike, most white Americans will fear the entry of blacks, any blacks, into their communities. And so long as that is the case, America's "most formidable evil" will continue to afflict the nation.

The other part of Tocqueville's prophecy—result in disaster—is less certain. Yet so long as we continue to tolerate the black ghetto, the prospect is for continuation of the two unequal societies described by the Kerner Report, and continued fear of blacks by white Americans. As long as that fear persists, whites will continue to treat black Americans as the feared Other. They are likely to continue to act fearfully and repressively, possibly to incarcerate still more black Americans in still more prisons. In that event, the Tocqueville prophecy of disaster may indeed become the American reality.

The alternative is to dismantle our black ghettos, replacing them wherever possible with mixed-income communities, thereby to lessen the fear and the fearful conduct they generate. Nothing can bring that about overnight, and any approach will be fraught with difficulty and uncertainty. But a national Gautreaux mobility program is a sensible way to begin a task that we postpone at our peril.

Commentaries

Gautreaux and the Vicious Circle of Racial Injustice

Paul L. Wachtel

To properly evaluate Alexander Polikoff's proposal for a nation-wide initiative based on the Chicago Gautreaux program, it is essential to be clear about the premises on which it is based. Without understanding those premises, it may be hard to appreciate why, although he clearly recognizes the importance of implementing a wide range of other approaches to addressing our persisting racial inequities, he nonetheless privileges the breaking up of the black ghetto as the single highest priority.

At the heart of Polikoff's vision, as I read him, is the same perception of a vicious circle of injustice begetting injustice that was at the heart of Gunnar Myrdal's analysis in *An American Dilemma* and that is central to my own analysis of our more contemporary racial impasse in *Race in the Mind of America*. And like many others as well, from Kenneth Clark to William Julius Wilson to Douglas Massey and Nancy Denton to George Galster, Polikoff sees as a crucial center of this self-perpetuating human tragedy the *de facto* restriction of the nation's black poor to neighborhoods characterized by neglect, minimal job opportunities, high crime rates and general social demoralization. Being trapped in such neighborhoods has an impact on the behavior of those who live there that is not only highly deleterious for them but contributes to the hardening of hearts and attitudes throughout our society. Without pulling punches, Polikoff states that America has gone through nothing less than a negative character change in recent decades and that that change has been fueled by reactions of fear and aversion to what is perceived to be characteristic behavior in our inner cities.

Those perceptions are, to be sure, highly distorted by the force of stereotype. But they are perpetuated as well by the actual behavior that can be evoked by the desperate circumstances and cruel absence of opportunity that the residents of these communities encounter. And their impact is further exacerbated when the behavior of poor blacks in the inner city becomes the filter through which *all* blacks are perceived and the basis for the "color-coding" that restricts so pervasively black Americans' opportunities for full participation and equal respect in our society.

The stereotypes that white Americans hold of the black residents of our poorest neighborhoods (much like the stereotypes they hold of blacks in general) are, of course, the product of centuries of injustice and the efforts of the perpetrators of that injustice to rationalize and justify it. But they are a *complex* product of those efforts. The image of the "ghetto black" is constructed mostly of myth and stereotype, but it is reinforced by some of the unfortunate realities that have accrued from our compressing a critical mass of misery into the fissionable space of our inner cities. And because Polikoff views that image as casting a shadow over race relations more generally, and as at the heart of the negative social character change he refers to, he sees the proposal he is making as having a dual impact. He aims not just to provide a better opportunity for those individuals and families who make the move, but, in essence, to defuse the generators of explosive misery and rage that have sent out shock waves to our entire society. He aims, it seems to me, at nothing less than another "character change" in American society, one much more congenial to justice and caring.

That character change will certainly not be easy to achieve in an era in which Americans are practically being told it is their Christian duty to be harshly judgemental, uncaring and self-interested. But it is important to appreciate that although political attitudes may appear to be fixed and singular, closer examination reveals that, like all facets of human psychology, they are the end result of a complex tangle of competing inclinations. Beneath what might seem to be monolithic opinions and dispositions, there lie emotionally powerful *conflicts* whose ultimate resolution or outcome is far from pre-determined. A key task for those of us committed to progressive social change is to make contact with the side of dominant white attitudes that might be more receptive to our message or our concerns than their present manifest stance might suggest.

The point is not that every racist or every greedy pursuer of self-interest has a hidden heart of gold. There are certainly people who are pretty thoroughly opposed to what progressives stand for. But many millions more are considerably more complex in their feelings than they themselves are aware of. The attitudes they manifest reflect the current resolution of conflicting forces; but as with a picture that comes crashing to the ground after hanging on the wall for years, a slight shift in the forces that have been invisibly contending can yield a dramatic change in the overall result.

The possibility exists for what Polikoff would call positive character change, notwithstanding all the discouraging indicators evident in our daily papers each day, because of the conflict that underlies *any* character configuration. Americans have not become converted in recent decades into totally different kinds of souls. The *balance of forces* in their psyches has shifted, a shift that for many is probably no more absolute or categorical than a 51 to 49 percent division in the electorate. In both instances, we must remind ourselves not to despair or to conclude that an irrevocable change has occurred.

Once any change in a complex configuration of visible and less visible forces or attitudes begins to occur, other things begin to alter as well, often in unpredictable ways. I have described in *Race in the Mind of America* how intricately connected and intertwined are the behavior and attitudes of blacks and whites. Each side responds to the other, and each, simultaneously, thereby partially "creates" the other to which it responds. This *reciprocal* (if mostly unwitting) participation in the perpetuation of a circular pattern of response and counter-response, with each side experiencing their behavior and attitudes as purely the product of the other's, has been at the heart of our continuing racial tragedy. Polikoff's proposal offers a way out of this pattern, a way to break into its dynamics by opening the pressure gauge in our inner cities. But it is crucial to note that Polikoff's proposal also emphasizes paying careful attention to the experience of people in the receiving communities as well. However valuable and essential it is to improve the lives of those individuals who are enabled to move, the national character change that we so urgently need will not occur if the receiving communities perceive themselves to be the losers in this exchange. In that sense, community-building and "revitalization" are almost as important to invest in in the receiving communities as it is in those communities more obviously in need.

If the program is not to fester into one more instance of the very phenomenon Polikoff identifies as a key source of our society's negative character change—fear and anger over "unwanted" and "undesirable" people forcing themselves into otherwise "good" neighborhoods—it is essential that the program be constructed in such a way that the people in the receiving community perceive something *positive* in the experience and be brought on board. There must be *incentives* for the receiving community, not the experience of something being rammed down their throat. My own proposal for "magnet neighborhoods" in *Race in the Mind of America* had very much this aim and structure, but Polikoff's emphasis on the link between white racial fears and the break-up of the liberal consensus gives it still greater urgency. There *has* been a moral decline in America, but it is not the one that conservatives trumpet. It is the coarsening and hardening of hearts and of social discourse, the narrowing of the bonds of compassion and mutual identification, the way in which American society itself has become a kind of gated community, with certain groups kept determinedly outside. Polikoff aims not just to reduce poverty and social inequity but, it seems to me, to address the social and psychological dynamics that contribute so powerfully to its perpetuation. It does not condone the injustices to understand the perceptions that contribute to maintaining them and the kernels of reality around which the destructive fictions become encrusted.

Needed: More Focus on Whiteness

john a. powell

Alexander Polikoff has written an important and timely challenge to America. He challenges us to deal with white racism toward blacks by adopting a nationwide mobility program. This program would be modeled after the famous Gautreaux program. This program came out of possibly the most important anti-discrimination housing lawsuit in United States history. Polikoff was the lead attorney in the case and is still involved with implementation of the suit. Among other things, the suit allowed for low-income blacks in the Chicago area to move to areas where there were few blacks and low poverty. While some have questioned the success of those black families who moved, the program is generally considered one of the most successful in addressing the deprivation associated with concentrated poverty and black confinement in areas of low opportunity.

Polikoff has been at the center of attempts to address racial injustice for almost four decades. He is a brilliant and courageous spirit whom the country has benefited from. He is also a good friend. His article should be looked at with seriousness and care. He warns us that failure to address the issue of racial inequality and injustice is not only wrong but, citing Tocqueville, that this failure could eventually destroy America. Polikoff finds the current racial arrangements partially responsible for loss of the New Deal. He cites exploitation of black fear by the Republican Party and their pandering to Southern prejudice in developing coded racial policies to enliven white fear and prejudice and to punish blacks while becoming a majority party. Dixiecrats are now solid Republicans. While other nonwhite groups experience discrimination, Polikoff argues that none have experienced the persistence and antipathy that blacks have from whites.

Many will find Polikoff's piece off-putting. He anticipates and attempts to answer some of his would-be critics. For example, he asserts that the ghettoization of blacks cannot be understood or addressed in race-neutral terms, citing the very different experience of poor whites in their housing, neighborhood and school lives. He also raises and rejects the position that black isolation is overstated because of the existence of the black middle class or the claim that this issue can be addressed through neighborhood revitalization instead of a Gautreaux mobility program.

Polikoff is to be commended for putting race—particularly anti-black racism—on the table when many liberals and progressives are at best confused about the continued significance of racism and too often flirting with the reductionist position that racism can be explain by class. Polikoff begins to suggest a new racial alignment that makes some sense out of today's racism. Three things are worth noting. First, it is the isolation of poor blacks that is the policy of our new racism. Second, coded racism, referred to as the Southern strategy, is working—liberals have not found an effective response. And third, as the 2004 election demonstrated, it is not just "the economy, stupid." We are complex beings with multiple values, not just economic beings. We understand this when multibillionaire George Soros supports Kerry instead of Bush for President, but we often forget this when trying to understand why poor and working-class Southern whites might support Bush by a large margin. If white anti-black prejudice is not *just* economic, then what else is at play and how should we think of it?

This last question takes me to Polikoff's article. He acknowledges that white anti-black feeling causes whites to adopt policies to isolate blacks from whites and then use this isolation and the conditions it engenders to justify anti-black feeling. But this "vicious circle" is not just a psychological error on the part of whites. It is more fundamental in the understanding of our being and our institutional arrangements. We have moved away from publicly accepting explicit racism towards accepting and promoting racial arrangements such as black ghettos and the protection of white space and white racial hoarding that limit the life options and meaning for poor blacks but also generally for all nonwhites. The present arrangement has ushered in a new white status and privilege without the articulated stigma of being a racist. How is it that there has been a substantial improvement in white racial attitudes while there has been an intensification of poor black ghettoization?

This question helps us see some of the limitations of Polikoff's suggestion. There is too little focus on whiteness and the inherent way it has been constructed and maintained. This is not just white attitudes but also white status, space and meaning. On the one hand, Polikoff states that it is white attitudes, anti-black hostility, that caused our current national policy of black confinement. Then he wishes to address white fear by limiting the number of blacks who will be allowed into any given white community. And these poor blacks will be certified before they move in. When stated like this, it might suggest that this plan is completely flawed. It is not. But it is limited and needs to be reframed. Certainly, there is dyfunctionality that comes out of concentrated poverty. But this is not the only aspect of our society that is dysfunctional. We must also understand and begin to address the dysfunctional spaces and practices that created the confinement in the first place. Are we confident that whites—collectively, functionally—have changed so they can now accept blacks not engaged in destructive behavior? And what of white behavior, attitudes and space? Will whites insist on dominating space and meaning? Anthony Downs explains this insistence in terms of middle-class domination, not just of poor blacks but also middle-class blacks. This need for dominance is one of the explanations for white flight as the nonwhite other "invades." The need for white domination cannot be adequately explained by class.

Maybe it is just too hard to think pragmatically about addressing white fear, white space or white hoarding. Maybe to talk about such things is what Gerald Torres calls a conversation-ending strategy. Whites may not allow it. These are difficult issues, but it does things that are beyond Polikoff's project. As DuBois and others have recognized, the race(ism) problem in the United States is largely the white problem. Certainly, racial arrangements and racism have changed. But even in its more gentle, non-signifying expression, white and anti-black policies dominate with a nod and a wink. I do not believe this can be addressed by just focusing on the manifestation of this new racial arrangement, Nor can we fix it by just focusing on the manifestation of it, black ghettos.

I have some concerns, but I strongly support Polikoff's project, with some changes. I would expand and reframe his project in term of opportunity, race and space. I have written about this in "Opportunity-Based Housing" (123 *J. of Affordable Housing and Community Development Law* 2 - 2003). I would also continue to think about dysfunctional practices, but I would not limit the discussion to the black poor. And, as Toni Morrison has suggested, I would look more carefully at how racism marks whites, but I would try to do it in a way that leaves the conversation open.

We Must Acknowledge How Poor People Live

Sudhir Alladi Venkatesh

Polikoff offers a persuasive proposal to dismantle America's ghettos. I leave to others a critique of its technocratic merits. Instead, I address the sociological underpinning, as it is a most elegant rendition of the liberal hymn for social justice.

Polikoff's spirited argument presupposes a folk model of the ghetto. "Folk" is not a pejorative label. All of us make claims about the social world that are based on our own largely untested assumptions. When they motivate policies to help others, they surely must be interrogated.

The ghetto, in his perspective, is the result of historic, institutionalized racism. True enough, but Polikoff knows from his life of public service that the black ghetto, like its Jewish predecessor, arose from the interplay of segregation and conscious preferences. To be sure, the dialectic was a perverse one. Black Americans' predilection for culturally/ethnically familiar spaces did not cause racism. Instead, discrimination and poverty created the conditions whereby comfort became a motive for mistreated souls to live near one another. In this era of near evangelical faith in the power of mobility vouchers, this basic structural feature of the black urban poor still makes liberals uneasy. Alas, the ghetto may not be dismantled until we renounce our bourgeois sensibility and acknowledge how poor people live.

Look, for example, at the goal of mobility proponents—exemplified in Polikoff's proposal for a "National Gautreaux Program." Namely, move the "family" out of the ghetto and into the "mainstream." First, the "family" may not be as meaningful to the poor as it is to the middle class. "Family" is an administrative/juridical designation affirmed by public policy. But the poor live in networks and households. These fluid ties, rooted in kin and the exchange of symbolic goods (e.g., intimacy) and commodities (e.g., babysitting), hold for white ethnics and Latinos as well as blacks. How to incorporate this variability in a voucher program? I'm not sure, but it would be nice if the leading minds would take it seriously.

Second, public housing families who move, voluntarily or not, continue to show strong connections to their old neighborhoods. My own study of Chicago relocatees shows one-third of families sending kids back to their familiar, decrepit schools—they trust teachers, draw on free day care nearby, get credit from stores. An even greater percentage are returning to their old areas after two years, even if they are leaving behind non-poor neighborhoods. We must do a better job of understanding why. FYI: only part of the answer involves improving relocation services.

Finally, Polikoff's embrace of the mixed-income vision is questionable. There is no evidence that mixed-income communities improve the lives of poor families—in fact, most exclude the poor because of unrealistic leasing criteria, such as strict work requirements. Polikoff's career displayed the courage not to trust the beneficence of government officials. Why does he now trust private-market developers ruled entirely by the profit motive?

None of these points necessarily invalidate a voucher program. I endorse much of Polikoff's proposal, in spirit and substance. But there are dangers to forging policies solely on the assumption of middle-class resources and perspectives. One is that we become blinded to their limits and we fail to appreciate when those who need the help do not accept it.

Getting the Politics Right on
a National Gautreaux Program

Sheryll Cashin

Alexander Polikoff has provided an important national service in identifying the black ghetto as a singular, nation-threatening challenge that is also eminently redressable. His essay resonated greatly with me when I read it. After three years of working in the Clinton White House on urban policy and five years of writing academic articles about race and class segregation in America, I came to virtually the same conclusion about the costs and consequences of the black ghetto. In my 2004 book, *The Failures of Integration: How Race and Class Are Undermining the American Dream*, I devoted an entire chapter to the subject, and my first public policy recommendation was to abolish the black ghetto through a combination of mobility vouchers and tax incentives for homeownership. So I wholeheartedly agree both with Polikoff's analysis of the devastating impact of the black ghetto on its residents and American race relations, and with his policy prescription: "mobility and ghetto-dismantling." I take issue, however, with his program design, largely because of the politics that are set against a rigid quota whereby half of the benefits would be available only to black people, albeit ghetto residents.

Beyond the serious constitutional challenges that will inevitably be raised against such a racial preference, I think that Polikoff's proposal would be extraordinarily difficult to sell to Congress. The Moving to Opportunity (MTO) program was a modest, small-scale demonstration effort that used class rather than race as the means of targeting, and yet its expansion was blocked after white community opposition in only one key Congressperson's district. The "reparations" justification Polikoff offers for his proposal is intellectually honest and consistent with our nation's history. There is an indelible trajectory from slavery, to Jim Crow, to the black ghetto. Following emancipation, with each succeeding generation America found different ways to suppress the racial minority it so greatly feared. However, given the political realities of a Republican-dominated Congress and White House—MTO was terminated when Clinton was President and Democrats led the Senate—I think there is a better way to pursue the ghetto-dismantling objective. I would use tight, geographic targeting as a rough proxy for race—i.e., residents of the highest-poverty communities would be substituted for blacks in Polikoff's proposal. And I would sell the program as an effort to eliminate concentrated poverty, not to give poor blacks more mobility. Like the diversity rationale that ultimately held sway with the Supreme Court in the *Grutter* case (upholding certain of the University of Michigan's affirmative action policies), I believe a forward-looking, optimistic account of what diverse American cities could be like is more likely to persuade in legal and policy arenas. Metropolitan and city life will be much better for everyone in a metropolitan America where all concentrated-poverty neighborhoods have been replaced with vibrant mixed-income neighborhoods and where the poor have meaningful housing options in middle-class settings. A nationwide Gautreaux program ultimately would mean that one day ordinary Americans will be able to live in a diverse society without fear because no neighborhoods would be overwhelmed by poverty.

Making a Nationwide Gautreaux Program More "Neighborhood-Friendly"

George Galster

Alexander Polikoff, in his famously lucid, engaging and persuasive manner, presents a compelling proposal for a national, Gautreaux-like voucher program as a solution for black ghetto poverty. In principle, I am a supporter of this proposal. However, despite its many prospective advantages, such a plan has the potential of being implemented in ways that might be economically, socially and politically counterproductive. These dire consequences would transpire if new voucher recipients were to move out of the ghetto but overwhelmingly concentrate in a few "almost ghetto" neighborhoods: those with moderate poverty rates with vulnerable housing markets. The consequences would transpire through two related mechanisms and would manifest themselves as an upsurge in a variety of socially problematic behaviors and falling property values in the destination neighborhoods where voucher recipients might cluster in this worst-case scenario. In this comment, I outline this danger and raise the challenges to policymakers in order to ensure that inappropriate clustering of new voucher recipients would not occur.

Distribution of the Poor and Overall Level of Social Problems in an Urban Area

The first potential problem from clustering arises due to the threshold nature of the relationship between the percentage of poor residents in a neighborhood and a variety of socially problematic behaviors that will be generated there, such as crime, out-of-wedlock teen parenting, dropping out of secondary school or not participating in the labor force. The research literature consistently suggests the existence of thresholds: critical values of neighborhood poverty, after which significantly different impacts on residents' behaviors occur with the addition of one more poor household. The literature identifies two thresholds. One appears at the intuitive demarcation between low- and moderate-poverty neighborhoods (approximately 15 to 20%) and denotes a point after which socially problematic outcomes begin to rise rapidly with increasing concentrations of the poor. The second appears at the demarcation between moderate- and high-poverty neighborhoods (approximately 30 to 40%) and denotes a point after which further concentrations of the poor produce no noticeable additional negative consequences. How rapidly the incidence of problems rises after the first threshold is exceeded appears to depend on the outcome indicator in question. Of course, the evidence consistently supports the conventional wisdom that the highest *level* of negative social impacts of all sorts occurs in the highest-poverty neighborhoods.

But, it is the relative *differences* in marginal impacts of one more poor households when they move between low-, moderate- and high-poverty neighborhoods that is the central consideration here. If social problems in the destination neighborhood to which the voucher-holders move rise in aggregate more than they decline in origin neighborhoods from whence they moved, society overall will be worse off. This circumstance is most likely if voucher-holders move from high- to moderate-poverty neighborhoods or, by concentrating in erstwhile low-poverty destinations, convert them into moderate- or high-poverty ones.

Threshold Effects for Negative Property Value Impacts in Destination Neighborhoods

The second mechanism, closely related to the first, is that, in sufficient concentrations, poor households with housing vouchers can have a deleterious effect on property values in the nearby neighborhood. In *Why NOT In My Back Yard* (2003), my colleagues and I report that stereotypical NIMBY concerns may be valid in certain (but not all) circumstances. The magnitude of impacts from the in-migration of voucher-holders was clearly contingent on neighborhood context and spatial concentration. There was a widespread pattern of threshold effects, whereby home price impacts became negative when more than a critical mass of voucher-holders was located in the vicinity. This danger of "re-concentration" was most acute in lower-value neighborhoods already possessing a modicum of poor households, especially where homeowners perceived a vulnerability to their quality of life and neighborhood's competitiveness. Indeed, in some especially vulnerable circumstances we observed that *any* additional voucher recipients would have harmful impacts on property values. But even in the most favorable neighborhood contexts observed, we estimated that a tiny number of such assisted households concentrated within 2,000 feet could lead to ensuing negative impacts.

Implications for the Implementation of a National Gautreaux Plan

Both potential concerns above lead to an implication about where recipients of a new voucher program should move in order to maximize the overall well-being of society. Clearly, they should move to low- (not moderate-) poverty neighborhoods, and even then at very low concentrations (not in large "Section 8 apartment complexes"). Polikoff suggests some recognition of this in his discussion of the "relatively few numbers of new voucher recipients compared to the hundreds of potential destination communities." But the programmatic challenge is greater than cursory consideration of "destination communities" alone. We must worry about the *neighborhood level* distribution of voucher-holders, for it is at this small scale where critically important consequences for social problems and property values emerge.

This raises several key operational questions. Will any conceivable mobility counseling program guarantee that all or even most new voucher-holders will move into (and remain in) low-poverty neighborhoods? Or, might it be more effective to tag these new vouchers with the proviso that they *only* may be used in census tracts with less than 10% poverty rates (including any voucher-holders already living there) and in locations at least minimally separated from other poor families? Will there be sufficient vacant units below HUD Fair Market

Rents in such neighborhoods, or will most voucher-holders be frustrated and ultimately be forced to turn in their voucher unused? If there are insufficient FMR housing units in these low-poverty areas, what would need to be done to increase the supply? Might all landlords be *required* to participate in the voucher program, perhaps by making it a federal fair housing violation to discriminate on the basis of source of income? And, will any local housing authority have the institutional capacity to micro-manage such a complex, neighborhood-sensitive program?

Clearly, these questions are easier to ask than answer. But if a national Gautreaux plan is to be contemplated seriously, it must be "neighborhood-friendly" and consider carefully how it will achieve the socially optimal destinations for new voucher-holders. To be economically and socially advantageous for the community as a whole, vouchers should only be used in certain types of neighborhoods in certain maximum concentrations. Failing that, the resulting problems will undoubtedly create a severe political backlash to curtail the program.

Needed Element: Laws Prohibiting Source of Income Discrimination

Libby Perl

I agree with the premise of Alexander Polikoff's proposal that housing vouchers are the best way to attack concentrations of poverty and segregation in urban communities. Yet Polikoff's worthy program is likely to fail unless the law governing housing vouchers is changed. As voucher law exists in most communities, landlords can and do refuse to accept vouchers. The high standards for the neighborhoods into which voucher tenants would move in Polikoff's proposal (less than 10% poverty, and non-minority impacted neighborhoods) could therefore present a problem. While Gautreaux moved tenants into neighborhoods that were not more than 30% black, it did not use poverty thresholds. And while it is true that Chicago has had continued success placing voucher tenants in less poor neighborhoods since Gautreaux, the program there still sets its poverty threshold at 24%, and does not use racial composition as a criterion. Finally, Moving to Opportunity families moved to low-poverty neighborhoods on a smaller scale without taking account of racial composition.

To assist in attacking concentrations of poverty, a nation-wide Gautreaux program should be accompanied by efforts to amend fair housing law to forbid landlords from refusing to rent to tenants based on their source of income, including housing vouchers. Although a national law against voucher discrimination may politically be a tough sell, if Gautreaux were to be a national program, efforts to prevent source of income discrimination should be national as well. In the meantime, it might be necessary to scale back the plan's expectations for neighborhood poverty and minority thresholds.

Currently, 12 states and the District of Columbia have laws that prevent source of income discrimination, although the language in some of the statutes makes it unclear whether housing vouchers are included. Various cities and counties also prohibit source of income discrimination. These laws improve the ability of voucher-holders to find housing. A November 2001 Department of Housing and Urban Development study found that voucher-holders in jurisdictions with laws prohibiting source of income discrimination had a probability of success in finding housing that was 12 percentage points greater (and statistically significant) than tenants in jurisdictions without such protection.

The refusal to accept vouchers often hides a malignant basis for denying housing to voucher tenants—the deformed fruits that Polikoff describes. Granted, laws that prohibit source of income discrimination will not stop this behavior; even though Chicago has a law prohibiting source of income discrimination, a study by the Lawyers' Committee for Better Housing found that 55% of landlords in areas preferred by the Housing Authority would not accept vouchers. Yet the laws give advocates a tool to begin discouraging discriminatory behavior, give tenants access to landlords who follow the law and do not discriminate, and could eventually bring about a change in attitudes toward voucher tenants and make them an accepted part of every community. Polikoff's idea to expand Gautreaux is a good one, I simply do not have as much faith that landlords in low-poverty communities would step forward and voluntarily rent their apartments to enough voucher tenants for it to work on a large scale.

Inclusionary Zoning—Gautreaux by Another Path

David Rusk

What my colleague john powell has termed creating "opportunity-based housing" is the goal of Alexander Polikoff's call for a sustained, Gautreaux-type program of 100,000 federal housing vouchers a year to relocate poor black families from high-poverty, opportunity-poor ghettoes to low-poverty, opportunity-rich communities.

We won't see such a commitment (political or fiscal) emerge from a Republican-controlled Congress and a second Bush Administration intent on further slashing federal taxes paid by corporations and wealthy Americans. Indeed, if the White House succeeds in making its tax cuts permanent, we probably won't see such a commitment ever. Even if a less conservative federal government develops the will, it won't have the way to do it in a post-Bush future. By 2004, just four federal programs—the Defense Department, Social Security, Medicare and payments on the $7.2 trillion national debt—accounted for two-thirds of all federal outlays. The first wave of baby boomers becomes eligible for Social Security payments in 2008 and for Medicare coverage in 2011; federal money for most other domestic needs will dry up. With one of the weakest Washington lobbies around, housing subsidies for poor families will be an early victim of a revenue-strapped federal budget.

Achieving Alexander Polikoff's admirable goal requires a strategy that does not rely on federal dollars. Fortunately, that strategy exists—inclusionary zoning laws.

Inclusionary zoning (IZ) uses market forces, not public dollars, to subsidize the creation of affordable housing. In higher-cost markets, homebuilders have a powerful, profit-driven incentive to build the maximum amount of market-rate housing on a given parcel of land. Local IZ laws mandate that 10% or 15% of new housing must be affordable for modest- and low-income families, but they also provide automatic density bonuses allowing builders to put up more homes than the underlying zoning would otherwise allow. The density bonus means that bonus units have zero land cost. A well-designed IZ law provides a large enough density bonus to lower the cost of inclusionary units and also to generate very profitable bonus market-rate units as well. An effective IZ law must be fair to for-profit builders as well as meet community housing needs.

Over 135 county and city governments have enacted mandatory IZ laws since Montgomery County, Maryland created the oldest IZ program in 1973. Most IZ laws have been enacted in high-cost markets like Northern and Southern California, the Washington, DC and Boston areas. However, IZ laws have been passed recently by communities in the Denver area, Illinois, Wisconsin and North Carolina. Some 13 million people—5% of the nation—live in communities that mandate mixed-income housing development.

Who qualifies for inclusionary housing? Local governments invariably set their income eligibility ceiling as a percentage of the annual, HUD-established Area Median Income (AMI). Several dozen California communities target a portion of their IZ units to 80-120% of AMI. That's far beyond the income of poverty-impacted ghetto dwellers. (Eligibility for federal housing subsidies tops out at 50% of AMI; the federal poverty ceiling is around 30% of AMI.) But half of all IZ jurisdictions earmark at least a portion of IZ units for families at less than 50% of AMI. And Montgomery County, Maryland and Fairfax County, Virginia pursue an even more targeted policy. By law, their county housing authorities buy one-third of all IZ units produced as a permanent inventory of homes to be rented to very-low-income families.

I've calculated what would have been the impact if, by waving some political magic wand, IZ laws had been in effect throughout the 100 largest metro areas over the past two decades. From 1980 to 2000, 30 million housing units were built in these 100 largest metro areas—almost all by private, for-profit builders. Let's assume that our hypothetical IZ law applies to new housing developments of ten or more units (the most common IZ standard); that means about 20% of all new units would be in smaller developments exempted from IZ requirements. Applying a 15% set-aside (also, the most common IZ standard) would have produced 3.6 million inclusionary housing units. That's three to four times the amount of affordable housing produced nationally through using Low Income Housing Tax Credits, which, HUD claims, were involved in 90% of all affordable housing produced during a comparable period. That's over ten times the amount of affordable housing aided nationally by LISC and the Enterprise Foundation, the two largest national affordable housing support organizations.

How could a significant proportion of these 3.6 million units best aid very-low-income families (less than 50% AMI)? By implementing the policy that a public housing authority buy or rent one-third of the IZ units. Some 1.2 million such IZ units would roughly equal the entire inventory of project-based units owned by the USA's 3,000 local public housing agencies. If implemented, such a program would cut the level of economic segregation in the USA's 100 largest metro areas by 40% and meet a substantial chunk of the affordable housing need.

This is all, of course, fantasy math. How do we get from here to there as a matter of practical politics and practical public finance? First, the political challenge: Sell IZ laws not as an issue of social justice but as an issue of sound economic policy. Sell IZ as an answer to the need for "workforce housing." Arguing for the need for affordable housing for a community's own teachers, police officers and firefighters (at 60%-80% of AMI) is easy. But IZ advocates have to champion the cause of the entire range of workers. We must change the public image from the stereotype of the "welfare queen and her drug-dealing boyfriend" to the reality of hard-working people you depend on every day in your community: your garbageman (50%-60% of AMI), the ambulance driver who responds to your 911 call (40%-50% of AMI), the nursing home aide taking care of your elderly parent (30%-40% of AMI), the clerk at the nearby dry cleaners or convenience store you've dealt with for years (20%-30% of AMI). Our rallying cry is, "Anyone good enough to work here is good enough to live here."

Second, the public finance challenge—a tough issue with federal housing subsidies drying up. However, creative housing agencies like the Montgomery County Housing Opportunities Commission have found a variety of ways to generate capital to purchase inclusionary units: capitalizing federal housing subsidies; using fees earned as the county's housing finance agency; securing modest county appropriations; using "in lieu of" fees paid by builders when technical site problems prevent producing IZ units; tapping into state housing subsidy programs, etc. It can be done, though it requires creativity and persistence.

Does such a program truly help move poor black residents out of inner-city ghettoes? Over time, yes. Labor markets are far less segregated and more mobile than housing markets or school systems. If the program could be tied partially to state "welfare to workfare" programs, progress would be accelerated.

Promoting "workforce housing" through IZ laws that serve the entire range of the workforce would ultimately achieve Polikoff's goal. Indeed, Business and Professional People in the Public Interest, which he founded, is a major advocate of inclusionary zoning. In short, we don't have to be "waiting for Gautreaux" outside the US Treasury. It's likely to be a long, long wait.

Response

Alexander Polikoff

None of the commentators opposes the basic idea—to dismantle or radically change black ghettos through a voluntary mobility program that would enable large numbers of ghetto residents to leave, thereby not only to improve life chances for the movers but—this is my focus—to end the poisoning effect black ghettos have on American attitudes, conduct and values.

The commentators do, however, raise questions about the suggested means. David Rusk says we won't get the needed federal dollars, and therefore proposes the alternate vehicle of inclusionary zoning. I am a strong supporter of inclusionary zoning (this, however, is not the place to discuss its benefits and the challenges to achieving it nationally). But Rusk apparently forgot my point that, by using "turnover" vouchers, the proposed mobility program wouldn't require any new vouchers at all. With this approach, the incremental program cost would be a negligible fraction (.0005) of just the military portion of our federal budget. An infinitesimal budgetary cost would not be the real reason for deep-sixing a program that could end the ghetto as we know it. The bottom line is that this isn't an either/or situation: We need a national Gautreaux program *and* inclusionary zoning. It's a mistake to set one against the other.

Rather than offering a different vehicle, other commentators propose adjustments to mine. Libby Perl would like a law prohibiting landlords from discriminating against voucher families. Without that, she fears, there won't be enough homes and apartments to satisfy demand. Such a law would be nice, but to link it to my proposal would add heavy political baggage. Nor is the evidence clear that such a law, if adopted, would make a major difference. Low Fair Market Rents are probably a bigger obstacle to getting enough units. My proposal would leap this higher hurdle by having Congress tell HUD, in the basic enactment creating the mobility program, to approve whatever rents were demonstrated to be reasonable—based on community comparables—for program participants.

George Galster says the program must be neighborhood-friendly. Going beyond my proposed requirements that program families move to very low-poverty, non-racially-impacted communities distant from ghettos, and a low annual ceiling on the number of families entering any city, town or village, Galster says to look at "almost ghetto" neighborhoods and make sure too many voucher families don't cluster in them. Although under my proposal it's unlikely that that would happen, Galster's right, and it's doable. There's a precedent in the Gautreaux Program for exactly this kind of neighborhood-sensitive program administration.

Sheryll Cashin writes that the politics of offering mobility vouchers solely to blacks won't work. Better, she says, to offer them to all ghetto residents. She too may be right. As I acknowledged in my article, "[O]ne can imagine that for reasons of policy or politics, Congress would choose to offer the mobility program to all residents of metropolitan ghettos."

There are disadvantages to this approach, however, one of which is blunting the programmatic thrust and rationale of ending the *black* ghetto. Another is considerably expanding scope and administrative complexity, creating the danger of watering down the program so it can't realize its ghetto-dismantling potential. Indeed, Cashin writes as if the purpose of a black-only program would be to "give poor blacks more mobility," rather than to eliminate the concentrated poverty of our worst ghettos. In fact, mobility is but the means to the end of dismantling, after which—as Cashin says—life will be better for everyone; the program should be sold on this ground, whether or not the vouchers are offered only to blacks. But if Cashin turned out to be right about the politics, offering mobility vouchers to all ghetto residents—provided the program weren't cut below the needed scale—isn't a bad prospect. Maybe starting on the high ground of ending black ghettos, as partial redress for slavery and Jim Crow, would lead to a later "compromise" that would include all ghetto residents.

Sudhir Venkatesh doesn't oppose my proposal, but he does say we need to learn more about and "acknowledge" how poor people in ghettos really live. Certainly. But if, as Venkatesh says, ghetto residents don't live in families as much as others do, that may be a consequence of the very intergenerational ghetto confinement we're hoping to end. And the notion that informal exchanges of goods and services, as opposed to market transactions, are more likely to be found inside than outside the ghetto seems suspect. Job networking, "old boy" contacts and the like are some of the very advantages sociologists cite when describing the disadvantages of ghetto isolation.

Venkatesh endorses "much" of my proposal, but he also seems to be asserting that liberal do-gooders just don't get it about the ghetto; discrimination and poverty may have created ghetto conditions, but people now live there for reasons of "comfort." Is he saying, leave the ghetto alone because people like it the way it is? I don't think so, yet the implication is that there are strengths and values in ghetto life that we don't perceive through our "bourgeois sensibility" and we had best tread carefully there.

Granted. But unless Venkatesh is more explicit, I will not put him in the camp of those who decline to acknowledge that many in the ghetto abhor it and would leave if they could, and who accuse those who seek to enable voluntary departure of the sin of blaming the victim. Too often ghetto romanticizers forget that white society created and today still maintains the black ghetto as a means of confinement and subjugation. Although there are testimonies to unbreakable human spirit to be found there, countless thousands of black men, women and children continue to pay a stupendous price, many with their lives, for what white society has wrought.

At bottom, Venkatesh's comments can be read as making the sound point that, as in all people-oriented government programs, administration had best be informed and sensitive. For a voluntary mobility program directed at ghetto residents, that includes post-move counseling informed by an understanding of the needs of human beings who will not only have suffered the trauma of moving, but who in many cases will have crossed a cultural divide as well.

The inevitable trauma of moving, especially across a cultural divide, calls for noting a point frequently made in mobility discussions: If mobility precedes community redevelopment, true housing choice will be denied—that is, many ghetto residents will only opt for mobility because the alternative of remaining in the ghetto is so bad. Redevelop first, the argument runs, and then the choice to leave or stay will be a fair one. However, as I believe my underlying chapter makes clear, in practice this approach will give us neither redevelopment nor mobility. With poverty deconcentration through mobility coming first, we can have both, and a responsible—albeit longer-term—means of addressing the needs of those who remain behind because they cannot, or decline to, participate in mobility.

Which leaves Paul Wachtel and john powell. A heroic warrior in race struggles, powell knows whereof he speaks when he emphasizes that we need more focus on "whiteness," that mobility alone won't fix whites' need for dominance, and that the race problem in the United States is largely the problem of (dysfunctional) whites and their racial practices and arrangements, which are today less overt, but with respect to poor blacks not much less effective, than they used to be. Understandably, powell points to the irony of a proposal that suggests addressing the problem by limiting black move-ins to an unthreatening number.

In defense, I turn to Wachtel. What we are really about, Wachtel says, is trying to defuse generations of misery (and, I would add, deeply entrenched patterns in whites' attitudes, conduct and values). This is not something conversation is likely to remedy.

When President Eisenhower was reluctant to enforce *Brown* because he thought it necessary first to change peoples' minds and hearts, and that laws and court decisions couldn't do that, he was dead wrong. As Wachtel says, "a slight shift in the forces which have been invisibly contending can yield a dramatic change in the overall result."

My thesis is that ghetto poison, relentlessly flowing into our body politic, is one of those invisibly contending forces shaping black-white relations. Over time, ending the ghetto would significantly alter those shaping forces, just as the "substantial improvement in white racial attitudes" powell notes is due partly to the enactment of the Fair Housing Act. Then, as Wachtel says, other things may begin to alter as well, often in unpredictable ways—maybe even some of the other things powell, and I, want to alter.

I share powell's anguish, but I have been in too many talk sessions to believe that the radical change he seeks will emerge from dialogue. "[T]o defuse the generators of explosive misery and rage," as Wachtel says, is a way to begin to *do*, not to talk. The *Brown* decision was something done, and it had profound beneficial effects on black-white relations even though it was a step, not a solution. Ending black ghettos would be another important step—albeit only a step —on the road to the kind of society powell, and the rest of us, hope America will one day become.

Chapter 25

The Power and Limits of Place: New Directions for Housing Mobility and Research on Neighborhoods

Xavier de Souza Briggs

In recent issues of *Poverty & Race*, some of the nation's leading practitioners and scholars have offered a compelling, well-updated case for housing mobility and related strategies, with the aim of "dismantling ghettos" and expanding housing choice and opportunity for the urban poor. They rightly understand segregation by race and income to be a linchpin of inequality in America, a problem that makes progress vastly harder on school failure, violent crime and a host of other problems that get more attention from the public and the media. Beginning with veteran civil rights attorney Alexander Polikoff's proposal for a national Gautreaux program, some of the commentators made the case for targeting disadvantaged blacks, others for targeting residents of high-poverty or high-risk neighborhoods generally. In this essay, I outline some new directions for policy and research, and I review emerging evidence that takes us beyond studies of housing mobility programs old and new. What's at stake is a clearer picture of the power and limits of place—not one to dissuade the mobility advocates whose commitments I share, but a picture, I hope, to make us more effective. Here I build, in particular, on the excellent research review by Margery Turner and Dolores Acevedo-Garcia, and I present ideas from a new book, *The Geography of Opportunity: Race and Housing Choice in Metropolitan America*, a volume I edited with support from the Harvard Civil Rights Project, which includes thoughtful analyses and proposals from a range of researchers, policy analysts and advocates.

Let me outline and explore three key ideas. First, most discussions of housing mobility—and of "locational opportunity" (access to better places) generally—focus far too little on the *repeat* mobility of American families and, in particular, the high degree of "bad mobility" by poor and minority renters. In plain terms, the debate tends to center (understandably) on helping people move *out*, overlooking how they move *on*—again and again, often from poor neighborhood to poor neighborhood or from non-poor ones back to poor ones—in a difficult housing market, with too few formal and informal supports. I want to sharpen our exchange on the issue of where and when the minority poor move, which several of the earlier commentaries briefly mentioned.

Second, as Turner and Acevedo-Garcia note, the effort to understand which families benefit from particular locations (and why) is in its infancy. I will outline a more dynamic view of what determines the benefits and burdens of living in particular places. It is a view that respects Sudhir Venkatesh's advice about designing policy to reflect certain realities of poor people's lives and preferences. This perspective has fairly clear implications for housing mobility, community development and other fields.

Third, there is the question of attitudes to support the sharing of neighborhoods (or tax-and-spend jurisdictions), across lines of race and class, to a degree that is unprecedented in America's history. As a matter of problem-solving, one cannot empty a bathtub merely by bailing out water (i.e., moving people out)—not if something is constantly refilling the vessel. America's local communities are changing fast, thanks in particular to immigration and continued economic restructuring, and this means that no conversation about ending the ghetto as we know it can proceed very far without considering the often segregative preferences of all Americans, including the immigrant groups (Hispanic, Asian and other) that tend, like whites, to place blacks on the bottom of their totem pole of racial others. It behooves any diverse coalition, particularly one eager to broaden its tent, to understand these attitudes. They are closely tied to white prejudice and discrimination, granted, but they will exert a force all their own as immigrants become more important in the nation's housing markets as well its political life.

Moving On (and On)

Americans are famously mobile. Every five years, about half the nation's population has moved, a Census-measured rate that has not changed much in the past half-century. What has changed is who moves often. About a third of the nation's renters move each year, and low-skill minority renters move more often still, with the poorest neighborhood choices. Sociologist Claude Fischer, analyzing Census data over decades ("Ever-More Rooted Americans," in *City &*

Community 1(2), 2003), found that low-skill workers are the only major demographic group for whom mobility has increased in the past few decades, and the most likely culprit is tighter housing markets and less affordable supply, alongside stagnant wages. Some moves are hugely beneficial: Non-local moves, in particular, tend to be moves to opportunity, whether low-skill or high-skill workers make them (e.g., moving out of state for more education or to take a new job). But other moves—in particular, frequent, local, "involuntary" moves—tend to reflect the conditions that are both cause and effect of persistent poverty: substandard housing units, difficult or exploitative landlords, fractured relationships, the need to isolate kids from gang violence at school and in the neighborhood, being unable to stay on the job (or get a new one in time to pay the bills), child-rearing responsibilities, illness and other problems. Local managers of HUD's Section 8 program tell me that repeat mobility by low-income renters is a major pattern, not to mention a burdensome one, and we desperately need good national and region-specific evidence on this. Clearly, moving frequently makes it harder for families to leverage the value of a positive new location. I see ample evidence of this in the ethnographic fieldwork and in-depth interviewing Susan Popkin, John Goering and I have done over the past year among very-low-income, mostly minority renters in the Moving to Opportunity experiment in metro Boston, Los Angeles and New York.

But the nature of the sender and receiver neighborhoods is at issue as well, and to date, there has been surprisingly little evidence on what kinds of neighborhoods families are exposed to *over time*, as they move about and neighborhoods change around them. Using a nationally representative sample of blacks and whites in the 1980s, sociologist Lincoln Quillian found that exposure to poor neighborhoods over time is more closely associated with race than with income or household type (in general, female-headed families are at greatest "locational risk"). Quillian found that most blacks, but only 10% of whites, lived in a poor neighborhood at some point in the decade and that little of the difference was accounted for by racial differences in poverty rate or family structure. For example, when blacks in female-headed households with income below the poverty line were compared with whites in comparable households, 57% of blacks, but only 27% of whites, spent at least half of the ten-year period in a poor neighborhood. By this measure, even blacks in male-headed households with income *above* the poverty line face more risk (39%) than whites in female-headed, poor households (27%)—and far more than whites in comparable households (3%). Blacks leave poor neighborhoods often, but they fall back into such neighborhoods much more often than whites, leading Quillian to conclude, "For African-Americans, the most difficult part of escape from a poor neighborhood is not moving out but staying out." (See his 2003 article, "How long are exposures to poor neighborhoods?: The long-term dynamics of entry and exit from poor neighborhoods," in *Population Research and Policy Review*, 22:3.)

Notably, mobility patterns contributed much more than neighborhood change to increases and decreases in families' neighborhood poverty exposure.

That is, it's where one moves more than what happens when one gets there that predicts exposure to neighborhood poverty, and with it associated risks, over time.

In a new study, I am checking to see whether these patterns continued into the 1990s, when the geographic concentration of poverty dropped markedly in many regions, and also analyzing patterns for Hispanics for the first time (data limitations make it hard to measure representative, long-run Hispanic patterns and, for now, make it essentially impossible to measure comparable Asian ones). I find, using a simulation model, that even dramatic changes in the 1980 patterns uncovered by Quillian—for example, doubling the rates of exiting poor places and halving the rate of re-entry ("falling back") into them—would leave many families exposed to poor neighborhoods for long periods of time. This leads to the second main idea—about rethinking the power of place, and what we really owe families, in the context of such barriers.

Leveraging the Power of Place: A More Dynamic View

Prior research has emphasized the kinds of mechanisms that *may* affect *some* families *once* they are living in particular neighborhoods. But in general, three dynamics shape the consequences of place in our lives: the life course (because our needs change from cradle to childhood, adolescence, young adulthood and so on); *neighborhood change* ("churning" through exits and entries, as well as in-place gains and losses by those who stay put); and *family-managed exposure and adaptation* to risks and resources. Turner and Acevedo-Garcia implicated the last-mentioned dynamic in distinguishing families who seem remarkably resilient even in the riskiest places (often because they buffer and restrict families members' activities in order to isolate them from risks in the immediate environment) from those families who are overwhelmed regardless of where they live.

Notwithstanding the well-founded assertion that we should shrink and, in time, eliminate ghettos because of the intolerable costs they impose, it is also true that the value of wider housing choices for disadvantaged families seems *extremely* variable, so variable that we need much more attention to what the Annie E. Casey Foundation and other innovative institutions have termed "family strengthening" strategies. In this view of what it takes to enable families to *leverage the value* of a place, not merely to get there, our task is helping families cope, buffer, connect and adapt wherever they live—this *at least as much* as helping them to relocate. Yes, pre- and post-move counseling are part of the answer, but, as other commentators have suggested, so are health and human service linkages, school choice counseling and transportation aid to help families "source" aid widely, across a metropolitan area (e.g., with car ownership promotion programs, also known as "car vouchers," linked to housing vouchers).

Choosing Neighbors in a Rainbow Nation

Accounts of segregation's costs, and of what produces and reproduces it, rightly emphasize the impact of white attitudes and behaviors, from direct acts of discrimination in the marketplace to the perfectly legal "self-steering" through which whites avoid certain communities, at least as places to live. But with our society fast becoming the most racially and ethnically diverse in human history, our discussions of housing choice and the geography of opportunity must evolve—and soon. Not only is the white/black paradigm terribly incomplete, but the hopes for a new, majority-minority-led coalition powerful enough to change the rules of the housing game may be naïve. Simply posed, what if fast-growing immigrant groups adopt prejudice and avoidance faster than the nation can undo our long color-coded geography, which reproduces itself? This is more than an alarmist hypothetical. In our new book, sociologist Camille Charles ("Can we live together? Racial preferences and neighborhood outcomes") offers the best-available evidence on evolving racial attitudes and neighborhood racial preferences—i.e., whom we would prefer to share neighborhoods with and whom we'd just as soon avoid—in a multi-ethnic America; and she reminds us that preferences, according to recent economic analyses, are not just what-if's offered to survey researchers but actually predict residential outcomes.

The evidence is sobering: Blacks are on the bottom of every other group's hierarchy of preferred neighbors, and immigrant Hispanics and Asians report many stereotypes of black people similar to those held by whites, albeit to a more modest degree (groups report certain stereotypes, including flattering ones, of all other groups, but blacks suffer the most consistently negative and widely held ones). This is not a portrait cut in stone, of course, and, as Paul Wachtel argues in his reply to Polikoff, shaping attitudes is a crucial part of social change. Sometimes, bold policy has to lead, not follow, a breakthrough in attitudes. But this evidence should disabuse us of the simple notion that immigration-led diversity will produce communities that are generally more inclusive. It should remind us to place well-informed discussions of desegregation, mobility and inclusionary housing in a rapidly evolving racial context that brings with it new hope, new risks and much uncharted terrain.

Chapter 26

Democracy's Unfinished Business: Federal Policy and the Search for Fair Housing, 1961-68

David M.P. Freund

The following chapter is excerpted from a longer research paper and will appear in David Freund's forthcoming Univ. of Chicago Press book, Colored Property: State Policy and White Racial Politics in the Modern American Suburb. *The research paper, with the same title as this chapter, was prepared as part of a PRRAC project, "Housing and School Segregation: Government Culpability, Government Remedies." Other research papers for that project, by urban historians Arnold Hirsch and Raymond Mohl, as well as the full Freund paper, are available on PRRAC's website, www.prrac.org.*

In July of 1963, the Administrator of the federal Housing and Home Finance Agency (HHFA), Robert Weaver, spoke to a meeting of his agency's Intergroup Relations Service (IRS), the "race relations" staff charged with promoting non-discrimination in federal housing programs. His talk came at a time of dramatic change in the federal government's relationship to metropolitan development. After three decades of condoning and actively promoting racial segregation in both the private and public housing and development sectors, federal officials began, in the early 1960s, to declare their commitment to fair housing. During the 1960 presidential campaign, John F. Kennedy promised to eliminate housing discrimination with "a stroke of the presidential pen," and soon after his election appointed Weaver—a former "race relations" officer, a long-time critic of federal policy and outspoken advocate of equal housing opportunity, and a black man—to run the HHFA. And in November of 1962, Kennedy made good on his campaign promise, issuing Executive Order 11063, which prohibited racial discrimination in some federally-supported housing development. Its symbolic importance notwithstanding, the new Executive Order had a very limited reach, in the end covering less than 1% of the nation's housing units. But Weaver and other like-minded reformers—particularly his colleagues in the IRS—interpreted the Order much more broadly, repeatedly distinguishing between its "letter" and its "spirit." They viewed it as part of a larger reform effort—particularly in light of Kennedy's amendment of another Executive Order that banned discrimination in federal employment practices—and felt they now had a mandate to pursue a quite radical re-orientation of both federal policy and practice.

Weaver used his appearance before the IRS in the summer of 1963 to outline this vision for reform, explaining what would be required to alter the government's impact on metropolitan development and to remedy the results of policies that for decades had both discriminated and segregated. Most important, he declared, was that the pursuit of "fair housing" become a responsibility of *all* housing officials, a goal integral to the day-to-day operations of all HHFA units, rather than a special assignment relegated to the IRS. He argued, in effect, for transforming the culture of the housing bureaucracy, for changing the way its agents thought about the impact of federal interventions, both past and present, and about the issue of racial equity in housing. "[T]he implementing of the President's [Executive Orders]," he explained, in a formal statement to IRS officials,

> is a responsibility of all associated with the HHFA. The head of each constituent agency is held responsible for the implementation over the programs under his jurisdiction, and all line staff have the primary responsibility of carrying out the requirements and purposes of these Orders just as they have with respect to all other policy and program objectives and requirements. In other words, the President's Orders will be carried out through the operations of the total staff and not through a new or separate operational staff.

This would require that the administrators and employees of the Federal Housing Administration (FHA), the Public Housing Administration (PHA), the Urban Renewal Administration (URA) and the Federal National Mortgage Association (FNMA) actively commit themselves to disrupting patterns of discrimination and to channeling resources to populations long denied the benefits of federal largesse. And it was the IRS's job to facilitate this, Weaver explained, by "work[ing] closely with and, through the heads of Agency units," to "encourage key staff member[s] to...make the fullest contribution toward the achievement of equal opportunity."

But merely shifting "policy and program objectives and requirements," he continued, was not sufficient. Equally important was a change in the very language of federal policy, in the ways federal officials conceived of their mission and portrayed it to the public. "There is no place under our equal opportunity policy goals," the Administrator continued, "for usage of concepts and statements connoting separateness. Our usage should take on appropriate alternatives such as housing open to or available to or accessible to Negroes, or nonwhites or minorities in lieu of 'Negro housing,' 'nonwhite housing,' 'minority housing,' etc."

Weaver's vision was informed by decades of personal engagement with the policies he was now charged with re-making. Thus, his reform efforts represented, on one level, an important victory for critics of federal housing policy. Since the early 1930s, Weaver was among the civil rights activists and a small group of federal officials who had been challenging a wide range of government interventions in both the public and private markets for residence, documenting how these programs favored white applicants, denied resources to minorities and maintained a strict "color line" in most of the nation's metropolitan areas. Weaver and others were well aware that, since the Depression, the state had helped build a two-tiered, or "dual," housing market, a market that segregated both space and material resources by race. And critics like Weaver were intimately familiar with the role federal interventions had played in normalizing popular discussions about this dual market. They recognized not only that the state had promoted segregation, but that an acceptance of the racially segregated market for homes was literally inscribed within federal policy and practice. They saw it as the mission of a reformed HHFA to change both the ways that the government shaped urban outcomes and the ways Americans conceived of the market for homes.

These reformers' new prominence was not enough, however, to alter the course of federal programs. When Weaver ended his service as the nation's chief housing official in 1968, he had far from achieved the hoped-for transformation in both government operations and thinking. There were, to be sure, several important victories during his tenure, including passage of Title VI of the Civil Rights Act of 1964, which confirmed prohibitions against racial discrimination in federal housing, and the elevation of HHFA to cabinet-level status in 1965 (creating the Department of Housing and Urban Development, which he headed, as the nation's first African-American cabinet member). Still, by 1968 the structure of the agencies that Weaver oversaw had barely changed, and the assumptions about the dual housing market, so long entrenched in practice and in bureaucratic culture, continued to guide federal policy. Indeed, not until 1967 did the PHA abandon a controversial tenant placement practice that was facilitating the continued segregation of public housing sites, and that year an internal FHA investigation revealed what realtors and homebuyers alike had long recognized: that the agency continued to deny mortgage insurance to most nonwhites, in defiance of the Executive Order. On top of this, Title VI of the 1964 Civil

Rights Act did not apply to federal programs of insurance or guarantee, thus excluding from its purview all private homes financed with the assistance of the FHA or Veterans Administration—the market for housing that benefited most from New Deal-era reforms. Finally, the fast-growing "conventional" market for home mortgages, while overseen and indirectly subsidized by federal regulatory agencies, including the Federal Home Loan Bank Board, remained untouched by fair housing law.

Given Weaver's expertise and experience, why was the HHFA and later HUD unable to implement substantive and effective reform? Why, in an era that saw the federal government commit itself to protecting civil rights, did the new "fair housing" mandate prove to be so inadequate? Congressional, bureaucratic and private sector opposition to open occupancy was certainly an important obstacle, as many observers have long noted. And the federal government, through decades of support for the two-tiered housing market, had provided crucial momentum for opponents of integrating housing. But to fully appreciate the legacy of past federal actions, one must consider both the structural and ideological impacts of government policy, which together transformed the ways that countless whites came to understand the politics of race and residence in metropolitan America.

First, when Weaver and other federal officials attempted to re-make government policy in the early 1960s, they inherited a vast federal bureaucracy—oversight and regulatory programs, mortgage insurance programs and a public housing program, among others—that had supported segregation for three decades, that had created a powerful new market for private housing for white people (to the exclusion of minorities), and that was very resistant to change. The programs that restructured the market for private housing and that built and managed a new market for public housing had been grounded in the principle that "separate but equal" was perfectly acceptable. And of critical importance, the flourishing market for private housing had by the early 1960s become foundational to post-war economic growth, in part by fueling a massive "flight" to the ever-expanding suburbs, which in turn further insulated countless whites from minority communities seen as threatening to families, communities and property values. In short, federal policies had been instrumental to building a political and economic constituency deeply resistant to change. To alter these government programs would require more than executive orders and legislative prohibitions against discrimination.

At the same time, HHFA and HUD officials inherited a powerful ideological legacy that would further obstruct their efforts. Throughout the first three decades of federal intervention in the market for residence, most public officials and their private sector allies had insisted that the development of the "two-tiered" market was a natural, market-driven development, merely the product of consumer choice, and thus in no way shaped by federal interventions themselves. In short, they had insisted that the federal government was not directly responsible for the segregated outcomes its programs had helped produce. Thus, when Weaver and others were charged with reforming a system of programs that, for 30 years, had discriminated by race, they were faced with widespread resistance from public and private sector leaders deeply invested in the myth that the state was not culpable for the spatial and economic segregation that had come to characterize the post-war metropolis. In the eyes of countless political leaders, federal officials and white homeowners, there was simply no evidence that the federal government had helped create the problem. Why then, they asked, should the government be responsible for finding a solution?

Chapter 27

Some Lessons from *Brown* for the Fair Housing Movement

Philip Tegeler

The trends are disturbing: Some 50 years after *Brown v. Board of Education*, schools are again becoming increasingly segregated by race and income. A 2004 study by the Harvard Civil Rights Project (Gary Orfield and Chungmei Lee, "*Brown* at 50: King's Dream or *Plessy's* Nightmare?") found school segregation in 2001 at its highest level since 1968. This trend is partly attributable to the abandonment of desegregation orders in many Southern districts, but it is also a function of continuing residential segregation in the Northeast and Midwest. Since the Supreme Court, in the mid-1970s, backed away from the problem of metropolitan-wide segregation in Northern schools, residential poverty concentration has become increasingly severe, peaking in the 1980s, and now continuing to consolidate and spread across wider areas, even as it declines in the most poverty-concentrated census tracts (see the May 2003 Urban Institute report, "Concentrated Poverty: A Change in Course," by G. Thomas Kingsley and Kathryn Pettit). In spite of this trend, federal and state housing programs continue to foster dual housing markets in separate school systems, one for the suburban middle class and one for the urban poor.

As researchers, we strive to understand the underlying causes and consequences of racial segregation and poverty concentration. As advocates, we have developed strategies for attacking the systems that continue to promote segregation. As proponents of progressive fair housing policies, we know that there are government interventions that can work to reverse these trends. Part of the

Brown spotlight reflects on the fair housing movement: What more can we do? Some answers can be found within the *Brown* decision itself:

Brown as History Lesson

The legal system attacked in *Brown v. Board of Education* was one of *de jure* (legally mandated) school segregation throughout the South, beginning after Reconstruction and continuing to at least 1954. *Brown* should also remind us of the state-sponsored history of housing segregation in this country. Both before and after *Brown*, this system of state segregation was replicated in federal, state and local housing policy. (For new research on the historical roots of segregation, see "Housing and School Segregation: Government Culpability, Government Remedies," on PRRAC's website—www.prrac.org.)

The history of state-sponsored housing segregation is not as well known as the history of *Brown*. But it was well understood in 1966 by Dr. King as he marched in Chicago, and it was recognized several years later by the Kerner Commission and the drafters of the Fair Housing Act, who understood that the ghetto was never a naturally occurring phenomenon: It was state-created and state-supported, and perpetuated by federal and state policy. This history is not taught in our schools today, and it is not routinely reflected in the media. But the historical perspective is necessary to justify remedial steps and to mobilize public support for desegregation.

Brown and the Problem of Intent

We need to come to terms with the reasons for *Brown*'s failure to achieve its own aspirations, and the implications for federal housing and civil rights policy. One important failure is the legal system's insistence on a standard of "intent" to define constitutional liability for structural racism. In the first two decades after *Brown*, as the cases moved from the South to equally segregated Northern cities lacking a written legal code of segregation, some courts were open to finding *de facto* segregation unconstitutional, even where there was no direct evidence of intent to create segregation. These courts reasoned that the harms of segregation were the same, regardless of the cause, and that, as the overseer of the system of student assignment, the state bore responsibility.

But the Supreme Court put an end to this logical extension of *Brown* in decisions in 1972 (*Keyes v. School District #1*) and 1976 (*Washington v. Davis*), which ultimately required proof of discriminatory intent by public officials before a constitutional violation could be found. This standard led to increasingly expensive and sometimes futile searches for the "smoking gun" in school districting, housing and zoning decisions spanning decades. But the result was the same whether or not the smoking gun could be found: In the absence of carefully planned school districting and assignment decisions, segregated neighborhoods create segregated schools.

In contrast to this increasingly strict standard of proof in constitutional cases, federal civil rights statutes (such as the Fair Housing Act) adopted during the first two decades after *Brown* reflected the sense that discriminatory "impact" could be a basis for liability in housing, employment and certain government programs, and this continues to be the legal standard today. But this standard is increasingly threatened by conservative courts, which have already stripped Title VI of much of its enforcement power (see the Supreme Court's 2000 *Alexander v. Sandoval* decision), and by a federal Administration that is increasingly reluctant to prosecute discriminatory impact claims in housing. In light of the history of enforcement of the *Brown* decision, it is crucial that fair housing law continue to permit a finding of liability where facially neutral housing policies have the effect of perpetuating segregation.

Brown and Jurisdictional Fragmentation

Brown's ultimate demise in the North was not just about the Supreme Court's requirement of a finding of "intentional" segregation—it was about the Court's reluctance to extend liability to "independent" suburban jurisdictions outside the segregated central city. This problem is well known to fair housing advocates, and its legal origins can be traced in part to the 1974 Supreme Court decision in the Detroit schools case (*Milliken v. Bradley*): Unless a finding of discrimination could be made against each suburban school district participating in a segregated regional system of education, those suburbs could not be ordered to desegregate. This decision had the effect of privileging suburban white flight and set the bar for meaningful school desegregation so high that it has rarely been hurdled since.

Although the Supreme Court, in Chicago's *Gautreaux* case, ultimately stopped short of applying this principle directly to housing desegregation litigation, jurisdictional fragmentation remains a key barrier to meaningful fair housing enforcement. And the delegation of land use, zoning and public housing administration to small local jurisdictions is one of the basic building blocks of segregation in this country. We must find housing solutions that successfully overcome (or transcend) these jurisdictional barriers.

Brown and the Duty to Affirmatively Further Fair Housing

The history of *Brown's* implementation in the South underscores the need to affirmatively dismantle segregation, not simply to remove discriminatory practices. In the initial decade after *Brown*, when *de jure* segregation was eliminated throughout the South, little true desegregation was achieved. In many areas, "freedom of choice" plans were adopted that replicated segregation almost perfectly. It was not until passage of the Civil Rights Act of 1964 and rulings in the *Green* and *Swann* cases in 1968 and 1971 that the courts recognized the need to eliminate segregation "root and branch" and take sweeping remedial steps to "disestablish" segregation and affirmatively promote integration, using the full remedial power of the federal courts.

The Fair Housing Act's mandate that federal and state agencies "affirmatively further fair housing" is a recognition of this reality: that the structures of segregation are deeply rooted and can only be eliminated through affirmative government measures, not simply policies of non-discrimination. A case involving the scope of the "affirmatively furthering" mandate is being tested in a case involving public housing desegregation in Baltimore; in challenges to state administration of the Low Income Housing Tax Credit Program in New Jersey and Connecticut; and in public housing demolition and relocation cases in Chicago and elsewhere. As the school desegregation cases have shown us, without this additional "affirmative" duty to promote integration, it is unlikely that the effects of decades of segregative government policies can be undone.

Brown and International Law

It has often been observed that the *Brown* decision had a great deal to do with the Cold War and with America's need to appear true to its own announced principles of liberty and equality in its global moral and strategic competition with the Soviet Union. (An early proponent of this view was James Baldwin, in *The Fire Next Time*.) Today, international human rights standards continue to be a powerful potential tool to influence United States policy, even though US courts and policymakers resist the notion of being bound by outside legal standards, and the Senate routinely places unnecessary "reservations" on international human rights accords that come before it.

Several standards adopted by the UN (and ratified, in part, by the US) speak directly to American housing and school segregation. The Convention on the Elimination of All Forms of Racial Discrimination (CERD) holds that its signing countries "particularly condemn racial segregation and apartheid and undertake to prevent, prohibit and eradicate all practices of this nature in territories under their jurisdiction." CERD further requires signing countries to "...take effective measures to review governmental, national and local policies, and to amend, rescind or nullify any laws and regulations which have the effect of creating or perpetuating racial discrimination wherever it exists." In 2003 testimony before the Inter-American Commission on Human Rights, former Under Secretary and General Counsel of the US Department of Education Judith Winston testified that:

> Today, racial discrimination in the public schools is a vestige of the
> legally sanctioned racial apartheid that existed prior to the landmark
> Supreme Court decision in 1954—*Brown v. Board of Education.* The
> existence and continuation of racial segregation in our schools is also
> a stark indication that the deeply ingrained negative racial stereotypes
> and racial prejudices that were at the core of 19th and 20th century
> racism affect the treatment and quality of education students of color
> receive in 21st century US public schools. This modern day discrimi-
> nation, however, is not often exhibited as intentional racial animus
> but is more deeply hidden in institutional racism that defies the tradi-
> tional legally enforceable means of eradication.

Fair housing advocates need to take advantage of these international forums
in a more proactive way in the coming years, to focus international attention on
state-sponsored segregation here in the US.

Brown as a Faith-Based Initiative

In his 2004 book, *A Stone of Hope: Prophetic Religion and the Death of Jim
Crow*, David Chappell reminds us of the religious foundations of *Brown* and the
ways in which religion sustained and helped to define the Civil Rights Movement in the 1960s. Similarly, one of the greatest sources of hope for today's fair
housing movement comes from the new, ecumenical coalitions that are reforming around regional equity, smart growth and educational equity issues,
bringing together inner-city and suburban congregations effectively for perhaps
the first time since the 1970s. Some of the leading examples of these coalitions
have joined together in a network sponsored by the Chicago-based Gamaliel
Foundation (see www.gamaliel.org).

Conclusion

The fair housing movement stood somewhat outside of the spotlight during the
50th anniversary year of the *Brown* decision. And we stand here knowing that it
is largely the *disconnect* between housing and school policy, and our collective
failure to dismantle housing segregation, that have placed our society in such
jeopardy. As we move forward in our housing work, we would do well to always keep schools in mind and remember these lessons of *Brown*.

Chapter 28

Race, Poverty and Homeowner Insurance

Gregory D. Squires

"No insurance, no loan; no loan, no house; lack of insurance thus makes housing unavailable." So said the Seventh Circuit Court of Appeals in *NAACP v. American Family Mutual Insurance Company*, a case that resulted in a 1995 settlement worth $14.5 million, including subsidized home purchase loans, greater access to insurance policies, and other forms of reinvestment for black neighborhoods in inner-city areas of Milwaukee, Wisconsin.

Evidence of insurance redlining persists in low- and moderate-income neighborhoods and minority communities generally, undercutting homeownership and wealth accumulation for residents of those areas. But given severe limitations in publicly available information, nobody can say with certainty how pervasive the problem is or how much progress has been made in recent years. With the industry now asking the federal government for help on at least two fronts, it's time to close the information gap.

Some 30 years ago, when redlining and racial discrimination were widespread in the mortgage lending market, the federal government responded by passing the Home Mortgage Disclosure Act (HMDA), requiring most lenders to publicly reveal a range of information about their mortgage-lending activity, including the number of loans in each census tract in which they were making loans. Two years later, the Community Reinvestment Act (CRA) was passed, banning redlining. HMDA and CRA are credited by the National Community Reinvestment Coalition with generating over $4 trillion in new loans for older urban neighborhoods around the country. Several reports, including "The 25th

Anniversary of the Community Reinvestment Act," from the Harvard Joint Center for Housing Studies, released in 2002, indicate that the CRA has directly led to increased lending activity to racial minorities and low- and moderate-income borrowers, as well as increases in property values in low- and moderate-income communities.

Redlining and discrimination have also long permeated property insurance markets, but nothing close to even minimal disclosure requirements has ever been required for this industry by the federal government.

The Federal Government to the Rescue?

In recent years, the industry has looked for help in dealing with the unpredictability of potentially billions of dollars in liability due to terrorist attacks. Not surprisingly, it has looked to the federal government for that help. President Bush signed a "bailout" or "backstop" bill that will provide private insurers with public money in the case of future terrorist attacks. Taxpayers could be on the hook for as much as $100 billion per year.

Some insurers and trade groups, including the American Insurance Association, which generally represents large insurance companies, are also seeking dual chartering legislation that would permit companies to choose to be regulated by either a federal agency or state insurance commissioners. Another approach under consideration is the creation of uniform federal standards (e.g., solvency requirements, rate regulations) that would be enforced by state insurance commissioners. This constitutes a significant break from the industry's almost universal and long-standing support for state regulation and reflects in part industry consolidation. Proponents contend that dealing with one regulator is more efficient and will help consumers by making it easier and quicker to bring new products to market. Whatever the argument, this would constitute a second form of assistance the industry would receive from the federal government.

Since the federal government is providing the bail-out or back-stop the industry has requested and may grant a dual chartering option, the public is entitled to some protections in return. At a minimum, the industry should inform the public about whom it is currently serving and whom it is not serving. Specifically, this means requiring HMDA-like disclosure for the property insurance industry.

Redlining, Insurance-Style

The costs of insurance redlining were captured by the President's 1968 *National Advisory Panel on Insurance in Riot-Affected Areas* when it concluded:

> Insurance is essential to revitalize our cities. Without insurance,
> banks and other financial institutions will not—and cannot—make

loans. New housing cannot be constructed, and existing housing cannot be repaired. New businesses cannot expand, or even survive. Without insurance, buildings are left to deteriorate; services, goods and jobs diminish. Efforts to rebuild our nation's inner cities cannot move forward. Communities without insurance are communities without hope.

The issue of mortgage redlining has received far more attention in research and public policy arenas. But insurance redlining has also long been a critical piece of the institutional infrastructure of dual housing markets. When, for reasons unrelated to risk, households cannot get insurance or have to pay more for inferior products, they are unfairly denied the opportunity to buy homes, and the market value of the homes they can purchase is unjustly reduced. Wealth accumulation, consequently, is undercut. For homeowners, on average, approximately 50% of their net worth comes from the equity in their homes. Working families and racial minorities are even more dependent on their homes as a source of wealth.

Evidence of urban insurance availability problems has surfaced, despite the absence of ongoing, systematic public disclosure of where policies are, and are not, written. The National Association of Insurance Commissioners examined the distribution of property insurance policies in 33 metropolitan areas. Their researchers found that the number of policies and the cost of policies were statistically significantly associated with the racial composition of neighborhoods, relationships that held even after taking risk exposure and loss experience into account.

Fair housing groups around the country have conducted paired-testing audits (where equally qualified black and white or Hispanic and white "testers" shop for insurance from the same agents) and have frequently found illegal discrimination in their investigations. In one nine-city national testing project, the National Fair Housing Alliance found discrimination in at least 32% of the tests in every city, with the frequency of discrimination reaching 83% in one city. Agents often offer policies with less coverage yet higher prices to the minority tester; refer the application to the home office for the minority tester but provide immediate coverage for the white tester; refuse to insure older or lower-valued homes; and commit other sins of commission or omission, with the result being less service to minority communities.

These investigations have led directly to the settlement of formal discrimination complaints against several major property insurers, including State Farm, Allstate, Nationwide, Liberty and American Family. These agreements call for increased marketing efforts in older urban communities, changes in underwriting rules, and funds to subsidize home purchase and home improvement loans in older, inner-city and predominantly minority neighborhoods. HUD, as of 2004, was investigating 15 additional discrimination complaints against property insurers.

Although progress has been made, racial discrimination persists, albeit in more subtle forms today. Most major insurers now utilize credit reports in their underwriting of applications and pricing of policies, which has an adverse disparate impact on racial minorities because of their relatively lower average credit scores. Racial discrimination may not be the intent, but it is the effect. The days of widespread, overt discrimination may be over, but race still matters. Fifteen years ago, a sales manager for the American Family Mutual Insurance Company advised an agent, in a tape-recorded conversation: "Very honestly, I think you write too many blacks...you got to sell good, solid, premium-paying white people." Today, a question one major insurer asks some of its agents is whether the kids in the neighborhood play basketball or hockey.

What We Don't Know and Why We Don't Know It

To the extent that insurance is regulated, the industry is regulated by state governments. But on the issue of redlining, state regulators have been missing in action. State insurance commissioners and state legislators simply have not regulated in this area. Most discouraging is the disclosure data that are available, particular compared to what the federal government requires of mortgage lenders.

Under HMDA, lenders are required to publicly disclose information on the race, gender, income and census tract of all applicants; whether or not the application was approved; the type (e.g., conventional, government-insured) and purpose (e.g., home purchase, improvement) of the loan; and for high-cost loans pricing information must be reported. Much of the information is available for free online and for minimal cost on compact disks or in hard copy. (To access this information, go to the web page of the Federal Financial Institutions Examination Council—http://www.ffiec.gov/hmda/default.htm.)

For property insurance, the picture is quite different. Only eight states collect any insurance disclosure data at all, and they are collected at the zip code rather than census tract level. (Zip codes are much larger and more heterogeneous than census tracts.) Data on individual insurers are available in just four of these states. The rest provide aggregate data on the larger insurers in the state. Six states provide information on the total number of policies issued and type of policy in each zip code. Loss information (the number of incidents— e.g., fires, thefts—where compensable losses occur, and the dollar amount of those incidents resulting in claims filed by policyholders for reimbursement) is made available in three states, and cost data are available in five. No state makes loss and cost data available at the individual company level. And no state provides information on the race or gender of applicants.

State insurance authorities have rarely pursued consumer protections aggressively. One important factor is the proverbial revolving door between the industry and its regulators. State insurance commissioners routinely come from major insurance companies and return to them after their short stints of "public service." In 1995, the Consumer Federation of America found that in ten large states, almost 20% of legislators who serve on insurance oversight committees are either owners or agents of insurance businesses or attorneys in lawfirms with substantial insurance practices. State regulation of insurance is anything but arms-length.

From Redlining to Reinvestment

There have been some positive developments in the insurance redlining debate, despite the reticence of state regulators. Pressure applied by fair housing groups, utilizing the leverage of fair housing laws, led to the settlements and additional complaints noted above. These actions have led to "voluntary" steps on the part of some within the insurance industry. The National Insurance Task Force of the Neighborhood Reinvestment Corporation, which includes most major insurers, has launched loss prevention partnerships with community-based organizations in six metropolitan areas, where insurers advise homeowners on steps they can take to reduce the likelihood they will experience a loss (e.g., installation of smoke alarms and security systems), thus increasing their insurability, and where community groups help insurers find profitable business in previously underserved neighborhoods. The Independent Insurance Agents of America invited the National African American Insurance Association and the Latin American Association of Insurance Agents to participate in its 2000 annual convention, and is assisting minority agents in developing their businesses by aiding them in securing contracts with major insurers. In 2001, Congressional Representatives Tom Barrett (Dem., WI) and Luis Gutierrez (Dem., IL) introduced the Community Reinvestment Modernization Act, calling for HMDA-like disclosure plus a range of community reinvestment requirements for the property insurance industry. The bill did not pass, but elements of it have been enacted by some states.

Absent the systematic disclosure of where property insurance policies are being sold, it is difficult to determine how successful various voluntary and law enforcement initiatives have been and can be. Appropriate disclosure can provide the missing information and encourage additional reinvestment efforts in traditionally underserved communities. Such steps can increase access to insurance, reinforce fair housing initiatives and enhance wealth accumulation, particularly for residents of low- and moderate-income neighborhoods and racial minorities throughout the nation's metropolitan areas.

In reference to the impact of disclosure on mortgage-lending, Nicholas Retsinas and Eric Belsky, Director and Executive Director of the Harvard Joint Center for Housing Studies, observed: "Some banks say that the Community Reinvestment Act didn't spur them to loan outside their rigid boxes as much as the newspaper publicity on their past records. Banks that redlined had to face angry politicians and shareholders, as well as regulators."

John Taylor, President of the National Community Reinvestment Coalition, affirmed this message when he concluded: "The mere act of data disclosure motivated partnerships among lending institutions, community organizations, and governmental agencies for designing new loan products and embarking on aggressive marketing campaigns for reaching those left out of wealth-building and homeownership opportunities."

Disclosure constitutes a win-win strategy. It's time to let the sunshine in on the property insurance industry.

Chapter 29

The CLT Model: A Tool for Permanently Affordable Housing and Wealth Generation

Gus Newport

The gap between wealth and poverty is growing in the US, because policies to stabilize the lives of the poor and people of color do not focus on long-term solutions. Our economy is unstable, in an inflationary spiral that continues to raise the cost of basic goods, including food, gasoline, medicine and health care. Most depressing is the lack of affordable housing for the poor, working and unemployed, and seniors with limited retirement income. The severity of the shortage of affordable housing has multiplied in recent years. Barbara Ehrenreich demonstrated the stark reality of the situation facing low-income wage earners in her book *Nickel and Dimed in America*. She found from personal experience that in today's America, two incomes are required in order to live "indoors," let alone reside in safe, adequate housing. Insufficient amounts of affordable housing are being developed to fulfill the need, and most that is developed remains affordable only during the terms of the initial financing, due to relatively short-term subsidies, after which time it reverts to market rates. As a result, over the longer term, public affordable housing resources actually aid gentrification, eventually displacing the very people they were meant to assist.

The CLT Model

Some four decades ago, Bob Swann and Ralph Borsodi developed the Community Land Trust model, arising from their concerns related to poverty and land tenure. The model, drawn from the Indian *gramdan* land reform movement, was conceived as a democratically-controlled institution that would hold land for the common good of any community, while making it available to individuals within the community through long-term leases. Over the years, the model has evolved and been applied primarily to the development of permanently affordable housing within intentional communities and more broadly in urban, suburban and rural communities across the country. Terms within the ground lease balance community interests with those of the individual, providing an opportunity for lower-income people to earn equity, while limiting appreciation to ensure affordability for future lower-income homebuyers.

According to the classic CLT model, the trust is a geographically defined, membership-based, nonprofit organization created to hold land for public purposes—usually for the creation of permanently affordable housing. Like a conservation land trust, a CLT acquires land with the intention of holding it in perpetuity. A central feature of the model is a dual ownership structure whereby the CLT owns the land, but individuals, public or private organizations own the buildings located on the land. Through long-term, renewable ground leases, each party's ownership interest in the land is protected. The CLT retains the ability to repurchase any improvement on the land through a resale formula written into the lease, limits resale value to maintain affordability. The lease also enables the CLT to impose further restrictions which maintain housing quality and neighborhood stability—such as requiring that homes be owner-occupied, preventing absentee landlordism. The ground lease is equally protective of the individual homebuyer's interests, providing long-term security, while at the same time providing an opportunity to build equity and benefit from a portion (typically 25%) of the appreciation on the home, should property values increase.

By removing the cost of the land from the home price and bringing further cost reductions through government-provided affordable housing subsidies, the CLT brings homeownership within the reach of lower-income families (CLTs generally seek to serve families earning less than 80% of area median income). The interests of the individual homebuyer are balanced with the desire to maintain a permanent stock of affordable housing for future families in need. The homebuyer gains the opportunity to earn equity through monthly mortgage payments, rather than building the equity of an absentee landlord through rental payments. However, rather than gaining a one-time windfall should the home value appreciate substantially, the seller foregoes this full capital gain in order to retain affordability for the next CLT homebuyer. The CLTs long-term interest in the land and property assures that this balance of interests is maintained and community wealth is retained. The value of public subsidies used to develop the affordable housing is permanently tied to the housing, thus recycling subsidy dollars from owner to owner, assuring long-term affordability and community benefit.

The governance structure of the CLT is an important aspect of this steward-ship. The classic CLT structure has a community-based membership open to all adult residents within its defined geographic region—often a neighborhood, city or county. The CLT is governed by an elected, tri-partite board that shares gov-ernance equally among leaseholders residing on CLT-owned land; nearby resi-dents who do not live on CLT-owned land; and public officials, local funders, nonprofit professionals and others representing the public interest who bring to the board essential skills and abilities needed for effective nonprofit administra-tion.

The Dudley Street Experience

I first became aware of the Community Land Trust model during my tenure as the Director of Boston's Dudley Street Neighborhood Initiative (DSNI). This initiative grew out of the community's concerns about a new Redevelopment Area plan which was being brought forth supposedly to raise the quality of life for the residents, through improvements such as housing, open space, recreation and cultural institutions. When this planning process became public, the com-munity came out in large numbers to voice its opinion as to what the planning process ought to be, and why a method had to be imposed that would assure the community's input in all pertinent planning decisions and protect current resi-dents' ability to enjoy the improvements into the future.

The majority of residents in the Dudley area were low-income, and many of them remembered previous redevelopment processes in the West End and South End of Boston, which had resulted in massive displacement due to gentrifica-tion. The plans' promise of improvements to these neighborhoods was not real-ized by the residents, who were gentrified out due to rising housing costs and limited affordable rental housing. The Dudley area residents did not want to see this result repeated yet again, insisting on a process whereby they could partici-pate in designing the community plan and improvements. At the heart of their concerns was the desire to promote homeownership opportunities for the lower-income residents of the neighborhood.

Through a series of policy firsts, DSNI became the first community non-profit organization in the country to be awarded eminent domain powers over vacant land in a 1.3 square mile area of the city of Boston. Through a seldom-used statute on the books in Massachusetts known as "special study status," the community plan became the zoning plan for the area. Having received eminent domain rights over 30 acres of land, DSNI sought a mechanism to assure per-manent affordability and discovered the Community Land Trust model. We in-vited the Institute for Community Economics, the national intermediary for CLTs, to assist us with the process.

What we learned was that the CLT did much more than provide a mechanism to hold the land. It provided a means to stabilize lives and the community
through homeownership. As is the case for the majority of the nation's lower-
income inner-city residents, the families of the Dudley Street neighborhood had
little or no control over their own housing—the most fundamental aspect of
household security. With no opportunity to own their own homes, they were
forced to live in substandard absentee-owned rental housing, subject to displacement when and if rents increased beyond their means. In addition to the
stability of homeownership, Dudley area residents sought to take control of the
neighborhood outside their windows—to deal with abandoned property, to stop
illegal dumping, to stop providing havens for drug dealers and other criminal
activity.

Dudley Street has become a renowned example of the power of truly participatory community-building for the long term, which addresses the fundamental policies and practices that have caused poverty and decline in cities across
the country. Through the community-controlled land trust, the residents were
able to create a vibrant multicultural community, developing hundreds of affordable homes and providing an opportunity for residents to personally benefit
from the community revitalization they themselves planned. The land trust, with
its ground lease and resale formula, has been proven to empower people by providing an opportunity for homeownership and equity generation that is normally
out of reach for lower-income, largely minority residents.

The Racial Wealth Gap

In his highly acclaimed 2004 book, *The Hidden Cost of Being African American: How Wealth Perpetuates Inequality*, Brandeis Univ. sociologist Thomas
Shapiro presents his extensive analysis of the wealth gap from a perspective of
race and discrimination in America. His central argument is that family
wealth/inherited assets are the key source of the wealth gap, as the black-white
earnings gap due to income discrimination has narrowed considerably since the
1960s. As the primary asset for most families, housing is the most salient source
of the wealth gap. Lacking the "transformative" asset of family wealth, African-
American families must rely on their income and personal savings to qualify for
a home mortgage. In contrast to white families with a similar income level, who
often benefit from their parents' wealth through inheritance or other financial
assistance when the time comes to buy their first homes, African-American
families do not have access to this "leg up." They pay higher interest rates and
incur additional costs for mortgage insurance, and as a result build less equity
over time. With each successive generation, this gap increases.

As schools and social services are tied to residence location, the wealth gap
is effectively leading to ever greater racial segregation. The current way we fund
and provide access to services produces, in Shapiro's words, a "privatized no-

tion of citizenship in which communities, families and individuals try to capture or purchase resources and services for their own benefit rather than invest in an infrastructure that would help everyone."

By creating shared stewardship of land and a mechanism for the wealth generated through housing appreciation to be shared from one lower-income family to another, the CLT offers an antidote for these inter-related problems. The land trust can, in effect, substitute for inherited wealth, and thus has the potential to address the racial wealth gap in this country. Examples like Dudley Street demonstrate the ability of the CLT to change the dynamics, to provide opportunity for all residents, to prevent displacement, gentrification and the associated racial segregation.

Faced with an Administration that seems focused, more than any in recent memory, on increasing the wealth of the top few at the expense of the many, we have little choice but to find our own solutions and implement them. In my new role as Executive Director of the Institute for Community Economics, I hope to raise awareness about the potential for Community Land Trusts to level the playing field, creating opportunities for people of color. Dudley Street is the quintessential melting pot, a laboratory where the CLT model has been tested and proven to provide opportunity across race lines.

Chapter 30

Predatory Lending:
Undermining Economic Progress
in Communities of Color

Mike Calhoun and Nikitra Bailey

Only a few years ago, one of the most notorious and pernicious practices in American lending was redlining—the practice of systematically restricting mortgage-lending in minority communities. Redlining served as a major barrier to homeownership and wealth accumulation among communities of color. Today, access to credit has improved, but race still matters in a lending environment where abusive lending practices are rampant. Predatory lending restrains economic progress among vulnerable communities and helps preserve a troubling and persistent wealth gap between whites and people of color.

Predatory lending occurs when loan terms or conditions are abusive or when borrowers who could qualify for credit on better terms are steered into higher-cost loans. This type of abusive lending has found fertile soil for growth in today's two-tiered, separate-but-unequal financial services system. Wealthier borrowers, mainly white, are served by banks and other conventional financial institutions. Lower-income borrowers and persons of color are targeted by higher-cost lenders, including subprime mortgage lenders, check cashers, payday lenders and other fringe bankers.

Not all of these lenders are predatory, but nearly all predatory lending occurs in these markets. In some cases, lenders find ways to circumvent existing consumer protection laws. In most cases, current federal law provides insufficient protections against abusive practices.

A number of states have enacted anti-predatory mortgage-lending laws in response to unscrupulous mortgage-lenders who engage in lending practices that fall just below the thresholds set in 1994 by the federal Home Ownership and Equity Protection Act (HOEPA). In 1999, North Carolina became the first state to do so, and its landmark legislation became a model for many other state anti-predatory mortgage-lending laws. The North Carolina law, which reflects a consensus built among bankers, consumer advocates and civil rights leaders, provides meaningful protections for high-cost loans while preserving access to credit.

Today, such state laws are in danger of being preempted by weaker national legislation. Several proposals were floated in Congress during 2004, including a bill sponsored by Representative Robert Ney (Rep., OH) that seeks to override existing state laws and, on balance, weaken existing protections for borrowers.

If Congress revisits the issue of predatory lending, the stakes will be high for borrowers in the subprime market. The Center for Responsible Lending (CRL) estimates that predatory lending of all kinds costs borrowers over $25 billion each year—comparable to the amount spent by the US government on funding for Community Development Block Grants, Head Start and public housing programs combined. A disproportionate number of these borrowers are elders, African Americans, Latinos, women and rural residents. As described below, the majority of the money siphoned from these communities occurs in the subprime mortgage market and through payday lending.

The Wealth–Ownership Connection

In America, wealth (versus simple income) is critical to a family's economic stability and security. The wealth gap between whites and people of color is well established and growing. According to a recent report by the Pew Hispanic Center, in 2002 African Americans and Latinos had respective median net worths of $5,998 and $7,932—shockingly low, all the more so compared to whites' median net worth of $88,651. Moreover, the figures for African Americans and Latinos represent a decline from their median net worth levels in 2000, which were $7,500 and $9,750, respectively, compared to $79,400 for whites.

Homeownership is one of the most reliable and accessible ways for economically disadvantaged populations to close the wealth gap and obtain a secure position in the middle class. However, despite homeownership gains in recent years, less than 50% of African-American and Latino families have achieved homeownership, compared to roughly 75% of white families. This gap is significant, especially given the importance of home equity as a component of wealth. For example, when home equity is excluded from 2000 data, the median net worth of African-American and Latino families drops drastically, down to

$1,160 and $1,850, respectively. In other words, of the wealth that African Americans and Latinos possess, nearly two-thirds consists of home equity, compared to only one-third of the wealth of white Americans. These figures illustrate the fragile financial position of families in communities of color, and also the vital importance of home equity to their wealth.

Predatory Mortgage-Lending

Because of pervasive predatory mortgage-lending practices, the slender home equity gain made in communities of color is under attack. Unscrupulous lenders operating in the subprime mortgage market target the most vulnerable borrowers for costly refinances that strip home equity while providing no net benefit. CRL estimates that predatory mortgage-lending alone costs borrowers approximately $9.1 billion every year.

The threat posed by predatory lending is severe. Home equity is the only savings account that many low-wealth families possess. The rise in homeownership among women, African Americans and Latinos has resulted from great effort and sacrifices. This progress can be wiped away quickly by unscrupulous lenders who strip equity savings in order to collect exorbitant fees, lock borrowers in over-priced loans and close access to the judicial system through mandatory arbitration requirements.

African Americans and Latinos are over-represented in the subprime mortgage market and have borne the brunt of abusive practices. According to a 2004 study published by ACORN, African Americans were 3.6 times as likely as whites to receive a home purchase loan from a subprime lender and 4.1 times as likely as whites to receive a refinance loan from a subprime lender in 2002. In 2002, for both home purchase and refinance loans, Latinos were 2.5 times as likely as whites to receive a loan from a subprime lender.

These figures are even more disturbing when one considers the high prevalence of "steering" and "push marketing." Predatory lenders are known to steer borrowers into subprime mortgages, even when the borrowers could qualify for a mainstream loan. Vulnerable borrowers are subjected to aggressive sales tactics and sometimes outright fraud. Studies show that 30-50% of borrowers with subprime mortgages could have qualified for loans with better terms. This point is further illustrated by joint US Department of Housing and Urban Development-Treasury Department research showing that upper-income borrowers in predominantly African-American neighborhoods are twice as likely as low-income borrowers in predominantly white neighborhoods to have subprime refinance loans.

Similarly, borrowers in rural areas appear to be more vulnerable to predatory lenders. A recent CRL study showed that rural borrowers are more likely than similar urban borrowers to have subprime mortgages with prepayment penalties imposed for three years or longer. Such penalties force borrowers who later qualify for more affordable loans to give up equity or remain trapped in a higher-cost mortgage. Another CRL study showed that in high-minority communities, borrowers face 35% greater odds of receiving a prepayment penalty with a term of two years or more, compared to residents in zip code areas with a low concentration of minority residents. These studies contribute to growing evidence that predatory lending imposes proportionately higher economic burdens on the most vulnerable communities.

Payday Lending—Who Pays?

Payday lending is another form of predatory lending that greatly affects communities of color. This type of lending, sometimes called cash advance, is the practice of making small, short-term loans (typically two weeks or less) using a check dated in the future as collateral. Usually borrowers cannot repay the full loan amount by their next pay day, so they are forced to renew the loan repeatedly for additional two-week terms, paying new fees with each renewal. Over 5 million American families are caught in a cycle of payday debt each year, paying $5.6 billion in excess fees.

Payday lending targets people with steady but limited incomes, such as service workers, soldiers, government employees, clerical workers and retirees. According to a study published by researchers at North Carolina A&T State University, payday lenders tend to locate in urban areas with high minority concentrations. A recent CRL study showed that in North Carolina, African-American neighborhoods have three times as many payday lending stores per capita as white neighborhoods. The findings show that race matters, even when we control for other factors. Variables that the payday industry claims are key demographics of its customer base—income, homeownership, poverty, unemployment rate, urban location, age, education, share of households with children, and gender—do not account for the disparity.

A 2004 analysis by the *New York Times* reveals that at least 26% of military households have been caught up in payday lending. This has strong implications for African Americans and other nonwhite groups, since people of color make up well over one-third of enlisted military personnel.

Payday lending is generally marketed as quick cash for a short-term emergency. However, only 1% of all loans go to one-time emergency borrowers. The typical structure allows only two weeks for repayment, fails to consider the borrower's ability to repay, and operates on back-to-back transactions that can easily confuse borrowers into believing they are receiving additional funds when they actually are paying fees repeatedly on the same loan principal.

CRL research shows that borrowers who receive five or more loans a year account for 91% of payday lenders' business. The fees are high, but it is the debt trap that makes payday lending a faulty form of credit and a poor substitute for legitimate banking services in communities of color.

Conclusion

Access to healthy credit contributes to sustainable prosperity; destructive debt and equity-draining loans impose hardships on families and ultimately harm entire communities. Greater awareness of predatory lending and increased focus on financial education are helpful, but education campaigns alone are not enough. Borrowers need strong protections eliminating most predatory lending before it happens.

A number of states are successfully addressing predatory lending issues through laws that curb specific abusive practices while preserving access to credit in the subprime market. Federal legislation that nullifies these existing laws would seriously impair progress already made. Any new national mortgage legislation should provide a floor, not a ceiling, on consumer protections. It should eliminate excessive fees, broker kickbacks, "flipping" and abusive pre-payment penalties. It should also require mandatory counseling for all high-cost loans and preserve a borrower's ability to seek legal remedies in a court of law. Advocates and concerned citizens can play a key role by urging their Congressional representatives to support legislation that preserves state laws and strengthens protections for families vulnerable to predatory lending.

As long as predatory lending is permitted, much of the economic progress made in communities of color will be largely wiped out. To the extent that families own property, they have many more options and opportunities to build a better future. To the extent that hard-earned equity and other assets are stripped away, opportunities vanish, and the negative ripple effects are passed down to the families' future generations and the wider communities in which they live.

Chapter 31

Housing Quiz

California Newsreel

The Housing Quiz was developed by California Newsreel, in association with the Association of American Colleges and Universities. The myths and misconceptions it raise are explored in the three-part documentary series, *RACE – The Power of an Illusion,* available on video and DVD from California Newsreel at www.newsreel.org. For more information and background, visit the companion website at www.pbs.org/race. *Answers are on page 401.*

1. Of the $120 billion in new housing loans underwritten by the federal government between 1934 and 1962, what percentage went to white homeowners?
   A. 45%
   B. 64%
   C. 75%
   D. 88%
   E. 98%

2. Which of the following is *not* a result of federal government policies?
   A. Redlining
   B. Urban renewal
   C. Deterioration of inner cities
   D. Affirmative action quotas
   E. The wealth gap between black and white families

3. Today, the net worth of the average white family is how much compared to the average black family?
    A. Fourteen times as much
    B. Ten times as much
    C. Twice as much
    D. The same
    E. Half as much

4. When white and black families of similar incomes are compared, what is the difference in their net worth?
    A. No difference
    B. Black net worth is slightly greater
    C. White net worth is more than eight times greater
    D. White net worth is more than two times greater
    E. Black net worth is twice as great

5. According to a 1993 study, 86% of suburban whites lived in a community where the black population was:
    A. Less than 5%
    B. Less than 10%
    C. Less than 1%
    D. More than 10%
    E. More than 15%

6. Which is *not* an example of a government racial preference program?
    A. 1964 Civil Rights Act
    B. 1862 Homestead Act
    C. 1790 Naturalization Act
    D. 1934 Federal Housing Administration
    E. 1935 Social Security Act

Education

Chapter 32

The O'Connor Project: Intervening Early to Eliminate the Need for Racial Preferences in Higher Education

The following article first appeared in Judicature, *88:2, Sept.-Oct. 2004 and is reprinted with permission and thanks. It was extensively footnoted; readers interested in obtaining these source notes can find them at www.common-purpose.org.*

Over the half-century since the US Supreme Court's ruling in *Brown v. Board of Education*, our nation has struggled to fulfill its commitment to racial equality. In *Brown*, the Court recognized the indispensable role that equal education opportunity would play in achieving that goal. Yet, not long after *Brown*, the country's courts and political leaders seemed to agree that after centuries of slavery and racial exclusion, equal opportunity alone would not be enough to ensure African Americans an equal stake in our nation's social, cultural and economic life. Policies of racial preferences were implemented to provide African Americans greater access to educational, employment and other opportunities. By the end of the 20th Century, the backlash against these affirmative action policies threatened to bring progress toward racial inclusiveness to a halt.

In 2003, however, the US Supreme Court's decision in *Grutter v. Bollinger* (539 U.S. 306 [2003]) upheld the constitutionality and desirability of diversity programs that take race into account and which, in effect, accord racial preferences to African-American applicants to graduate school. In her opinion for the Court, Justice Sandra Day O'Connor emphasized the limited extent to which these preferences may be relied upon by university administrators. She also imposed a durational limitation on their use, declaring her expectation that racial preferences in higher education will no longer be necessary in 25 years.

Justice O'Connor's expectation is realistic if, and only if, the nation acts promptly to put in place the measures that would eliminate, or substantially reduce, racial disparities that occur between birth and young adulthood. Figuring out the actions needed is the easier part, because the knowledge about what works to reduce these disparities now exists, waiting only to be assembled and disseminated in actionable form. The hard part—mobilizing the political will to implement this agenda—will require a major effort by American opinion leaders, black and white.

Here is what we can and must do to reduce or eliminate racial disparities early in life and thereby eliminate the need for racial preferences at the university level:

- First, reduce racial disparities in birth outcomes.
- Second, reduce the disparities in school readiness.
- Third, attack racial disparities in the outcomes of kindergarten through 12th-grade education.
- Fourth, reduce significant racial disparities in the successful transition to young adulthood.

A fundamental tenet of the agenda laid out here, which I call "The O'Connor Project," is that in a nation in which a legacy of slavery and Jim Crow plays such a powerful and destructive role, no single, isolated change can bring about conditions where racial preferences will be unnecessary. What is needed, rather, is a combination of actions that would eliminate racial disparities at each decisive stage of development. As Harvard professor William Julius Wilson, leading scholar of urban poverty, has pointed out, to "drastically reduce and eventually eliminate the environmental differences that create the present gap in black and white achievement," we must "attack all aspects of the structure of inequality." This is a daunting challenge, but one that this nation can meet by building on widely shared and strongly held values—the importance of education, family responsibility and social justice.

One encouraging recent development is the establishment at Harvard University of the new Charles Hamilton Houston Institute for Race and Justice, headed by Harvard law professor Charles J. Ogletree Jr. The institute will help lead efforts to rally national support for the actions envisioned as part of The O'Connor Project.

Implementation of this agenda will change life trajectories as today's children become healthier, better educated and better prepared to succeed in good jobs and to be tomorrow's effective parents. This progress, especially in the context of economic growth, will produce further inroads against racism and discrimination.

What follows is a brief review of the state of understanding of the strategies that we must build on as we seek to reduce racial disparities in crucial outcomes between birth and young adulthood.

Disparities in Birth Outcomes

Damaging birth outcomes, such as low birthweight, are found twice as often among African-American babies as among whites and are associated with serious cognitive impairments, behavioral and learning disorders, and health problems—all of which predispose children to school failure. The causes of racial disparities in infant health can be environmental, such as an exposure to toxic substances; socioeconomic, including poor housing or nutrition, dangerous neighborhoods or lack of social support; behavioral, including the abuse of drugs or alcohol; or medical, such as the lack of access to prompt, high-quality prenatal care. In addition, unintended, unwanted or early pregnancies, also characterized by racial disparities, are associated with a greater risk of developmental delays, lack of stimulating home environments, and lower levels of cognitive and educational attainment.

A wealth of knowledge is available to improve birth outcomes and reduce teen births through, among other things, universal health insurance coverage; universal access to age-appropriate, reproduction-related health education; changes in the policies and practices of health care providers, including prenatal care and family planning services; and efforts to spread community norms that hold that all births should be intended and wanted, when young people are ready for parenthood.

Disparities in School Readiness

Perhaps the most dramatic race-based disparities occur before children enter school. Children who start behind as toddlers are likely to be left behind in the course of schooling. The number of words in a typical three-year-old black child's vocabulary falls below the 20th percentile of the national distribution. Similar disparities appear when the comparisons are by the occupational status of the children's families. In 2002, Kansas City three-year-olds in professional families knew an average of 1,116 words, while three-year-olds in families receiving welfare benefits knew an average of only 525 words. These are disturbing findings when one considers that early vocabulary development is strongly associated with later school performance.

By harnessing the tremendous growth in understanding of how children's later prospects are affected by their early physical well-being, and by the stimulation, caring relationships and supports they experience long before they enter school, we could significantly reduce the existing racial gap in how well young children are equipped for school learning.

The remedies here lie in improved child health care, and in strengthening the two domains in which young children spend their time: the family and out-of-home child care.

Improved child health care. In many American cities, health problems such as untreated vision and hearing defects, lead poisoning, poor nutrition and asthma—all of which interfere with normal development and learning—are found in African-American children at two to three times the incidence among white children. Moreover, racial disparities extend to medical care itself. For example, among children ages 1 to 5 with the same health conditions, African-American children are half as likely as white children to receive prescription medication.

The answer is to extend health insurance coverage to all children under 18 years of age, and to make competent, continuing and culturally sensitive health care available through a readily accessible source of care, which pediatricians like to call a "medical home," that is closely connected to other community resources.

Improved home environments. The family's role in providing the interactions and stimulation so crucial to school readiness is widely recognized, but there is much skepticism about how much change in the ways families deal with their children can be brought about from outside the family. It is encouraging, then, that a rich array of successful, albeit scattered, community-based efforts are already in place that show it can be done. On a small scale that can surely be expanded, these programs are daily enhancing the capacity and impetus of families to read to young children at home, to engage them in rich conversations and to limit television viewing.

In Harlem, new parents learn effective parenting techniques in nine Saturdays of "Baby College" and in home visits from trained parent educators. In Okolona, Mississippi, syndicated columnist William Raspberry's "Baby Steps" program shows parents how to use ordinary kitchen items to teach word recognition while inspiring an entire town to read to its children, tutor them and make its preschoolers "the smartest in northeast Mississippi." All over the country, parents are encouraged to read with their children by gifts of free children's books from pediatricians, libraries and family support centers, and through burgeoning adult literacy programs.

Higher-quality child care. Child care that meets high standards of quality and promotes social, emotional and cognitive development is an essential component of any school-readiness strategy. Because young children develop so rapidly between birth and school entry, many of the skills, abilities and dispositions that go into school readiness are learned in child care and early education programs. Once again, we have plenty of examples of where it's being done right, but systemic changes are required to build on these successes so that all children, especially African Americans, will have access to the high-quality early care and education programs that are most likely to have a positive impact. The characteristics these programs share include, among other things:

- Child groupings small enough, together with adult-child ratios low enough, to permit young children, especially babies and toddlers, to have one-on-one time with care-givers;
- Staff turnover low enough to allow stable, continuing relationships to develop between individual children and adults;
- Staff who are culturally sensitive and responsive to the interests and needs of families;
- Staff who encourage active involvement and participation by parents and provide support to mothers and other family members to strengthen their child-rearing capacities;
- Opportunities for children to interact socially with other children and adults in diverse situations, so that they learn to take turns, remember and follow directions, and use adults as sources of information, discipline and enjoyment;
- Staff and parents who have high, age-appropriate expectations for children's behavior and ability to learn and achieve; and
- Recognition that school readiness is more than a set of mechanical skills.

This last characteristic means less reliance on didactic, adult-directed teaching of isolated skills, such as naming letters, and more emphasis on instruction that is individualized and builds on children's current understandings, such as engaging them in problem-solving and manipulation of materials.

Disparities in K-12 Education

America's primary and secondary schools currently operate in ways that simply do not produce a high enough proportion of minority youngsters graduating from high school with the skills to succeed in four-year colleges, much less in graduate work. Compared with their white counterparts, black children enter schools that have larger class sizes, undertake less outreach to parents, have fewer well-prepared and experienced teachers, and are located in areas where safety is an issue. Many have such high mobility rates that a school with an enrollment of 1,000 pupils will have had to try to teach as many as 2,000 different children at some time during the year.

Of the approximately 1.2 million black and Hispanic 18-year-olds in the United States in the year 2000, only about half actually graduated from high school with a regular diploma. Only a quarter had taken the high school courses that would allow them to apply to even the least selective four-year colleges.

The remedies for this start with excellent teachers with high expectations and schools of a size where every child is known by a school adult. These are measures that will obviously benefit whites as well as blacks. But after that, the remedies must differentiate by context. In schools where students of color are in the minority, the most promising strategies to reduce racial disparities focus on recognizing and changing the subtle and complex institutional practices that perpetuate the gap in academic opportunities, and on convincing those who benefit most from existing arrangements that this is not a zero-sum game. Numerous studies have shown that minority students' progress can occur without detracting from the achievement of white students.

This is not, however, the situation for most black youngsters, nearly half of whom attend high schools from which the majority of students who enter ninth grade never graduate. Only 11% of white students attend such high schools. Thus, the biggest risk factor for dropping out of school before graduating is not a personal or even a family characteristic; rather, it is attending a high school in which graduation is not the norm.

A preponderance of research and experience now suggests that the strategies that would change outcomes in these predominantly poor and minority schools involve staffing them with the best and most experienced teachers and adopting a principle enunciated long ago by W.E.B. DuBois: the combination of strong social support with high levels of "academic press." The Consortium on Chicago School Research proposes that neither social support nor academic press alone is sufficient, but that the combination can significantly change outcomes. The Consortium has concluded that the most successful schools are able to create school and classroom environments that: (1) promote strong, caring and supportive personal relationships between students and teachers, parents and other students; and (2) place a heavy emphasis on high expectations for academic success, rigor and conformity to specific standards of achievement.

Of course, it is not easy to create schools with these characteristics, but as more and more education leaders around the country become engaged in precisely this enterprise, the lessons from experience are accumulating and showing the way, so that not only individual schools but whole districts will be able to reorganize on the basis of these principles.

Disparities in Transition to Adulthood

The greatest risk factors that stack the odds against a smooth transition into adulthood are: dropping out of school, becoming an unmarried teen mother, becoming involved with the juvenile justice or foster care system, and living in a neighborhood of concentrated poverty and unemployment. Each of these risk factors occurs disproportionately among African-American youth.

This essay has already explored some of the actions needed to reduce racial disparities with regard to school drop-out and teen parenting. What follows are some proposals for reducing racial disparities resulting from the prevailing practices of the foster care and juvenile justice systems and from the persistence of neighborhoods of concentrated poverty.

The foster care and juvenile justice systems, with a few exceptions, are not working well for most American youngsters, but young people of color are the worst off. For many, involvement with these systems not only fails to support healthy development, but actually adds more risk factors to the burdens they already carry. African-American youngsters are more likely to be in residential or group care instead of family foster care, they stay in out-of-home care longer, and they are least likely to be reunified with their families. The number of youth detained in secure detention facilities, which is perhaps the most significant predictor of a non-mainstream adulthood, has increased by almost 100% since 1985. Virtually all of this growth can be accounted for by the greatly increased rates of detention for youth of color.

Although they have rarely done so in the past, and despite the fact that these systems have proven inordinately resistant to change, they could, as a few such systems have demonstrated, partner with communities in ways that move them beyond a purely punitive to a supportive role in the lives of heretofore marginalized individuals and neighborhoods. They could do much to ensure that the young people over whom they exercise authority have or obtain, among other things, needed skills, education, and physical and mental health services; financial, vocational, entrepreneurial and recreational resources that connect them to mainstream prospects; and access to caring adults who provide them with the support they need to persevere in their pursuit of change, and to overcome their sense of exclusion and inadequacy.

Finally, we have learned much about how to reduce the risk factors facing the young people who live in neighborhoods of concentrated poverty and unemployment. Nearly four decades after federal legislation outlawed residential segregation, *de facto* segregation persists. Blacks continue to experience more severe racial isolation due to residence than any other racial group, as well as the accompaniments of racial isolation, including concentrated social and economic disadvantage, high rates of crime and unemployment, and deteriorated and unsafe housing. All of these factors contribute to the racial disparities in the transition to adulthood. All of them make it more likely that even strong families cannot protect their children against the magnetic pull of the streets.

The remedies here start with more jobs that pay a living wage and stronger income supports. Additional tools are community-based. Among them: programs to promote homeownership, which is linked to family and neighborhood stability, increased civic participation and social networks; community policing and other efforts to make disinvested neighborhoods safe and attractive; local initiatives to develop and maintain libraries, recreation centers, after-school programs, community centers, parks and play spaces; and local enforcement measures to eliminate abandoned buildings, drug houses and drug dealing, and violations by absentee landlords. Finally, systematic efforts at the community level are required to provide opportunities for youths to connect with and establish solid, trusting relationships with competent and caring adults from outside their own families.

****

There is little question that the agenda outlined in this essay would sharply reduce racial disparities in children's birth-related issues, health, school readiness and transition to young adulthood. It would thereby also help eliminate the need for racial preferences beyond the year 2028, as Justice O'Connor's decision in the *Grutter* case requires. Many of the answers about what to do exist, and need only to be put together in actionable form. Our understanding of how to do it may be less refined than we wish, but much of that learning can be assembled as we go. We undeniably have, today, the actionable intelligence we need in order to get started. Now we must mobilize the political will to implement this agenda of both structural and individual change, so that the nation can realize Justice O'Connor's goal for the nation by 2028.

Chapter 33

Why Is School Reform So Hard?

Linda Christensen and Stan Karp

With districts across the nation reeling from the impact of the No Child Left Behind Act (NCLB), which may put over 75% of the nation's schools on the "needs improvement" list, it's a good time to ask again why successful school reform is so hard.

Under NCLB, the federal government is using test scores to identify which schools will face an escalating series of mandatory "reforms," ranging from intervention by consultants to wholesale dismissal of school staff to the imposition of private management on public schools.

Yet even according to a 2003 study—"Can Failing Schools Be Fixed?"— from the conservative Thomas B. Fordham Foundation (an enthusiastic supporter of NCLB), the "reform interventions" mandated by the new law have a success rate of well below 50%. According to the study: "Several lessons can be drawn from America's previous experience with state and district-level interventions into failing schools:

- Some turnaround efforts have improved some schools, but success is not the norm.
- No particular intervention appears more successful than any other.
- Interventions are uneven in their implementation and always hard to sustain.

- It is nearly impossible to determine which interventions offer the most bang for the buck because they are attempted in very different situations."

These findings resonate with our own experience as classroom teachers and school reformers for over 25 years each in urban systems at opposite ends of the country: Portland, OR and Paterson, NJ. Together, we have been through state takeovers, school reconstitutions, site-based management, small-school restructuring, state standards and testing (and more testing), and "whole school reform" initiatives of all kinds. We've learned the hard way that while there are many model schools, model classrooms and model educators from which we can learn a great deal, there are no model districts, no model states and no model systems that have put in place and sustained the policies and programs needed to deliver quality education and outcomes to all children. Why should this be so?

We think the reasons have less to do with the specifics of any reform strategy or intervention than with the dual character of schools in our society.

School reform, especially in urban districts, often invokes a common rhetoric: "all children can learn," "high standards for all," "no child should be left behind." These sentiments resonate with all who care about schools and children. But such rhetoric can also hide the historic reality that schools have always had a dual character.

On the one hand, public schools remain perhaps our most important democratic institution. They are the product of decades of effort to give substance to the nation's promises of equal opportunity, self-improvement and success through hard work and achievement. Schools play a key role in American dreams of class mobility and generational progress, and their success or failure has a daily impact on the lives and prospects of millions of children and families.

At the same time, schools historically have been instruments for reproducing class and race privilege as it exists in the larger society. The low academic performance of schools in poor areas, the inadequate facilities, the endemic underfunding, the persistence of tracking and resegregation, the notorious administrative instability and shallow trendiness of reform efforts, the toleration of failure and disrespect for communities of color, all reflect real relations of inequality and injustice that permeate our society. Through ideology, gate-keeping, various forms of stratification, and bureaucratic, often authoritarian, administration, schools function as a large sifting and labeling operation that re-creates and justifies existing distributions of wealth and power. In many ways, schools reproduce the very inequality that American mythology professes they are designed to overcome.

This dual character of schooling—its democratic promise and its institutional service to a society based on class, race and gender privilege—invariably generates contradictory impulses when it comes to reform. At every turn, the gap between the promise and practice of schooling creates a tension: Should curriculum reflect a mainstream consensus or a multicultural pluralism? Should schools endorse traditional values or promote independent, critical thought? Are standards being raised to bar the door to some or assure better outcomes for all? Should parents and classroom teachers have as much to say about reform agendas as governors and corporate executives? Should schools be as concerned with promoting anti-racist attitudes as with marketable skills? Will new forms of assessment provide better ways to report and improve student performance or more effective ways to sort and label kids for predetermined slots in society?

To be sure, answers to complicated questions of educational policy cannot be reduced to either/or propositions. But the debate over policy options inevitably takes place within this context of the dual nature of schooling. The choices made push schools in one direction or the other along a continuum from promoting social justice to reinforcing the status quo. Whether any particular reform initiative improves or impoverishes life in the classroom often depends on how it fits into this larger context.

The dual character of schooling suggests that reforms cannot be judged by their self-proclaimed goals, rhetorical promises or short-term effect on test scores. Instead, they must be measured by their ability to deliver more democratic classroom experiences and more equitable results and outcomes across the system.

Take for example, the current enthusiasm in reform circles for small-school experiments. Small schools show promise in large part because they attempt to change the social relations of schooling; that is, they create a more human scale and more supportive environment for collaborative, personalized interaction among students, teachers and communities. They can nourish creativity and mutual accountability in powerful ways that large, traditional schools cannot. Small schools can also introduce elements of choice, pluralism and innovation into historically bureaucratized and stagnant systems.

But like most reforms, small schools can also be developed in problematic ways. They can become specialized magnets that "cream" the best students and most committed parents. They can claim a disproportionate share of resources for a relatively small slice of the student population. Instead of providing models that promote system-wide reform, they can be insulated pockets of privilege, resegregation and tracking. It all depends on which of the system's dual tendencies prevails.

This is one reason for keeping a sharp eye on the big picture and asking "who benefits and who does not?" whenever a reform proposal is put on the table. There are many educators, parents and concerned advocates at all levels pushing the system to realize its most ambitious and democratic possibilities. These heroic efforts need encouragement in the face of hard choices and daunting problems. But they also need a healthy dose of realism about the nature of the system we're trying to move.

Unfortunate as it may be, schools have never been just about educating children. They are also about constructing social and political power. Real school reform must be about challenging it. Until we find the political will and vision to put social justice at the heart of the debate about public education, school reform will continue to be an exasperating tug of war with limited impact on the status quo.

Chapter 34

Socioeconomic School Integration: A Symposium

Socioeconomic School Integration

Richard D. Kahlenberg

Today, most of the education reform world, liberal and conservative, accepts as a given that American children will attend schools that are largely segregated by class and race. There is a strong policy consensus that concentrations of poverty, whether in public housing or in public schools, reduce life chances, and an equally strong political consensus that we can't do much of anything to alleviate those conditions. Those institutions that remain devoted to bringing about the important work of school integration—for example, the NAACP Legal Defense and Educational Fund and the Harvard Civil Rights Project—define the issue primarily through the lens of race, and they are facing an increasingly frustrating uphill battle. Whereas a focus on segregation by race made eminent legal sense for years, as the Supreme Court decision in *Brown v. Board of Education* sought to correct the gross injustice of racial apartheid, today courts use *Brown* to say that all classifications by race are inherently suspect, striking down even voluntary race-conscious efforts to promote integration.

For those of us who care about equal educational opportunity and integration, the times demand a new approach that goes beyond trying to make separate but equal work, on the one hand, or simply pursuing a failing legal race-based integration strategy, on the other. This new approach seeks to integrate students by economic status, such as eligibility for free or reduced price lunch. Because much of the nation's concentration of poverty is the result of racial discrimination in housing, any plan to reduce economic isolation will produce, as a positive byproduct, a fair measure of racial integration. Moreover, the economic integration strategy helps create in all schools the single most powerful predictor of a good education: the presence of a core of middle-class families who will insist upon, and get, a quality school for their children. In order to be politically sustainable, this new strategy should avoid forced busing and instead ride the popular wave of greater school choice. While private school vouchers undercut equal opportunity, programs of public school choice, if properly implemented, can be a powerful vehicle for overcoming residential segregation by race and class.

Why Integration?

Why should we care about integration at all? A recent Public Agenda survey found that most parents, black and white, prioritize quality schools over integrated schools. Many blacks have come to see racial desegregation as essentially insulting: Why do black kids need to sit next to white kids in order to learn? As Clarence Thomas put it: "It never ceases to amaze me that the courts are so willing to assume that anything that is predominantly black must be inferior." Alternatively, under the new economic integration, what good does it do poor kids to sit next to rich kids?

The answer is that the separation of poor and middle-class children is the fountainhead of a host of related inequalities of educational opportunity. Specifically, here are ten reasons why socioeconomic integration matters:

- Good schools require an adequate financial base (as measured against student needs) to provide small class size, modern equipment and the like. Low-income schools, on average, spend about half of what more affluent schools spend per pupil.
- Good schools require that money is spent wisely, on the classroom rather than on bureaucracy. In low-income areas, pressure is intense to make education a jobs program, so bureaucracies are more likely to be bloated.
- Good schools require an orderly environment. Low-income schools report disorder problems twice as often as middle-class schools.
- Good schools have a stable student and teacher population. High-poverty schools see more than twice as much student mobility as low-poverty schools, and teacher mobility is four times as high.
- Good schools have a solid principal and well-qualified teachers trained in the subject they are teaching. Teachers in high-poverty schools are more likely to be unlicensed, more likely to teach out of their field of

expertise, more likely to have low teacher test scores, more likely to be inexperienced and more likely to have less formal education. Even when paid comparable salaries, most teachers consider it a promotion to move from poor to middle-class schools, and the best teachers usually transfer out of low-income schools at the first opportunity.

- Good schools have a meaty curriculum and high expectations. Curriculum in high-poverty schools is more watered down; and expectations are so low that the grade of A in a low-income school is often the same as a grade of C in middle-class schools, as measured by standardized tests results. In many low-income schools, AP classes and high-level math are not even offered.
- Good schools have active parental involvement. In low-income schools, parents are four times less likely to be members of the PTA and much less likely to participate in fund-raising.
- Good schools have motivated peers who value achievement and encourage it among classmates. Peers in low-income schools are less academically engaged, less likely to do homework, more likely to watch TV, more likely to cut class and less likely to graduate—all of which have been found to influence the behavior of classmates.
- Good schools have high-achieving peers, whose knowledge is shared informally with classmates all day long. In low-income schools, peers come to school with about half the vocabulary of middle-class children, so any given child is less likely to expand his or her vocabulary through informal interaction.
- Good schools have well-connected classmates who will help provide access to jobs down the line. Children attending high-poverty schools are cut off from access to informal connections that serve middle-class children well in finding jobs after graduation.

It is true, of course, that high-poverty schools can work, given a particularly charismatic principal or an unusually devoted teaching staff. The Heritage Foundation has published a report, *No Excuses*, which "found not one or two [but] twenty-one high poverty high performing schools." The problem, of course, is that the Department of Education has identified some 7,000 high-poverty schools nationally that are low-performing.

The one type of successful school that Americans have been able to replicate time and time again are those in which a majority of the students are middle-class. Study after study has found that low-income students do better, and middle-class achievement does not suffer, in economically integrated majority middle-class schools. In a nation in which two-thirds of students are middle-class (not eligible for free or reduced price lunch), it is entirely plausible to set a goal of making all schools majority middle-class.

Race vs. Class

If integration matters, the new emphasis should be on socioeconomic status. Except where a district is rooting out the vestiges of discrimination—in which case the use of race is appropriate, even constitutionally required—leading with socioeconomic integration offers three advantages.

First, from a legal standpoint, *Brown v. Board of Education* has largely run its course. The courts have made it clear that desegregation orders are meant to be temporary and with increasing frequency are releasing school districts from court supervision. Over the past 20 years, our schools have been slowly re-segregating. Today, 70% of black students attend majority minority schools, up from 63% in 1980. Thirty years ago, it made sense to lead with race because *Brown* found that purposeful racial segregation is illegal but said nothing about segregation by socioeconomic status. Now, however, the legal posture has changed 180 degrees. Conservative courts in Montgomery County, Maryland, Arlington, Virginia, and elsewhere have found that, absent the lingering effects of past discrimination, efforts to promote school diversity by considering a student's race may itself be unconstitutional. The Supreme Court has not definitively ruled on this issue, but the election of George W. Bush certainly makes it more likely that a future Court majority will continue down the path of requiring race-neutrality except where race is used as a remedy to past discrimination. Indeed, in Wake County, North Carolina, an income integration plan was recently adopted based on the fear that the existing racial balance plan was probably unconstitutional. By contrast, even Justices Antonin Scalia and Clarence Thomas have written that using economic status is perfectly legal.

Second, on the merits, the factors that drive the quality of a school have much more to do with class than with race. As Harvard University's Gary Orfield noted in his 1996 book, *Dismantling Desegregation*, separate is inherently unequal, not because "something magic happens to minority students when they sit next to whites," but because minority schools are so often "isolated high-poverty schools that almost always have low levels of academic competition, performance, and preparation for college or jobs."

Numerous studies have confirmed the findings of the 1966 Coleman Report that the "beneficial effect of a student body with a high proportion of white students comes not from racial composition per se but from the better educational background and higher educational aspirations that are, on the average, found among whites." This finding is confirmed by other studies that conclude that racial integration is much more likely to raise academic achievement of African-American students when the plan involves more affluent suburban whites, as in Charlotte-Mecklenburg, North Carolina, as opposed to poor and working-class whites, as in Boston, Massachusetts.

The data on the various factors that make for a difficult learning environment—peers who are disruptive, who cut class, watch excessive TV, and drop out of high school; parents who are inactive in the school—all track much more by class than by race. Even the widely touted issue of African-American students running down academic excellence as "acting white" turns out to be more closely associated with economic class (poor whites also denigrate achievement, on average).

Third, there is also a political advantage to leading with economic rather than racial integration. In some communities, like La Crosse, Wisconsin, local leaders believed that economic integration would go over better with the public, in part because poor whites would also benefit, and in part because it would prevent opponents of integration from playing the "race card." More broadly speaking, there is an argument that progressives have a particular political interest in leading with class, so that so-called "Reagan Democrats" would see a benefit to their children—and would seek an alliance with African Americans, rather than opposing them.

How to Get There

How should economic school integration be accomplished? Compulsory busing—which gives parents no say in their children's school assignment—is a political non-starter. A 1998 Public Agenda poll found that 76% of white parents, as well as a substantial minority (42%) of African-American parents, were opposed to "busing children to achieve a better racial balance in the schools." But we've learned a number of things since the racial desegregation era of the early 1970s about how to make integration more politically palatable.

The first lesson is to emphasize choice over coercion. Voucher proponents say it's unfair to trap kids in bad schools—a stunning admission for conservatives who once defended the neighborhood school at all costs. Vouchers are wrongheaded for a number of reasons, and they divide Americans politically, but there is consistently more than 70% support for greater school choice within the public school system. Choice empowers families where busing (or automatic neighborhood assignment) leaves them impotent.

The second lesson is to emphasize that economic integration is primarily about making schools effective and raising academic achievement. Last year, Wake County (Raleigh), North Carolina schools adopted a policy that no school is to have more than 40% of its students eligible for free or reduced price lunch (family income less than 185% of the poverty line) or have more than 25% of its students reading below grade level. The purpose of the Wake County program is not to rectify historic discrimination or to promote a utopian vision of an integrated society but to create quality schools and raise academic achievement. Says Wake County schools attorney Ann Majestic, it's "educational engineering," not social engineering.

The third lesson is to give educational incentives for middle-class families to buy in to integrated schools. It is important to offer middle-class families something in return, a reason to venture beyond local schools, whether that be smaller class size or an emphasis on the arts. We should capitalize on the common-sense notion that in education one size doesn't fit all.

The most promising mechanism is a system of assignment known as "controlled choice," used in Cambridge, Massachusetts and elsewhere. Automatic assignment based on what neighborhood people can afford to live in is abolished. Officials poll parents and find out what kinds of schools they'd like. Then they make every school within a given geographic region a magnet school, providing special signatures or themes (computers, arts) or special pedagogical approaches (e.g., Montessori, back to basics). Families rank preferences, and those choices are honored by school officials in a way that will also ensure that all schools are majority middle-class. Schools that are under-chosen get extra help, just as a lagging professional football team gets a first-round draft pick. The same 1998 Public Agenda poll that found strong opposition to busing found substantial support for racial integration combined with choice. Asked whether they favored or opposed "letting parents choose their top three schools, while the district makes the final choice, with an eye to racial balance," 61% of white parents favored the approach (35% disapproved), while 65% of black parents approved (34% opposed).

The era of court-ordered racial desegregation is coming to an end. But to give up on racial and economic integration altogether—pouring greater and greater resources into making separate but equal a little more equitable—is to concede almost all of the problem. Greater public school choice is in our future. The question is whether progressives can harness the choice movement to help overcome the massive inequalities inherent in a system that educates poor and middle-class children separately.

Commentaries

Not the Same as Racial Integration

Gary Orfield

Socioeconomic integration is a good idea, but it is not the same as racial integration, may not provide some of the important advantages, does not have any enforceable basis in law, and often has been extremely controversial.

It is true that students in isolated high-poverty schools and neighborhoods suffer disadvantages regardless of race, but the fact is that there are few such schools and communities that are white. The basic reality is that race is related to but different in some critical ways from class. Middle-class blacks and Latinos face discrimination on racial grounds, poor blacks and Latinos face dual discrimination, and even upper-class blacks tend to live in segregated patterns and experience differential treatment on the basis of race. My black students at Harvard are often followed in stores and treated unequally not far from Harvard Square. Middle-class blacks often live with and attend school with more poor children than poor whites do because of differential housing practices and various forms of discrimination. Even in elite settings, their children are often placed in lower-track classes, based on racial assumptions by counselors and teachers. Class-based solutions do not consider the fact that white resistance to being in predominantly black neighborhoods is independent of class and that the highest-income black families are as segregated from white counterparts as the lowest-income.

A variety of experiments with class-based integration show shortcomings. It failed to integrate Lowell High school, a selective school in San Francisco; it failed miserably in the UCLA Law School; it has been a very partial and inadequate substitute for affirmative action in many institutions of higher education, which have had to rely on a variety of proxies for race, such as segregated high schools, to make up some of the losses due to affirmative action bans.

The assumption that it will be more politically popular than race-based desegregation is questionable. All the battles against suburban housing exclusion, about zoning and land-use policies that excluded affordable, rental and subsidized housing, were class-based, but they were often interpreted in racial terms and almost always defeated politically. Class-based desegregation lacks the history of discrimination argument as well as a legal basis, because economic discrimination is not considered illegitimate in American law or ideology, since economic status is considered a result of individual attainment rather than group position. When class-based school desegregation was tried in Duluth years ago and in Wausau, Wisconsin, it produced an intense political reaction and was ended. School boards have always had the authority, plus some good educational reasons, to do this, but almost none do. The interest in it today is mostly from those desperate to retain some of what they see as beneficial racial desegregation threatened by hostile courts.

Anyone seriously considering class-based desegregation or class-based affirmative action needs to be skeptical about any claims that it will do the same thing or be readily accepted. Obviously, class-based desegregation is much better than none and has real educational benefits, but those expecting to achieve and maintain integration through this method would do well to try to include specific definitions of class that are more related to race—like persistent poverty and isolation in areas of concentrated residential poverty—and to think hard about the effects of cutting off middle-class blacks and Hispanics from the reach of civil rights remedies. Otherwise, class-based remedies can have the effect of helping the temporarily poor whose families have strong human capital, such as recent highly educated immigrants or recently divorced or downsized suburban families whose long-term prospects are very positive without special attention and who are not the victims of discrimination.

And we should realize that there are particular benefits that come from racial integration, in terms of learning and preparation for adult and community life, that do not come from economic diversity. In surveys we are conducting in high schools around the country, we find students reporting clear evidence of such benefits. We know almost nothing about whether or not class integration lowers or increases racial and class prejudice.

I agree that social class desegregation needs exploration. Such exploration should include a careful sorting out of a variety of experiences and dilemmas. Until that work is fully done, and Kahlenberg's is only a first step in that direction, there is often a tendency to over-generalize from limited information. It would certainly be foolish to give up race-based remedies, particularly where they, unlike class-based responses, can be linked to a remedial context and at least partially protected from local politics. Parents of lower-class students usually have very little influence and even less organization than minority parents and communities, and the continuation and support for good class-based remedies will be entirely dependent on political systems in which the poor are largely unrepresented. Class integration may be all that is left if the Supreme Court continues to dismantle race-conscious remedies, so it is very important that we have a sober and realistic analysis of its possibilities and real limitations.

My basic view is that a class-based remedy has to come from the elected branches of government in a society that denies class as a significant category, and that one which really helped with race would often have to be done in a way that would be attacked both as a subterfuge for race and as unfair to whites and Asians of similar income levels. The work I am doing with the group of scholars working with John Stanfield of Morehouse College on the reasons for the educational failure of black and Latino middle-class students has strongly reinforced my view that it is a terrible failure to leave this issue off the table or to assume that class integration (defined by free lunch status, for example) of middle-class and poor blacks would produce a good solution rather than just accelerate out-migration of whites and the black middle class.

Nothing in my teaching and work on housing makes me think that addressing class without race will help much on the problems that we face. New Jersey's Mt. Laurel litigation built more than 30,000 units and almost none of them went to urban minorities. Without something very specific like the Chicago's Gautreaux remedy, the class approach has consistently led to funding white departure and spreading housing segregation for minority families. This was apparent in the low-income homeownership program (Sec. 235) and in the private market voucher-type programs (Sec. 8). You can produce a great deal of housing for the poor and only intensify segregation, confining the black and Latino poor in areas with the kinds of schools that will keep them poor.

A good class-based remedy, just like a strictly limited and targeted voucher plan serving only minority kids in terrible schools, could be a very good thing, but my analysis of both the history of related policies and the total unwillingness of policymakers in any branch of government to make and enforce complex definitions, plus my strong belief that unorganized constituencies of powerless people are consistently treated poorly, makes me believe that such policies would usually be poorly drawn, usually have weak effects, and would not long be able to retain targeted funding for transportation, recruitment and other key elements to make a desegregation plan succeed.

None of this means that we should not try class-based plans where there is a will and no better alternative. I think we should. But it would be very wrong to think, on the basis of existing evidence, that they would be likely to be nearly as good for minority students, and, for social integration, as good as race-based remedies. It might be best considered as a supplement to rather than a replacement for race-targeted remedies.

White Racism: The Core Issue

Theodore M. Shaw

I join Gary Orfield's observations in response to Richard D. Kahlenberg's chapter on socioeconomic school integration. I write to articulate an analysis that may be implicit in Orfield's observations and that is absent or ignored in Kahlenberg's. Both chapters failed to confront the core of the school integration issue, whether it is defined by race or by class: white racism directed at people of African decent.

This contention flies in the face of the prevailing contemporary liberal racial paradigm, which properly eschews the exclusively black-white analysis that has dominated race relations throughout most of American history, and it stands in direct conflict with the undeniable progress achieved within the United States over the last 50 years. Most Americans undoubtedly would subscribe to the central principle of *Brown v. Board of Education*—that government-sponsored racial segregation and discrimination violates the Constitution's equal protection clause and is otherwise morally reprehensible. Non-discrimination principles are irrevocably imbedded in America's normative values in a manner that transcends the originally hypocritical Jeffersonian egalitarian vision. Americans genuinely abhor racial discrimination. Yet they cannot let go of the demon of racism, especially against black people. Thus, the paradox of race in America at the dawn of the 21st Century is segregated integration: The edifice of formal American apartheid has been dismantled, and black Americans have achieved a level of integration their parents could only dream about, yet racial segregation remains an intractable and seemingly permanent characteristic of American life.

As a nation, we honor *Brown v. Board of Education* more in principle than in practice. The days of court-ordered school desegregation appear to be coming to a close. In the end, it seems that enforcement of *Brown* was a process by which school boards that practiced racial segregation were required to achieve a degree of desegregation for a period of time, during which a judicial snapshot would reveal a picture of integration that justified judicial absolution. Once these school districts are declared unitary, the judicial fiction goes, the causal links between past segregation and discriminatory practices and the post-unitary status segregation attributed to residential segregation has been broken. Segregated demographic patterns reflecting new population growth in heavily white suburbs are deemed to be wholly unrelated to pre-unitary status conditions.

The truth about school desegregation in the United States hinges on these two facts: 1) school desegregation, even when successfully accomplished, has been limited in scope and duration by the refusal of the majority of white parents with school-age children to enroll them in public schools with significant black populations; and 2) many, if not most, white parents of school-age children have a level of tolerance for black enrollment in their children's schools beyond which they are unwilling to go, regardless of the economic class of those black students.

Race continues to mean something within the United States. Its meaning is distinct from, even if connected to, the significance of class. Because of a national weariness with issues of race and a misplaced vision of a civil rights struggle with a goal of color-blindness instead of racial justice, even many liberals and progressives are advocating abandonment of race-conscious policies and practices. They are wrong because class-based policies, while worthy of consideration on their own merits, are not guaranteed to reach those impacted by racial discrimination. The majority of the intended beneficiaries of such policies in this country continue to be white, and color-blind, class-conscious policies are not designed to reach black and brown people. And they are wrong because abandonment of race-conscious policies and practices is unjustified, given the historical and continuing significance of race. There is no other issue on the American agenda that we propose to address by not talking about it. While Americans' compulsive denial of historical and current realities of race is so strongly entrenched that the path of least resistance (in Kahlenberg's case, class) is attractive, the abandonment of race-conscious policies is a stunning and unwarranted surrender. We must continue to talk about the significance of race as long as race continues to be significant, and race will not become insignificant simply because we refuse to talk about it.

Socioeconomic school integration is a worthy goal, but it is not a substitute for racial desegregation. Kahlenberg's ten reasons supporting socioeconomic school integration are indisputable; everyone wants good schools and all they bring for their children. For many white parents, good schools are those that are not too black. If we are abandoning the effort to desegregate America's public schools and if we are comfortable in doing so, let's be honest about it. If we are not, let's say what we do and do what we say.

Nothing in our national experience demonstrates that public school racial integration will be accomplished serendipitously.

Class Cannot Be a Substitute for Race

Makani Themba-Nixon

Richard Kahlenberg's might actually be the smart alternative to racial integration he asserts it is if it weren't for one troublesome thing—racism. While not repeating Gary Orfield's fine critique of the piece, let me say that Kahlenberg appears to be unaware that racism is more than low income or limited access, that class cannot be a substitute for race. Additionally, the "evidence" he submits to support his argument has serious flaws.

Race and class are certainly both important factors in education policy, but there are plenty of issues to be dealt with outside of the space where the two intersect. Teacher expectations, fair student treatment, student sense of belonging, the presence of teachers of color, and culturally appropriate, culturally relevant instruction are all important elements of quality education that cannot be addressed without race-conscious remedies. The inarguable fact is that we can never hope to achieve quality education for all without addressing racism. Socioeconomic integration "by choice" is not only a poor substitute for addressing racism, it is an inadequate approach to addressing economic inequities.

Kahlenberg is partially correct when he writes that the presence of a core of middle-class families acting as advocates is the "single most powerful predictor of a good education." Aside from the fact that there is no single, most powerful predictor of a good education, broad political will to do what's necessary is critical to creating good schools. However, white middle-class families (and most certainly rich families) don't have to advocate as hard or as consistently for decent education as people of color have to. It is assumed that white middle-class children are deserving of quality education, and that their parents will make a fuss if they don't get one whether they advocate or not. People of color, regardless of class, must often work tirelessly for even substandard education. They are the folk who crowd the school board meetings and plea for books instead of worksheets, classrooms with light fixtures, and teachers who will treat their children fairly. Clearly, if advocacy alone is what gets a kid a good education, there would be a lot more highly educated poor kids of color and many more neglected middle-class students.

Race not only plays a factor in the efficacy and necessity of advocacy, it often determines the kind of information parents receive about their children's education so they know what they should advocate about. Parents of color are less likely to be formally engaged by teachers and less likely to be considered partners or peers in the educational process. Although part of the problem is that poorer schools often lack the infrastructure to provide formal, ongoing feedback on student progress beyond minimum district requirements, race has long been established as a factor in communication challenges between teachers and parents of color, regardless of class.

Adequate funding, well-trained teachers, involved parents, high expectations and modern equipment are among the necessary elements of a quality education. Who has these resources and why isn't limited to education policy. It is part and parcel of the sociopolitical context that created the inequities in the first place. Poorer schools have greater needs. There are more kids requiring remedial education, special education and other services. Before one even gets to administrative "bloat" (administrative abuse is not limited to high-poverty schools as Kahlenberg suggests), high-poverty schools' administrative infrastructures are necessarily larger and salaries are often higher because many of these schools are in urban centers where it costs more to do business. Any school that significantly increases its share of "high maintenance" students will have to either increase its funding to keep up or fall woefully behind. That is the unavoidable reality that has dogged previous experiments with socioeconomic integration as well as racial integration—few parents with a choice want to see their school's resources stretched between their kids and the children they perceive as "the troubled others." All of which demonstrates the underlying folly of assuming that somehow socioeconomic integration can happen without the same political fallout of racial integration.

The problems with Kahlenberg's argument are only compounded by his view that such integration should be accomplished by "choice." All over the country, choice programs are creating greater inequities between and *within* schools. In Roanoke, Virginia, where my four children attended school for three years, magnet programs developed priority slots for white students and reorganized special academic programs so that program participants had little contact with the school's "regular students." Addison Middle School's Challenge Program, for example, takes white kids regardless of their academic performance. Challenge students have their own staircase, corridor and section in the cafeteria. Addison is not alone. School districts all over the country are touting such measures in order to assuage parent concerns about student "safety" at urban schools. Although these magnet programs seem to create integrated schools, they are instead creating two separate but unequal schools within a school that focus the most resources on students with the least need. In fact, inequality at magnet schools has become such an issue that a number of civil rights groups have petitioned the federal government to investigate.

"Good schools" and "bad schools" are both products of a complicated mix in which racism and, more accurately, white privilege plays a major role. As evident throughout the excellent collection *In Pursuit of a Dream Deferred: Linking Housing and Education Policy* (eds. powell, Kearney & Kay), it's impossible to consider any kind of school integration looking at school policy alone.

Institutionalized white privilege and racism undermine quality education. The policies designed to maintain these systems of privilege and oppression serve to segregate people geographically and culturally in order to reserve the best resources for whites. Of course, there are some people of color who manage to benefit under this system and some whites who don't, but it's clear that the intention and outcomes of these policies are racially biased, and this bias must be remedied. Due to the over-concentration of poverty in communities of color as a result of white privilege, there are certainly benefits to be gained by interventions that seek to address class inequities. However, Kahlenberg's proposal seeks to ignore race *and* withdraw the power of law from efforts to address class. Both are wrongheaded and ignore the basic problem.

Poor schools are poor because they have inadequate resources to address the challenges they face—and racism greatly compounds these challenges. Affluent schools are better because they have more resources and fewer challenges—and white privilege greatly enhances their resources. The real problem is marshalling the political will to address the obvious. These are "only" poor kids of color, and that, sadly, is the point.

It Won't Work

john a. powell

There has been a long and largely unproductive debate in this country about the primacy of racial subordination or class to address our society's growing inequality. Over the last several years, a growing number of scholars have persuasively demonstrated that these two hierarchical structures in our society are powerfully related, but nonetheless differ. Addressing the problem of class isolation in schools is certainly a necessary and important task, but it is only a partial and weak response to racial segregation. While it is true that racial hierarchy has socioeconomic dimensions, it cannot simply be reduced to class and cannot be addressed by only using class. Both for analytical and pragmatic reasons, race must be central to any serious effort to confront racism.

It is a reflexive move within the dominant society to try to avoid discussions about race or racism. To the limited extent that we are willing to talk about racism, we are likely to find it a psychological event where the perpetrator is just as likely to be a racial minority holding negative stereotypes about innocent whites as the other way around. Never mind that racism was called into being to create a system of white superiority that is very much reflected in our institutions and structures. This system was not and could not have been put together just by the individual private acts of whites. Racism in our country has largely been and is about white superiority and white supremacy that is reflected in the creation and distribution of resources.

By locating racism in our structures and institutions, I am not suggesting that whites and people of color do not harbor negative racial thoughts. What I am suggesting is that our institutions and structures have produced and reflect white hierarchy. This expression of white superiority (and conversely, minority inferiority) that is visited on nonwhites is not something that is largely dependent on the expressed or proven intention of any individual.

The creation and maintenance of the modern suburbs provide an example of this structural racial hierarchy. There are a number of reasons why whites may live in the suburbs that are not explicitly anti-nonwhite. But nonwhites, and particularly blacks, were excluded from choosing the 'burbs. New home, good school, clean environment away from the city were available only to white Americans. These structures were put in place, funded and protected against minority intrusion by the government. When we talk about the impossibility of changing the pattern of spatial segregation, the obvious question is why. Whites who took advantage of government's arrangement may not be guilty of harboring racial animus, but they still are the beneficiaries of a system of white supremacy. Even if they are not guilty, they certainly are not "innocent," as Justice Powell and others have insisted. We need to move beyond the guilt and innocence paradigm and begin to challenge racism on a deeper, institutional level.

In one of the most important cases in United States history, *Dred Scott*, Chief Justice Taney stated that no blacks, slave or free, had any right protected by the Constitution. He went on to assert that blacks only had the rights that whites were willing to give them. Many historians have stated that *Dred Scott* helped push the country into the Civil War. After the Civil War and passage of the Civil War Amendments, the Supreme Court in *Plessy v. Ferguson* upheld the doctrine of separate but equal, holding that isolating blacks did not violate the Constitution's Equal Protection Clause.

What both of these cases represent is that blacks and other minorities were not recognized as full citizens, and that their rights can be abbreviated in the interest of whites. This is what racial segregation meant in 1896, and that is what it means today.

In reading these cases, the Court does not discuss socioeconomic status. But this is wrong on a number of counts. Racial hierarchy cannot be either adequately explained or corrected by income alone, and class is not just income. The ideology of white supremacy was not reducible to class in *Plessy* or *Dred Scott*, and it is not reducible to class now. While it is true that one of the consequences of a system of white supremacy is to depress the economic wealth and class status of blacks and others, it was never a system where all blacks were necessarily poorer than all whites, based on a single indicator. Consider voting: It did not matter how much wealth a black had in Mississippi. For much of this country's history, this person could not vote, regardless of his or her income resources. Racial profiling is another poignant example of racial exclusion not explained by class. Even if one were to pick a single economic indicator, wealth is a much better indicator of disparity than income, as demonstrated by Melvin

Oliver and Thomas Shapiro in *Black Wealth/White Wealth*. The correlation of wealth and access with opportunity in education and other areas is much stronger than free and reduced lunch or income. While both income and free and reduced lunch tell us something, they both understate the persistent inequality between whites and nonwhites.

The Nobel Prize-winning economist Amartya Sen observes that in considering equity, one must look not just at resources, but the ability to translate those resources into utilities. In a system where opportunity is distorted by discrimination, the disfavored groups' ability to translate economic resources into opportunity will be limited. What this means is that if there is discrimination against blacks in, for example, mortgage lending or purchasing a car, blacks will pay more for a mortgage or a car than whites. This is a subordination tax levied against blacks that discounts their resources.

These are just a few examples of the limitations of using class to address issues of race. In the school context, Federal Judge Robert Carter observed that segregation is only the symptom of the disease of white supremacy. I maintain that neither the disease nor the symptom can be adequately treated by simply using class or free and reduced lunch to overcome the racial isolation of students. There are a number of reasons for this. First of all, a strategy of class integration will not be effective in addressing the racial isolation, and even where physical isolation is reduced, this will not address the problem of white supremacy and move us to true integration.

Empirical evidence backs up these claims. There have been a number of efforts to address racial subordination and segregation by simply folding them into a class response. Virtually all of them have failed, and some of them have caused greater racial isolation.

Justice O'Connor in *The City of Richmond v. Crowson* suggested that it would be better to use class rather than race for "set-aside" contracts in the construction industry. However, the evidence is clear that while it may benefit poor whites, this approach does not address the problem of the lack of minority contractors. It is important to note the O'Connor and other conservative Justices are not trying to address the problem set out by Judge Carter. They have largely rejected the claim that racism remains a serious problem in our society and are in the business of demanding greater and greater proof. Instead, they assert that racial classification is the evil that must be avoided, not racial hierarchy.

In New Jersey, the state Supreme Court took a housing segregation case that was largely about racial discrimination and turned it into a case about class. In the most far-reaching housing case dealing with low-income residents, the Court ordered the entire state to provide a fair share of low-income housing. About 25,000 housing units have been created under this plan. However, it has been administered in such a way as to actually *increase* the racial segregation of minorities in New Jersey. When we think about it, it is clear: Middle-class whites' reluctance to live with poor whites is not nearly as strong as their reluctance to live with blacks. Given the choice between the two, you get the results in New

Jersey. It is also instructive that many advocates argued that because minorities were over-represented in the pool of low-income tenants, they would receive the largest benefit from a class-based approach. They wrongly assumed there were no other factors that would continue to disadvantage minorities or the ingenuity of whites to find creative ways to exclude people of color. In essence, they believed that the present dynamic of racial subordination would be reduced to class.

To try to reduce racial subordination to a single cause has repeatedly and consistently failed. The current conservative Supreme Court has limited racial discrimination in education to the intentional acts of a school board. They have refused in most cases to look at housing or the drawing of jurisdictional boundaries. They have treated housing and municipal segregation as "nature" and beyond the scope of consideration for addressing discrimination in schools. A growing number of commentators have recognized the relationship between concentrated poverty neighborhoods and high poverty rates in school. But even some of these have not examined why 75% of those living in high-poverty neighborhoods are minorities. Poor whites in urban areas are much more likely to live in white middle-class neighborhoods. We sort people by both race and class. And although most commentators recognize that blacks and other minorities are over-represented in the low-income and low-wealth categories, they fail to tie this sorting process to race and class. But as Oliver and Shapiro remind us, this process is both the consequence and the product of racialized wealth. Once this system is in place, it does not require racial animus to reproduce itself.

According to Professor George Lipsitz, there is ambivalence in America. We are willing and even want to pursue racial justice in our society but only to the extent that whites' expectation of privilege and hierarchy is not disrupted. He calls this "the possessive investment in whiteness." But in order to achieve racial justice, the very thing that is called for is disruption of this expectation. Lipsitz looks at examples of major civil rights laws, from education to housing to employment, and asserts that each set of laws as policies was designed to create some accommodation without dis-establishing the material and cultural privileges associated with whiteness. In the school context, we see the Court narrowing the scope of *Brown* to achieve this ambivalent balance. We can promise minorities desegregated schools, not to be confused with integrated schools, while maintaining the reality of racially segregated schools in response to whites' fears all across the country.

If this is accurate, why do people keep pushing class in our capitalist society to address the problem of racism and white supremacy? It may be that some really believe it will work. Others clearly know that it will not, but it gives the appearance of doing something while avoiding the issue. For the latter, group, it is what some theorists have called "whitespeak." It is another iteration of the ambivalence noted above, while maintaining white privilege. So, we can have fair housing laws as long as they allow for the continuation of white enclaves. And we can have judicial repudiation of segregated schools as long as we have a system of *de facto* segregation. There is an attempt to explain these segregation patterns in neutral sounding terms like "private choice" and "the market." Anything but racial discrimination. For those who follow the jurisprudence of the Supreme Court in education and housing law, it is clear that the Court has decided to accommodate neo-segregationists in the school and housing context. While doing so, the Court invites us to consider class after it has already found that there is very little judicial remedy for class-based inequalities.

There are many important issues raised in the call to use class as a surrogate for racial integration. From a pragmatic standpoint, I have argued, based on prior examples, that it will not work. This need not disturb us unless we believe that racial integration remains an important goal. Unfortunately, we do not have a clear concept of what is meant by integration. At times, we seem to confuse integration with either desegregation or assimilation. Although Kahlenberg tells us that he supports racially integrated schools, he does not tell us why. All the reasons he lists for supporting integrated schools are about class and not about race. He cites Justice Thomas' rhetorical question as to why it is necessary for black and white children to be together to learn. The only answer he suggests is class, not race. Of course, the need for students to be together or (more accurately) not separated varies in importance, depending on what we think students are to learn and what they are learning by the separation. Should we then be satisfied if we had economically integrated schools that remained racially segregated?

Dr. King understood integration to mean more than simply having students in the same classroom. Unlike many detractors of integration, he understood that integration is not assimilation or desegregation:

> We do not have to look very far to see the pernicious effects of a de-segregated society that is not integrated. It leads to "physical proximity without spiritual affinity." It gives us a society where men are physically desegregated and spiritually segregated, where elbows are together and hearts are apart. It gives us spatial togetherness and spiritual apartness. It leaves us with a stagnant equality of sameness rather than a constructive equality of oneness.

And as Gordon W. Allport prefigured in his 1950s book *The Nature of Prejudice,* the nature of contact between students and the surrounding environment matters greatly in terms of whether the school is truly integrated or has just succeeded in putting bodies next to each other.

True integration embraces a multicultural conception of social interaction. Social interaction is constitutive of the individual and the collective identity of the community. Assimilation envisions the absorption of minorities into the mainstream. Integration envisions the transformations of the mainstream. Thus, real integration is measured by the transformations of institutions, communities and individuals. Real integration involves fundamental change, among whites, blacks and other minorities as people and communities. Rather than Euro-centric or Afro-centric education, integration necessarily implies a curriculum that respects and values cultural difference, while building community. It is about integrating the mind and heart. In our society, it is about dis-establishing white supremacy.

A truly integrated education is not just about putting students together, as important as this might be. It is about building, if not a beloved community, at least a democratic community. As John Dewey suggests, the primary role of education is not about test scores or access to employment, even though both can be important. Fundamentally, it is about citizenship. The problem that persists in this country is that we have a racialized concept of who belongs, based on white superiority, that undermines our democratic community.

I have already touched on many complicated issues. But I want to at least raise one more: Justice Scalia, in some of his opinions, has rhetorically asked the question, *"What is race?"* He suggests that it is socially-constructed and not biologically real. But for him and for many others, this means that we should not discuss race, and that racial categories are problematic and must be avoided. There is a lot of confusion in this popular and increasingly judicial position.

If race is socially constructed, it does not follow that it is not real. Instead, it means that it gains its reality and significance from our social practices and arrangements. How can whites claim that race does not exist and yet assert the desire to be around whites? Glenn Loury has suggested that if race is socially constructed, then so are any disparities that exist between the races. The significance of race will only change when these disparities in education, income, housing and life opportunities cease to exist. This is a social, not individual, project.

The current project to avoid race is not a project to address white superiority, but is instead likely to entrench it. Our country's history has been about racial hierarchy. This system of hierarchy is a web constructed by society. If it is to be deconstructed, we must avoid reducing it to a single thread. Racial subordination cannot be addressed by avoiding race and racism, nor can we sneak through the agenda of racial justice under the cover of class. I am ready to sign on to a struggle to reduce poverty and class inequities in our society, but I am not prepared to endorse a position that asserts we will only embrace racial justice after we have become a classless society. That position is not racial progress but the depth of our attachment to racial hierarchy.

Both

S.M. Miller

After reading Kahlenberg and Orfield, my reaction is: You are both right!

Clearly, judicial decisions continue to undercut school racial integration. The likelihood is that racial integration will fade away as an objective and practice of most schools systems. Moreover, it hasn't worked very effectively, as shown in Gary Orfield's data on the recent increase in school segregation. We can't go on as before.

Class integration has a nice ring to it, but can it work? Residential segregation is high, as Orfield points out. Won't busing and other devices be needed to bring about class integration in schools? Will such devices be politically or juridically acceptable? Doubtful. Could great pools of money attract school systems to pursue economic integration? Possibly. That money would have to come from the federal government, as local and state tax revenues are inadequate. Unlikely.

What is needed are new legal, political and organizational innovations to promote integration. Of course. But what might they be? Human Rights? Segregation (and low-quality schools) as deprivation of property or social capital? New ways of organizing schools? New legal and political strategies and principles are needed. What organizations are developing them?

A major issue is how to improve schools with high racial-ethnic populations that are not integrated, while pushing to integrate racially within schools. We need to deal with the present while trying to shape the future.

Kahlenberg has the virtue of facing the issue of declining pressure for school racial integration. His solution would be most difficult. I am not aware— my ignorance?—of steps toward racial integration that seem to have judicial, political and organizational possibilities.

The 2005 articles on "class" in the *New York Times* and the *Wall Street Journal* highlight economic, social and cultural divides in the USA. Perhaps we are emerging into a political discussion space where issues of class differences, discrimination and obstacles can be raised without the responding thunder of an un-American, divisive "class conflict" accusation.

Class, race and gender might again gain prominence and offer hope. As in so many arenas, those seeking change have to think anew, not content with old solutions that are stymied or outworn. To think anew is what now is needed.

The US and the Republican Party changed enormously in the last 40 years. Progressives and the Democratic Party have not faced, responded to, nor built on or away from these changes. We have a lot of catching up to do, especially in the battle over ideas, direction and strategy. Racial and class school segregation is a key area to rethink.

Race-Conscious Measures Remain Available

Thomas J. Henderson

Richard Kahlenberg suggests that the economic integration of our public schools —or, more specifically, their transformation into "majority middle-class" schools—is both the necessary and achievable response to our society's inability, and unwillingness, to achieve the racial desegregation of its schools and its housing patterns. Social science research demonstrates that economic integration is desirable and could yield substantial educational benefits. However, the notion that America's congenital malady of racial discrimination can be cured by focusing instead on income is ill-conceived, at best, and troubling. The proposition that economic integration is widely accepted and, therefore, substantially more feasible than racial integration is contradicted by our national experience.

The economic integration of schools *can* be helpful, for many of the reasons listed in Kahlenberg's chapter. However, essentially all of the benefits that are predicted to flow from the integration of middle-class and poor students will be realized only if middle-class and poorer students are afforded the same educational programs and resources *within* the school, i.e., receive the same challenging instruction, in the same "meaty curriculum," with the same teachers and the same genuine expectations that all students can achieve and progress at high levels. Unfortunately, research documents that this is not how schools are organized. Even within mixed-income schools (and almost all schools have some income heterogeneity), poorer students (together with most African-American and Latino students) are placed in separate lower-level, non-academic classes, with instruction and expectations based on negative stereotypical assumptions. Thus, creating school populations that are economically integrated alone will not solve the problem Kahlenberg recognizes: "that the separation of poor and middle-class children is the fountainhead of a host of related inequalities of educational opportunity."

Similarly, the proposition that we can solve our seemingly intractable problems of racial segregation and inequality by attempting to change the subject from race to class is at least naive. Fulfilling the unrealized promise of *Brown v. Board of Education* will not be furthered by submerging, or attempting to deflect public attention away from, race.

Although it is possible that there is relatively less support for desegregation now than 30 years ago, current support should not be underestimated, nor the capacity for increased support in response to appropriate and determined efforts. As to the very real problem of an unsympathetic judiciary, we must recall that, except in the face of the most egregious forms of discrimination or resistance, courts rarely have been generous in affording remedies for racial discrimination. Resort to the courts should not be abandoned simply because they may be relatively unsympathetic. If that course had been followed in the past, *Brown* would never have been decided. Instead, both the courts and the public need to be further informed as to the inequities and larger effects of segregation and of needed remedial efforts.

As to the courts, concerted effort to define more fully and demonstrate the inequalities *Brown* held were inherent in segregation is one available avenue. The "separate but equal" doctrine of *Plessy v. Ferguson* was premised on the profoundly disingenuous assumption that racial segregation in America carried with it no harm. When *Brown* overruled *Plessy*, the premise was reversed—the harms associated with segregation were not only assumed, but recognized as "inherent." Thus, implementing *Brown* required no further examination and identification of the particular injuries and inequalities associated with segregation and discrimination. At this point, fuller analysis and persuasive illustration of the manner in which the organization and delivery of public education discriminates against racial minorities, and the role of government in maintaining and re-creating segregation and inequality, can serve to re-orient and more fully define unlawful conditions and the remedies needed to achieve racial equality.

Race-conscious measures remain available as remedies for discrimination. Demonstrating the relationships between existing inequalities and governmental policies and actions—past and present—will distinguish the harms associated with various forms of governmental discrimination and segregation from the curious category of "general societal discrimination" that the Supreme Court has held to be beyond the reach of the courts. Further social science and public policy research and other evidence revealing the harms associated with racial segregation and inequality must be developed, articulated and presented to educators, policymakers and the courts.

As to public and political support for efforts to secure real racial equality, both have come only as the hard-won result of concerted efforts to inform the public and the political process and appeal to the enduring principles of equality to which the nation aspires. Our society is all too inclined to amnesia regarding the ugly and uncomfortable truth of slavery and of the calculated discrimination pervading all aspects of society that followed in its wake and persists into the present. This, together with the formal legal, if often superficial, equality that has been established leads Americans to the assumption that racial discrimination and its effects have been eliminated. The needed response is not to abandon express efforts to eliminate racial segregation and discrimination by focusing instead on class. Progress is made only through determined efforts to expose discrimination and promote understanding of its effects, and to insist that our society and government—including in the selection of judges—act to address them.

Also, the suggestion that class-based integration enjoys wide support and is therefore achievable is belied by current conditions and experience. Kahlenberg holds up as his model "one type of successful school that Americans have been able to replicate time and time again...those in which a majority of the students are middle-class." Ironically, those majority middle-class schools are largely the product of economic as well as racial segregation in housing patterns that has created isolated middle-class suburban districts or middle-class enclaves within cities. Schools are a powerful factor in housing choice, and middle-class families have gone to great lengths and substantial expense to isolate themselves in relatively homogeneous middle-class communities removed from schools with a significant presence of poorer students.

In addition, demographically, race and class are nearly impossible to separate. Indeed, this is a major premise of Kahlenberg's proposal: "Because much of the nation's concentration of poverty is the result of racial discrimination in housing, any plan to reduce economic isolation will produce, as a positive byproduct, a fair measure of racial integration." It is simply unrealistic to presume that integrating poor children into middle-class schools will be perceived as anything different than integrating by race. When HUD's "Moving to Opportunity" program proposed to move a modest number of individual residents of predominately African-American Baltimore public housing into individual market-rate units across the suburbs, the outcry led otherwise liberal members of Congress to shut the program down.

Moreover, because residential racial segregation is related to economic segregation, present barriers to racial desegregation apply as well to economic integration. Where large numbers of poor and minority students are isolated in urban school districts, and middle-class and white students are isolated in suburban districts, even the redistribution of students with different incomes to different schools within their respective districts will not achieve appreciable economic or racial integration. Both school district boundaries and the distances from which these communities are removed from each other represent formidable barriers to integration.

In the end, housing segregation and the organization and financing of public education are nearly insurmountable obstacles to racially and economically integrated schools. Real efforts are needed to desegregate our nation's housing, led by the federal and state governments that are so extensively involved in housing and lending markets. As well, characteristics of good schools, such as those in Kahlenberg's list, and the economic and racial integration he advocates, should guide a re-examination and restructuring of public education. Too often, the structure and delivery of public education serve unfairly to stratify children, isolating poor and minority students from their middle-class and white peers, and apportioning grossly unequal resources, curricula, instruction and expectations. Separate and unequal has been unconstitutional at least since *Plessy* and has always been unjust. Public education should be redesigned to promote the equitable and effective development of all children, consistent with our mutual interest and democratic values. Research, policy initiatives and advocacy should be directed to developing and executing structural reforms to achieve truly democratic forms of public education.

Response

Richard D. Kahlenberg

The responses to my chapter, "Socioeconomic School Integration," make a number of important points that are themselves deserving of a reply. I group my comments around six themes:

1. Using Race in K-12 School Integration vs. Higher Education Affirmative Action

In the context of K-12 schooling, I argue for "leading" with socioeconomic integration because I think it is the central determinant of quality education. Having said that, I also believe, where it is legally permissible, that it is appropriate for school districts to consider race in student assignment. I think the US Supreme Court is likely to strike down the use of race in student assignment in the very near future—except where race is used to remedy the vestiges of *de jure* segregation—but until it does, I believe school districts in judicial circuits that continue to allow the use of race should do so. In the context of K-12 education, when Gary Orfield says class should be "a supplement to rather than a replacement for" race, I agree.

The K-12 situation can be distinguished from affirmative action at selective institutions of higher education (where I do think class should replace considerations of race), because attending a non-selective elementary or secondary school doesn't raise issues of "merit." No student can be considered to have "earned" his or her way into a non-selective K-12 institution; they are democratic institutions open to all. (The flip side is that because no testing is involved in non-selective primary and secondary education, the "racial dividend" of economic integration—the degree to which economic integration produces racial integration—will be greater in the K-12 context than in the higher education context.)

2. Social vs. Academic Reasons for Integration

Broadly speaking, there are two sets of reasons to favor integrated schools: academic (integration will raise student achievement) and societal (integration will make students better citizens and more tolerant individuals and make the country more unified). In my chapter, I emphasized the first objective, raising academic achievement, which is mostly a matter of integrating by class. There is little reason to think blacks need to sit next to whites in order to learn, but there is ample reason to think low-income students of all races will benefit from a middle-class school environment. Take a few of the ten points I raised in my original chapter: Schools do better when parents serve as powerful advocates for improvements. Who is likely to be better at getting school needs met: an African-American lawyer or a white waitress? Studies find that resources flow not by race but by class. According to the US Department of Education's *Condition of Education 1998,* in the 1993-94 school year, high-income districts expended $7,027 per pupil, compared to $5,634 for low-income districts. But districts with high percentages of minority students actually spent somewhat more than districts with low percentages ($6,847 vs. $6,347). To take another example, highly motivated peers have a positive influence on any given child's education. Conservatives make a big deal out of the finding that some low-income African Americans deride achievement as "acting white," but according to Philip Cook and Jens Ludwig's national study, included in the 1998 Brookings volume, *The Black-White Test Score Gap,* acting white has more to do with class than race. Controlling for class, they found that blacks do not cut classes, miss school or complete fewer homework assignments than whites.

(Of course, minority students and parents are more likely to be low-income —more likely to be waitresses than lawyers. Moreover, as john powell notes, "75% of those living in high-poverty neighborhoods are minorities." That's precisely why economic integration will produce a fair amount of racial integration.)

john powell's commentary is right to highlight the larger societal issue: that education is more than about test scores—it's about citizenship, too. In my 2001 book *All Together Now: Creating Middle-Class Schools Through Public School Choice* (Brookings), I discuss the important benefits of both racial and economic integration in teaching students the meaning of democracy. This is all the more relevant after September 11th. Integration by race is essential if we want to teach tolerance; anyone who thinks white racism is a thing of the past is demented. I agree with Theodore Shaw that race continues to have meaning that "is distinct from, even if connected to, the significance of class" and with powell that "integration envisions the transformations of the mainstream."

3. Segregation Between Schools vs. Segregation Within Schools

Thomas Henderson notes the goals of integration may be defeated if integrated school buildings are re-segregated by classroom. Gary Orfield also raises the issue that "children are often placed in lower-track classes, based on racial assumptions by counselors and teachers."

Likewise, Makani Themba-Nixon points out that magnet schools can sometimes be segregated, so that certain students have "their own staircase, corridor and section in the cafeteria." In *All Together Now,* I spend a fair amount of space addressing the complicated issue of ability grouping and tracking within integrated schools. I am strongly opposed to separate magnet programs within larger schools, and I believe tracking must be tempered by equity considerations. I'm also strongly supportive of using Title VI of the 1964 Civil Rights Act to ensure that ability grouping practices that have a disparate impact on minority students must be fully justified as educationally valid.

4. Politics vs. The Law

I agree with the critique that says socioeconomic integration is politically difficult to accomplish, though I think it's marginally less difficult than racial integration and that creative use of public school choice can overcome much of the opposition to forced "busing." Gary Orfield cites the example of the failed effort to promote socioeconomic integration in Wausau, Wisconsin as evidence of the difficulty of achieving the goal. In fact, Wausau's unsuccessful effort coupled integration by race and class; and its failure is contrasted to a contemporaneous success in nearby La Crosse, Wisconsin, where a straight socioeconomic integration plan was adopted and remains in place. Teachers proved crucial to the political success of that program and will be important allies in the political fight for economic school integration.

Having said that, it's also important to look at the courts to promote integration. Orfield claims that socioeconomic integration "does not have any enforceable basis in law," while Themba-Nixon contends I would "withdraw the power of law from the efforts to address class." In fact, I agree with S.M. Miller that we should seek new legal devices to promote integration. While there is no federal constitutional right to economically integrated schools, there is some intriguing state law that could be used to fashion an argument for socioeconomic integration on a state-by-state basis. In roughly half the states, state supreme courts have found that state constitutions require either equal educational opportunity or an adequate education. This is an affirmative right that has been interpreted to require changes in school financing within states, across district lines. But if finances are but one of ten factors important to getting an equal education (as outlined in my chapter), then state constitutions may be read to require that poverty concentrations be addressed. The Connecticut Supreme Court came close to saying that. I also very much like Thomas Henderson's suggestion that new efforts should be made to enforce *Brown* by pointing to documented harm that comes from segregation, now that courts no longer seem to believe those harms are "inherent."

5. Choice vs. Coercion

I agree with Themba-Nixon that choice in education by itself won't produce integration, even though it theoretically frees us from school assignment that reflects housing segregation. School vouchers will make things worse. And even public school choice must be "controlled choice"—choice conditioned on the promotion of integration. Ideally, choice should take place across district lines, as Henderson notes. Having said that, even integrating the suburbs would be important. While powell is correct to say that in the past "blacks were excluded from choosing the 'burbs," today, 75% of African Americans in the Washington, DC area live in the suburbs. In Atlanta, the figure is 78%.

6. Housing Remedies vs. School Remedies

I also agree with powell and Henderson that in addition to school integration, we must address the larger issue of housing segregation. But we must also acknowledge that housing integration is marginally more difficult to accomplish. Philosophically, middle-class Americans appear more willing to redistribute opportunity (education) than results (housing); and they may be more willing to send their children to integrated schools than to live next door to low-income families.

Conclusion

I will close where I began my chapter, in observing that anyone who cares about integration at all—by race or class—is up against a powerful political consensus that what matters is quality, not integration. Discussions about the relative salience of race and class are important, but it is significant that all seven of us agree that school integration—by race and class—will make our country and our people stronger. I happen to believe that for a variety of reasons, class is the central inequality; while my six colleagues argue that race is prior. Either way, the law can't be ignored, which is why a number of progressive communities that have strongly supported racial integration—from San Francisco, to Charlotte, to Cambridge—are looking at the socioeconomic alternative. What we have been doing hasn't taken us far enough; we have to explore new alternatives.

Chapter 35

Schools and the Achievement Gap: A Symposium

Richard Rothstein summarized for P&R *the argument in his 2005 book* Class and Schools, *following which we asked a wide range of education experts to provide comments.*

Even the Best Schools Can't Close the Race Achievement Gap

Richard Rothstein

The achievement gap between poor and middle-class, black and white children is an educational challenge, but we prevent ourselves from solving it because of a commonplace belief that poverty and race can't "cause" low achievement and that therefore schools must be failing to teach disadvantaged children adequately. After all, we see many highly successful students from lower-class backgrounds. Their success seems to prove that social class cannot be what impedes most disadvantaged students.

Yet the success of some lower-class students proves nothing about schools' power to close the achievement gap. There is a distribution of achievement in every social group. These distributions overlap. While average achievement of low-income students is below average achievement of middle-class students, there are always some middle-class students who achieve below typical low-income levels. Some low-income students achieve above typical middle-class levels. "Demography is not destiny," but students' family characteristics are a powerful influence on their relative *average* achievement, even in the best of schools.

Widely repeated accounts of schools that somehow elicit consistently high achievement from lower-class children almost always turn out, upon examination, to be flawed. In some cases, "schools that beat the odds" are highly selective, enrolling only the most able or most motivated lower-class children. Some are not truly lower-class schools—for example, schools enrolling children who qualify for subsidized lunches because their parents are poorly paid but highly educated. Some schools "succeed" with lower-class children by defining high achievement at such a low level that all students can reach it, despite big gaps that remain at higher levels. And some schools' successes are statistical flukes—their high test scores last for only one year, in only one grade and in only one subject.

While the idea that "if some children can defy the demographic odds, all can" seems plausible, it reflects a reasoning whose naiveté we easily recognize in other policy areas. In human affairs, where multiple causation is typical, causes are not disproved by exceptions. Tobacco firms once claimed that smoking does not cause cancer because we all know people who smoked without getting cancer. We now consider such reasoning specious. We understand that because no single cause is rigidly deterministic, some people can smoke without harm, but we also understand that, on average, smoking is dangerous. Yet despite such understanding, quite sophisticated people often proclaim that success of some poor children proves that social disadvantage does not cause low achievement.

Social Class and Learning

Partly, our confusion stems from failing to examine the concrete ways that social class actually affects learning. Describing these may help to make their influence more obvious.

Overall, lower-income children are in poorer health, and poor health depresses student achievement, no matter how effective a school may be. Low-income children have poorer vision, partly because of prenatal conditions, partly because, even as toddlers, they watch too much television both at home and in low-quality day care settings, so their eyes are more poorly trained. Trying to read, their eyes may wander or have difficulty tracking print or focusing. A good part of the over-identification of learning disabilities for lower-class children is probably attributable simply to undiagnosed vision problems for which therapy is available and for which special education placement should be unnecessary.

Lower-class children have poorer oral hygiene, more lead poisoning, more asthma, poorer nutrition, less adequate pediatric care, more exposure to smoke, and a host of other health problems—on average. Because, for example, lower-class children typically have less adequate dental care, they are more likely to have toothaches and resulting discomfort that affects concentration.

Because low-income children are more likely to live in communities where landlords use high-sulfur home heating oil, and where diesel trucks frequently pass en route to industrial and commercial sites, such children are more likely to suffer from asthma, leading to more absences from school and drowsiness (from lying awake wheezing at night) when present. Recent surveys of black children in Chicago and in New York City's Harlem community found one of every four children suffering from asthma, a rate six times as great as that for all children. Asthma is now the single biggest cause of chronic school absence.

Because primary care physicians are few in low-income communities (the physician to population ratio is less than a third the rate in middle-class communities), disadvantaged children (even those with health insurance) are also more likely to miss school for relatively minor problems, like common ear infections, for which middle-class children are treated promptly. If in attendance, children with earaches have more difficulty paying attention.

Each of these well-documented social class differences in health is likely to have a palpable effect on academic achievement. The influence of each may be small, but combined, the influence of all is probably huge.

The growing unaffordability of adequate housing for low-income families also affects achievement—children whose families have difficulty finding stable housing are more likely to be mobile, and student mobility is an important cause of failing student performance. A 1994 government report found that 30% of the poorest children had attended at least three different schools by third grade, while only 10% of middle-class children did so. Blacks were more than twice as likely as whites to change schools this much. It is hard to imagine how teachers, no matter how well trained, can be as effective for children who move in and out of their classrooms.

Differences in wealth are also likely to affect achievement, but these are usually overlooked because most analysts focus only on annual family income to indicate disadvantage. This makes it hard to understand why black students, on average, score lower than whites whose family incomes are the same. It is easier to understand this pattern when we recognize that children can have similar family incomes but be of different economic classes: Black families with low income in any year are likely to have been poor for longer than white families with similar income in that year. White families are likely to own far more assets that support their children's achievement than are black families at the same income level, partly because black middle-class parents are more likely to be the first generation in their families to have middle-class status. Although median black family income is now nearly two-thirds of white income, black family assets are still only 12% of whites'. This difference means that, among white and black families with the same middle-class incomes, the whites are more likely to have savings for college. This makes white children's college aspirations more practical, and therefore more commonplace.

Child-Rearing/Personality Traits

Social class differences however, amount to more than these quantifiable differences in health, housing, income and assets. There are powerful social class differences in child-rearing habits and personality traits, and these too cause average differences in academic achievement by social class.

Consider how parents of different social classes tend to raise children. Young children of more educated parents are read to more consistently, and are encouraged to read more by themselves when they are older. Most children whose parents have college degrees are read to daily before they begin kindergarten; few children whose parents have only a high school diploma or less benefit from daily reading. White children are more likely than blacks to be read to in pre-kindergarten years.

A five-year-old who enters school recognizing some words and who has turned pages of many stories will be easier to teach than one who has rarely held a book. The latter can be taught, but the child with a stronger home literacy background will typically post higher scores on reading tests than one for whom book reading is unfamiliar—even if both children benefit from high expectations and effective teaching. So, the achievement gap begins.

If a society with such differences wants children, irrespective of social class, to have the same chance to achieve academic goals, it should find ways to help lower-class children enter school having the same familiarity with books as middle-class children have. This requires re-thinking the institutional settings in which we provide early childhood care, beginning in infancy.

Some people acknowledge the impact of such differences but find it hard to accept that good schools should have so difficult a time overcoming them. This would be easier to understand if Americans had a broader international perspective on education. Class backgrounds influence *relative* achievement everywhere. The inability of schools to overcome the disadvantage of less literate homes is not a peculiar American failure but a universal reality. Turkish immigrant students suffer from an achievement gap in Germany, as do Algerians in France, as do Caribbean, African, Pakistani and Bangladeshi pupils in Great Britain, and as do Okinawans and low-caste Buraku in Japan.

An international survey of 15-year-olds, conducted in 2000, found a strong relationship in almost every nation between parental occupation and student literacy. The gap between literacy of children of the highest status workers (like doctors, professors, lawyers) and the lowest status workers (like waiters and waitresses, taxi drivers, mechanics) was even greater in Germany and the United Kingdom than it was in the United States. After reviewing these results, a US Department of Education summary concluded that "most participating countries do not differ significantly from the United States in terms of the strength of the relationship between socioeconomic status and literacy in any subject." Remarkably, the Department published this conclusion at the very time it was guiding a bill through Congress—"No Child Left Behind"—that demanded every school in the nation abolish social class differences in achievement within 12 years.

Urging less educated parents to read to children can't fully compensate for differences in school readiness. If children see parents read to solve their own problems or for entertainment, children are more likely to want to read themselves. Parents who bring reading material home from work demonstrate by example to children that reading is not a segmented burden but a seamless activity that bridges work and leisure. Parents who read to children but don't read for themselves send a different message.

How parents read to children is as important as whether they do; more educated parents read aloud differently. When working-class parents read aloud, they are more likely to tell children to pay attention without interruptions or to sound out words or name letters. When they ask children about a story, questions are more likely to be factual, asking for names of objects or memory of events.

Parents who are more literate are more likely to ask questions that are creative, interpretive or connective, like "what do you think will happen next?," "does that remind you of what we did yesterday?" Middle-class parents are more likely to read aloud, to have fun, to start conversations, as an entree to the world outside. Their children learn that reading is enjoyable and are more motivated to read in school.

There are stark class differences not only in how parents read but in how they converse. Explaining events in the broader world to children, in dinner talk, for example, may have as much of an influence on test scores as early reading itself. Through such conversations, children develop vocabularies and become familiar with contexts for reading in school. Educated parents are more likely to engage in such talk and to begin it with infants and toddlers, conducting pretend conversations long before infants can understand the language. Typically, middle-class parents "ask" infants about their needs, then provide answers for the children ("Are you ready for a nap, now? Yes, you are, aren't you?"). Instructions are more likely to be given indirectly ("You don't want to make so much noise, do you?"). Such instruction is really an invitation for a child to work through the reasoning behind an order and to internalize it. Middle-class parents implicitly begin academic instruction for infants with such indirect guidance.

Yet such instruction is quite different from what policymakers nowadays consider "academic" for young children: explicit training in letter and number recognition, letter-sound correspondence and so on. Such drill in basic skills can be helpful but is unlikely to close the social class gap in learning.

Soon after middle-class children become verbal, parents typically draw them into adult conversations so children can practice expressing their own opinions. Lower-class children are more likely to be expected to be seen and not heard. Inclusion this early in adult conversations develops a sense of entitlement in middle-class children; they feel comfortable addressing adults as equals and without deference. Children who want reasons rather than being willing to accept assertions on adult authority develop intellectual skills upon which later academic success in school will rely. Certainly, some lower-class children have such skills and some middle-class children lack them. But, on average, a sense of entitlement is social class-based.

Parents whose professional occupations entail authority and responsibility typically believe more strongly that they can affect their environments and solve problems. At work, they explore alternatives and negotiate compromises. They naturally express these personality traits at home when they design activities where children figure out solutions for themselves. Even the youngest middle-class children practice traits that make academic success more likely when they negotiate what to wear or to eat. When middle-class parents give orders, they are more likely to explain why the rules are reasonable.

But parents whose jobs entail following orders or doing routine tasks exude a lesser sense of efficacy. Their children are less likely to be encouraged to ne-gotiate clothing or food. Lower-class parents are more likely to instruct children by giving directions without extended discussion. Following orders, after all, is how they themselves behave at work. So their children are also more likely to be fatalistic about obstacles they face, in and out of school.

Middle-class children's self-assurance is enhanced in after-school activities that sometimes require large fees for enrollment and almost always require par-ents to have enough free time and resources to provide transportation. Organized sports, music, drama and dance programs build self-confidence (with both tro-phies and admiring adult spectators) and discipline in middle-class children. Lower-class parents find the fees for such activities more daunting, and trans-portation may also be more of a problem. In many cases, such organized athletic and artistic activities are not available anywhere in lower-class neighborhoods. So lower-class children's sports are more informal and less confidence-building, with less opportunity to learn teamwork and self-discipline. For children with greater self-confidence, unfamiliar school challenges can be exciting; such chil-dren, who are more likely to be from middle-class homes, are more likely to succeed than those who are less self-confident.

Homework exacerbates academic differences between middle- and work-ing-class children because middle-class parents are more likely to assist with homework. Yet homework would increase the achievement gap even if all par-ents were able to assist. Parents from different social classes supervise home-work differently. Consistent with overall patterns of language use, middle-class parents—particularly those whose own occupational habits require problem-solving—are more likely to assist by posing questions that decompose problems and that help children figure out correct answers. Lower-class parents are more likely to guide children with direct instructions. Children from both strata may go to school with completed homework, but middle-class children gain more in intellectual power from the exercise than do lower-class children.

Twenty years ago, Betty Hart and Todd Risley, researchers from the Uni-versity of Kansas, visited families from different social classes to monitor the conversations between parents and toddlers. Hart and Risley found that, on average, professional parents spoke over 2,000 words per hour to their children, working-class parents spoke about 1,300, and welfare mothers spoke about 600. So, by age three, children of professionals had vocabularies that were nearly 50% greater than those of working-class children and twice as large as those of welfare children.

Deficits like these cannot be made up by schools alone, no matter how high the teachers' expectations. For all children to achieve the same goals, the less advantaged would have to enter school with verbal fluency similar to the fluency of middle-class children.

The Kansas researchers also tracked how often parents verbally encouraged children's behavior, and how often parents reprimanded their children. Toddlers of professionals got an average of six encouragements per reprimand. Working-class children had two. For welfare children, the ratio was reversed, an average of one encouragement for two reprimands. Children whose initiative was encouraged from a very early age are probably more likely, on average, to take responsibility for their own learning.

Social class differences in role modeling also make an achievement gap almost inevitable. Not surprisingly, middle-class professional parents tend to associate with, and be friends with, similarly educated professionals. Working-class parents have fewer professional friends. If parents and their friends perform jobs requiring little academic skill, their children's images of their own futures are influenced. On average, these children must struggle harder to motivate themselves to achieve than children who assume that, as in their parents' social circle, the only roles are doctor, lawyer, teacher, social worker, manager, administrator or businessperson.

Even disadvantaged children now usually say they plan to attend college. College has become such a broad rhetorical goal that black eighth-graders tell surveyors they expect to earn college degrees as often as white eighth-graders respond in this way. But despite these intentions to pursue education, fewer black than white eighth-graders actually graduate from high school four years later, fewer eventually enroll in college the year after high school graduation, and even fewer persist to get bachelor's degrees.

A bigger reason than affordability is that while disadvantaged students say they plan on college, they don't feel as much parental, community or peer pressure to take the courses or to get the grades to qualify and to study hard to become more attractive to college admission officers. Lower-class parents say they expect children to perform well, but are less likely to enforce these expectations, for example with rewards or punishments for report card grades. Teachers and counselors can stress doing well in school to lower-class children, but such lessons compete with children's own self-images, formed early in life and reinforced daily at home.

Culture and Expectations

Partly, there may be a black community culture of under-achievement that helps to explain why even middle-class black children often don't do as well in school as white children from seemingly similar socioeconomic backgrounds. Middle-class black students don't study as hard as white middle-class students, and blacks are more disruptive in class than whites from similar income strata. This culture of under-achievement is easier to understand than to cure. Throughout American history, many black students who excelled in school were not re-warded in the labor market for that effort. Many black college graduates could only find work as servants, as Pullman car porters or, in white-collar fields, as assistants to less qualified whites. Many Americans believe that these practices have disappeared and that blacks and whites with similar test scores now have similar earnings and occupational status. But labor market discrimination, even for blacks whose test scores are comparable to whites, continues to play an im-portant role. Especially for black males with high school educations, discrimina-tion continues to be a big factor.

Evidence for this comes from the continued success of employment dis-crimination cases—for example, a prominent 1996 case in which Texaco settled for a payment of $176 million to black employees after taped conversations of executives revealed pervasive racist attitudes, presumably not restricted to ex-ecutives of this corporation. Other evidence comes from studies finding that black workers with darker complexions have less labor market success than those with lighter complexions but identical education, age and criminal records. Still more evidence comes from studies in which blacks and whites with similar qualifications are sent to apply for job vacancies; the whites are typically more successful than the blacks. One recent study trained young, well-groomed and articulate black and white college graduates to pose as high school graduates with otherwise identical qualifications except that some reported convictions for drug possession. When these youths submitted applications for entry level jobs, the applications of whites with criminal records got positive responses more often than the applications of blacks with no criminal records.

So the expectation of black students that their academic efforts will be less rewarded than efforts of their white peers is rational for the majority of black students who do not expect to complete college. Some will reduce their aca-demic effort as a result. We can say that they should not do so and, instead, should redouble their efforts in response to the greater obstacles they face. But as long as racial discrimination persists, the average achievement of black stu-dents will be lower than the average achievement of whites, simply because many blacks (especially males) who see that academic effort has less of a payoff will respond rationally by reducing their effort.

Helpful Policies

If we properly identify the actual social class characteristics that produce differences in average achievement, we should be able to design policies that narrow the achievement gap. Certainly, improvement of instructional practices is among these, but alone, a focus on school reform is bound to be frustrating and ultimately unsuccessful. To work, school improvement must combine with policies that narrow the social and economic differences among children. Where these differences cannot easily be narrowed, school should be redefined to cover more of the early childhood, after-school and summer times when the disparate influences of families and communities are most powerful.

Because the gap is already huge at age three, the most important new investment should probably be in early childhood programs. Pre-kindergarten classes for four-year-olds are needed, but barely begin to address the problem. The quality of early childhood programs is as important as the existence of programs themselves. Too many low-income children are parked before television sets in low-quality day care settings. To narrow the gap, care for infants and toddlers should be provided by adults who can create the kind of intellectual environment that is typically experienced by middle-class infants and toddlers. This requires professional care-givers and low child:adult ratios.

After-school and summer experiences for lower-class children, similar to programs middle-class children take for granted, would also likely be needed to narrow the gap. This does not mean remedial programs where lower-class children get added drill in math and reading. Certainly, remediation should be part of an adequate after-school and summer program, but only a part. The advantage that middle-class children gain after school and in summer likely comes from self-confidence they acquire and awareness they develop of the world outside, from organized athletics, dance, drama, museum visits, recreational reading and other activities that develop inquisitiveness, creativity, self-discipline and organizational skills. After-school and summer programs can be expected to have a chance to narrow the achievement gap only by attempting to duplicate such experiences.

Provision of health care services to lower-class children and their families is also required to narrow the achievement gap. Some health care services are relatively inexpensive, like school vision and dental clinics that cost less than schools typically spend on many less effective reforms. A full array of health services will cost more, but likely can't be avoided if there is a true intent to raise the achievement of lower-class children.

Policies to make stable housing affordable to low-income working families with children and policies to support the earnings of such families should also be thought of as educational policies—they can have a big impact on student achievement, irrespective of school quality.

The association of social and economic disadvantage with an achievement gap has long been well known to educators. Most, however, have avoided the obvious implication: To improve lower-class children's learning, amelioration of the social and economic conditions of their lives is also needed. Calling attention to this link is not to make excuses for poor school performance. It is, rather, to be honest about the social support schools require if they are to fulfill the public's expectation that the achievement gap disappear. Only if school improvement proceeds simultaneously with social and economic reform can this expectation be fulfilled.

Commentaries

Social Class, But What About the Schools?

Pedro A. Noguera

Long before publication of *Social Class and Schools*, I was a fan of Richard Rothstein's work. As a *New York Times* columnist for several years, Rothstein's commentaries on education were distinguished by his ability to bring common-sense insights to complex policy issues. In a field where policy typically is driven by ideology and the latest reform fad, Rothstein's perspectives were frequently a breath of fresh air, and I often found myself clipping the articles to share with students and colleagues.

Hence, I was not surprised to find myself in complete agreement with most of the arguments in his new book. In fact, many of the points he raises about the ways in which poverty influences the academic performance of poor children I have made myself (my 2003 book, *City Schools and the American Dream*). Like Rothstein, I have often taken issue with those (like the Thernstroms and The Heritage Foundation) who assert that there are "no excuses" for the achievement gap between Black and white, or middle-class and poor children. As Rothstein makes clear, lack of health care, inadequate nutrition or inability to secure stable housing has an effect on the achievement of poor students, and those who claim that children whose basic needs have not been met should do just as well as more privileged children are either lying or delusional.

Despite my concurrence with Rothstein on a number of educational issues, there are at least two disturbing aspects to his main argument that I take issue with. First, there is substantial evidence that the schools poor children attend are more likely to be overcrowded, underfunded and staffed by inexperienced teachers. Poor children of color are also more likely to attend schools that are segregated by race and class; less likely to have access to the rigorous math and science courses needed for college; less likely to have access to computers and the Internet; and less likely to be in a school that is safe and orderly. Rothstein does not argue that improving these conditions would not help poor children; he simply suggests that this is not where the emphasis for change should be placed. He focuses instead on the family background of poor children and the multi-faceted effects of poverty, factors that clearly have an influence on achievement but which are harder to address. Rothstein argues that improving school conditions would not lead to elimination of the achievement gap. While this may be true, I find it hard to understand how any reasonable person could argue that improving the abysmal conditions present in so many schools serving poor children would not have a positive effect on learning outcomes.

My other point of disagreement with Rothstein concerns his argument that some of the money being spent to improve schools should be redirected to address issues such as health care and housing that contribute to the hardships experienced by poor children in America. My disagreement on this point is political rather than substantive. While I agree that much more needs to be done to address the needs of poor children in America, such as providing access to quality early childhood programs, I also know that there has not been much political will or support for taking on these issues since the War on Poverty in the 1960s. There is, however, substantial popular support for the idea of improving public education and using it as a vehicle to promote opportunity and social mobility. Like Rothstein, I agree that schools cannot be expected to address the effects of poverty on children alone, but from a tactical standpoint I believe it makes sense to support the idea of advancing equity by expanding educational opportunities, rather than dismissing such efforts as unrealistic or hopelessly unattainable. Put more simply, reducing poverty and improving schools should not be treated as competing goals. Both are necessary, but for the time being at least, there is far greater support for improving education.

There are other parts of Rothstein's argument that I also take issue with: his arguments regarding minority student attitudes toward school (I contend that oppositional attitudes are often produced in school); his narrow focus on Black and white students at a time when Latinos and Asians are the fastest growing groups nationally; and his lack of attention to the difference that highly qualified teachers can make in influencing student outcomes.

But most of all I am troubled by his dismissal of the high-performing/high-poverty schools that have been documented by The Education Trust and others. While there may indeed be a bit of exaggeration about some of these schools, I know from my own research and experience (see my article "Transforming High Schools" in the May 2004 issue of *Educational Leadership*) that such schools do exist, and while they may not close the achievement gap as some have claimed, they do succeed in reducing academic disparities. The existence of such schools is the most important evidence available that the quality of schools poor students attend does matter. I'm not sure if Rothstein would argue against this point or why he does not weigh in more heavily on the need to do more to improve schools. In all likelihood, it is because his goal is to call for greater attention to the effects of poverty rather than seeing so much emphasis placed on reforming schools. While I don't have a problem with that emphasis, I do think it is important to show what effective schools can do to promote student achievement. This ultimately is where Rothstein and I disagree, and while I strongly endorse the attention he directs toward the effects of poverty on achievement, I believe that the book he's written is not really about schools, it's about what he thinks schools cannot do. The limitations he identifies are certainly real and profoundly important, but what he pays insufficient attention to is the extraordinary difference that good schools can make for students who are lucky enough to get access to them.

Don't Lose the Battle
Trying to Fight the War

John H. Jackson

Richard Rothstein's article highlights the importance of our nation's commitment to address people of color's socioeconomic ills as a tool for addressing and closing the racial achievement gap. In theory, I wholeheartedly support that it is not by accident or outrageous misfortunes that many of the areas that have the lowest achievement levels are urban areas populated by poor people of color who are confronted with many social challenges—people who often also have the lowest opportunity levels. This has been a challenge that has begged for an answer for over a century.

Immediately following passage of the 1964 Civil Rights Act, in 1965, Dr. Kenneth Clark, noted expert social scientist in *Brown v. Board of Education*, described, in his classic text, *Dark Ghetto: Dilemmas of Social Power*, the psychology and pathology of urban life. Like Rothstein's, Dr. Clark's analysis highlighted the outcomes rooted in historical and contemporary forms of discrimination against populations who were blocked access to educational and economic opportunities. That same year, Senator Daniel Moynihan headed up a commission which issued a report, *The Negro Family: The Case for National Action*, that again, like Rothstein's work, indicated that the lack of socioeconomic opportunity led to family instability in poor black communities and gave rise to a "culture of poverty" which often leads to unfavorable sociological outcomes.

Thus, while Clark, Moynihan and now Rothstein provide an accurate diagnosis of the symptoms that lead to the racial achievement gaps we see in school systems across the nation, the remedy is not as simple as Rothstein indicates. Rothstein's approach underestimates the institutionalized policies and practices that lead to racial achievement disparities among blacks and whites regardless of socioeconomic status. At its core, Rothstein's approach assumes that wiping out the social challenges that exist in urban communities will also wipe out racial achievement gaps. Its underlying tone suggests that many of the educational barriers that produce the achievement gaps are centered in the student's sociological background rather than in the institutions that are charged with educating all students—regardless of socioeconomic background. For example, Rothstein asserts that African-American students are "more disruptive" in class than their white peers. His assertion is likely rooted in the fact that these students are more often referred to the office for discipline and penalized more than their white peers. However, as research by the Harvard Civil Rights Project and The Advancement Project indicates, African-American students are more often sent to the office for "subjective" offenses and are more often penalized for offenses for which their white peers are not penalized. In this case, the bulk of the problem lies less with the student's actions than the system of discipline which labels a similar act "disruptive" on the one hand and "acceptable" on the other. Here, the answer lies in ensuring that teachers have the professional development needed to understand and educate the population that sits before them. Furthermore, removing students from this "culture of poverty" won't alone close the achievement gap, as numerous studies have proven that even minority students in wealthier areas, on average, have lower test scores than their white peers in similar areas.

While Rothstein's approach to addressing the problem identifies a significant barrier in addressing the gap, it does not account for the gap, nor should it absolve schools of their responsibility to ensure that there are highly qualified teachers in the classrooms, appropriate class sizes and adequate resources.

If history is to be our guide in addressing this challenge, in 1964, President Lyndon B. Johnson launched a national War on Poverty. One of the first steps he took to address it was working to pass the Elementary and Secondary Education Act, which outlined the federal government's role in ensuring equal educational opportunities for all children—through teacher quality, resource equity (Title I) and other components. In addition, through Title VI of the Act, it prohibited racial discrimination in educational programs and services and vested the Office for Civil Rights (OCR) in the Department of Education with enforcement powers. Today, more than 40 years later, the number of racial discrimination violation complaints resolved by OCR are down, Title I is yet to have been fully funded, and in 2004 President Bush and Congress failed to fully fund reauthorization of the Act (the No Child Left Behind Act)—falling more than $8 billion short of the resources required to give states and districts what is needed so that teachers can teach and students can learn in all communities. Yet in FY2004, the Administration chose to invest more than $480 billion in defense spending to aid efforts to fight wars in Iraq and Afghanistan, while ignoring our domestic war on poverty.

Thus, it remains difficult to measure the true weight the "culture of poverty" has on the racial achievement gap in education when the first battle—addressing the "culture of implementing policies and practices that blatantly ensure educational opportunities to some and deny them to others"—has yet to have been won. Nonetheless, the strength of Rothstein's current work is not in his diagnosis of the war on poverty that stills needs to be fought, but the context that his work provides to energize stakeholders to pick up arms to address the battle that exists in their local schools and districts—the battle to ensure equal access to a high-quality education for all students. If we win enough of these battles, we will surely win the war on poverty.

Simplistic and Condescending

Jenice L. View

Pity the low-income person who, by virtue of lousy wages alone, is considered an incompetent parent. Let's patronize the woman who is unworthy of talking with or reading to her child or helping with homework (following a 16-hour shift or her second job) because she cannot be relied on to do it correctly. And, should the low-income parent feel too fatigued or too defeated by racism at the end of a hard day's work, let's nevertheless encourage his kids to address him "as an equal and without deference" in order to promote the same sense of entitlement that middle-class kids feel and use to their academic advantage.

Simplistic and condescending? No less than Rothstein's chapter. So, to give Rothstein the benefit of the doubt, let's first assume that the supporting evidence for some of the more outrageous claims about urban, low-income African-American families are contained within the book's endnotes, and are more current than the 20-year-old data he cites on (rural? white?) Kansas families. While he seems to have no direct experience with low-income African-American families, we can hope that the citations include information about the cultural supports and transformations of the last 40 years in the wake of legal desegregation, including those within the Black church.

Secondly, his international comparison is not credible because the chapter fails to address native language literacy of dark-skinned immigrants to Europe and Japan compared with the native language literacy of white Europeans. In addition, it is not clear if the data he cites on parental occupation and student literacy hold constant for language proficiency.

Thirdly, the impact on urban communities of the crack cocaine epidemic of the 1980s and 1990s cannot be overlooked, leaving behind children with impaired health and leaving grandparents to compensate for the failings of addicted parents.

Finally, if the wealth gap between middle-class whites and middle-class Blacks is indeed shrinking, and if many of the current Black achievers are first-generation middle-class, from where did they all come? How do we explain the circumstances of their birth and their low-income parents and the differences in outcomes? In other words, how is it that being poor one generation ago was less of a barrier to achievement than now? Perhaps it is due to the worsening income and wealth gaps between rich and poor of all races and ethnicities, a fact that is neither irrelevant nor in the control of parents or teachers. The final paragraph of Rothstein's chapter makes the most sense:

> The association of social and economic disadvantage with an achievement gap has long been well known to educators. Most, however, have avoided the obvious implication: To improve lower-class children's learning; amelioration of the social and economic conditions of their lives is also needed. Calling attention to this link is not to make excuses for poor school performance. It is, rather, to be honest about the social support schools require if they are to fulfill the public's expectation that the achievement gap disappear. Only if school improvement proceeds simultaneously with social and economic reform can this expectation be fulfilled.

Inequality and the Schoolhouse

Stan Karp

Richard Rothstein asks how much schools can be expected to overcome the staggering inequality that continues to define our society. It's the right question. Educational inequality—whose manifestations go well beyond test score gaps— is perhaps the central problem our schools face. How we deal with it will go a long way toward determining whether our society's future will be one of democratic promise or growing division.

Weighing the ability of schools to compensate for the inequality that exists all around them is a question of balance, and there are dangers to be found on both sides of the equation. There's little doubt that schools could do more to bridge gaps between students whose affluence provides private tutors and summer camps and those whose poverty or language status adds only extra burdens. They could use the inadequate resources they receive more efficiently and equitably. They could provide more academic supports, more engaging curriculum and more effective, high-quality instruction They could move beyond a superficial multiculturalism that "celebrates diversity" toward a deeper anti-racist practice that helps uncover why some differences translate into access to wealth and power, while others become a source of discrimination and injustice. Schools could also design better systems for encouraging multi-sided accountability and promoting democratic collaboration with parents and communities. To do any of this, schools need pressure from inside and out to make reducing educational inequality a more visible and more urgent priority.

That said, it seems to me that Rothstein is essentially correct when he argues that schools face unreasonable expectations from those who demand schoolhouse solutions to the political, economic and social inequality that we allow to persist. Currently, the achievement gap, narrowly defined by test scores and, more recently, by NCLB's absurd "adequate yearly progress" formulas, is being used to label public schools as failures, without providing the resources and strategies needed to overcome them. To expect schools to wipe out long-standing academic achievement gaps while denying them substantial new resources and leaving many of the social factors that contribute to this inequality in place is not a formula for providing better education to those who need it most. Instead, it's a strategy for eroding the common ground that a universal system of public education needs to survive.

It's one thing to document academic achievement gaps. It's quite another to use those data, as NCLB and many of its supporters do, to promote a punitive program of test-driven sanctions, privatization and market reforms which have no record of success as school improvement strategies and which promise to do for schooling what the not-so-free market has done for health care and housing. (Just how serious this privatization agenda is and how cynically concern for achievement gaps is being manipulated to advance it is currently a major point of difference among those who otherwise share a common interest in addressing issues of educational inequality.)

Fifty years after *Brown v. Board of Education* schools are being rightfully taken to task for failing to deliver on its promises. But the bill for that failure, as Rothstein's book shows, needs to be itemized to include the appalling gaps in income, health care, nutrition, family support, housing, school funding and other factors that translate into inequality in classrooms. Yes, we need to press our schools to do a better job. But until society as a whole picks up the tab for the equality it so often invokes as a goal, we will all continue to pay a heavy price.

Even the Best Schools Can't Do It Alone

Wendy Puriefoy

At a time when the No Child Left Behind Act all but monopolizes the debate on school reform, Richard Rothstein raises important points that underscore the broader context of public education—a context that deserves to be taken seriously now more than ever. To be sure, schools will benefit when policymakers and communities pay attention to the role that race and class disparities play in shaping the all-too-predictable patterns of academic achievement.

Unfortunately, Rothstein uses his astute observations about the manifestations of these disparities to suggest that the causes of the achievement gap are personal or cultural, rather than deeply systemic. In its focus on the victims of the system rather than the system itself, Rothstein's scrutiny smacks of the old "cultural deprivation" accounts of unequal success rates, the idea that we can somehow explain away the achievement gap by finding fault with the lifestyles of those who end up on the wrong end of it. The trouble with this line of thinking is that it often discourages comprehensive, systemic reform in favor of "reforming" those who would benefit from it. If we are serious about creating lasting and effective reforms, we must look for problems within schools, not pathologize children and families.

Rothstein's analysis represents a particular barrier to comprehensive reform because it fails to rise above a set of superficial choices, reinforcing a rhetorical dichotomy that plays directly into the hands of those for whom supporting public education is not a priority. The fallacy of this dichotomy becomes clear when we realize that solving social disparities and improving public education are not competing aims, but two parts of the same large one. Suggesting that we can either reform schools *or* address inequalities in health care, housing, wealth and parental attention presents us with a set of false choices that all of us, and underprivileged communities in particular, have a vested interest in reconciling. The danger of ignoring school-based variables in favor of child-based variables is that it can have the flavor of resigning underprivileged communities to a fate, instead of engaging them and others to take an active, participatory role in the function of local schools. In other words, the problem is not, as Rothstein claims in his title, that "Even the Best Schools Can't Close the Race Achievement Gap." The reality is that Even The Best Schools Can't Do It Alone.

Public schools rely on public involvement. Nonprofit organizations like local education funds play a vital role in fostering both awareness of, and responsibility for, education issues at the local level. When we engage communities in generating assets and ideas for public education, we help dispel the myth that a scarcity of resources forces us to choose between preparing our children at home and in our communities or educating them in the classroom.

Of course, this is not an easy process. The first step towards building broader support for public education is seeing public education as a broader issue, and at their best, Richard Rothstein's observations help us to do just that. But contrary to their author's implications, the observations are relevant to school reform not because they expose its limits, but because they expand its potential. Only when we fully recognize the relationship between community health, economic vitality and academic achievement can we work towards solutions equal to the complexities of the task. Such a commitment to a shared public education may well be the first step towards a coherent new vision ensuring that every child can benefit from a quality education.

What Teachers Know

Mark Simon

For teachers, the most disheartening aspect of the Administration's "No Child Left Behind" agenda is the dishonesty in the goals and supposed success stories. No responsible educator disagrees with the stated purpose of leaving no child behind and closing the achievement gap, but we must begin with the truth.

The myth perpetrated by conservative education reformers is that we can abandon the war on poverty while expecting the children of the poor to achieve middle-class success in school simply by "raising expectations." NCLB has provided cover for growing social inequality, de-funding of the public sector, a privatization agenda increasingly unjustified by any research, and a blame game that scapegoats the teacher work force. The liberal-conservative compromise that created the NCLB act seems premised on an assumption that teachers aren't really trying. The most talented teachers particularly resent the message. Rothstein's book provides ammunition for teachers and principals to respond to the hype.

I recently gathered a group of accomplished teachers to discuss *Class and Schools*. They agreed that the book helped them to articulate what teachers already know—that teaching well in challenging, urban, high-poverty environments is tougher than teaching more privileged kids. Rothstein reminded these teachers exactly why it was so difficult. The book doesn't lessen their commitment to closing the achievement gap. It did lead them to want to personally take new steps—walking tours of their school community and other strategies to get to know their students and families better; political activism to fight for expansion of Head Start and other pre-school programs that help prepare students and families for school; and initiating school- and district-wide conversations to reconsider decisions that had narrowed the focus of education to what is tested—de-valuing important non-cognitive aspects. (This is not covered in Rothstein's summary here, but was an important point in the book.) Most importantly, they talked of the weight it lifted from their shoulders, allowing them to celebrate human-scale improvement rather than perpetually feeling bad about their work.

It is surprising how little we know about teaching practices that cause students to succeed, particularly in high-poverty schools. Ironically, the hyped myth-making success stories promoted by The Education Trust, Heritage Foundation and purveyors of 90-90-90 schools (90% poverty, 90% minority and 90% meeting high academic standards), by making it sound so easy, have actually distracted educators from recognizing the more nuanced successes that need to be documented and replicated. *Class and Schools* should allow us to more realistically analyze what teacher behaviors, beliefs and school practices actually improve student achievement and expand student potential.

Rothstein makes clear (not in his summary here but in the last pages of the book) that part of his intent is to provide an antidote to the demoralizing atmosphere that is driving the most creative, accomplished teachers out of teaching, particularly fleeing schools with high-poverty students. This is a significant issue. The class/race disparities represented by vastly different teacher working and student learning conditions have widened to crisis proportions. Rather than dismissing the need to correct the unequal distribution of teacher talent as "politically and financially fanciful," as he does in the book, Rothstein should have included it under "Helpful Policies." In all other respects, *Class and Schools* brings the realities of what teachers instinctively know to the policymaking table, hopefully before it's too late.

Family and School Matter

Krista Kafer

Richard Rothstein is right. His new book *Class and Schools* underscores what researchers like James Coleman, Derek Neal and Christopher Jencks have been saying for decades: Life outside of school is the greatest predictor of success in school.

It should come as no surprise that adults' decisions impact their children's academic progress. A child born to married parents is less likely to have developmental delays or behavioral problems, repeat grades or be expelled. Parents who read regularly to their children will see them grow as readers. It is equally true that conflict and instability at home will seep into a child's performance in the classroom.

Even so, demography is not destiny, and Rothstein admits as much. However, he discounts the power of a good school to make a difference. He attributes the success of high-poverty/high-performing schools identified by The Education Trust, The Heritage Foundation and others to selectivity or statistical anomaly. He believes such models may serve a few but are not the answer for most.

His pessimism, however, is unfounded. Research shows that the greatest in-school predictor of academic success is the quality of teaching. What happens 33 hours a week, 180 days a year matters.

The late James Coleman, groundbreaking researcher on the primacy of socioeconomic influence, also found that Catholic and other private schools achieved greater academic results with poor students than public schools serving their peers. Similarly, albeit more recently, Harvard University's Paul Peterson found poor black students using vouchers to attend private schools outperformed their public school counterparts.

Successful schools are not limited to the private sector. Educators are replicating public school models like KIPP Academies around the country because they raise achievement among low-income students. Whether public or private, such effective schools have much in common. Led by strong principals and talented teachers, these schools create an environment focused on learning and character development. They build a solid foundation in the basics before moving to higher-level material. Faced with many challenges, they often use a longer school day or school year to get the job done.

While a school can never fully fill the space left by a deprived home life, it can go a long way. Giving kids access to schools of excellence will make a difference.

Unfortunately, Rothstein's solution—to enact a host of new Great Society programs—is unlikely to make a difference. After almost four decades of Head Start, welfare, and federal academic and after-school programs, there is little to show for the effort.

The focus has been in the wrong place. Since family is the greatest determinant of academic success, followed by teaching quality, these should be the focus of change. Policies that encourage marriage, parental responsibility and access to good schools will narrow the gap between poor students and their middle-class peers. A healthy family and a good school are what a child needs most.

Schools Count

Dianne M. Piché and Tamar Ruth

In *Class and Schools*, Richard Rothstein suggests that school reform will not produce results unless and until the entire liberal social and economic agenda is fully enacted. He has summarized a one-sided collection of unsurprising and not very new studies about the impact of poverty, discrimination and class-related child-rearing practices on student outcomes. His purpose is clear: to make a case that schools cannot be expected to produce the dramatic improvements demanded by increasing numbers of parents and voters, and called for under the No Child Left Behind Act, because there is very little schools can do to mitigate achievement gaps caused primarily by non-school factors.

Rothstein is wrong about the potential and power of schools, and here's why:

First, education continues to be the single most important and effective "equalizer" of opportunity in our society. If there is one place progressives can and should put their energy and see results, it is in improving public schools, because despite the persistence of race and sex discrimination in the job market, education remains the most promising ticket into the middle class for black and

Latino children. For example, in the years following enactment of the Civil Rights Act of 1964 and the inception of Head Start and Title I programs in 1965, along with court-enforced desegregation, we saw dramatic narrowing of the gap between African-American and white children on the National Assessment of Educational Progress.

Certainly there are "non-school" factors that are difficult or outside the power of schools to overcome, as Rothstein describes. Rather than write off the potential of schools, however, we should redouble our efforts to ensure that all children have access to schools that work, including: qualified teachers; a safe and supportive learning environment; and, critically, instruction that is not dumbed down but rather matched with the same high standards taught in the suburbs and required now by growing numbers of states in order to graduate. If states and school districts are not willing or able to desegregate schools with high concentrations of poverty (and the Prospects study conducted for the National Assessment of Title I, as well as other credible research, has made it clear that one of the worst educational environments is high poverty concentration in the classroom), they and the federal government should provide additional, carefully targeted resources to such schools and their students to enable them to succeed, including: highly-qualified teachers; extended time (e.g., high-quality summer and after-school programs); additional highly-trained professionals (e.g., reading specialists, master teachers/coaches); professional development in reading and other core subjects that is aligned with the state's standards; and sufficient pay or other incentives for good teachers to remain in these schools. While a certain amount of racial and economic isolation in schools is outside the control of school officials (the result of entrenched residential segregation), school boards retain control over student assignment and attendance policies and ought to do all in their power to reduce poverty concentration in classrooms; magnet schools, controlled choice and compliance with NCLB's new transfer provisions can all help reduce isolation and improve learning outcomes.

Second, Rothstein's contention that most successful high-poverty or high-minority schools are flukes, statistical outliers or selective academies is not supportable. Despite Rothstein's effort to deflate and discredit as many success stories as he can, our own experience in teaching and advocacy is completely consistent with The Education Trust reports on successful schools and the belief that success is possible in far more schools (http://www2.edtrust.org/edtrust/), and for many more students, than currently reported. There are success stories on an individual, school and community-wide basis all across the country, and we each have been fortunate to live, witness and celebrate success everywhere we go. For example:

- Last year, every single one of co-author Ruth's students (all nonwhite, most eligible for free or reduced price meals, and many new to learning English) met the school district's benchmark in reading, and most far exceeded the standard. Her experience as a classroom teacher and her prior work with poor Latino toddlers refutes Rothstein's notion that only a handful of poor children can "defy the odds." Rather, her own experience both as an "at-risk" child growing up, and now as an educator, speaks powerfully to the fact that students can succeed if we believe in and support them.

- In the larger community of eastern Montgomery County, MD, where both authors live, the public schools are majority nonwhite and enroll large numbers of poor and immigrant children. Under the superintedent's leadership, a program of sensible, coherent instructional programs and interventions targeted to poor neighborhoods and schools is dramatically closing the gap, erasing many of the preschool literacy deficits Rothstein asserts are responsible for the gap at the get-go. In one Title I school where author Piché volunteered and sent her own children, the system's intensive and balanced literacy initiative brought nearly all low-income and non-English-proficient second graders to or above level on the district's early reading assessment, including a number of children who might otherwise have been consigned to special education.

- In St. Louis, where author Piché has represented schoolchildren in an ongoing desegregation case, we have seen results from strategies to improve achievement. Specifically, over the last two decades, thousands of poor black children from St. Louis transferred to majority white and middle-class suburban districts, where their parents could not afford to live. Under this program, the largest public school choice program in the nation, the students achieved graduation and college-going rates enormously higher than the city schools they otherwise would have attended.

- In California, one of the most underfunded states, with huge numbers of poor and immigrant students, Education Trust West has identified increasing numbers of high-poverty schools making or exceeding state achievement targets. The Citizens' Commission on Civil Rights met with and interviewed educators at some of these schools (and many others across the country) as part of our Title I monitoring project and found some common themes: 1) an overarching belief among staff that all children could succeed (and with it a refusal to make excuses or to blame parents); 2) a relentless focus on literacy and getting all students to read on grade level by the third grade; 3) continuous examination and use of data, including periodic assessment in reading and math, to implement instructional improvements and changes; 4) a strong principal and senior staff who respect teachers, encourage collaboration and celebrate success but who also communicate and enforce high standards; and 5) a sense of connection to a larger community (e.g., through parent involvement, adult volunteers, business partners and support from clergy and faith communities). Significantly, very few of these schools received any "extras" above and beyond their regular district allocations for staffing and materials and their Title I grants. But what they did with their resources was to use them in the smartest, most efficacious ways to improve achievement.

Finally, Rothstein fails to address how schools and school officials themselves are often responsible for perpetuating and exacerbating achievement gaps. Many more kids would succeed in school and huge parts of the gaps would be erased if adults in charge of schools ended policies and practices we know are bad for kids, including the following:

1. The persistent, widespread inequitable distribution of education resources, including teachers. In many parts of the country, rich students get more and poor students get less. We are dismayed that in an entire work on the achievement gap, Rothstein makes light of perhaps the most consequential maldistribution of resources, that of good qualified teachers. He writes off closing the well-documented teacher quality gap as "politically unrealistic" (p.132 of the book). But this "in-school" problem is one of the largest contributing factors to the achievement gap in the first place. An extensive and growing body of research by Richard Ingersoll (Univ. of Penn.), Jennifer King Rice (Univ. of Md.), William Sanders (Univ. of Tenn.) and others has established that teacher quality is the most signficant in-school variable that influences student achievement.

2. Tracking and academic-content gaps. Rothstein acknowledges that poor and minority students have the same educational aspirations as middle-class and white students: to go to college and make a good living. But with a set of widespread practices that expand rather than close gaps, schools themselves make attainment of these goals virtually impossible for many students. These practices include: a) tracking poor and minority students into whole classes or, in the earlier grades, groups, where expectations and standards are low and remain low throughout students' educational careers; b) counseling and steering similarly situated minority students into less challenging and dumbed-down high school classes, while white students are encouraged to take honors, Advanced Placement and other more rigorous courses; c) in some schools, not requiring, encouraging or even offering a full sequence of college-preparatory classes; and d) the failure of states and districts to ensure that the same courses (e.g., algebra, biology) in fact have the same or comparable rigor across school class and race lines.

3. Bad adult behavior toward children and their parents. In many high-poverty communities, there are adults working in and supervising schools who are downright disrespectful of students and their families. Rothstein addresses the impact of discrimination occurring off school premises, but neglects to acknowledge the poisonous impact of within-school discrimination and other demeaning conduct. Under the category of "bad adult behavior," we include both overtly and covertly biased remarks and practices, schools that are managed as if they were prisons and not places of learning, and school environments that are unwelcoming to both students and parents. We also include the persistent over-

use of suspension, expulsion and so-called "zero tolerance" policies that, as applied, deny students an ongoing opportunity to learn and often have an adverse and disproportionate impact on minority and male students.

4. Dishonest grading and promotion practices. While we do not favor large-scale retention, we also know, as reported by the National Assessment of Title I, that in general students in poor urban schools receive "A's" for work that would only pass for a "C" in the better-off suburbs. Children do not ultimately benefit when they are promoted from grade to grade without having attained the grade-level mastery of reading and math skills necessary to do core subject coursework (including comprehending more complex texts) in succeeding years. Intervention and additional assistance should be immediate and targeted to prevent an accumulation of deficits that ultimately will lead to drop-outs or failure to meet graduation standards.

To his credit, Rothstein does acknowledge the persistence of and harm caused by segregation, and calls for school and wider community (e.g., residential) integration, proposals with which we agree. In addition, his recommendations for addressing poverty through progressive policies in the areas of pre-school and child care, health care, housing and income security are all very important. We do not disagree with any of them.

But, as discussed above, we disagree completely with his thesis in *Class and Schools* that schools themselves can do little to close achievement gaps.

Not only is Rothstein's thesis incorrect, it also provides ammunition to an entrenched, retrograde education establishment desperate to excuse achievement gaps at a time when there is a growing public consensus that such gaps are neither inevitable nor morally defensible. This "establishment" includes some (though by no means all) public officials, school administrators and classroom teachers who are challenged, and in some cases personally threatened, by the gap-closing promises and requirements of the bipartisan NCLB. It also includes many middle- and upper-class parents and voters who, historically, have been reluctant to send their tax dollars to the other side of town to improve the schools of poor and nonwhite students.

Ironically, 50 years after *Brown v. Board of Education*, those very provisions in NCLB that call for racial and economic justice in the provision of educational resources (including high-quality teaching) are among the most threatening to some otherwise moderate to liberal constituencies, including the nation's largest teachers' union. These NCLB provisions include the requirement that states put all schools on a trajectory to ensure that all children, including poor and minority students, can read and do math at the state's own levels of proficiency within 12 years (a timeline decried as unrealistic by many in the education establishment, but way too long for most parents whose children will have fallen far behind, or dropped out, by the time the deadlines roll around). Less widely discussed (perhaps because the Bush Administration has been complicit in state and local disregard of these provisions) are additional requirements in NCLB to redirect resources to the schools with greatest needs, including closing the well-documented "teacher quality gap" between rich and poor schools. Compliance with this provision (which was supported by a coalition of civil rights organizations but opposed by the teachers' unions) could involve the redeployment of highly qualified teachers at well-off schools to those with high concentrations of poverty and/or the provision of economic and other incentives for good teachers to remain in high-needs schools.

Most of us who support a broad progressive economic and civil rights agenda know the playing field in and out of school very likely will not be leveled in our lifetimes, nor during the school careers of millions of poor African-American and Latino children now in or about to enter the public school system. But we refuse to give up on a generation or even a classroom of children, or to stop pushing lawmakers, school administrators and other educators to do their very best, even as the Right Wing pushes for more shredding of the safety net and the Left backs off its commitment to enforcing racial equality in education. It is not only reasonable but also morally imperative that we expect all schools to do right by all students.

Response

Richard Rothstein

Several commentators charge that I devote too much attention to social reform and not enough to school improvement as a strategy for equalizing outcomes between blacks and whites. Getting the balance right is difficult, but the biggest obstacle to doing so is an excessive emphasis on the role of schools. Were the obstacles reversed, I would have written a different book.

My summary for *P&R* of *Class and Schools* insisted that both are needed:

> Improvement of instructional practices is among [policies to narrow the achievement gap], but alone, a focus on school reform is bound to be frustrating and ultimately unsuccessful. To work, school improvement must combine with policies that narrow the social and economic differences between children....Only if school improvement proceeds simultaneously with social and economic reform can [the gap be closed].

In *Class and Schools*, I explain that I devoted this work primarily to the social and economic causes of the achievement gap, not because school inadequacies are unimportant, but because our public discussion of school and socioeconomic effects is now so imbalanced: Volumes are produced weekly on how schools should improve (and with many of them I agree), leaving me little to add. But silence on the complementary importance of social and economic reform is deafening.

In neither my summary nor my book do I deny that schools like KIPP, or those cited by The Heritage Foundation or The Education Trust, are better than most and succeed in narrowing the achievement gap. What I do deny is the claim of some of their fans that such schools can close the achievement gap without simultaneous social and economic reform. Interestingly, leaders of these schools, when pressed, almost never make such claims. They realize, as many policy analysts do not, that their efforts alone can be only modestly successful if socioeconomic deprivation remains unaddressed.

Some of the commentators (Pedro Noguera, for example) appreciate the need for complementary work on both socioeconomic reform and school improvement, but think I have gotten the balance wrong. Perhaps so. But clearly the emphasis in public policy today is so exclusively on schools that a correction is in order. If, in some unimaginable (in today's political environment) future it swings too far in the direction of social and economic justice, my book may serve a less useful purpose.

Other commentators, however, who claim to have read both the summary and the book, stubbornly misrepresent the argument as "school reform will not produce results unless and until the entire liberal social and economic agenda is fully enacted" (Dianne M. Piché and Tamar Ruth). These commentators go on to assert, with no evidence whatsoever, that "education continues to be the single most important and effective 'equalizer' of opportunity in our society." Is educational improvement more effective than full employment, anti-discrimination policies in housing and labor markets, progressive taxation, adequate public health and unionization? Perhaps so, but I'd like to know the basis for such a claim. Recent research on intergenerational mobility suggests that we are less mobile than we thought and less mobile than other advanced countries—most of which pay more attention to social and economic equality than we do. The conundrum is that it is difficult to overcome class differences using a tool—schools—whose outcomes are themselves heavily influenced by social class.

As to Piché and Ruth's historical illustration, their memories are short. They correctly note that "in the years following enactment of the Civil Rights Act of 1964 and the inception of Head Start and Title I programs in 1965, along with court-enforced desegregation, we saw dramatic narrowing of the gap between African-American and white children on the National Assessment of Educational Progress." But they fail to note that these were also years in which Medicare and Medicaid were enacted, in which the minimum wage was higher (in real terms, and relative to the median wage) than it is today, when affirmative action in employment was aggressively pursued, when suburban housing was opened for the first time to black families, and when black family size decreased (giving children more parental time and attention). Did these play no role? Surely, school improvements such as Title 1 were important, but the years when the gap on the National Assessment narrowed were those when school and socioeconomic policies to address inequality were pursued simultaneously. In the 15 years from 1965 to 1980, the poverty of black children declined by over a third (from 66% to 42% of all black children). Subsequently, black children's poverty continued to decline, but at a much slower rate. The 1965 to 1980 period provides no support for believing that school improvement can close gaps without complementary progress in the social and economic conditions experienced by poor and minority children. (Piché and Ruth cite Head Start in support of their complaint about my thesis, but as my summary and book stress, I regard expansion of early childhood programs as one of the most important initiatives we can take. Whether this is considered an educational or social reform is beside the point.)

I frequently encounter caricatures of my argument, such as that of Piché and Ruth, by liberals who retain, with the Bush Administration and other conservatives, a belief that the only important barrier to equality worth addressing is schools' "soft bigotry of low expectations" and other failures, such as inadequate financing, classes that are too large, and teachers who are too poorly trained. While these are certainly barriers, I wonder why there is such resistance to acknowledging that there are other barriers outside of schools and that these are also worthy of attention. One need not let schools off the hook and deny that our educational system is unequal in order to contend that schools are not unique in their inequality.

For conservatives, the reason for an emphasis on schools is obvious. Schools are tax-supported institutions, and an attack on the public sector is at the core of a conservative agenda. Public sector employees (both administrators ["bureaucrats"] and unionized workers) are enemies conservatives love to have. Proposals to narrow income inequality, or to intervene in the private housing, employment or health sectors, are attacks on private interests at the core of the conservative base. Far better to blame schools for all our ills.

But why do liberals join in this distortion? Is it because an excessive focus on school reform brings the flattering support of conservative allies? Truthfully, I don't know the answer.

Pedro Noguera offers a possible explanation. He agrees that both socioeconomic and educational policy are necessary to enhance equality, but thinks that school improvement is more politically practical: "for the time being at least, there is far greater support for improving education." He worries that, in the present political environment, when public funds are scarce, advocacy of social and economic reform will undermine support for school improvement, leaving funds for neither.

In response, I urge him to consider two points. First, in the long run, effective public policy cannot proceed from a myth. Denying the obvious importance of socioeconomic conditions in perpetuating inequality may, in the short run, build support for school improvement efforts, but these quickly degenerate into an excessive attack on schools, as in present federal policy with its exaggerated emphasis on testing, basic skills and accountability, and its nonchalance about the need for better and more equitable school funding. We also set schools up for failure when we discuss closing the achievement gap with schools alone. Even if school improvement were our exclusive concern, would we achieve it by establishing goals (closing the gap) that can't be achieved and that make no distinction between progress and failure?

Second, I think Professor Noguera may not be making the best estimate of political practicality. We've not, after all, been so successful to date in improving schools to the point where they come anywhere close to generating equal outcomes for children from different social classes. And reforms like universal health care, full employment policy, more progressive taxation, adequate housing (consider the Section 8 program) are not wild pie-in-the-sky ideas but policies that are very much part of a practical agenda, and very much needed. Certainly, the present Administration has no interest in them, but the prior Administration made some progress in all of them, despite daunting political opposition. If, by some chance, advocates of social and economic reform can win greater power in our political institutions, we can hope that they will not be hindered by arguments of liberals that only schools can make a difference.

Finally, I am gratified by the reaction of Mark Simon's teacher group to my book. One reason I wrote it was that I have been troubled by the demoralization I have encountered among dedicated, highly skilled and indefatigable teachers in schools serving disadvantaged children. They know that they make a difference and bitterly resent being labeled "failures" and considered indistinguishable from teachers who are far less qualified, only because their students don't achieve at the same level as privileged suburban children. If my book can help, in a small way, make them feel better about their selfless and unrecognized dedication, it will have been worth it for that reason alone.

Chapter 36

High Classroom Turnover:
How Some Children Get Left Behind

Chester Hartman and Alison Leff

A 1994 US General Accounting Office study reported that by the end of the third grade, one out of six children had attended three or more schools, and that students often changed schools more than once during the school year. For many schools, over a four-year time period, overall school stability can fall under 50%. Certain populations—in particular, low-income, minority, immigrant, homeless, farmworker and foster care children—are disproportionately represented in the pool of transient students, and the inadequacies of the education received by such students are grossly magnified.

What triggers potentially damaging educational moves may be categorized as either external or internal to the school situation and environment. The former category—accounting for the majority of school transfers—consists primarily of residential changes on the part of the student's family, mainly caused by the workings of the housing system or (less frequently) by changes is the household situation, such as family break-up. The latter refers to a range of reasons, including expulsion by school authorities and problems or dissatisfactions on the part of the student and his/her family that lead to transfers.

For low-income, minority, homeless and farmworker children, residential changes usually are not under the families' control, or, in the case of farmworkers, are dictated by expected and planned changes in employment location. Over recent years, the supply of affordable housing has dramatically decreased. For families of color, this dearth of housing is compounded by overt and covert discrimination on the part of various housing gatekeepers. These factors leave low-income and minority families hard-pressed to find acceptable, affordable and stable living situations. Homeless families commonly move three to four times a year, and residency rules and lack of transportation often do not allow them to stay in one school as their families search for stable housing. Migrant students and students in the foster care system also change schools more frequently than their peers.

High mobility rates negatively affect the educational outcomes of transient students, as well as their stable classroom peers. For high-mobility students, the long-term effects of transiency include lower achievement levels and slower academic pacing. A review in the *Journal of Research and Development* concluded: "[T]he educational research literature seems quite consistent with regard to findings that high student transiency rates are strongly and negatively associated with academic attainment at school." Over a period of six years, students who have moved more than three times can fall a full academic year behind stable students. Stable students in such changing classrooms suffer academically as well: In shifting environments, such students fall behind half a year compared to stable students in stable classrooms. Evidence also shows that high mobility reduces the likelihood of high school completion. Nationally, while 86% of high school students graduate, the graduation rate is 60% for students who changed high schools at least twice.

High mobility rates also place a strain on school resources, influencing staffing and resource utilization decisions, as well as inducing teachers to become more review-oriented, resulting in an overall flattening of curricula. Student mobility can also constrain staff time, detract from per-pupil resources, and slow school-improvement and community-building efforts.

In sum, there is a clear need for recognition of the problem of school transiency: its pervasiveness, incidence, causes and deleterious results. Based on that knowledge, there is a concomitant need to mount a serious attack on the problem, reducing it where possible, handling it in the most constructive manner where it persists. A crucial threshold step is making policymakers in a variety of areas, as well as the general public (parents in particular), aware of the prevalence and severity of the problem, and of the ways it can inadvertently cause or be exacerbated by various policies. New and improved policies are needed at all levels of government and in far more areas than just the sphere of education.

With respect to education policy, the federal accountability framework should provide adequate safeguards, and enforce them strictly, to ensure that state and local entities protect the educational rights of highly mobile students. States should mandate standardized collection and reporting of school mobility data, as a vital tool in understanding the nature of the problem and devising solutions. Accountability standards need to be evaluated to make sure that schools are not given incentives to transfer "problem" students out as a method of excluding these students from school data.

While federal and state governments have key roles to play in mandating responsibility and providing necessary resources, it is at the local level that changed practices are needed and where effective improvements will manifest themselves. School districts should make every effort to retain students. Schools should focus on creating school communities that parents and students value and would think twice about leaving. Students who move a short distance and homeless students should be provided with transportation assistance if it would enable them to stay at their original school, at least until the end of the academic year.

While there is overwhelming evidence that the majority of school mobility is a function of housing mobility, the school mobility literature has paid surprisingly little attention to housing policy reform—virtually all recommendations focus on school policies. The greatest boost to residential stability—hence to school stability—would come from a vast increase in the supply of decent, affordable housing. Such a change would create a situation where pressures to move—demand exceeding supply, gentrification, unaffordable rent increases—would be markedly reduced.

Policies regarding evictions need to better reflect the disastrous impacts such forced displacements have on children's education. Local public housing programs (such as HOPE VI, which is displacing tens of thousands of residents in order to create new, mixed-income developments), community development corporations and other nonprofit housing sponsors should take school relocation issues into account when they feel they must force tenants to leave. In terms of the more complicated task of regulating privately-owned housing, rent and "just cause" eviction controls, condominium conversion and demolition controls, and mortgage foreclosure prevention programs can do a great deal to increase residential stability. In the upcoming welfare reauthorization, dollars could be allocated to help families avoid or delay evictions. Expanding the protected categories under various federal, state and local anti-discrimination laws could also help create residential stability.

The few existing federal categorical programs that support educational stability and academic success for homeless, migrant and other "at-risk" students should be preserved, expanded and adequately enforced. Information about successful state and local models should be widely disseminated and replicated. Child welfare, in particular foster care, is another area where increased sensitivity to student mobility is needed. Wherever possible, children's placements should avoid the need to change schools, especially during a school year. To help ease the burden on transitioning families and the new schools and teachers they come to, the US Department of Education must be more aggressive in ensuring that electronic interstate records systems are put into place.

Clearly, student mobility is an area where additional research is needed. Among the questions we have initially identified are:

- What are the impacts of a highly mobile classroom on the stable students in that classroom?
- What are the impacts of a highly mobile classroom on teachers?

- What are the ways in which welfare reform impacts the classroom?
- What are the ways in which the child welfare/foster care system impacts classroom mobility?
- What financial costs are imposed on school systems as a result of high classroom mobility?
- How does high mobility impact new federal and state accountability systems?
- What is the experience of private/parochial schools with classroom mobility?
- How does the Department of Defense deal with classroom mobility in the schools it runs?
- To what degree do proposed reforms—e.g., higher teacher qualifications, smaller schools/classrooms—reduce classroom mobility?
- What litigation possibilities—in the housing area as well as the education area—exist to force needed change: What are the legal theories, with respect to housing policy and other relevant areas, that might produce desirable results?

A multipronged approach to addressing classroom mobility should seek to support family stability by instituting shared responsibility for mobile students among families, communities, schools, school districts and government at all levels. Raised awareness of the centrality and connectedness of school transiency will help create an impetus for changes in the housing, welfare, education, homelessness, migrant worker and foster care policies aimed at reducing and addressing the effects of harmful school mobility.

Chapter 37

Race, Poverty and Special Education: Apprenticeships for Prison Work

Rosa Smith

Where have all of our Black sons gone? Some might say to war, my dear. Others would say to jail, my dear. I would say yes to both of these and add that they are first sent to Special Education programs, which for all too many African-American boys are not doorways to opportunity, but trapdoors sending them willy-nilly to war, to jail, to lives of unfulfilled promise.

According to *A New Era: Revitalizing Special Education for Children and Their Families*, the July 2002 report of the President's Commission on Excellence in Special Education: "Many of the current methods of identifying children with disabilities lack validity. As a result, thousands of children are misidentified every year...." And whom does this most affect? "African-American children are twice as likely as whites to be identified for the mental retardation category. In the emotional disturbance category, black students are about half more likely than white students to be classified in this category" (*Minority Students in Special and Gifted Education*, National Research Council, 2002).

Are we surprised?

The IQ Test Bias

The reasons for this pervasive misidentification and referral of African-American children were found by the President's Commission to include "reliance on IQ tests that have known cultural bias" and the fact that "minority children are much more likely to be placed in the emotional disturbance category because of behavioral characteristics associated with the cultural context in which a child is raised."

The mental retardation category of Special Education is under the control of specialists too often using IQ tests that were developed with a concern for their validity with White populations and sub-groups, but with no concern for their validity with minority populations. When their originators found that girls were doing better than boys on early versions of the test, they changed the tests rather than their ideas about the relative skill of girls and boys at such tasks. But when it was found that the tests failed to deal equitably among ethnic and racial groups, the test developers took this to be a confirmation of the tests' validity. This is not news. It is now generally acknowledged that IQ tests, and the very concept of IQ, were deeply implicated in early 20th Century racist theories. And yet they continue to be used.

Teacher Referrals

If the over-classification of African-American children and other minorities as mentally retarded is performed out of sight by "scientifically trained" experts, classification of children as in need of Special Education because of emotional disturbance, on the other hand, is overwhelmingly based on teacher referrals. According to President Bush's Commission on Excellence in Special Education, teachers "refer more than 80 percent of children who are placed in a high-incidence category.... To the extent that teachers are not prepared to manage behavior or instruct those with learning characteristics that make them 'at risk' in general education, minority children will be more likely to be referred."

State-by-State Differences

One of the most important findings of the National Research Council study is the enormous difference in the way the system operates across the states. For example, in 1998 five states categorized over 5% of their Black students as mentally retarded (Massachusetts, Alabama, Arkansas, Iowa, Indiana), while five states classified less than 1% of their Black students as mentally retarded (Alaska, Maine, New Hampshire, New Jersey, New York). In Washington, DC, the odds of a Black student being declared as mentally retarded are over nine times those for a White student. It seems most unlikely on the face of it that the frequency of mental retardation of any group in Massachusetts is six times that of the same group in New Jersey or neighboring New Hampshire, or that in the nation's capital, home of one of the largest concentrations of middle-class African Americans, nine times as many of their children as those of their White neighbors are mentally retarded.

The suspicion of systematic bias is reinforced by the fact that, nationally, 6.6% of all children are placed in gifted and talented programs, but only 3% of Black children receive such placement. Of course, much placement in such programs is done with reference to IQ tests.

Nationally, approximately 12% of all children—nearly two million girls and four million boys—are classified as Special Education students. For most groups, placement in Special Education for emotional disturbance is three times as high for male as for female students, which means that when we look at the intersection of race and gender bias in emotional disturbance placements, for example, we find that Black male students are referred at more than five times the rate for White female students. As a result, in many parts of the country up to 30% of African-American boys of school age are to be found in Special Education programs. It is common knowledge that once children are placed in Special Education classes, their chances of graduating on time and pursuing education beyond high school are greatly reduced.

Jail-Bound

The Harvard Civil Rights Project, in its September 2002 report, "Racial Inequity in Special Education," tells us that "To the extent that minority students are misclassified, segregated or inadequately served, Special Education can contribute to a denial of equality of opportunity, with devastating results in communities throughout the nation." Partially as a consequence of over-assignments to Special Education, in many large cities 70% or more of African-American boys do not graduate from high school with their peers. The consequences for those young men, for their communities and for the country are disastrous. Most dramatically, the racial bias that permeates the justice system helps exacerbate other factors—such as inadequate education—to criminalize black youths. Racial bias in the criminal justice system is present in response to crime, disparate enforcement of laws such as drug laws, the creation of criminal histories through racial profiling, and disparities in prosecution and sentencing. A 1997 study of Massachusetts drug-law enforcement found that in that "liberal" state, Blacks were 39 times more likely to be incarcerated for a drug offense than Whites. According to the 2000 Census, nationally 60% of incarcerated youths age 18 and under are African-American, nearly four times their representation in the general population.

According to Marc Mauer in his 1999 book *Race to Incarcerate*, young African-American men are more likely to be in jail—or otherwise involved with the courts—than to go to college. A Black boy born in 1991 stands a 29% chance of being imprisoned at some point in his life, compared with a 16% chance for a Hispanic boy and a 4% chance for a White boy. As a result, in some states, one-quarter of Black men cannot vote because of a felony conviction. Perhaps the most disturbing aspect of this trend is the enormous racial disparity among those on death row.

The social consequences of poverty and race are vividly apparent in the continuum from over-assignment to Special Education for Black boys to prison statistics for Black men. If Black boys were assigned to Special Education at rates comparable to those of White boys, drop-out rates would decline, graduation rates would rise and the school-to-prison pipeline would flow less swiftly. Part of the problem is in the misuse of IQ tests, part in the fear that teachers have of Black boys "disrupting" classrooms. Much of the origin of the problem is to be found in the fact that the schools impoverished African-American (and other minority) children attend are less well-funded than those attended by more privileged students. Such schools are less likely than those in the suburbs to have experienced, well-trained teachers. Per-student expenditures in those schools are often lower, while common sense would indicate that the needs of poor children require higher levels of per-pupil expenditure and better trained, more experienced teachers who can deliver high-quality instruction while practicing effective classroom management that minimizes chaos, rather than reaching for the Special Education referral form.

The Need for Early Intervention

Many believe that the system must be changed at an even earlier point. Too many African-American boys and other disadvantaged children do not have the opportunity to experience quality early childhood education. As a consequence, they come to school poorly prepared and not ready to learn, and thus are more likely to be placed in Special Education classes at an early age. Once there, students of color "are less likely than their white counterparts to receive counseling and psychological supports when they first exhibit signs of emotional turmoil and often go without adequate services once identified," according to the Harvard Civil Rights Project report noted above. "This lack of early intervention and support correlates highly with drop-outs and suspension or expulsion and helps explain why minority school-aged children are over-represented in the juvenile justice system."

Classified as mentally retarded by culturally biased IQ tests and called emotionally disturbed by teachers who find it easier to ask for students to be removed from their classrooms than to teach them, African-American boys are thrown off the classic American path to achievement. The large numbers of African-American boys who do not graduate from high school, the large numbers of African-American men who go through the criminal justice system, are then pointed to as "proof" of the validity of the biased systems that have failed them.

From a social policy point of view, the entire Special Education-to-prison system in which all too many African-American men are placed is irrationally costly. It would be much better, much more "efficient," to spend even a small fraction of those funds so as to provide universal pre-kindergarten and kindergarten, higher salaries and better training for inner-city classroom teachers, and universal after-school and summer programs for children at risk of not achieving their full academic potential.

I suggest that we do so.

Chapter 38

Race, Poverty and Virtual Learning

Sharon Johnston and Michelle Kinley

Florida Virtual School (FLVS), an innovative educational opportunity, breaks the mold of traditional education. Our virtual learning environment allows students to choose the time convenient for them to "attend class." Our online courses offer a choice for all learners. FLVS students consist of public school, home-school and private school students, athletes, performers and students with scheduling conflicts or medical problems. For the 2004-05 school year, 68% of the students served were from public schools, 25% were home-schoolers and 7% were private and charter school students. The program serves middle and high school students, with no immediate plans to serve elementary school students, out of concerns for how educationally appropriate this mode of instruction is for younger children. FLVS is part of the Florida Public Schools, and public school students who participate in its activities are required to get sign-off from their geographical school in order to enroll. The signature of the guidance counselor is used by FLVS only to verify that the desired course is appropriate, based on the student's academic history, grade level and age. Most public school students take just one or two online courses from FLVS as a supplement to their regular curriculum.

The primary reasons for developing FLVS were to give students a choice in how, when and where they learn, with the intended outcome of increasing student achievement and ensuring that all students in Florida have equal access to all courses, especially the high-level courses.

Teaching is not just about the curriculum, it's about connecting with students. FLVS has designed its courses and instruction to maximize the student-teacher-parent relationship. All of the 173 full-time and 100 adjunct teachers have state certification in the field they are teaching, and there is an intensive, ongoing staff development program covering FLVS pedagogy, technology, policies and procedures. For the first year, teachers have a veteran FLVS teacher as a mentor. FLVS instructors are available to students via cell phone, pager, email, chat rooms and instant messaging throughout the day, week and weekends. We have created an online environment that gives students the opportunity to receive individualized attention from their instructor, resulting in a mastery of learning approach. By providing parents instant access to their child's grade book, progress reports and instructional comments, FLVS has built a model in which the student receives instruction from a highly qualified instructor while receiving support at home from his or her parents.

FLVS launched its first online courses in 1997. In 2000, the Florida Legislature established FLVS as an independent educational entity with a separate governing board. In most respects, FLVS now has a legal status comparable to the 67 school districts that make up Florida's public school system.

For the 2005-06 school year, it is estimated that FLVS will serve over 40,000 enrollments (a figure representing all courses taken) in more than 85 online courses. Current course offerings include a full middle school curriculum, regular and honors-level high school credit courses covering all curriculum areas, AP courses and high-stakes test preparation courses. Through creation of a partnership with eight school districts, FLVS has also developed three courses specifically targeted for adult high school students, as well as the state's first fully online GED preparation course.

Educational leaders across the nation are being challenged as never before to create opportunities to meet the varied needs of students. Many leaders are beginning to implement online education as a part of their solution to meet a wide range of challenges. These challenges include such issues as providing educational choice, promoting the use of technology in learning, dealing with large increases or decreases in student enrollment, and producing students who have the knowledge and skills to immediately succeed in their post-secondary pursuits or the workforce. FLVS has received international attention for its work in distance learning, and, beyond Florida, provides courses and/or instruction in 28 states as well as serving tuition enrollments from nine countries.

A Resource for Underserved Populations

To reach the underserved populations, FLVS hired an e-learning manager who connects with minority groups to promote access for minority and disadvantaged students. By working with One Florida, a state initiative that "unites Floridians behind a shared vision of opportunity and diversity," FLVS is involved in projects that promote educational and technological equity throughout the state. One Florida has the goal of providing the same level of high-quality services to all students and their families, regardless of where they live, the wealth of their family or the color of their skin. Some of the groups involved in One Florida that are working with FLVS to pave the path for minority students are The Hundred Black Men, NAACP, the Digital Divide Council, The Work Force Innovation Boards, The Florida Education Fund, and the Office of Equity and Access. A major challenge has been to find ways to provide equal access as well as connectivity to those in need. Businesses and organizations that are One Florida members have been locating or creating local community centers or hubs that can provide Internet access for students. Despite the group's effort, the demand for computers and connectivity outweigh the supply. Calls come in each day with requests for connectivity to the Internet, computers new or old, as well as computer parts (printers, scanners, etc.).

By establishing a priority registration process, allowing minority students top priority in registering for courses, FLVS has witnessed the minority population increase to 35%. To reach into the community, FLVS offers several workshops and trainings free of charge.

FLVS Minority Student Speaks:

My name is Jalon Dardy and I am an African-American young lady who is currently a senior at Palm Beach Lakes High. Four of the students that took the FLVS AP Microeconomics course with me lived with a single mother. Three of them were black. All four students' fathers had left their families and only one of the black students had no sibling(s). Yes, none of us had the money to buy three computers, pay $700 a month for a car, or go to the mall every week, but we all at least had the chance to take a free accelerated course online. Online learning opens a door to the future and closes a door of the past.

Regardless of race and poverty, online learning has given students the chance to challenge themselves, try something new, obtain a higher level of freedom, earn a college credit early, and display intelligence and potential. Although minority students facing poverty may have a little more difficulty in obtaining these benefits, we are not at all discouraged from reaching our goals. In fact, our disadvantages help us to reach higher and stretch further for the advantages.

Chapter 39

Race, Poverty and Residential Schools

Heidi Goldsmith

> "Boarding schools are among the oldest institutions in the country. This educational choice has been reserved for the rich. Boarding schools for the affluent have been celebrated. But somehow it is controversial when we say choice for all children. Every child wants very much to succeed. The introduction of boarding schools is nothing more than another educational choice."—Former Minnesota Governor Arne Carlson, at First National Conference on Residential Education for Disadvantaged Children and Youth, October 2000.

Parents who live in nice, safe neighborhoods and have the financial means often send their teenagers, with pride, to residential preparatory ("prep") schools. Youth from economically and socially disadvantaged homes rarely have that choice. In fact, it is actually counter to current public policy to "place" —i.e., enroll—an abused, neglected or poor youth in anything other than a "family." Youth in the child welfare system can only live in what *looks* like a family —i.e., a foster family or a group home with no more than 18 residents. At age 18, they are then "emancipated," meaning they must now fend for themselves, with no one to support them. Current public policy for foster care youth strongly favors any number of foster care placements over enrollment of a foster youth in a boarding school.

Currently, there are approximately 80 boarding schools for economically and socially disadvantaged children in the US. Over 50% of the students at these schools are children of color. While there are over 300 "prep" schools in TABS, The Association of Boarding Schools, only three have more than a few scholarship students from economically disadvantaged backgrounds. Two of these, Girard College in Philadelphia and Piney Woods Country Life School in Piney Woods, Mississippi, have student populations that are 85% and 99% African-American, respectively. Most of these students—at Girard College, 100%—are from low-income, zero- or single-parent backgrounds. Yet their success rates are astounding: 90% of their graduates go on to four-year colleges.

Residential Education

"Residential education" is the umbrella term for an out-of-home setting where a young person both lives and learns. It encompasses boarding schools, "prep" schools, orphanages, youth villages, residential academies and, most recently, residential charter schools. These 24-hour educational, future-focused settings become students' "second homes." Students are housed and fed in a safe, nurturing setting where they receive a quality education with smaller class sizes than in most public schools, and can take advantage of sports teams, computer clubs, leadership programs, community service and more. They learn social skills, such as conflict resolution, have positive adult role models and gain a positive sense of what their lives can be. Values and lessons learned are consistent 24 hours a day—what is taught in the classroom is reinforced in the dorms or cottages, and vice versa. The focus in these environments is on students' potential and futures.

CORE: the Coalition for Residential Education is an advocacy group for and association of residential schools that serve youth whose homes and communities cannot meet their needs. Specifically, these schools aim to serve:

- Youth who don't live in safe homes—homeless youth and those in abusive homes.
- Youth who have bounced around from foster home to foster home, or who would likely fare poorly in the foster care system.
- Youth whose well-meaning parents, struggling to make ends meet, beg the residential schools to accept their children, to keep them safe and away from the drug culture.
- Youth whose parents won't enter residential drug treatment programs because they are afraid to place their children in the foster care system. Enrolling their children in residential schools would be good for the children, face-saving for the parent, and halt the destructive cycle of abuse and neglect.

An internal survey of students attending CORE schools found that approximately 65% are youth of color; 81% are economically disadvantaged.

Most students spend at least two years at these residential education programs. According to practitioners across the country and in other countries, this is the length of time young people need until they finally understand they are in charge of their own life outcomes. They need this longer-term, stable setting until they grasp that they need not be a victim anymore. A light goes on in a young person's eyes at this approximately two-year point, and their motivation skyrockets. The child now believes he or she can become a "somebody," a valuable member of society, a productive citizen.

Most residential education programs for children from economically and socially disadvantaged backgrounds meet a student's educational and living needs at a cost of approximately $30,000 per year. This is less than half the cost most juvenile delinquency facilities incur, where many of these youth are likely to land absent significant intervention, and a third to a fifth of the cost of residential/psychiatric treatment centers, which are short-term, intensive and focus on the youth's pathologies.

Funding for existing residential education programs falls into three categories:

- Publicly funded: The federal government funds three programs run by different agencies: the Department of Labor, the Department of Interior's Bureau of Indian Affairs and the Department of Defense. Two states (Pennsylvania, with the Scotland School for Veterans' Children, and Indiana, with the Indiana Soldiers' and Sailors' Home) provide funding as well, in both cases Civil War relics and available only to children of veterans.
- Privately funded: Philanthropists such as Stephen Girard and Milton Hershey funded residential schools in their names; American Honda recently funded a residential school in Colorado; individual visionaries founded and began private fundraising for their dream residential schools.
- Public-private partnerships: This is the most popular recent method of funding, which includes residential charter schools, of which there are now four nationally. Public funds pay for some elements, such as the education component and/or the per diem on behalf of enrolled foster care youth. The remaining funds are raised from private sources.

I was personally inspired to make this option available for at-risk American youth after seeing Israel's network of 60 youth villages, which are used as a national tool of rehabilitation and social inclusion. These villages are based on a hybrid between a kibbutz and an English boarding school. Israelis tell the youth in the villages, "What your family cannot do for you, your community will." Some of Israel's most successful politicians, business leaders, artists, teachers and other citizens are graduates of the youth villages and attribute much of their success to them. Many Americans agree that a similar network of residential education programs would be extremely effective in the US.

The New National "Residential Education Movement"

The idea of residential schools for economically and socially disadvantaged youth is gaining momentum. A national movement, in its relative infancy, believes a young person needs to live in a setting, such as a residential school, that behaves like a family—providing basic food, clothing and shelter, physical and emotional safety, consistent love from caring adults, stability, belonging and encouragement to achieve one's best. New schools are being planned and opened across the country by public servants, private individuals, corporations and existing youth-serving organizations. In addition to assisting new school development across the country, CORE is taking these additional steps:

- Creating a nationwide network of residential schools;
- Campaigning to change public understanding of what these places are and can be;
- Advocating for more supportive public policy so that young people from the most disadvantaged backgrounds, including foster youth, can attend.

Challenges: Money, Myths and Myopia

The new residential education movement faces significant ideological and public perception challenges. It is less expensive, in the very short term, to let a youth drop out of school and "do his own thing" than to invest approximately $30,000 per year to send him to a residential school. In the long term, however, it is likely to be cost-effective—and good for the youth, their families and our communities. Funding for prevention-focused programs for low-income youth, however, remains a low priority.

There are misperceptions of what these residential education programs are—and are not. The Dickensian image of harsh institutions is a far cry from today's reality. Yet people wanting to open new residential schools still encounter this bias and face formidable NIMBY challenges—based on fears as to what the new schools and their students will do to surrounding neighborhoods. These fears are often reinforced by people who do not want youth of color and those who are economically disadvantaged in their neighborhoods. Another challenge is that the majority of the current child welfare establishment is strongly anti-"institutional." According to those who perpetuate this belief, anything large (i.e., a residential school housing and educating 70 to a few hundred youth) is bad, even though they have not checked out these programs.

The San Pasqual Academy, which opened in 2001 in San Diego, will ultimately be the home and school for 250 teenagers from the foster care system who have already been in 7–25 foster homes and whom the courts have determined cannot be reunited with their families. One thousand children in San

Diego County alone are eligible. Yet, a number of child welfare advocates have objected to this setting, and some have even sued.

There are some downsides and challenges inherent in this option for youth. One is that students need to learn to live in "two worlds"—within the world and norms of the residential school, and the world they came from, visit and to which they likely will return. This is sometimes enough to cause students to drop out of their residential school. Conversely, teachers at these schools often complain that it takes a day or more for the students to be "teachable" again after a visit to their homes. Another challenge for students in residential schools is adjusting to life after graduation. Regular life, with all its choices, is very different from the safe, structured environment of a residential school students are accustomed to.

Research Needs and Questions

There are no evaluative studies of residential education as a whole—something that is sorely needed. However, there are thousands of success stories from alumni and poignant testimonies of students currently attending residential schools. Over and over again, students in schools I visit tell me they are the only one among the friends they grew up with who is not in jail or dead. Sometimes youth even arrive at the entrance to the residential schools on their own accord ("pilgrims"), often from hundreds of miles away, with a modern version of the bandana on a stick over their shoulders, and plead, "Please take me in." These anecdotes speak to the success of these residential programs.

However, skeptics and supporters alike ask for proof, outcomes and statistics that residential education is effective and cost-effective. The lack of such information is an obstacle to increasing the number of residential schools, to changing public policy and to changing public opinion about this option for youth. Some of the questions needing study are:

- Who are best served in these settings?
- What is the "value added" of the residential component? Which is the most expensive and controversial part?
- What aspects of these programs make the most impact?
- How are children's lives improved in these programs?
- How do students in these settings fare compared with students of similar backgrounds and talents who live in foster homes, group homes, or those who remain in poverty-stricken neighborhoods?
- What are the effective practices and policies of other countries that would contribute to those in the US?

Long viewed as a desirable option for youth from wealthy backgrounds, boarding schools should also be viewed as a "normal," high-quality and sometimes desirable choice for low-income children, regardless of race. Low-income youth and their families need this choice at least as much as those living in more comfortable circumstances. These settings are especially needed for youth who, through no fault of their own, lack a stable, supportive, loving, stimulating home. This option for youth should be accepted, both as a matter of policy and practice.

Chapter 40

Race, Poverty and Community Schools

Ira Harkavy and Martin J. Blank

Listening to the ongoing debate about the "No Child Left Behind Act" and education reform, it would be easy to assume that the only things that matter are annually testing for all children, having a qualified teacher in every classroom in four years and allowing parents to move their children out of persistently failing schools.

Nonsense.

High academic standards, aligned tests, clear incentives and strong professional development are important, but they're not sufficient to meet the lofty goal of educating all children.

Largely ignored in this debate, and early implementation of the Act, are the highly visible, morally troubling, increasingly savage inequalities experienced by far too many poor children in predominantly minority urban schools, as well as in underserved, under-resourced rural schools, and their respective communities. The school-community connection is evident in the relationship between the multiple interrelated plagues: poverty, violence, ill health, broken families, unemployment, and drug and alcohol abuse—and academic failure.

Discussion of these issues seems to be outside the present education reform framework. Paul Barton of the Educational Testing Service, in his 2001 study *Facing the Hard Facts of Education Reform*, suggests an alternative view. He argues that "our reluctance to address important nonacademic factors stems from a fear that to consider such factors may cause us to lose focus,...and provide excuses for not raising standards and achievement....[H]owever, we do so at our peril. The seriousness of our purpose requires that we learn to rub our bellies and pat our heads at the same time."

From our perspective, rubbing our bellies and patting our heads means creating comprehensive community schools. While the community school approach is applicable to all students, it is particularly important for poor children of color, whose assets and talents tend to be overlooked, and who bring the largest challenges to the schoolhouse door.

A Vision of Community Schools

Here is a vision of a community schools supported by the Coalition for Community Schools, an alliance of more than 170 national, state and local organizations. This vision explicitly recognizes the shared responsibility of schools, families and community for the education of all our children:

> A community school strategically combines community resources with the assets and expertise of educators and schools to better meet the learning and development goals of students and schools, and to support families and communities. Individual schools and the school system work in partnership with community agencies and organizations to operate these unique institutions. Families, students, principals, teachers and neighborhood residents decide together what happens at a community school.
>
> Community schools are open to students, families and community members before, during and after school, throughout the year. They have high standards and expectations for students, qualified teachers and a focused, engaging curriculum.
>
> Community schools use the community as a resource to engage students in learning and service, and help them become problem-solvers in their communities. The school also sees itself as a resource to the community, sharing its facilities, equipment and other assets to support community-building efforts.
>
> Before- and after-school programs build on classroom experiences and help students expand their horizons, contribute to their communities and have fun. Family support centers help with parent involvement, child rearing, employment, housing and other services. Medical, dental and mental health services are readily available. Parents and community residents participate in adult education and job training programs, and use the school as a place for community problem-solving. Volunteers come to community schools to support young people's academic, interpersonal and career success.

Strategically, when community schools bring together school and community assets, they create six conditions for learning, conditions that are especially vital for poor, minority children:

- **Condition #1**: A core instructional program with high standards, qualified teachers, and a focused, engaged curriculum provides for academic
  excellence.
- **Condition #2**: The basic medical, mental and physical health needs of
  young people and their families are addressed.
- **Condition #3**: Families are actively engaged in supporting and making
  decisions affecting their children's learning.
- **Condition #4**: The school climate, strengthened by community engagement, promotes safety, respect and connection to a learning community.
- **Condition #5**: Students are motivated and engaged in learning in and
  out of school.
- **Condition #6**: The community provides a resource for learning and
  civic participation.

These conditions summarize a growing consensus on what research, practice and common sense suggests it takes for all young people to succeed.

In our vision of community schools, educators are major partners, but they
do not do everything. A capable partner organization—a youth development
organization, a college or university, a child and family services agency, a
community development corporation, a family support center, for example—can
serve as the anchor partner for a community school. The partner organizations
work with the school to mobilize and integrate the resources of community and
school. This allows principals and teachers to focus on their core mission: improving student learning.

Asset-based and strengths-based practices that have emerged in the fields of
community-building, youth development, family support and related human
services fields complement one another at a community school, providing students, their families and neighborhood residents with multiple pathways to success. The totality of the work of a community school represents an important
anti-poverty strategy.

In the past decade, community school expansion has largely been in poor
urban and rural settings with large minority populations. There are national approaches, such as the work of Children's Aid Society and Beacon Schools, initiated in New York and now being adapted in many cities; Communities in
Schools, reaching students and families in more than 2,300 schools; and the
West Philadelphia Improvement Corps, started in Philadelphia, in partnership
with the Center for Community Partnerships at the University of Pennsylvania,
is now operating in more than 20 communities.

There are many more locally grown models, distinguished by the creation
of community leadership groups that bring together representatives of various
stakeholder groups concerned with the well-being of children, families and
communities—e.g., Campaign for Community Schools, Chicago; Bridges to
Success, Indianapolis; Local Investment Commission, Kansas City, Missouri;

Schools Uniting Neighborhoods, Portland/Multnomah County, Oregon; and the Community Learning Centers Initiative in Lincoln, Nebraska. In rural communities, the community school strategy emphasizes place-based education—engaging the community, the school and its students in active learning and community problem-solving. Each of these approaches has different emphases, but they all share the broad vision of a community school.

Results in Community Schools

Do community schools work? Absolutely. Evaluation data compiled by the Coalition for Community Schools in *Making the Difference: Research and Practice in Community Schools* demonstrate the positive impact of community schools on student learning, healthy youth development, family well-being, school functioning and community life. Results include students doing better on tests, students improving their attendance and behavior, and families having their basic needs met and being more involved in their children's education. Moreover, principals and teachers in community schools testify that deep and intentional relationships with community partners are not a distraction, but rather a significant source of support, giving teachers more time to teach and students more opportunity to learn.

The Public's Perspective

A 2002 poll by the Knowledge Works Foundation in Ohio provides evidence that the public supports the community school approach. Eighty-four percent of respondents supported community use of schools during afternoon, evening and weekend hours for activities like health clinics, recreation activities, and parenting and adult education classes. Seventy-two percent agreed that adult fitness, community activities and parenting classes should be located in public schools. Seventy-nine percent agreed that schools should offer mental health services for students, and 65% agreed that community social services for children like health services, dental services and after-school programs should be located in public schools. We suspect there is similar support around the country.

Keys to Community Schools

There are five keys to creating community schools: leadership, partnership, community voice, financing and management.

Leadership

As Atelia Melaville writes in her 1998 study, *Learning Together: The developing field of school-community initiatives*, leadership provides "fuel and direction; community school initiatives that last are led by people committed to the well-being of poor children and families, and who know where they want to go and have the position, personality and power to make others want to come along." This leadership is creating permanent coalitions to improve results for children through community schools.

Partnership

Partnerships are essential to mobilizing, galvanizing and integrating the enormous untapped resources of communities for the purpose of improving schooling and community life. These partnerships, bringing together stakeholders across the public, private and nonprofit sectors and including community voices, are part of a "democratic devolution revolution" that is slowly restructuring the way communities make decisions affecting their residents. Through these partnerships, the ongoing work of local institutions (e.g., higher education; health and human services agencies; youth development and community development groups; civic, business and religious organizations) changes and adapts to the needs in particular community school settings.

Community Voice

Organized and vocal support from students, parents and neighborhood residents ensures that the community school is responsive to their concerns and helps to convince stakeholders across the community of the importance and effectiveness of the community school strategy. These individuals participate on a planning team that develops, oversees and assesses the performance of the community school.

Financing

Money does matter in a community school. Government and public school systems, in particular, as well as philanthropy and United Ways and other institutions, have key roles to play in helping to finance the cooperation among the sectors of society that must come together in a community school strategy. The work of the partnership at the community or school district level, and the coordination work at the school site, generally require new investments or the use of existing funds in new ways.

Management
Linking community resources to the school and helping the school become a resource to the community is real work. Community schools work because someone does that work—a community school coordinator hired by the school or in many urban centers by community-based organizations (CBOs). More and more places are turning to CBOs for this work because they have deeper roots in neighborhoods and bring an expertise in youth development and community development that schools do not have.

Barriers to the Community Schools Movement

The benefits of community schools are becoming clearer and clearer. Yet there are numerous challenges to expanding the community schools approach as an anti-poverty approach and education reform strategy:

Differences in Philosophy and Practice
Practitioners in education, youth development, health, mental health, family support, community development and related fields often have their distinct philosophy and practice of what works best to help young people succeed. The cultural distance between school and community remains wide. To shorten that distance, inter-professional development programs are needed that help educate practitioners able to work across sectors and with schools and communities.

Preparation of School Leaders
Superintendents and principals learn little about working with family and community at institutes of higher education. They are trained to manage their buildings, not to be leaders and partners in the education of children.

Community Leadership
The number of leaders who are able to initiate and guide a partnership-driven community school strategy, especially involving working across race and class, is still limited. More efforts must be made to develop leaders committed to a collaborative community problem-solving culture.

Categorical Funding
Narrowly crafted public funding streams separate people and organizations. They make it more difficult to integrate resources in ways that are consistent with a community school strategy. Needless to say, resources remain insufficient

to meet the needs of all students even if they were used more strategically; at the same time, much more can be done with what is available.

Financing

Funding is still insufficient to develop community schools that can create the conditions for all children to learn. We now find ourselves in a budgetary crisis at the federal level that is leading to significant reduction in programs that assist low-income children and families. Even if Title I continues to receive increases, cuts in other education programs and in the budgets of HHS, USDA, HUD and other federal agencies pose a major threat to the well-being of children.

The continuing expansion of community schools across the country in the face of these barriers demonstrates the power and potential of this idea.

Action Steps

Stakeholders in many sectors must act to create and sustain community schools. The following six action recommendations focus on the federal and state government:

- Develop and promote a **vision** for improving student learning that incorporates the critical role of families and communities, as well as schools.
- Support broad-based, local coalitions or multi-agency commissions to advance, develop and sustain community schools.
- Ensure that federal and state programs and policies focus on supporting student learning and are subject to the guidance of a local coalition of such multi-agency commissions. This means coordinating categorical grant programs across agencies to improve student learning, and providing incentives for coordination at other governmental levels.
- Substantially **increase funding** for the supports and opportunities that poor children need to succeed, with a focus on those that build on the assets of young people, their families and communities.
- Make targeted **investments** in community schools to increase the effectiveness of existing programs and resources. This includes funding community school coordinators to facilitate effective partnerships, sustain funding over time, and support local planning and partnership-building processes.
- Build schools as centers of community. As state and local government and school districts pay to rehabilitate or construct new schools, they

should build community schools that meet not only the needs of students and schools, but family and community as well.

Conclusion

Organizational development expert Peter Senge argued in the Summer 2001 *Community Youth Development Journal* that "until we go back to thinking about school as the totality of the environment in which a child grows up, we can expect no deep changes. Change requires a community—people living and working together, assuming some common responsibility for something that's of deep concern and interest to all of them—their children."

Community schools can help build the kind of caring, compassionate, responsible community Senge describes. Community schools are an environment-changing institution that engage children, their families, neighbors and local institutions in active work to improve the quality of life and learning of all members of the community. Needless to say, community schools have a particular contribution to make in helping to change the appalling conditions facing far too many of America's poor and minority children.

Chapter 41

Education Quiz

Derrick Z. Jackson

This quiz, slightly shortened here, first appeared in the June 30, 2000 Boston Globe *and is used with permission of and thanks to the author. MCAS (the Massachusetts Comprehensive Assessment System) is a test (in English, math, science and social studies) given to all fourth-, eighth- and tenth-graders in the state's public and charter schools (including special education students and students whose first language is not English). A passing grade now is required for graduation. Fifty percent of the tenth-graders failed the math test.*

Recently I published questions from the MCAS tenth-grade history test, criticizing them as being grossly Eurocentric and of questionable relevance for today's job-seekers.

Of course, many readers saw nothing wrong with the questions. One wrote that surgeons, construction workers and software designers may not need to know about the Edict of Nantes or the Treaty of Tordesillas at work but that such events "are not trivia—they are part of the framework within which we try to evaluate our own nation's attempts to shape the world."

Let us be nice and assume the reader is correct. But if you are going to be correct about how our own nation shaped itself, you have to have other questions that are not on the MCAS tests:

1. According to Gorée Island's slave museum, the number of stolen Africans is the equivalent of emptying out the current metropolitan areas of:

    A. Milwaukee
    B. Tokyo
    C. Los Angeles
    D. New York, Los Angeles, Chicago, Washington, San Francisco and Philadelphia combined

2. According to most histories, the number of stolen Africans who actually made it alive to the Americas is the equivalent of:
    A. New York, Los Angeles, Chicago, Washington, San Francisco and Philadelphia combined
    B. New York, Los Angeles and Chicago combined
    C. Los Angeles and Chicago combined
    D. Just San Francisco and Philadelphia

3. The conservative value of slave labor to the American economy, when it was analyzed in 1983, is nearly the equivalent of the 1999 spending budget for:
    A. Wisconsin
    B. The Rolling Stones Tour
    C. The New York Yankees
    D. The United States

4. The World War II generation will bequeath $8 trillion to its children. In the years 1929 to 1969, wages lost by African Americans to discrimination were:
    A. nothing, because we are now a color-blind society
    B. $1.6 billion
    C. irrelevant because Michael Jordan owns part of the Washington Wizards and Magic Johnson owns part of the Los Angeles Lakers
    D. $1.6 trillion, nearly equal to 1999 federal budget of $1.7 trillion

5. One result of post-slavery discrimination is that the average white baby-boomer and the average black baby-boomer will respectively inherit:
    A. $50,000 and $42,000
    B. $80,000 and $50,000
    C. $20,000 and $15,000
    D. $65,000 and $8,000

6. Under "40 Acres and a Mule," about 40,000 newly freed slaves were given Southern coastal land that had been abandoned by unpardoned Confederate families. These black people held the land for two years before angry white people stole it through beatings, torture and legal chicanery. During those two years, the black occupants were known for:

    A. being lazy and shiftless

    B. being top local athletes

    C. wanting back the good old days, where you could depend on a bowl of gruel and a watermelon from massa

    D. fine crops and self-governance

7. New England is far from cotton fields and sugar plantations. Thus, it is interesting that Brown University:

    A. created a chair in honor of abolitionist John Brown

    B. named its music department after James Brown

    C. named its graduate school of business after Ron Brown

    D. was founded by the Browns of Rhode Island, who profited from the triangular slave trade

8. In Lowell, Mass., in 1835, politicians, law enforcement, lawyers, doctors and shopkeepers signed petitions to:

    A. call for the end of slavery

    B. volunteer to go south for a Freedom Summer to understand the plight of the slaves

    C. build a new Fenway Park for the Red Sox

    D. oppose abolition because the textile mills depended on slave-picked cotton

9. African Americans fought in every US war, hoping their participation would result in equality. After the Civil War, World War I and World War II, black sacrifice for America and the world was rewarded with:

    A. full voting rights

    B. free tickets to Jack Johnson and Joe Louis fights

    C. free coupons for watermelons

    D. lynchings and white race riots

By the way, the answer is (D) on all questions.

Health

Chapter 42

What Works: A Fifty-Year Retrospective

David Barton Smith

Three watershed events in the struggle to end divisions by race in the United States recently marked major anniversaries: the 1954 *Brown v. Board of Education* decision, the Civil Rights Act of 1964 and the 1965 Medicare-Medicaid legislation. While we have fallen far short of the vision of the movement that produced these events, what has worked? I list concrete examples of five general strategies that have given good returns on investments.

    1. *Visibility:* Nothing happens until the inequities and disparities are made visible. The Medicare-Medicaid legislation was passed only after disparities in access to care by race and income began to be documented by regular national surveys. Since the 1989 revisions of the Home Mortgage Disclosure Act of 1975, residential mortgage lenders are required to publicly report detailed information, including the race of loan applicants. Nationally, loan approval rates, unadjusted for risk, are substantially lower for blacks than whites. The Federal Reserve Bank of Boston in 1992 did the first "risk-adjusted" study. The study concluded that minorities in the Boston area were rejected for loans 56% more often than equally creditworthy whites. After scathing headlines, heated industry rebuttals and lending agency efforts to improve the fairness of their loan application processes, the number of loans approved nationally for blacks has increased and rejection rates have declined. Public disclosure reports by race for individual lending institutions are available both in hard copy and from the website of the Federal Financial Institutions Examination Council (www.ffiec.gov). As a re-

sult, lenders concerned about their public image have a strong incentive to demonstrate good faith by following such best practice loan fairness guidelines.

2. *Testing:* Making disparities visible, however, rarely forces change. There are just too many more comfortable, moralistic and victim-blaming alternative explanations. Randomized testing varying only the race of the testers clears away this ideological underbrush. By the 1970s, testing was being used by fair housing agencies to determine the validity of housing discrimination complaints. In 1979, the Department of Housing and Urban Development sponsored the first national testing study of discrimination in housing markets. The study demonstrated the feasibility of such surveys and the persistence of a high degree of discrimination in the housing market. This has been followed by a series of regular testing studies that have kept pressure on and have documented progress in reducing the level of discrimination. Perhaps reflecting these pressures, the Census documents a modest decline in residential segregation in most metropolitan areas over the last 20 years.

3. *Gold:* The golden rule in America is that those who have the gold rule. Title VI of the Civil Rights Act attempted to impose the condition of integration and non-discrimination on all organizations receiving federal funds. Unwavering commitment to this principle in implementation of the Medicare program worked. Almost 1,000 hospitals integrated their accommodations and medical staff in a period of a few months. The visible symbols of Jim Crow in the nation's hospitals disappeared almost overnight, and gross racial disparities in access to services gradually disappeared over the next decade.

4. *Regionalism:* Patterns of geographic and residential segregation limit the ability to reduce unequal treatment. Treatment may be integrated and equal within school districts or health systems but unequal between. The more affluent and predominantly white suburban areas do better. Health systems and school districts that don't overlap such boundaries can do little to reduce the overall level of segregation and are limited in their ability to address treatment disparities. For a brief period in the 1970s and 1980s, federal regional health planning certificate of need requirements forced integration of specialized health services in many metropolitan areas. Metropolitan areas that had been operating under city-suburban court-ordered desegregation have achieved a greater degree of integration. In general, metropolitan areas whose schools or health systems are regionalized have fewer disparities and better overall outcomes.

5. *Universality:* "Freedom of choice" was the rallying cry of the segregationists in the 1960s and is embedded within market/competitive solutions to schools and health care. The initial success of the Medicare program in integrating hospitals was based on a single universal program (all persons over 65) and a restructuring of the hospital system to restrict consumer choice. This meant one entrance, one waiting room and race-blind room assignment. The goals of desegregation and equity trumped individual consumer choice. Choice was viewed as the wolf in sheep's clothing that would undermine the goal of integration.

These five general strategies have worked because the majority of Americans believe (or at least can be shamed into saying they believe) in equal opportunity, and that segregation and discrimination should not be tolerated. Yet, the sheep's clothing arguments of the wolf of segregation have blunted the effectiveness of each of these strategies. Visibility has been fought with privacy objections, testing by raising the specter of costly government intrusion, regionalization by the rhetoric of community empowerment and entrepreneurship, and universality by appeals for consumer choice and competition. The vision of the Civil Rights Movement will be realized to the extent that the wolf is named for what it is and the long-term impact of such alternatives on the cost and quality of life for all citizens made clear.

Chapter 43

Why is HHS Obscuring
a Health Care Gap?

H. Jack Geiger

Over the past four years, my colleagues and I have read and reviewed more than a thousand careful, peer-reviewed studies documenting systematic deficiencies and inequities in the health care provided for African Americans, Hispanics, Native Americans and members of some Asian sub-groups. The evidence is overwhelming. Unfortunately, the Department of Health and Human Services seems intent on papering it over.

This is the only conclusion that can be drawn from HHS's recent treatment of the first national report card on disparities in the diagnosis and treatment for this country's most vulnerable populations. The Department edited and rewrote the report's summary until it reflected nothing close to reality.

The reality is this: If you are an African-American man with one form of lung cancer, you are far less likely than a similarly ill white patient to receive a surgical procedure that would cut your chances of early death nearly in half, from 95% to 50%—even if you have the same health insurance coverage and are in the same hospital. If you are a Hispanic trauma victim with multiple bone fractures, you are less likely to be given adequate pain medication—or any at all. If you are a low-income or minority child with severe asthma, your chances of getting the most effective drug combinations are slimmer, and you endure repeated attacks of the disease and hospitalizations. Native Americans with diabetes, or Asian/Pacific Islanders with HIV-AIDS, all too often experience such disparities in care. The pattern extends over the full range of medical conditions.

304

The reasons are complex. Patients often mistrust the medical system because of perceived past discrimination. On the physicians' side, poor communication, lack of cultural understanding, and subconscious negative racial and ethnic stereotyping can be involved. Much needs to be learned. But even though there are at least eight major reviews of all this evidence, including the Institute of Medicine's landmark 2001 study, "Unequal Treatment," there has been no overall national assessment of the scope of the problem. So it was a welcome development when Congress mandated HHS's Agency for Healthcare Research and Quality (AHRQ), a body with an impeccable track record of expertise and honesty, to produce the first annual national report card on disparities.

The AHRQ did its job well. Its draft report was a clear and massive presentation of the data on disparities in care associated with race, ethnicity and socioeconomic status. Its summary was blunt, noting that such disparities are "national problems that affect health care at all points in the process, at all sites of care, and for all medical conditions," affecting health outcomes and entailing "a personal and societal price."

After "review" by HHS, those truthful words are gone, as are most references to race and ethnicity, now described as problems that existed "in the past." Prejudice is "not implied in any way." Disparities are simply called "differences," and—incredibly—"there is no implication that these differences result in adverse health outcomes."

What of the thousand or more studies to the contrary? The new summary says: "Some studies and commentators have suggested that a gap exists between ideal health care and the actual health care that Americans sometimes receive." Worse, the new summary begins with a short list of relatively minor health areas in which minority and poor populations do slightly better than the majority (because, an AHRQ spokesman said, "Secretary [Tommy] Thompson likes to focus on the positive.")

There is a pattern here. All of the different institutes that make up the National Institutes of Health released their draft "strategic plans" to overcome racial and ethnic disparities in health status—the burdens of greater illness and shorter life expectancies of America's minority populations. Disparities in health care obviously contribute to those burdens. But only three of the NIH's 14 institutes even mentioned them.

A recent report by a panel of experts convened by Physicians for Human Rights recommended corrective steps to be taken by government at every level, as well as by the medical profession, hospitals, HMOs, community groups and civil rights organizations. But the federal government has an especially critical role to play in collecting and honestly analyzing data, supporting a more diverse health workforce, and ensuring enforcement of civil rights in the health care system. To avoid the truth, or cloak it in more comfortable words, is to abandon that responsibility.

When confronted at a Congressional hearing with the evidence that the 2004 AHRQ disparities report had been censored to suppress the findings on racial and ethnic disparities in care, then-Secretary Thompson asserted that this was a "mistake" made by his staff, and authorized the release of the original—uncensored—report.

In 2005, AHRQ issued its second annual disparities report card, without apparent interference by HHS. It described small gains in some areas of care, but emphasized that racial and ethnic disparities persisted, and that much remained to be done to reduce and eliminate them.

However, the absence of overt censorship and denials of racially different health care—and health status—has not been followed by vigorous federal efforts to collect and analyze Medicare and other pertinent data by race/ethnicity, or done enough to support diversity in the health workforce, nor supplied the policy, funding and staff for vigorous enforcement of civil rights and equity in health care. On the first crucial step, mandating the collection of all clinical data by patients' race and ethnicity, HHS has remained ominously silent.

The Rev. Martin Luther King, Jr. understood what is at issue here. "Of all the forms of injustice," he said, "discrimination in health care is the most cruel."

Chapter 44

Race, Poverty and New Strategies to Control the Obesity Epidemic

Anthony Robbins, Wendy E. Parmet and Richard Daynard

Obesity, and perhaps some efforts taken in the name of combating it, constitute serious dangers to poor and minority populations in this country. Obesity has reached epidemic levels in the United States. This epidemic poses a first-order health threat to the population, particularly young people. The prevalence of obesity and its gravity continue to increase. Obesity contributes to severe health impairments—heart disease, Type 2 diabetes, osteoarthritis, hypertension, plus colon and post-menopausal breast cancer—and death. For many of these problems, economically disadvantaged and minority populations suffer most heavily. Obesity's direct and indirect health care costs are approaching $100 billion a year, the same order of magnitude as tobacco-caused health expenditures.

A Cause of the Epidemic

Overweight results from consuming more food energy than activity expends. Overweight and obesity are the natural response of a population to the environment that features inexpensive, tasty, convenient and highly caloric foods. Many elements of that environment have their greatest impact on poor and minority populations. Food industry processing and marketing practices have encouraged excessive food consumption. In a country with an overabundance of food and where the raw materials that go into processed foods are very inexpensive, food companies increase their return on investment by selling products where the "value" they add through marketing, processing and packaging is a large part of the final price. Foods that encourage greater consumption not only capture a larger share of the market but induce individuals to eat more than they need to maintain an appropriate weight. How is this done? Super-sized portions offered at small price increments over regular-sized portions attract people to buy more at a lower unit price. Convenience—food that takes little time or effort to prepare—is attractive. Tastes, such a sweetness, fattiness and saltiness, produce satisfying effects. And the food industry's marketing targets the young, attempting to establish profitable eating habits early in the naïve population of children. Schools, starved for resources, are now complicit, through their contracts with food companies, in teaching children to eat and drink high-calorie processed foods.

Assigning responsibility for obesity to the food industry conflicts with our nation's strong tendency to attribute "lifestyle" choices to individuals. Even the 2001 Surgeon General's analysis of obesity focused on how to help people change their own behaviors or habits. Members of disadvantaged groups understand that poverty constrains choices, including "lifestyle" choices about what to eat. Limits of time and money, and habits learned at an early age, condemn many poor Americans to an excessively generous diet of processed and fast food. Perhaps "comfort food" is not misnamed. The distribution of obesity by income is similar to the distribution of tobacco use in the population—greater prevalence with lower income, as well as racial disparities.

Legal Strategies

Just as lawyers successfully challenged the tobacco industry for selling a product that manufacturers knew to be deadly, litigators have recently filed lawsuits on behalf of obese people who believe they are victims of food industry marketing that encouraged over-consumption. And, like the early tobacco litigation, it is hard to predict the outcome until the lawyers learn what the food marketers knew about causing obesity and when they knew it.

We have little doubt that many food processors and restaurants have very extensive knowledge about what makes their products attractive, what encourages more consumption. Although food manufacturers and sellers will portray eating habits as matters of personal choice, these personal choices have been shaped and influenced by the marketing tactics of the food industry. Have these marketing practices been deceptive or misleading—and perhaps deliberately so? For example, does labeling a product "low fat" encourage over-consumption by people who fail to realize that the product, although low in fats, may still be highly caloric? Does advertising high calorie-density/low nutrition-density foods on children's television programs violate state law prohibitions against unfair or deceptive acts or practices? Does the placement of soda machines in school corridors, with the attendant increase in adolescent consumption of empty calories, violate these prohibitions? We expect that legal discovery will pierce the secrecy to disclose just how much the food industry knew and when they knew it, just as that process led to finding clear evidence in the tobacco litigation.

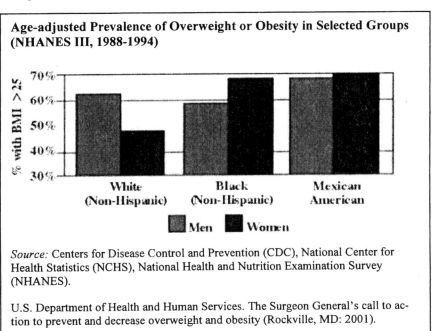

Age-adjusted Prevalence of Overweight or Obesity in Selected Groups (NHANES III, 1988-1994)

Source: Centers for Disease Control and Prevention (CDC), National Center for Health Statistics (NCHS), National Health and Nutrition Examination Survey (NHANES).

U.S. Department of Health and Human Services. The Surgeon General's call to action to prevent and decrease overweight and obesity (Rockville, MD: 2001).

Some Cautionary Words

If this is true, some lawsuits will successfully hold food producers and sellers at least partly responsible for obesity and its health consequences. But will the outcome of litigation be good for public health, for others in the population beyond the plaintiffs? There are reasons to be concerned. The few plaintiffs who receive large payments are unlikely to regain their good health. But the critical question relates to protecting the rest of the population who can still avoid the consequences of overeating. Will the industry be asked to change its practices, and how?

For tobacco, the desirable public health goal was always to reduce cigarette smoking to the greatest possible extent—an addiction dangerous at all times. For food, the goal is not elimination of food, but limited consumption to eliminate obesity. It is not too soon to begin strategic planning to assure a good public health outcome, as we cannot expect the plaintiffs' attorneys to represent the interest of the population at large. We must:

- Define the public health objectives so that any judgment or settlement can be assessed by its effect on the obesity epidemic and its health consequences. Having a measurable objective is important because the industry will certainly argue that voluntary changes in marketing will suffice.
- Explore ways to extend legislation and regulation of foods, from the immediate safety of the products to the health consequences of the entire food production, processing and marketing system.
- Study the disproportionate effect of food marketing on children and vulnerable populations in order to prevent further damage from any changes proposed by litigation, regulation, legislation or the industry itself.

The goal must be to change corporate behavior and thus a population of individual behaviors.

The Other Edge of the Sword

A less than well-coordinated attack on the corporate behavior that contributes to overweight and obesity can have a downside. The obesity epidemic may provide a new opportunity for the Bush Administration to cut assistance to poor people. Food Stamps and school lunches are the immediate targets. Conservatives have hit on the idea that food programs encourage recipients to overeat. The *New York Times* (Feb. 23, 2003) quotes Douglas J. Besharov, director of the American Enterprise Institute's Project on Social and Individual Responsibility: "We are feeding the poor as if they are starving, when anyone can see that the real problems for them, like other Americans, is expanding girth."

As a start, House-passed legislation would allow up to five states to do as they wish with the federal Food Stamp program, frozen at the current funding level. The Administration also proposes to enforce income rules more strictly in the school lunch program that now provides 28 million students with $7 billion worth of food per year. "In recent pilot programs in which families were asked to document household income, approval for free lunches fell by 21% and by 8.8% for reduced-price lunches," reported in the same day's *New York Times*.

Now is the time for two populations of advocates to come together: public health professionals who know that overweight and eating habits are not principally a matter of individual choice and advocates for disadvantaged populations who can keep the public health community from inadvertently harming poor people and minorities.

Chapter 45

The Contribution of Black-White Health Differences to the Academic Achievement Gap

Richard Rothstein and Tamara Wilder

The health characteristics of African Americans and their access to good health care are systematically poorer than those of white Americans. These systematic differences begin before birth, continue through early childhood and school years, and continue into adulthood.

These health and health care differences partially explain the inability of black students to achieve academically at levels comparable to whites. Because there has been so little research on the topic, including a failure to conduct feasible experiments, we can't say how much of the black-white test score gap is attributable to health and health care differences. Health disparities themselves may stem from inferior schooling for black students—for example, if black students have less adequate physical education, or if inferior education in the prior generation led to greater adult economic insecurity which, in turn, causes poor health for both parents and children today.

Yet despite our inability to be precise about causal relationships between poor health and the academic achievement gap, the poorer health and access to care of African Americans certainly contributes to the gap. Children with more exposure to toxins (children with lead poisoning, for example) or more nutritional inadequacies (iron deficiency anemia, for example) have inferior cognitive ability—lower IQs. Children with poorer vision cannot read as well; children less likely to be immunized and more likely to be ill have higher school absenteeism rates; children with more discomfort, from ear infections or toothaches, or with labored breathing from asthmatic attacks, are less able to pay attention to classroom lessons. Parents in poor health are less able to care for their children and less likely to guide their children to good health habits. Each of these average statistical health differences between black and white children and their parents may make a tiny contribution to the achievement gap, but their cumulative effect is bound to be significant.

In what follows, we describe some of these differences, in life cycle sequence, beginning before a child's birth, and continuing into adulthood. In each case, data are from the most recent year available, which may vary from indicator to indicator.

Pregnancy, Childbirth and Neonatality

Inequality begins shortly after conception. One indicator of a child's healthy birth, making other lifetime outcomes more likely to be successful, is whether mothers get early medical attention during pregnancy. Twenty-five percent of black mothers get no prenatal care during the first trimester, while 11% of white mothers get none. For black mothers, 6% get no prenatal care at all (or get it only during the last trimester, when it is almost too late), but only 2% of white mothers, one-third the number of blacks, get no or too-late care. These data, describing only care during pregnancies that end with live births, probably understate the disparity.

We have no good data on unsuccessful pregnancies, but it is probable that black women also miscarry more frequently than whites. Data on neonatal deaths strengthen this conclusion. For black newborns, there are 9 deaths within the first month for every 1,000 live births. For whites, there are only 4 such deaths. Considering infant mortality during the first year of life, there are 14 deaths for blacks and 6 whites. Adequate prenatal care could have prevented some of these.

Infant mortality and morbidity are continuous, so the higher rate of black infant mortality suggests a similarly higher rate of black infants who survive with unhealthy conditions that make school and lifetime success more difficult.

These differences in pregnancy and childbirth are reflections of *racial* inequality itself and are not eliminated by controlling for maternal education. For black mothers who are high school drop-outs, 15 of every 1,000 live births die within the first year; for white drop-outs, 9 do so. For mothers who graduated from high school but got no further education, infant deaths are 13 for blacks and 6 for whites. And for mothers with at least one year of college, infant deaths are 12 for blacks and 4 for whites.

Racial differences in pregnancies and live births are paralleled by differences in birthweight. Low birthweight predicts special education placement, lower academic achievement, emotional maladjustment and likelihood of criminal behavior. For blacks, 3% of newborns have very low birthweight (less than 1,500 grams—3 lbs., 5 oz.), the condition most likely to lead to adverse educational and lifetime outcomes. For whites, the rate is only one-third as great. For low birthweight (less than 2,500 grams—5½ lbs.), a condition still putting children at risk, 13% of black babies have this disadvantageous start, versus 7% of whites.

Again, these disparities narrow only slightly after controlling for education. For black mothers who are high school drop-outs, 15% of live births are low birthweight; for white dropouts, it is 9%. For mothers who graduated from high school but got no further education, 14% of live births are low birthweight for blacks and 7% for whites. And for mothers with at least one year of college, the rates are 12% for blacks and 6% for whites.

Black mothers are less likely than whites to follow practices recommended for the best infant outcomes. For example, 54% of black mothers breastfeed their infants in the early postpartum period, compared to 73% of white mothers. When infants are six months of age, the relative disparity is even greater: 19% of black mothers breastfeed, compared to 36% of white mothers. At one year of age, the rates are 12% and 21%, respectively.

Some of these indicators are more important than others. For example, if we closed the gap in prenatal care, the low birthweight gap might, at least partly, solve itself. Nonetheless, we can roughly summarize the overall black disadvantage in pregnancy, childbirth and neonatality. The summary requires two oversimplifying assumptions: that each indicator we've mentioned describes normally distributed characteristics, and that each is equally important. We can then say that the average black experience with healthy pregnancy, childbirth and neonatality is at the 37th percentile of the experience of all US mothers and babies, while the average white experience is at the 53rd percentile.

This distribution is only somewhat more equal than that of black and white test scores in elementary school. In an average of black and white fourth- and eighth-grade student performance on the most recent administrations (in all subjects) of the National Assessment of Educational Progress, black students are at the 28th percentile of achievement, while white students are at the 60th percentile. Certainly other factors besides pregnancy, childbirth and neonatal experiences are involved, but life's earliest experiences of inequality are not easily overcome.

Access to Health Care

Partly, racial inequalities in pregnancy and infancy stem from inequalities in health insurance. For children under 18, 14% of blacks lack health insurance, including Medicaid or CHIP (federally-subsidized children's insurance), whereas for whites, 7% lack coverage.

These numbers understate inequality—less health insurance for black families is compounded by inaccessibility of primary care physicians, even when families have insurance. In many low-income minority communities, insurance cards in practice confer only the right to wait in lines at clinics or emergency rooms, because few obstetricians, pediatricians or other primary care physicians practice in these communities. We have no national data on this, but a California analysis found that urban neighborhoods with high poverty and concentrations of black and Hispanic residents had one primary care physician for every 4,000 residents. Neighborhoods that were neither high-poverty nor high-minority had one per 1,200.

Black children are thus less likely to get primary and preventive medical care than whites. Eighty-seven percent of black children (under 18) have seen a doctor in the previous year, compared to 90% of whites. Keep in mind that this relatively small disparity does not reflect the much larger disparities in the average number of doctor visits or in the type of medical facility visited. This inequality also has both a racial and socioeconomic aspect. Relatively more poor black children lack medical care than do poor whites, and relatively more non-poor black children lack medical care than do non-poor whites.

Similar inequalities characterize oral health: 69% of black children age 2-17 have seen a dentist in the previous year, compared to 79% of white children.

These inequalities in access to health care compound the inequalities of birth outcomes to contribute to differences in health between black and white children that, in turn, contribute to differences in educational and lifelong outcomes. By the age of 35 months, 25% black children have not received standard vaccinations for diptheria, tetanus, pertussis, polio, measles and influenza. For whites, the non-vaccinated share is 16%.

Ear infections afflict all children, but disadvantáged children are less likely to get prompt treatment. Parents rarely take children to emergency rooms for common ear infections; if primary pediatric care is unavailable, parents are more likely to let the infection take its own course, and it will, most probably, take care of itself. But before then, children with earaches are more likely to miss school, or be inattentive or irritable from pain. Forty-five percent of black children have received antibiotics for ear infections by age 5, compared to 65% of whites.

Again, assuming that each of these indicators reflects normally distributed characteristics and each has equal weight, black children, on average, are at the 43rd percentile in the distribution of children's access to good health care, while white children, on average, are at the 56th percentile.

Health of Young Children

Black children get less adequate nutrition—lacking not calories, but some essential nutrients. For example, iron deficiency anemia, which adversely affects cognitive ability and predicts special education placement and school failure, is more prevalent among black children. In federal programs for low-income children, 19% of blacks under the age of 5 are anemic, versus 10% of whites. Iron deficiency anemia also predisposes to lead absorption, further depressing cognitive ability.

Educational inadequacy also results from disparities in vision—not only in near- or farsightedness, but also in poor eye-muscle development, leading to less facility in skills needed for reading, like tracking print, converging and focusing. Optometrists who have tested children in low-income black communities report that as many as 50% of the children may come to elementary school with vision difficulties that impair reading ability, compared to 25% of children in non-poor communities. These difficulties do not always require correction with eyeglasses; eye exercise therapy may suffice, but such therapy is generally unavailable to low-income children.

Disparate rates of lead poisoning also exacerbate the academic achievement gap. Children who live in older buildings have more lead dust exposure that harms cognitive functioning and behavior. High lead levels also contribute to hearing loss. Three percent of black children but only 1% of whites age 1-5 have blood lead levels that are dangerously high.

We have made great progress in eliminating lead from children's blood; 15 years ago, 11% of very young black children had dangerously high lead levels, compared to 2% of whites. The reduction to today's lower levels is mostly attributable to the elimination of leaded automobile fuel, and to a 1978 prohibition on lead-based paint in residential construction. Yet low-income and minority children still today are more likely to live in poorly maintained, pre-1978 buildings with peeling older layers of paint. And the higher lead poisoning levels of only a decade ago still affect the academic potential of children who are now in the upper grades. Urban children are also more likely to attend older schools, built when water pipes contained lead. New York City, Baltimore and Washington, DC have recently found it necessary to shut off school drinking fountains because lead exceeded dangerous levels.

Other serious diseases are also more common for young black children. Twenty-six of every 100,000 black children under age 2 contract bacterial meningitis; for whites, less than half that number do, 11 of 100,000. Bacterial meningitis is treatable, but requires prompt diagnosis. Although a small number of children, black or white, get the disease, for those who do it can lead to death or, for survivors, hearing loss, mental retardation, paralysis and seizures. So it, too, makes a contribution to the academic achievement gap.

Similar inequalities characterize children under 5 for other bacterial diseases, such as pneumonia and ear, blood stream and sinus infections. For black children under 5, 155 of every 100,000 get such infections each year; for whites, only 63 do.

At this early age, racial differences in oral health are relatively small. Twenty-five percent of black children between the ages of 2 and 5 have untreated dental cavities; for whites, it is 23%. As we will see below, however, these small disparities grow large as children mature.

Summarizing these indicators of young children's health, again assuming that each reflects normally distributed characteristics and has equal weight, young black children, on average, are at the 41st percentile in good health characteristics, while young white children, on average, are at the 52nd percentile.

Health of School-Age Children

Mentioned above was that black children enter school with a rate of vision difficulty that makes reading difficulty more probable. For children under 18, for the most severe cases of blindness and vision difficulty that cannot be corrected by eyeglasses, the rate for blacks is 2.6%; for whites, 2.3%.

Because the environmental conditions in neighborhoods where disadvantaged children reside contain more allergens, minority and low-income children are more likely to suffer from asthma. Eighteen percent of black children suffer from asthma, versus 11% of white children. (Because black children get worse primary medical care and are less likely to be diagnosed, these numbers may understate the disparity.) Again, this is a racial and socioeconomic disparity; although poor children suffer from asthma more than non-poor children, the disparity for poverty (15% for poor children, versus 12% for non-poor) is smaller than the racial disparity.

Asthma is the single largest cause of chronic school absenteeism. It keeps children up at night, and, if they do make it to school the next day, they are likely to be drowsy and less attentive. Middle-class asthma sufferers typically get treatment for its symptoms, while disadvantaged children get relief less often. As a result, low-income asthmatic children are about 80% more likely than middle-class asthmatic children to miss more than seven days of school a year from the disease. Children with asthma refrain from exercise and so are less physically fit. Irritable from sleeplessness, they also have more behavioral problems that depress achievement.

Perhaps because of environmental factors, asthma increased for children overall by 50% from 1980 to 1996. But it increased twice as rapidly for black children, perhaps partly because their environments are worse, or partly because their low rate of diagnosis is improving. Unequal increases in asthma, with its impact on children's attendance and behavior, will undermine other efforts to raise black student achievement.

We noted above that although lead poisoning has diminished, black preschoolers have three times the rate of whites. Disparities in blood lead levels continue during the school years. There is no clear cut-off between dangerous and safe blood lead levels. Many school-age children have less than "dangerous" levels that still have subtle depressing effects on cognitive ability. In particular, school-age children with levels even half as high as those considered dangerous have lower reading scores, lower math scores, lower non-verbal reasoning scores and less short-term memory. For black and white children age 6 to 16, 22% of blacks have this half-dangerous level, more than three times the white rate of 6%.

Perhaps because of differences in diet, perhaps because of differences in sports and physical activity opportunities, black children are more likely to be overweight than whites. In the elementary school years, 21% of black children are overweight, versus 14% of whites. Including those heavy enough to be seriously at risk of overweight, 35% of black elementary school children are either overweight or at risk of being overweight, compared to 29% of whites. In high school, 18% of black students are overweight, compared to 12% of whites; 36% of black high school students are either overweight or at risk of being overweight, compared to 26% of whites.

Black students are more likely to engage in risky sexual behaviors than whites. Nine percent of black high school students have either been pregnant or gotten someone pregnant, compared to 2% of whites. Although white students are somewhat more likely to use contraception than blacks (mostly because white students are more likely to take birth control pills; condom use is similar for black and white teenagers), most of the difference is attributable to the fact that 49% of black high school students are sexually active, compared to 30% of whites. As a result, 9% of black and 4% of white high school students are sexually active without practicing regular contraception.

Black teenagers are diagnosed with new cases of AIDS at nearly 20 times the annual rate of whites—for every million black teenagers, there are 29 new cases; for every million whites, 1.5 new cases.

Another mortal danger is firearms. Each year, of every 100,000 black teenagers (age 15 to 19), 27 are victims of homicide by firearms. For whites, the rate is only 2 per 100,000. Black teenagers are also more likely to be suicidal. Four percent of black high school students require medical attention annually for a suicide attempt; only 2% of white high school students require it.

We reported above that black preschoolers are only slightly less likely to have healthy teeth than whites. But by school age, the gap has widened. Seventy-two percent of black children 6 to 17 have healthy teeth (with no untreated dental cavities), compared to 82% of whites. Not only does pain, including toothaches, make it more difficult for children to learn, but their poor oral health makes serious oral diseases more likely when they become adults.

All these add up to overall inequality in the health status of schoolchildren. Black parents report that 74% of their school-aged children are in overall good health, compared to white parents who report that 87% are in good health. These parent-reported data are consistent with what we find from a simple average of the other indicators we've presented on schoolchildren's health.

In a few important respects, the health of black teenagers is superior to that of whites. For example, black high school students are less like to engage in substance abuse (smoking, alcohol and drugs) and less likely to die in automobile accidents than whites (perhaps partly because black youths, less likely to consume alcohol, are less likely to drive when under its influence, and perhaps partly because black youths are less likely to own cars).

Notwithstanding these few contrary indicators, if we again assume that children's experiences are normally distributed on each of the indicators of school-aged children's physical and mental health, and weighting each indicator equally, we conclude that black school-aged children, on average, are at the 47th percentile in a distribution of favorable health characteristics, while white children, on average, are at the 55th percentile.

Health of Adults

Health inequalities, for which foundations are laid in early childhood and the school years, continue and, in some cases, grow for young adults who, then, are less able to care for their own children and pass good health habits on to the next generation. The poor health of parents is, therefore, another determinant of children's lower achievement.

For adults in prime childbearing years, age 18-34, only 68% of blacks are covered by health insurance, compared to 79% of whites.

Of every 100,000 young (age 20-24) black adults, 18 are newly diagnosed each year with AIDS. For whites, there is only 1 such diagnosis per 100,000.

Differences in overweight, established in childhood, continue into adulthood. Sixty-three percent of black young (age 20-39) adults are overweight, compared to 55% of whites. Considering only those who are obese, 36% of blacks and 24% of whites are in this category.

Unequal exercise habits also persist into adulthood. Fifty-one percent of black young (age 18-24) adults engage in the minimal amount of physical activity recommended for good health (including recreational exercise or activity integrated into household work or employment); for whites, 61% of young adults do so. Considering adults from 25 to 34 years old, 44% of blacks engage in the minimal amount of physical activity, compared to 54% of whites.

These data are consistent with adults' overall health conditions. Eighty-one percent of black adults consider themselves to be in excellent or good health, compared to 90% of whites. These subjective reports reflect a reality that black adults are more likely to die prematurely from cardiovascular disease and cancer than whites. Of every 100,000 black adults age 45 to 54, 181 die from heart disease, more than twice the number (88) of whites who do. Forty-one blacks in this group die of stroke, nearly four times the number (11) of whites. One hundred and eighty-two die of cancer, nearly half again as many deaths as the rate for whites (124).

Summarizing these adult health indicators, with the same simplifying assumptions used previously, we conclude that black adults, on average, are at the 42nd percentile in a distribution of favorable health characteristics, while white adults, on average, are at the 54th percentile.

As noted at the beginning of this chapter, it is impossible to say precisely to what extent these inequalities in health, extending from before birth to adulthood, contribute to black-white educational inequalities, and to what extent educational inequalities perpetuate disparities in health. It would be hard to argue, however, that causality does not run in both directions. For blacks and whites to have equal chances of academic and lifetime success, remedying health inequalities must be part of the solution.

This chapter provides preliminary estimates of black-white differences in health and access to health care. These estimates are subject to ongoing revision as new data sources become available, as we gain better understanding of the distribution of health outcomes among blacks, whites and the general population, and as we apply a more sophisticated weighting system to the various indicators we describe.

Chapter 46

Eliminating the Slave Health Deficit: Using Reparations to Repair Black Health

Vernellia R. Randall

As an African American and as a nurse-practitioner, I can clearly assert that: "Being Black in America is dangerous to our health!"

That current health disparities are directly traceable to slavery is a fact that is not well understood. African Americans still suffer from the generational effects of a slave health deficit. And reparations could repair that deficit.

But before we can engage in a discussion around the "slave health deficit," I need to lay out a clear definition of reparations. To many—Black, white and other—reparations is viewed as a paycheck, some undetermined amount of money for some long-ago harm. In my view, that is an incomplete and destructive view of reparations. Rather, reparations should be viewed as an obligation to make the repairs necessary to correct current harms done as a result of past wrongs. This is a much more expansive view than merely calculating the economic harm and writing a check. Under this view, reparations becomes a process that restores hope and dignity and rebuilds the community. Writing about the relationship of Japanese-American redress to African-American claims, Eric Yamamoto concludes, "[R]eparations for African Americans, conceived as repair, can help mend this larger tear in the social fabric for the benefit of both Blacks and mainstream America." This view allows for both responsibility and action by all parties. It allows for healing to begin by allowing the souls of

Blacks and Whites to be cleansed. Thus, when I speak about reparations, I am talking about taking up the burden to repair the harm—that is, to eliminate the "Black health deficit."

African Americans lag behind on nearly every health indicator, including life expectancy, death rates, infant mortality, low birthweight rates and disease rates. African Americans are sicker than European Americans. We have shorter lives—we are quite literally dying from being Black! This Black health deficit is directly traceable to the slave health deficit.

The enslavement of Africans was abnormally hazardous, and there were health hazards and high death rates during every phase: during the interior trek, the middle passage, the breaking-in period and the enslavement. The slave health deficit that was established during slavery was not relieved during the Reconstruction period (1865-70), Jim Crow era (1870-1965), the Affirmative Action era (1965-80) or the racial entrenchment era (1980 to present). Thus, repairing the health of African Americans will require a multifaceted, long-term financial commitment and effort.

Another way to think about the kind of commitment needed is to consider that of the total time that persons of African descent have had a presence in the New World, 64% of that time was as chattel slavery and another 26% of that time was spent in *de jure* or Jim Crow segregation. For less than 10% of the total time in the United States have persons of African descent had full legal status as citizens. From a health perspective, 64% of the time was spent establishing and maintaining a health deficit, and at no point has that deficit been removed. Thus, the burden of a slave health deficit has been continuous.

Elements of a Program

The slave health deficit will be removed only if the United States makes a significant and sustained commitment—undertaking whatever actions are necessary. Specifically, to eliminate the slave health deficit, the government will need to:

- Eliminate the disparities in morbidity and mortality
- Assure access to quality health care
- Eliminate racial discrimination in health care and health research

Eliminate the Disparities in Morbidity and Mortality

This will require, among other things: (1) a focus on education and prevention through targeted services; (2) provision of a livable wage or income for all persons and families; and (3) elimination of environmental hazards in African-American communities.

Target Services

Until recently, eliminating health disparities has not been a goal. For instance, the goals promulgated by the US Department of Health and Human Services in *Healthy People 2000* focused on reducing disparities, not eliminating them. It was not until *Healthy People 2010* that eliminating health disparities became a goal, and the same health goals for Whites were set for African Americans. Targeting health care services to African Americans would focus resources on the specific health problems confronting them. States could take steps to target services toward African Americans. In particular, a focused and sustained effort must be undertaken to eliminate health disparities in diabetes, cardiovascular disease, maternal and infant mortality, HIV/AIDS, cancer, oral health, mental health, drug, alcohol and tobacco addiction, asthma and violence (including domestic violence).

An essential public health approach will need to be taken which includes primary, secondary and tertiary care. Primary care involves services that prevent harm by changing behavior of individuals and others. Primary services would focus on education and prevention. For instance, outlawing the sale of alcohol within ten miles of neighborhoods or schools would be a primary service, since it would impact the actual use of alcohol. Secondary services are services designed to intervene early and minimize the harm done. For instance, early prenatal care can be used to assist pregnant women to stop drinking early in their pregnancy, thus reducing the harm done to the unborn child. Tertiary services involve measures after harm has been done and can include steps that invoke punitive policy or legislative action. For instance, tertiary services would include alcohol treatment programs, and if the pregnant woman was reluctant to use the services it could involve civil commitment. For an effective approach to eliminating health disparities, there must be a full range of public health services and actions.

Provide a Livable Wage or Income

Health status is caused by complex interaction of many factors, including individual behavior. However, recognizing the importance of individual behavior in health status does not minimize the need to focus on systemic influences such as poverty and racism. Poverty affects housing choice, job choice, food and education. Since African Americans are disproportionately poor, the elimination of poverty becomes essential to improving their health status.

Poverty is also a problem for the "working poor," likewise disproportionately African-American. The working poor are people whose full-time, year-round earnings are so meager that, despite their best efforts, they can't afford decent housing, diets, health care or child care. Assuring everyone in the United States a "livable wage," not merely a minimum wage, could eliminate poverty and the problems of the working poor.

A livable wage provides enough income to pay for the basic necessities of daily living: shelter, food, clothing, health care, child care and transportation.

Without a livable wage income, people suffer not only a lack of dignity, but also a variety of social and health problems. In a 2000 study, the San Francisco Department of Public Health reported that livable wages diminished mortality rates, decreased unnecessary hospitalization of the poor, eliminated some costs associated with caring for the homeless and saved lives.

Thus, livable wages become a cornerstone to eliminating the slave health deficit, and reparations should be in the form of assuring a livable wage.

Eliminate Environmental Hazards in African-American Communities

One particularly important consideration for health is the location of environmental hazards and toxic dumps in Black communities, workplace hazards, and hazards in the home. Studies have documented that hazardous waste landfills are disproportionately placed in African-American communities. Such studies have concluded that race—more than poverty, land values or homeownership —is a predictor of the location of hazardous facilities. Race is independent of class in the distribution of air pollution, contaminated fish consumption, location of municipal landfills and incinerators, abandoned toxic waste dumps, cleanup of Superfund sites, lead poisoning in children, and asthma. In 1987, more than 15 million (57%) of the United States' 26 million African Americans resided in communities with one or more uncontrolled toxic-waste sites. African Americans faced with a polluting industry moving into their back yard often have the least mobility because of limited financial resources and discrimination in employment and housing.

In addition, African Americans are disproportionately represented in jobs with the highest environmental hazards, such as pesticide-intensive farm labor, rubber-making, coke production, battery manufacturing, lead plating and smelting, and industrial laundering. In the workplace, African-American men have a 27% greater chance than White men of facing safety hazards and a 60% greater chance of facing health hazards. Even controlling for the level of job-training and education, African Americans find themselves in substantially more dangerous occupations than Whites.

Finally, for African-American children, lead poisoning in the home is a significant health issue. The blood lead levels in urban African-American children under the age five significantly exceed the levels found in White children of the same age living in the same city. This disparity persists across income levels. Thus, for families with incomes less than $6,000, 68% of Black children, compared to 36% of White children, had unsafe blood levels. In families earning more than $15,000, 38% of Black children and 12% of White children had excess lead levels.

Given the above, reparations should be used to remove toxic dumps and landfills from African-American communities or completely relocate such communities to a safe environment; to make workplaces safer; and to eliminate lead paint from housing.

Assure Access to Quality Health Care

Eliminating morbidity and mortality disparities will require access to quality care. Assuring access to quality care will require: (1) assuring universal health care; (2) locating adequate health care facilities within the Black community; (3) assuring a competent health care workforce in Black communities; (4) assuring the cultural competence of the health care workforce; and (5) increasing knowledge about health and health of Black persons and translating it into effective clinical practice.

Provide Universal Health Care

The United States and South Africa are the only major industrialized nations without a universal health insurance system that guarantees access to health care for all of their citizens. What the United States has instead is a scheme of employer-financed insurance and government programs that still leave more than 41 million Americans without the financial resources to pay for health care. The lack of health insurance is a particular issue for African Americans, who are less likely to have employer-financed insurance. While public programs, such as Medicaid and Medicare, are important sources of health care coverage for many low-income African Americans, they do not reach anywhere near all of the uninsured poor. In fact, one-fourth of African Americans have no source of health coverage. Even more disturbing is that the number of uninsured African Americans is increasing. While from 1977 to 1987 the proportion of uninsured non-elderly European Americans increased from 12% to 15%, the proportion of uninsured non-elderly African Americans increased from 18% to 25%.

Since private health insurance coverage is linked to employment, racial barriers to employment are one explanation for the significant difference in insurance coverage. For example, in 1990 the African-American unemployment rate was 240% higher than the European-American unemployment rate. However, even where employed, African Americans are more likely to be in lower-paying jobs that do not provide employer-based health insurance. Another factor affecting insurance coverage is the higher percentage of African-American families with only one adult. Families with two working adults are more likely to have at least one adult with employer-based insurance.

While the absence of health insurance is much more likely among those with lower incomes, race is an independent factor. In fact, the racial difference in proportion of uninsured is most marked at higher incomes. For example, poor/low-income African Americans are uninsured at about the same rate as poor/low-income European Americans; however, middle-/high-income African Americans are almost twice as likely to be uninsured as higher-income European Americans.

Reparations should be used to expand insurance coverage so that all African Americans have either employer-based or government-based insurance.

Locate Health Facilities in Black Communities

Racial barriers to health care access are based in large part on the unavailability of services in a community. Hospitals that serve the African-American community are closing, relocating or becoming private. In 1982, Alan Sager reported to the United States House of Representatives that during the 1937-77 period the likelihood of a hospital's closing was directly related to the percentage of African Americans in the population. Throughout the 1980s, many hospitals relocated from heavily African-American communities to predominantly European-American suburban communities.

This loss of services to the community resulted in reduced access to care for African Americans. Geographic availability and proximity are important determinants to seeking health care services early. If African Americans fail to seek early health care, they are more likely to be sicker when they do enter the system; and the cost for the patient to receive services and for the system to provide services at that point is likely to be greater. Thus, not only does the loss of services significantly increase health care costs to African Americans, it also increases health care costs to the society.

Another devastating trend that affects the access of African Americans to health care is the privatization of public hospitals. Quite a few hospitals (public and nonprofit) have elected to restructure as private, for-profit corporations. As public hospitals, many were obligated under the Hill-Burton Act to provide uncompensated care. As private hospitals, these institutions are most likely to discontinue providing general health services to the indigent populations and essential primary health care services to serve African-American communities.

The problem of limited resources is not new and has plagued the African-American community since slavery. Historically, African-American communities attempted to address the problem by establishing African-American hospitals. At one point, more than 200 hospitals were located in predominantly Black communities. African Americans relied on these institutions to heal and save their lives. Now these institutions are almost non-existent. By the 1960s, only 90 African-American hospitals remained. Between 1961 and 1988, 57 African-American hospitals closed and 14 others merged, converted or consolidated. By 1991, only 12 hospitals remained, struggling daily just to keep their doors open. As a result of these closures, relocations and privatization, many African Americans are left with limited services and difficult access to hospitals.

Reparations should provide hospitals, clinics, alcohol and drug detox centers, dental health clinics and mental health clinics in the African-American community.

Assure a Competent Health Care Workforce in Black Communities

Another important aspect of access to care is the availability of health care providers who serve the African-American communities. Providers include physicians, nurses, pharmacists, dentists, as well as the many other health care professionals who serve a community. It should go without saying that proximity increases utilization. African-American physicians have been important in fill-ing the availability gap. Very few White physicians have offices in the African-American community. Without physicians and providers in their communities, African Americans are likely to delay seeking health care. That delay can result in more severe illness, increased health care costs, increased mortality and in-creased costs to society.

Despite being 12% of the population, African Americans are seriously un-der-represented in every health care profession. Only 3% of physicians, 2.5% of dentists and 3.6% of pharmacists are African-American. In fact, 75% of African-American physicians practice in or near African-American communities, 90% had patient loads that were at least 50% African-American. Of European-American physicians, only one in every 163 (.61%) had a 90% African-American patient load. Thus, this shortage of Black health care providers results in sicker individuals and an increase in overall health care costs. If African Americans are sicker, they need more physicians, not fewer. Yet we see the same limited availability of providers, as of hospitals, to serve African-American communities. In addition, even programs such as Medicaid do not necessarily expand access, since many primary care providers either do not ac-cept Medicaid patients or limit the number of such patients they will accept. It is only natural to look to the African-American physicians to fill this gap.

With so few African-American health care professionals, the control of the health care system lies almost exclusively in European-American hands. The result is an inadequate, if not ineffective, voice on African-American health care issues. This lack of African-American voice leads to increased ignorance on the part of European Americans regarding issues pertaining to African-American health. When health care issues are defined, policymakers' ignorance results in their overlooking African-Americans' health concerns.

Clearly, a significant issue for eliminating health disparities is increasing the availability of providers in African-American communities. This lack of African-American representation in health care is traceable to slavery, racism and segregation. An African American did not receive a degree in an American medical school until 1847. While a few White medical schools admitted African Americans prior to the Civil War, most did not. Even in 1971, 21 medical schools out of 85 still had no African-American students. The American Asso-ciation of Medical Colleges reported that between 1950 and 1998, out of the 125 US medical schools, 12 graduated 30% of all minority physicians. And for Black physicians, medical schools at Howard, Meharry and the University of Illinois graduated the most.

Reparations should be used to increase the availability of providers in the Black community. This should be done by providing scholarships for Blacks to enter health care professions; by providing grants to universities and colleges to increase the graduation rate of persons who will work in urban areas; by in-creasing the capacity of historically Black colleges to train and graduate stu-dents; by increasing health care reimbursement for services provided to inner-

city residents; and by providing economic incentives to doctors and other health care professionals to locate in African-American communities.

Assure Cultural Competence of the Health Care Workforce

A person does not have meaningful access to health care if that person is not provided health care within the context of his or her cultural background. Merely providing a person with a piece of paper (insurance) or a provider does not mean that the person will receive health care that assists in improving the person's health status. For centuries, Americans indulged in the fantasy that all persons (Native Americans, immigrants and slaves) blended into one great "melting pot" to become Americans. While it is true that there are unique American cultural similarities that cut across all groups, this country has always had a diverse population of races, ethnic groups, subcultures and religions.

Unfortunately, the medical care system represents one subculture: the middle-class, middle-aged European American. For instance, the system focuses on individual autonomy rather than family involvement. It assumes a basic trust in the health care system, instead of distrust. It relies on a Western, European-American concept of communications. It is built on a Western European concept of wellness, illness and health care. Consequently, the more a patient differs from the cultural prototype, the more likely the person will not have meaningful access to quality health care.

One barrier to culturally competent care is physicians' own negative perceptions about African Americans. Because they have differing needs and problems in accessing care, physicians tend to see African Americans as less compliant and more difficult to care for. The problem, however, is not African Americans, but the health care system's inability to provide effective care to diverse populations. If increased compliance and improved health status are the goals, then the health care system must be flexible enough to match a community's cultural, ethnic, lifestyle and socioeconomic needs.

Through reparations, culturally competent care can be assured by requiring: (1) health professional schools to train providers from diverse backgrounds; (2) that all physicians have a rotation during their internship and externship focusing on providing culturally competent care; (3) that providers take continuing education units in cultural competency; (4) that health care facilities and managed care organizations complete and submit to a regulatory agency on a regular basis cultural competency assessments; (5) that health care be provided in accordance with realities of the needs of the various "classes" of the Black community.

Increase Knowledge About Health of Black Persons and Translate It into Effective Clinical Practice

Despite volumes of literature suggesting the importance of race, ethnicity and culture in health, health care and treatment, there is relatively little information available on the racial, ethnic and biological differences that affect the manifestations of certain illnesses and their treatments. Billions of dollars are spent each year on health research ($35.7 billion in 1995). However, a strikingly minute percentage of those funds are allocated to research on issues of particular importance to minorities and women, and to research by African-American and women scientists (21.5% and 37%, respectively). In response to years of exclusion of minorities and women, several statutory requirements have been enacted to ensure that research protocols include a diverse population. The health condition of African Americans will continue to suffer until they are included in all types of health research. The information from that research has to be translated into clinical practice without becoming just another stereotype.

Reparations should be used to assure that health care research and development is focused on the health issues of African Americans.

Eliminate Racial Discrimination in Health Care and Health Research

Federal laws related to eliminating racial discrimination in health care delivery are limited to Title VI of the Civil Rights Act. Racial inequality in health care persists in the United States despite laws against racial discrimination, in significant part because of the inadequacy of Title VI. Although required by regulation to produce data, the Department of Health and Human Services' Office for Civil Rights (OCR) Title VI enforcement effort has produced few consistent data for evaluating Title VI compliance. Moreover, there has been little uniformity in how different states handle Title VI requirements, little guidance, little analysis of the information collected by this process, and no research and development. Title VI also lacks specific definitions of prohibited discrimination and acceptable remedial action. Finally, OCR has relied on individual complaints as a means of enforcement, particularly troubling when most discrimination and harm is hidden from the individual.

Even if the provisions of Title VI were improved and data collected, the legal system within which Title VI operates would still be inadequate for the particular difficulties presented by the health care system. That is, the legal system has had difficulty addressing issues of "unthinking discrimination"—that is, discrimination that results from acting on biases and stereotypes. While legal standards for discrimination have not always centered on intent, they do so now. Thus, to prove a disparate treatment claim, an individual must show that the defendant intentionally discriminated. Such a standard means that few of the discriminatory acts that occur in the health care system can be successfully litigated, since most occur from "unthinking" or "unconscious" biases. As long as the law requires a conscious discriminatory purpose for disparate treatment liability, individual discrimination claims cannot address the issue of unconscious prejudice.

The health care system presents several additional problems. First, as with the situation when racial minorities use housing and lending institutions, individuals may be totally unaware that the provider or institution has discriminated against them. Second, because of the very specialized knowledge required in medical care, individuals may be totally unaware that the provider has injured them. Third, the health care system, through managed care, has actually built in incentives that encourage "unconscious" discrimination. Because of these issues, an appropriate legal structure is essential to eliminating institutional/cultural racism.

In an effective public health policy, appropriate state and federal laws must be available to eliminate discriminatory practices in health care. Thus, the crux of the problem, given managed care, the historical disparity in health care and "unthinking" discrimination, current laws do not address the barriers faced by African Americans; and the executive branch, the legislatures and the courts are singularly reluctant to hold health care institutions and providers responsible for institutional racism. As the United States Commission on Civil Rights found in a 1999 report:

> There is substantial evidence that discrimination in health care delivery, financing and research continues to exist. Such evidence suggests that federal laws designed to address inequality in health care have not been adequately enforced by federal agencies...[Such failure has]...resulted in a failure to remove the historical barriers to access to quality health care for women and minorities, which, in turn, has perpetuated these barriers.

Authorize and Fund the Use of Medical Testers

To discourage health care discrimination, an aggrieved person should be redefined to include not only the individual who has been injured, but also one who believes that he or she will be injured, as well as individuals engaged as testers and organizations engaged in testing. In testing, persons pretending to be patients, who share common traits or symptoms except for their race, are sent to health care facilities or providers in order to prove that patients of a particular race receive different treatment. This is important because much of health care discrimination goes undetected and unreported.

Require Data Collection and Reporting

Current data collection efforts fail to capture the diversity of racial and ethnic communities in the United States. Disaggregated information on sub-groups within the Census Bureau's five racial and ethnic categories is not collected systematically. Further, racial and ethnic classifications are often limited in surveys and other data collection instruments, and minorities often are misclassified on vital statistics records and other surveys and censuses. It is important to collect the most complete data on African Americans and other subpopulations, to fully understand the health status of all individuals, as well as to recognize the barriers they face in obtaining quality health care. The lack of data on providers and institutions makes it difficult to conduct research studies and comparative analyses. Furthermore, the lack of a uniform data collection method makes obtaining an accurate and specific description of race discrimination in health care difficult. Existing data collection procedures do not allow for regularly collecting race data on provider and institutional behavior.

As a part of reparations, a Health Care Anti-Discrimination Act should be enacted which, among other things: (1) authorizes and funds testers; (2) recognizes disparate impact; (3) assures fines and regulatory enforcement; (4) requires a health scorecard for each health agency, provider or facility; and (5) requires data collection and reporting.

Conclusion

In its broader, most expansive sense, reparations restores hope and dignity because it provides current descendants a way out of their seemingly dead-end lives caused by the lingering effects of slavery, racism and segregation. Reparations ultimately is about social justice, since it is about undoing the harm that has been done to one group in society. Reparations is not a one-way action; it requires the African-American community to undertake action and to rebuild itself. Reparations will rebuild community and cleanse the soul of the nation. Most importantly, reparations could restore the health of people of African descent in America.

Resources on the Slave Health Deficit

Bullard, Robert D. "The Legacy of American Apartheid and Environmental Racism" (*St. John's Journal of Legal Comment,* 1994).

Byrd, Michael & Linda A. Clayton. *An American Health Dilemma: A Medical History of African Americans and the Problem of Race, Beginnings to 1900* (Routledge, 2000).

Lado, Marianne Engelman. "Unfinished Agenda: The Need for Civil Rights Litigation to Address Race Discrimination and Inequalities in Health Care Delivery (*Texas Forum on Civil Liberties & Civil Rights,* 2001).

Smedley, Brian D., Adrienne Y. Stith & Alan R. Nelson, eds. *Unequal Treatment: Confronting Racial and Ethnic Disparities in Health Care* (Institute of Medicine, 2002).

Chapter 47

Health Quiz I

Health Policy Institute

Answers are on page 402.

1. Heart disease and stroke are the leading causes of death for all racial and ethnic groups in the US.
    True or False

2. While health disparities have not decreased in the US, the nation's infant mortality rate has remained stable over the last two decades.
    True or False

3. According to a 1999 report from the National Center for Health Statistics at the Centers for Disease Control and Prevention, what was the US rank in infant mortality among 37 nations?
    A. 10th
    B. 23rd
    C. 28th
    D. 30th

4. In the US, the life expectancy for white men is 74.8 years. What is the life expectancy for African-American men?
    A. 67.9 years
    B. 68.2 years

    C. 68.9 years
    D. 70.1 years

5. In 2001, the age-adjusted death rate for cancer was how much higher for African Americans than for white Americans?
    A. 12.5 %
    B   17.7 %
    C. 23.4%
    D. 25.4%

6. How much higher is the incidence rate of cervical cancer for Vietnamese-American women compared to white American women?
    A. twice
    B. three times
    C. four times
    D. five times

7. Research has shown that medical doctors rated African-American and white American patients equally based on intelligence, education, their likelihood to abuse drugs and alcohol, and compliance with medical advice.
    True or False

8. What is the death rate for African Americans from HIV/AIDS as compared to white Americans?
    A. 7 times higher
    B. 8 times higher
    C. 9 times higher
    D. 10 times higher

9. What is the age-adjusted death rate for HIV for Puerto Ricans living on the mainland US, compared to non-Hispanic white Americans?
    A. 7 times higher
    B. 9 times higher
    C. 11 times higher
    D. 13 times higher

10. Minorities are under-represented in the health care professions.
    True or False

11. In 2002, 20.2% of African Americans were uninsured, compared to 11.7% of whites. What was the percentage of uninsured Hispanic/Latinos during that year?
    A. 19.1 %
    B. 25.3 %

C. 30.6 %
D. 32.4 %

12. Sudden infant death syndrome (SIDS) rate is the highest among which population group?
    A. American Indians/Alaska Natives
    B. Asian Americans/Pacific Islanders
    C. African Americans
    D. White Americans

13. Research has shown that when racial/ethnic minorities are insured at the same levels comparable to whites, they receive the same level of quality of health care for the same health conditions.
    True or False

14. Which population group had the highest tuberculosis case rates in 2001?
    A. American Indians/Alaska Natives
    B. Asian Americans/Pacific Islanders
    C. African Americans
    D. White Americans

15. How much of every health care dollar does the US spend on health promotion and public health research?
    A. less than one cent
    B. one cent
    C. between one cent and two cents
    D. three cents

Chapter 48

Health Quiz II

David Barton Smith

Answers are on page 404.

1. Nonwhites still tend to use different hospitals than whites. In what region of the country has hospital care become the most racially integrated?
   - A. Midwest
   - B. Northeast
   - C. South
   - D. West

2. Medicare provides almost universal health insurance coverage to those over 65, but few under 65 are covered by Medicare and most have to rely on private insurance. Roughly what is the difference in the percentages of whites and blacks under 65 with private health insurance?
   - A. 8%
   - B. 18%
   - C. 28%
   - D. 38%

3. Most people under 65 who are covered by private health insurance obtain this coverage through their employment. Among those under 65, about what is the difference between the percentage of Hispanics and the percentage of non-Hispanics who receive health insurance coverage through employment?
   - A. 3%

B. 13%
C. 21%
D. 33%

4. The Medicaid program provides "safety net" coverage to those under 65 who, because of low income, can't afford private insurance or because of poor health are ineligible for private insurance coverage. What is the difference between the percentage of blacks and the percentage of whites dependent on coverage through this program?
   A. 1%
   B. 11%
   C. 21%
   D. 31%

5. Avoidable admissions are hospitalizations that could potentially be avoided by high-quality outpatient care. Rates of such hospitalizations for the under 65 population are higher among blacks. The gap between black and white rates between 1980 and 1998:
   A. Remained the same
   B. Narrowed
   C. Was closed
   D. Widened

6. In the only study ever done approximating a randomized "testing" of discriminatory physician behavior, those shown videos of blacks, with identical scripts, presenting the same cardiovascular symptoms as whites did, were:
   A. More likely to be referred for cardiac catheterization
   B. Just as likely to be referred for cardiac catheterization
   C. Likely to be referred only 60% as often
   D. Likely to be referred only 20% as often

7. Reported blood pressure monitoring rates and Pap-testing rates among the black population in the United States are:
   A. Half of white rates
   B. Somewhat lower than white rates
   C. About the same as white rates
   D. Somewhat higher than white rates

8. Death rates for blacks in the United States, adjusted for age, are:
   A. Lower than white rates
   B. About the same as white rates
   C. About 10% higher
   D. About 30% higher
   E. More than 50% higher

Democracy

Chapter 49

From Slave Republic to Constitutional Democracy: The Continuing Struggle for the Right to Vote

Jamin Raskin

"Why is George Bush in the White House? The majority of Americans did not vote for him. I tell you this morning that he's in the White House because God put him in there." (Lieutenant-General William Boykin, Deputy Undersecretary of Defense for Intelligence, United States Department of Defense)

In their indispensable book, *Radical Equations*, Bob Moses and Charles Cobb describe the epiphany the 26-year old Moses had in 1960 when he arrived as a volunteer in Mississippi and got to know Amzie Moore, president of the NAACP in Cleveland, Mississippi. Moore was not interested in sit-ins to desegregate restaurants or lawsuits to enforce *Brown v. Board of Education*. In an area where violence and oppression had left 98% of African Americans off the voter rolls and too terrified to register, Moore "had concluded that at the heart of Mississippi's race problem was denial of the right to vote," Moses writes. "Amzie wanted a grassroots movement to get it, and in his view getting that right was the key to unlocking Mississippi and gaining some power to initiate real change. I had not given that idea any thought at all; I didn't know before I began talking to Amzie that the Mississippi where he lived was a Congressional district that was two-thirds black."

The voting rights movement launched in Mississippi nearly got Moses killed, but it led to the Voting Rights Act of 1965 and the creation of some long-suppressed majority-African-American and Hispanic Congressional districts (that would later be attacked by the Rehnquist Court). Knocking on doors in apartheid Mississippi, Moses developed the visionary rhetoric of "one person, one vote." This "radical equation" captured the imagination of the Warren Court in the early 1960s redistricting cases like *Baker v. Carr* and *Reynolds v. Sims*, and later infused democratic movements from Poland to South Africa. The many thousands of college and law students who went out to monitor the polls and participate in "election protection" in 2004 are part of this legacy of struggle for democratic rights.

That struggle is as important today as it was four decades ago, but the mechanisms of disenfranchisement have grown more complex and insidious. Racial minorities are no longer disenfranchised by white primaries, poll taxes and literacy tests, but rather by a series of background structural exclusions and dilutions, as well as the resilient dirty tricks and sleight-of-hand that reappear at election time. Moreover, convincing people of the efficacy of voting remains a problem: While basic voting rights remain *necessary* to generate upward social motion for people at the bottom of the society, they hardly seem to be *sufficient* to do so. Indeed, Bob Moses himself has thrown his own magnificent energy over the last many years into the Algebra Project, whose thesis is that movement-style math education is a key project for social change in the age of high technology.

Even if other concerns, like algebra education and health care for all, command urgent attention today, voting rights remain not only the paradigmatic expression of first-class citizenship and social standing, but also the crucial currency of democratic politics and the pre-condition for instrumental public action on other problems. But achieving universal suffrage, as we shall see, is still a maddeningly elusive goal, with millions of American citizens, a majority of them African-American and Hispanic, disenfranchised by law, and basic democratic principles in constant danger on the ground. To understand why basic voting rights are still contested terrain, we need to revisit the basic dynamics and institutions of our political history.

A Slave Republic of Wealthy Christian White Male Property-Owners

Our last great Republican President—Abraham Lincoln—gave poetic definition to the American vision of democracy: a government "of the people, by the people and for the people." But this tantalizing ideal has little to do with our beginnings, as Lincoln knew. We began as a slave republic of wealthy Christian white male property-owners. The Constitution established no popular right to vote but left suffrage requirements up to the state legislatures, which imposed a gauntlet of race, gender, religious, property, wealth and age qualifications. It also vested in each legislature the power to appoint two United States Senators for the state, thus giving smaller slave states like South Carolina or Alabama the same US Senate representation as large Northern states like New York, Pennsylvania or Massachusetts.

The character of the US House of Representatives was defined by Southern resolve to entrench slavery in the Constitutional fabric. The first trick was to count slaves in the process of determining how many seats in the US House of Representatives each state would be apportioned. So millions of slaves, none of whom could vote (obviously), were used to inflate the size of the Southern Congressional delegations controlled by their masters. Indeed, the Southern states argued that slaves should be counted as full persons in the Census, while the Northern states argued that the slaves, being disenfranchised, should not be counted at all. The two sides settled on the infamous "Three-Fifths" provision —counting each slave as three-fifths of a person for the purposes of reapportionment, a clear and ominous victory for political white supremacy. As Garry Wills has shown in *The New York Review of Books*, the resulting Southern delegations to Congress, swollen with the "slave power," checkmated any moves against slavery.

With both the House and Senate institutionalizing America's original sin, Article II of the Constitution fused and reproduced these pro-slavery features in the design of the Presidential selection process. The Electoral College system awards each state a number of Presidential electors equal to the number of US House members it has, plus an extra two "add on" electors for its US Senators. In the event of a failure of any candidate to assemble an Electoral College majority, the President is chosen in a "contingent election" in the House of Representatives where each state, regardless of size, casts one vote, thus again making the states, rather than the people, the functional base of the system.

Southern blueprints to rig our political architecture worked like a dream. The "slave power" proved extremely effective at both dominating Congress— which for decades enforced a rule against even raising slavery as an issue—and also winning and manipulating Presidential elections. Four of the first five US Presidents were Virginia slave masters who brought their household slaves with them into the Presidency: George Washington, Thomas Jefferson, James Madison and James Monroe. And the reign of slave power continued on and off until the nation plunged into Civil War.

Even after the Civil War, the Electoral College propped up white supremacy and thwarted its opposition. In the 20th Century, Southern politicians cleverly used the Electoral College to block civil rights for African Americans. Racist Southern Democrats like Strom Thurmond (1948), Harry Byrd (1960) and George Wallace (1968) practiced the quadrennial art of leaving the Democratic Party to run for President as Independents, taking substantial chunks of Presidential electors with them and sending a sharp message to the national Democratic Party about the political perils of racial integration. LBJ presciently remarked after passage of the Voting Rights Act of 1965 that the Democratic Party would lose the South for a generation—and so it has.

Today, the Solid South provides a majority of Electoral College votes in the Republican Party's Presidential coalition. If you glance at a red-blue map of 2000, you will find that the old Confederacy is the beating heart of George W. Bush country. Furthermore, because of the nation's racial demography and geography and the winner-take-all method of allocating electors still used by all states except Maine and Nebraska, most votes cast by African Americans in Presidential elections will count literally for nothing. In 2000, more than 90% of African Americans voted for Democrat Al Gore, but 58% of all African Americans lived in states that gave 100% of their Electoral College votes to Bush. This means that, in 2000, most African Americans voted in states where their ballots ended up having no effect on the election outcome. The one Southern state where the African-American vote clearly could have made a critical difference in 2000 was Florida, which makes all of the devious strategies to cancel out African-American votes there both entirely comprehensible and deeply appalling.

The civil rights struggle dismantled American apartheid but did not establish an affirmative Constitutional right to vote.

Through the process of social and political struggle, the American people have taken down many barriers to voting. The most significant changes have been embodied in Constitutional amendments, although often that alone has not been enough to overcome elite resistance to voting by the poor and racial minorities. The 15th Amendment banned race discrimination in voting (1870), but we still had to follow through with the Voting Rights Act of 1965; the 17th Amendment gave us direct election of US Senators (1913)—a populist victory that Justice Scalia recently lamented at Harvard Law School; the 19th Amendment banned sex discrimination in voting (1920); the 23rd Amendment gave citizens living in the District of Columbia the right to participate in Presidential elections (1961); the 24th Amendment banned poll taxes in federal elections (1964); and the 26th amendment lowered the voting age to 18 for qualified voters in the states (1971).

But this *ad hoc* sequence of democratizing and anti-discrimination amendments for particular groups still does not add up to an affirmative universal right to vote, the kind that the International Covenant on Civil and Political Rights calls for and that, for example, post-apartheid South Africa actually has. The South African Constitution defines the new Republic as a "sovereign democratic state" with "universal adult suffrage" and a "multiparty system of democratic government." In South Africa, "Every adult citizen has the right to vote in elections for any legislative body established in terms of the Constitution."

What difference does it make that our Constitution has never made a declaration like that? After all, most people think that we already do have a "right to vote," and billions of dollars were spent in 2004 telling people to exercise it. But, in truth, this void deep in the heart of our Constitution leaves us with a major democracy deficit that poses the three following problems for democratic legitimacy in America:

Within the Electoral College system, the individual citizen has no Constitutional right to vote for President, and the people have no right to control the selection of the state's electors.

Most Americans dimly understand that the popular vote does not control who wins in the Presidential election—thus, Vice-President Gore had 500,000+ votes more than Bush in 2000 but still lost. Yet most people also assume that a majority popular vote controls which candidate captures the Electoral College votes in their own state. But the 2000 Presidential election taught us that this is false.

In 2000, the Florida Supreme Court ordered a state-wide manual recount of 175,000 ballots that for various reasons could not be read by the state's obsolescent punchcard machines. At that point, leaders of the Republican-controlled Florida legislature in 2000 declared that the legislature would not be bound by this recount and would independently select the state's Electoral College members. This announcement stunned many Americans. Harvard Kennedy School of Government Professor Alexander Keyssar, in the *Political Science Quarterly* (Summer 2003), likened it to "a half-forgotten corpse" that "had suddenly been jarred loose from the river bottom and floated upward into view."

But in its opinion in *Bush v. Gore*, the Supreme Court's majority emphasized that the Florida legislature was acting well within its powers. The Court stated that the "individual citizen has no federal Constitutional right to vote for electors for the President of the United States." Thus, even when legislatures grant the people the right to vote in Presidential elections, they can always revoke it and "take back the power to appoint electors." Even if the people seek to bind themselves in their state constitutions to abide by a popular vote for President, they cannot restrain legislatures that resolve in the future to appoint electors of their own choosing.

The events of 2000, however extreme they seemed at the time, may prefigure the collapse of already fragile democratic norms in close Presidential elections. As the nation's demographics shift, undermining the natural strength of the contemporary Republican Party, we can expect to see aggressive partisan tactics by its leaders in state legislatures—and their lawyers in the Supreme Court and other tribunals—working to accumulate 270 electors by hook or by crook. Indeed, the Texas Constitution was amended shortly after the 2000 election to provide that if the popular vote seems ambiguous or difficult to count, the Texas legislature shall have the right to immediately appoint electors of its choosing. This provision is redundant, of course, given the Court's analysis of the problem, but it is properly read as a statement of collective political intentions by a flagship Republican legislature that, in 2003, with ferocious partisan precision, also moved heaven and earth to "gerrymander" US House districts to favor Republicans. If any state legislature decides to take advantage of the ample confusion and controversy in the electoral system to appoint electors without regard to the popular vote, the people will have little structural recourse.

The Electoral College presents a massive challenge to democratic values and a standing invitation to political mischief. But, even if we assume that we are stuck with it for the time being, the electors should at least be directly chosen by the people of each state. The only way to strip the legislatures of their dangerous power over selection of the electors and establish real popular control of each state's electoral votes is by way of Constitutional amendment.

In every election, millions of Americans entitled to vote are disenfranchised by bad technology, voter registration obstacles and tactical suppression of voting, which are problems engineered or tolerated by state election managers who operate with relative impunity under current laws.

Because America has no Constitutional right to vote, it also has no national electoral commission to protect voting rights and fair elections. Rather, we have hundreds of partisan officials at the state and local level supervising our elections—people like Florida's Secretary of State in 2000, Katherine Harris, who co-chaired the Bush for President campaign in Florida, or Ohio Secretary of State Kenneth Blackwell, who co-chaired his state's Bush for President campaign in 2004. We have no national ballot but a maze of state ballots. We have no single system of voting but everything from punchcard machines to the "optical scan" method to the paranoia-inducing "black box" computers without paper receipts. Our election systems are increasingly designed, not by public agencies but by private corporations, many of them run by political activists. The CEO of the Diebold Corporation, which is the largest maker of the new voting computers, spent a weekend at President Bush's ranch and wrote a fundraising letter to fellow Republicans in which he pledged to deliver Ohio's Electoral College votes to President Bush.

In this electoral jungle, voting rights are weak but voting wrongs are everywhere. Our votes are lost, miscounted, passed over and suppressed in every election. This reality was shown by the outrageous practices that came to light in Florida in 2000. Journalist Greg Palast, in *Harper's*, has documented that more than 50,000 persons—half of them African-American or Latino—were falsely accused of being felons and then illegally removed from the state voter registration list before the election by a private company with which Secretary of State Katherine Harris contracted to purge felons from the rolls. These citizens were beyond the 600,000 convicted felons who were already disenfranchised by law. After the election, the state promised to restore the illegally purged voters and not to do it again.

There were other irregularities. Thousands of Florida voters who actually made it into the voting booth lost their votes to that masterpiece of design error, the Palm Beach "butterfly ballot." Tens of thousands more "overvote" ballots— where voters followed ambiguous instructions and checked off the name of "Al Gore," for example, and then also wrote it in separately—were cast aside and forgotten. Above all, more than 175,000 ballots were simply left uncounted when they failed to register on the punchcard ballot tabulations. Although the Florida Supreme Court ordered all of the ballots to be counted, a 5-4 majority on the US Supreme Court quickly moved in to stop the vote-counting.

Florida was illustrative of our electoral practices, where we all belong to a reserve army of the disenfranchised that can be mobilized in different places at different times. According to the July 2001 report of the CalTech and MIT Voting Technology Project ("Voting: What It Is, What It Could Be"), "between four and six million presidential votes were lost in the 2000 election." Some 2 million votes were simply never counted, primarily because of "faulty equipment and confusing ballots"; between 1.5 and 3 million votes were lost in the maze-like vagaries of the voter registration process; and up to 1.2 million votes were lost "because of polling place operations"—meaning technical malfunctions, problems with lines and hours, negligence, understaffing and underfunding. Significantly, this study reports that these problems are even worse in state elections than federal ones.

After 2000, many were convinced that all we needed was technological reform to improve the picture. The Help America Vote Act of 2002 (HAVA) put billions of dollars into state efforts to replace the punchcard machines with electronic voting and, most positively, required state provisional voting laws that will allow voters to cast challenged ballots if there is a problem at the polls.

But HAVA did not fundamentally change the picture of official indifference to voting rights and in fact made certain things worse. The statute created no legal redress for voters who are wrongfully excluded from the voter rolls, nor did it pass any criminal or civil penalties for officials who actually violate a person's right to vote. There are no real teeth in the statute when it comes to defending voting rights against government misconduct. And it has created some practices and implications unfriendly to voting. Several courts this year upheld the power of states under HAVA to toss out provisional ballots cast by *bona fide* voters who vote in the wrong precinct. This would be unthinkable if the fundamental right to vote were rooted in the Constitution rather than the grace of state legislatures.

We also face the recurring problem of the modern Republican Party practicing scare tactics to intimidate minority voters. Just as Southern white Democrats suppressed black voting in Mississippi, today's Republicans are always looking for ways to intimidate and deter racial minorities in the political process. A seminal example took place early in the Reagan years, in New Jersey's 1981 gubernatorial election. The Republican National Committee launched a National Ballot Security Force, which sent letters to registered Democrats in African-American and Hispanic communities. Any letters returned as undeliverable became the basis for challenging voters and trying to get them deleted from the rolls. "On election day," Laughlin McDonald writes in *The American Prospect*, "the security force dispatched armed off-duty police officers wearing official looking armbands to heavily black...precincts in Newark, Camden and Trenton."

They patrolled the polls and posted signs advertising a $1,000 reward for anyone offering information leading to the arrest and conviction of people violating election laws. This kind of "ballot security" operation has become standard operating procedure in today's Republican Party, which understands, as one of its Michigan state legislators put it in 2004, that victory depends on suppressing the black vote.

More than 8 million American citizens, a majority of them African Americans and Hispanics, remain absolutely or substantially disenfranchised by virtue of exclusionary voting policies that the courts have found Constitutionally acceptable or even obligatory.

Unlike the haphazard disenfranchisement that randomly affected millions in 2000, there is a larger institutionalized disenfranchisement taking place that rarely enters the headlines. More than 8 million Americans, a majority of them racial and ethnic minorities, still belong to communities that are absolutely or substantially disenfranchised by law. This is a population of voteless persons larger than the combined populations of Wyoming, Vermont, Alaska, North Dakota, South Dakota, Montana, Delaware, Maine and Nebraska. The unrepresented fall into three groups:

There are 570,898 US citizens, subject to normal rules of taxation and military conscription, living in the District of Columbia who lack any voting representation in the US Congress. Although Washingtonians pay more federal taxes per capita than the residents of every state but Connecticut, are subject to military conscription and can vote in Presidential elections under the terms of the 23rd Amendment, they have been continually frustrated in their efforts to achieve voting representation in the United States Senate and House of Representatives. This is a double injustice, since Congress acts not only as their national legislative sovereign but ultimately as their local legislature as well under the terms of the Constitution's "District Clause" (US Const. art. I, 17, cl. 8), which confers upon Congress "exclusive Legislation" over the District. District residents have only a non-voting Delegate in the House, Rep. Eleanor Holmes Norton, who has been brilliantly nimble but so far unsuccessful in promoting equal voting rights for her constituents against the frosty indifference of most politicians.

The District's effort to climb up to a level of equal membership in America has been a lonely one, and the Constitution has been effectively mobilized as an enemy to the cause. In the early 1990s, a bill to grant a petition for statehood for DC failed by a 2-1 margin in the House of Representatives and never saw the light of day in the Senate. Members of Congress repeatedly invoked the Constitution itself as the warrant for continuing disenfranchisement.

In 2000, just a few months before its decision in *Bush v. Gore*, the Supreme Court rejected an Equal Protection attack on Congressional disenfranchisement of the District by affirming a 2-1 decision of the United States District Court for the District of Columbia in a case called *Alexander v. Mineta* (90 F.Supp.2d 35

[D. D.C. 2000], aff'd by 531 U.S. 940). The plaintiffs in the suit, which was brought by the District's lawyer, alleged that their disenfranchisement in the US Senate and House of Representatives was unconstitutional. The District Court majority found that: "The Equal Protection Clause does not protect the right of all citizens to vote, but rather the right of all *qualified* citizens to vote." To be a "qualified" citizen for purposes of national legislative representation, you must live in a state and have the state grant you the vote. Thus, the District population, nearly 70% of which is African-American, Hispanic and Asian-American, is simply in the wrong place.

The effort that has come nearest to accomplishing voting rights in Congress for District residents was the proposed DC Voting Rights Constitutional amendment, which would have treated the District constituting the Seat of Government as though it were a state for the purposes of Congressional representation. The proposed amendment passed Congress in 1978 by more than a two-thirds majority in both the House and Senate, with overwhelming Democratic support and substantial Republican backing as well. It failed in the states when it found itself desperately short of national allies against a ferocious conservative opposition.

There are 4,129,318 American citizens living in the federal Territories of Puerto Rico, Guam, American Samoa and the US Virgin Islands who have no right to vote for President and no voting representation in the Congress. These 4+ million US citizens living in the Territories are subject to the sovereignty of Congress under the "Territorial Clause" of the Constitution (art. IV, 3, cl. 2). But they have no mechanism for participation in federal elections and no voting representation in national government. The largest Territorial population is in Puerto Rico, home to 3,808,610 people as of the 2000 Census. In 1917, the Jones Act gave all Puerto Ricans US citizenship, and in 1952 the island gained "Commonwealth" status. But, like the District's Eleanor Holmes Norton, the Puerto Rican "Resident Commissioner" still acts only as a non-voting Delegate in the House of Representatives. Also like residents of the District of Columbia, Territorial residents are shut out of the Senate completely. Unlike Washingtonians, Puerto Ricans have no voice even in Presidential elections.

Citizens living in the Territories have all the responsibilities of other American citizens except that they do not pay federal taxes (unless they work for the federal government). Some people believe that this exemption justifies complete disenfranchisement. This is certainly not the view of Puerto Ricans and other Territorial residents, who pay heavy local taxes, serve in the armed forces, are subject to the draft and consider themselves part of the country. According to the US Court of Appeals for the Second Circuit, the "exclusion of US citizens residing in the territories from participating in the vote for the President of the United States is the cause of immense resentment in those territories— resentment that has been especially vocal in Puerto Rico" (*Romeu v. Cohen,* 265 F.3d 118, 127 [2d Cir. 2001]). As Judge Pierre Leval observed in that case, the political exclusion of Puerto Ricans "fuels annual attack on the United States in hearings in the United Nations, at which the United States is described as hypo-critically preaching democracy to the world while practicing nineteenth-century colonialism at home."

Yet repeated lawsuits against the disenfranchisement of Puerto Ricans in Presidential elections have failed. The Constitution makes no provision for Ter-ritorial residents to be represented in the national government and therefore re-duces citizens living in Territories to colonial status. This second-class citizen-ship is a central obsession of Puerto Rican politics and equally significant in other Territories. There is little sympathy for seeking independence from the US, which seems an ever more far-fetched option. But Congress has refused to act in an effective way to grant Puerto Ricans a real choice among statehood, independence, the status quo and "enhanced commonwealth" status. The politi-cal rights of citizens in the Territories should not wait any longer for a choice of political forms that never emerges. The 23rd Amendment, which gave residents of DC the opportunity to vote in their first Presidential election in 1964, set a precedent for using Constitutional amendments to enfranchise citizens who have no residence in a state and to recognize them as a permanent part of the national community.

There are more than 4 million citizens disenfranchised, many of them for the rest of their lives, in federal, state and local elections as a consequence of a felony criminal conviction. According to The Sentencing Project and Human Rights Watch, in their report, "Losing the Vote: The Impact of Felony Disen-franchisement," citizens who have been disenfranchised in their states because of criminal convictions amount to about 2% of the country's eligible voting population. In four states—Florida, Mississippi, Virginia and Wyoming—citizens disenfranchised because of their criminal records constitute fully 4% of the adult population.

Felon disenfranchisement is less a strategy of individual moral rehabilita-tion than mass electoral suppression. This analysis seems unavoidable when we consider that 1.4 million ex-offenders, mostly African Americans, are perma-nently disenfranchised in eight states. In Florida in 2000, 600,000 voteless citi-zens were *former* felons who already did their time and paid their dues to soci-ety. They will never get their suffrage rights back under current law, which op-erates like a political death sentence, unless they beg for, and receive, electoral clemency from the state's Governor, presently Jeb Bush.

As one might expect in a period of racially-tilted law enforcement, these policies have dramatic effects on the composition of the electorate. In Florida, a shocking 31% of all African-American men are permanently disenfranchised. In both Delaware and Texas, 20% of African Americans are disenfranchised. In Virginia and Mississippi, about 25% of the black male population has been per-manently locked out of the electoral process.

Felon disenfranchisement is at odds with the principle of universal suffrage, which is why the policy has begun to fall around the world. Last year, the Cana-dian Supreme Court, in *Sauve v. Canada (Chief Electoral Officer)*, struck it down as violative of Canada's constitutional right to vote, holding: "Denial of the right to vote on the basis of attributed moral unworthiness is inconsistent with the respect for the dignity of every person that lies at the heart of Canadian democracy."

But our Constitution creates the contrary implication. In 1974, the US Supreme Court in *Richardson v. Ramirez* (418 U.S. 24, 56 [1974]) found that felon disenfranchisement does not violate the requirement of "equal protection" in Section 1 of the 14th Amendment because Section 2 explicitly authorizes states to disenfranchise persons convicted of "rebellion, or other crime" without losing any Congressional representation. Unless this decision is reversed, only a Constitutional amendment can enfranchise more than 4 million people who have been convicted of felonies and stripped of their voting rights or, at least, the 1.4 million ex-offenders who have served their time but are likely to remain disenfranchised until they die.

Catching Up to the World—and Ourselves

Americans are waking up to a central and surprising flaw of American politics— our deeply vulnerable right to vote. But, in a certain sense, this only scratches the surface of our difficulties, which include: runaway partisan gerrymandering that destroys competitiveness in most US House races and gives us an incumbent re-election rate often exceeding 95%; a US Senate with (as of 2005) a single African-American member; winner-take-all elections that systematically cancel out the voting strength and interests of tens of millions of people; blatant official discrimination against third parties and independents in ballot access rules and debate participation; the continuing dominance of big money in government and elections; and the unnecessary disenfranchisement of non-citizens in local elections.

But these second-generation issues will be difficult to address until we deal with the primary fact that we have not protected voting as an affirmative Constitutional right. In the global context, this departure of American constitutionalism from well-established international norms is ironic. For the United States was the first nation conceived in popular insurgency against tyranny and in favor of representative constitutionalism. It was Bob Moses and our modern civil rights activists, battling the political oppression of apartheid Mississippi, who produced the slogan of "one person, one vote" that swept the earth at the end of the 20th Century.

Today, our political Constitution looks frail and incomplete in the face of modern universal suffrage principles visible all over the world. We are the only nation on earth that disenfranchises the people of its capital city. Our felon disenfranchisement policies are backward compared to those of other advanced democracies. Our election systems are raggedy, and our electoral practices disfavor real electoral competition and diverse representation.

The world was shocked to witness our electoral train-wreck in 2000, and many of us were astonished to read the Supreme Court's pronouncement that we have no Constitutional right to vote for President. But no one should have been surprised, for the evidence is all around us. A right-to-vote Constitutional amendment is necessary, not only to redeem the demoralizing chaos we experienced in the 2000 election but to maintain the trajectory of our democratic development against competing forms of government also lurking within our society, such as empire and national security state. Already the entire Congressional Black Caucus has endorsed a right-to-vote Constitutional amendment proposed by Congressman Jesse Jackson, Jr. Dozens of other members of Congress have voiced their support as well.

The history of the United States can be read as a struggle for inclusive democracy against structures of domination and exclusion. Many of the amendments we have added since the Bill of Rights have been suffrage-expanding or democracy-deepening amendments. But they have had a sharply limited effect. Without a universal Constitutional right to vote granting every possible presumption in favor of the people, almost any electoral policy can be turned against the electorate by partisan state election officials. We need to show the political maturity as a nation now to inscribe the people's right to vote directly into the people's covenant.

Resources on the Right to Vote

The Center for Voting and Democracy, the nation's leading voting reform organization—www.fairvote.org.

* * *

Hill, Steven. *Fixing Elections: The Failure of America's Winner Take All Politics* (Routledge, 2002).

Keyssar, Alexander. *The Right to Vote: The Contested History of Democracy in the United States* (Basic Books, 2000).

"The Long Shadow of Jim Crow: Voter Intimidation and Suppression in America Today" (People for the American Way Foundation & NAACP).

McDonald, Laughlin. "The New Poll Tax," *The American Prospect*, 2002.

Moses, Bob & Charles Cobb. *Radical Equations: Math Literacy and Civil Rights* (Beacon Press, 2001).

Overton, Spencer. *No Backsliding* (W.W. Norton, 2006).

Chapter 50

Voting Rights for Immigrants

Catherine Tactaquin

In recent times, the notion of immigrant civic participation has been emerging as a significant trend in community enfranchisement. In cities around the country, especially where there are significant concentrations of immigrants, community organizations and immigrant rights coalitions have mustered energy and resources to conduct voter registration drives and to mobilize immigrant voters. The substantial growth of the immigrant population throughout the country was a key factor fueling these and other initiatives, including proposals for "noncitizen" voting in local elections, such as school boards.

An October 2004 report by the Immigration Policy Center, a division of the American Immigration Law Foundation, called attention to the potentially significant role an energized immigrant electorate could play in local, state and national elections. In "Power and Potential: The Growing Electoral Clout of New Citizens," author Rob Paral wrote: "In highly competitive electoral environments, the rapidly growing ranks of 'new citizens'—foreign-born individuals who become 'naturalized' U.S. citizens—are increasingly important political players."

That report described the dramatic growth of immigrant populations over the last decade: Some 13 million people immigrated into the US during the 1990s. In the 2000 elections, 6.2 million new citizens had registered to vote, and over 85% of them voted—a proportion far higher than turnout among all voters.

The National Association of Latino Elected and Appointed Officials Education Fund, which has predicted Latino voter turnout quite closely in the last two

Presidential elections, had projected that "one million more Latinos will vote in November 2004 than in our last Presidential election, a new record for the Latino community." NALEO and other Latino groups stated that naturalized Latino voters—the new immigrant voters—may be key, given the increased numbers of newly registered voters and the pattern of these voters actually going to the polls on Election Day. The Pew Hispanic Center found that an estimated 7.6 million Latinos voted in the November 2004 elections.

Asian Pacific Islander communities were also expected to significantly gain new voters and presence at the polls. With over 12 million people, API communities are poised to become a formidable electoral force. API immigrants have a fairly high rate of naturalization—over 40%—a source of potential new voters. Between 1996 and 2000, the number of Asian voters had increased by 22%.

Despite these trends, certain factors have continued to diminish the potential participation of immigrant voters. Jeffrey Passel of The Urban Institute's Immigration Studies Program notes: "About 62 percent of Latinos could not register to vote in 2000 because they were either too young or not U.S. citizens; 59 percent of Asians could not register. In contrast, only 35 percent of blacks and 25 percent of whites could not register to vote for demographic reasons." And the Asian American Legal Defense and Education Fund found in its exit polling in several cities that over 40% of Asian voters were limited-English proficient, and that almost half of the voters—usually first-time voters—needed voting assistance.

Presence in Swing States

While the foreign-born population overall is just over 11% of the entire US population, the concentration of immigrants in several states has produced considerable political interest for tapping into a rapidly increasing pool of votes. While immigrant voters in the traditionally large foreign-born states of California, Florida, Illinois, New Jersey, New York and Texas are expected to contribute votes to the Democratic Party, in the swing states the impact of immigrant votes is less certain. Prior to the November 2004 elections, Rob Paral projected: "In all, six battleground states may be identified where new-citizen voters can make a difference in a two-candidate race even if the difference in percentage points separating the candidates is as high as five points. These states are Arizona, Florida, Nevada, New Mexico, Pennsylvania and Washington."

Although the overall foreign-born vote is only about 5% of the entire electorate nation-wide, it is in particular areas of the country—with large immigrant populations or with dramatic increases in population size—where the vote will have increasing impact. However, in the 2004 Presidential election, immigrant community organizers were often frustrated by the fleeting recognition given to potential immigrant voters. As political strategists typically zeroed in on likely and undecided voters in swing states, resources for voter registration, education and mobilization did not, as a whole, flow to immigrant communities.

Increasing the Voice of Immigrants

Facing this reality, groups committed to both short-term and long-term goals of increasing immigrant community voices at the polls nonetheless rallied to build initiatives that would support immigrant civic participation in the elections and beyond. These initiatives have given attention to the significant challenges and barriers to engaging immigrants from numerous ethnic and language backgrounds and homeland experiences. Many initiatives build on ongoing organizing and advocacy, particularly on controversial immigration policy issues.

Many groups recall the upsurge in naturalization applications and immigrant voter registrations prior to and after California's infamous anti-immigrant ballot initiative, Proposition 187, in 1994. At that time, many immigrants raised their concerns about important decisions being made about their lives, but without their voice. That concern was repeated in Arizona, where the anti-immigrant Proposition 200 passed in 2004 despite the rapid growth of "official" opposition among many sectors. Prop 200, which will require proof of legal status from anyone applying for a public service or registering to vote, also unleashed the introduction of 18 anti-immigrant bills in the state legislature (and inspired a slew of copycat bills in several states, including Alabama, Arkansas, Georgia and Colorado). Organizers against the initiative had included new citizen voter registration as a key component of their strategy. The state's population is about 13% foreign-born, and during the 1990s, the Latino population grew by 88%.

The 2003 Immigrant Worker Freedom Ride produced a campaign called "Freedom Summer," building on the historic work of the Civil Rights Movement in the South, to conduct voter registration in the key states of Arizona and Florida. For two months, 50 predominantly young activists worked with local organizations to register new voters, particularly among new citizens. Civic participation campaigns have been organized in several states by regional and state immigrant rights coalitions, as well as by such groups as the National Korean American Service and Education Consortium, National Council of La Raza, Center for Community Change, Gamaliel Foundation, ACORN and many more.

The Northern California Citizenship Project (NCCP—now PILA—Partnership for Immigrant Leadership and Action) led a new California collaborative—Mobilize the Immigrant Vote (MIV) 2004—to reach diverse immigrant communities. The initiative mobilized some 112 immigrant community groups and over 1,000 community volunteers who registered over 20,000 new immigrant voters and mobilized the vote in November. Although California was not identified as a swing state, its large and diverse foreign-born population—over 26% of the total population and almost 15% of the state's voters — is ripe for voter engagement. Generations of US-born members of immigrant families—a major demographic factor in California—are also targets for registration and get-out-the-vote activities. As with initiatives in other states, MIV identified the need to reach particular language groups, working with community-based organizations and others to produce multilingual "palm cards" on voting rights and information, and easily accessible voting guides with information and recommendations on ballot initiatives of particular concern and relevance to immigrant communities. MIV provided new voters with "how to" information, understanding that a lack of familiarity with the actual voting process—including where to find the correct polling location—can hinder participation.

According to Maria Rogers Pascual, NCCP/PILA Executive Director: "We are not only increasing voter turnout from immigrant communities, but we are helping to strengthen immigrant community leadership for ongoing organizing on critical issues." This has been a consistent theme of initiatives such as "One Voice, One Vote" in Massachusetts and "New Americans Vote '04" in Illinois, where the state immigrant rights coalition surpassed its pledge to register at least 25,000 new voters. The campaign focused on reaching out to the large Muslim community, whose civil liberties were particularly threatened by the 9/11 backlash.

The New York Immigration Coalition (NYIC), which has successfully spearheaded immigrant voter registration activities, has decried the loss of voting opportunities for immigrants whose citizenship applications have been bogged down in lengthy background checks in the Department of Homeland Security (DHS). According to NYIC, almost half of the more than 126,000 immigrants in New York with pending citizenship applications were in danger of not being able to vote in November 2004 due to the processing backlogs. In moving immigration servicing into the DHS when it was established in the wake of 9/11, President Bush had set a six-month standard for citizenship application processing, but in New York and elsewhere, the wait is much longer. In Miami, there is a 21-month backlog; in Arizona, 13 months.

Renewed Interest in Non-Citizen Voting

Problems such as these in moving towards citizenship, as well as a current impasse on setting up a new legalization program for undocumented immigrants, have stirred renewed interest in "non-citizen" voting—generally, the opening of voting rights in local elections, such as for school boards, to all residents of a given locale, regardless of citizenship or immigration status.

Particularly during the last decade or so, non-citizen voting initiatives have emerged throughout the country, and there are a few places where non-citizens can vote—such as in Takoma Park, Maryland, and even (at least until recently) in the school board elections in New York City. San Francisco voters in 2004 narrowly failed to pass Proposition F, to allow non-citizens to vote in school board elections. Proponents had argued that with at least one-third of the children in the school district having at least one immigrant parent, the proposition would fairly give representation in school matters to all parents. The school board had voted unanimously to support the proposition, but detractors claimed the proposition was just a back-door tactic—a "Trojan Horse"—to give citizenship rights to undocumented immigrants, under the guise of supporting education.

The issue of non-citizen voting will no doubt be a long and protracted debate with uneven results. Political scientists Ronald Hayduk at the Borough of Manhattan Community College argues that non-citizens should have voting rights, and says: it's legal (not precluded by the Constitution); it's rational—with good reasons for enfranchisement, such as notions of equal rights and treatment articulated in the suffragette and Civil Rights Movement; and it's feasible.

Hayduk and other proponents have pointed out that until the 1920s, in fact, non-citizens could vote in local, state and even national elections in 22 states! Then, the anti-immigrant movements and xenophobia following World War I ended the practice. Opposition to non-citizen voting went hand-in-hand with racist movements against the influx of darker-skinned immigrants, fanning fears about the progressive political influences these new immigrants might inspire.

Current calls for non-citizen voting certainly seem much more benign: Giving all parents the right to vote in school board elections gives them an opportunity to decide key issues in their children's education, and, it is argued, will encourage greater participation in their community—isn't that a classic American ideal?

Hayduk, as well as Wendy Shimmelman, offer three critical arguments for non-citizen voting—arguments that could just as well apply to the encouragement of today's new citizen voters. These arguments include: 1) democracy will thrive when it enfranchises all of its members—when they have representation (remember "no taxation without representation"—non-citizens, including the undocumented, do pay taxes); 2) discrimination and bias: Lacking voting rights, non-citizens are at risk of discrimination and bias by the majority, and their interests can be more easily ignored; and 3) common interests: Other members of society, particularly from the working class and communities of color, face many of the same issues immigrants face, and would benefit from non-citizen participation and integration. Their concerns and political power would be strengthened—certainly an argument against the wedge politics of the Right that have sought to align working people and other communities of color *against* immigrants over jobs, housing and so forth.

Whether non-citizen voting becomes a "right" for immigrants at any noticeable level, or whether new citizens are rallied to register and vote, the scope and scale of immigration currently and in the foreseeable future demands that these issues of enfranchisement be addressed—and soon—in yet another test for American democracy.

Resources on Immigrants and Voting

Grantmakers Concerned with Immigrants and Refugees, www.gcir.org, provides facts on immigration at state, national and international levels.

Immigrant Voting Project, http://www.immigrantvoting.org/index.html.

Mobilize the Immigrant Vote 2004, California campaign website provides immigrant voting rights materials in six languages, lists resources and website links for civic participation information, www.immigrantvoice. org/miv2004/index.htm

* * *

"The Asian-American Vote 2004: A Report on the Multilingual Exit Poll in the 2004 Presidential Election" (Asian American Legal Defense and Education Fund, 2005, www.aaldef.org).

Avila, Joaquin. "Political Apartheid in California: Consequences of Excluding a Growing Noncitizen Population" (UCLA Chicano Studies Center, 2003, http://www.chicano.ucla.edu/press/briefs/archive.html).

"California's Minority and Immigrant Voters" (Public Policy Institute of California, 2004, www.ppic.org).

Hayduk, Ronald. "Non-Citizen Voting: Pipe Dream or Possibility" (Drum Major Institute for Public Policy e-journal, 2002, http://www.drummajorinstitute. org/plugin/template/dmi/55/1694).

Paral, Rob. "Power and Potential: The Growing Electoral Clout of New Citizens" (*Immigration Policy IN FOCUS*, 2004, www.ailf.org).

Passel, Jeffrey S. "Election 2004: The Latino and Asian Vote" (2004, www.urban.org/urlprint.cfm?ID=8938).

Raskin, Jamin. "Legal Aliens, Local Citizens: The Historical, Constitutional and Theoretical Meanings of Alien Suffrage (*Univ. of Pennsylvania Law Review,* 1993).

Shimmelman, Wendy. "Local Voting Rights for Non-U.S. Citizen Immigrants in New York City" (1992, orders@nnirr.org).

Suro, Roberto, Richard Fry & Jeffrey Passel. "Hispanics and the 2004 Election: Population, Electorate and Voters" (Pew Hispanic Center, 2005, www.pewhispanic.org).

"Voting Rights," (Asian Pacific American Legal Defense and Education Fund, www.aaldef.org/voting.html).

Chapter 51

Bringing American Democracy to America's Capital

DC Vote

Most Americans are unaware that the 572,000 residents of the District of Columbia have no voting representation in Congress. When this is brought to their attention, however, the vast majority of people in the rest of the US support voting rights for DC—82% in a 2005 nationwide poll. And indeed, at a time when our government is avidly and aggressively attempting to implant democracy around the world, this homegrown example of disenfranchisement is particularly offensive.

The root cause, as well as a viable solution to this situation, stems from the interpretation of the US Constitution. According to Article 1, Section 8, Clause 17, the "District Clause," Congress has the power to "exercise exclusive legislation in all cases whatsoever" over the seat of government, the District of Columbia. Analyses from various legal scholars conclude that the Framers of the US Constitution plainly did not intend to deprive citizens of our nation's capital of the most basic right of the democracy they created—the right to vote. Georgetown law professor Viet Dinh, in 2004 Congressional testimony, reports that: "There are no indications, textual or otherwise, to suggest that the framers intended that Congressional authority under the District Clause, extraordinary and plenary in all other respects, would not extend also to grant District residents representation in Congress." Rather, because the nation's capital was not created until several years after the Constitution was written, the Framers left it to Congress to provide for citizens of the capital once it was created.

Over the years, there has been incremental progress in bringing democracy to the nation's capital. In 1961, a Constitutional amendment giving District residents the right to send three voting representatives to the Electoral College was ratified by Congress and the requisite number of states. In 1964, for the first time, DC residents were allowed to vote in a Presidential election. In 1968, Congress permitted DC residents to elect their own Board of Education. Two years later, in 1970, the DC Election Act gave DC a non-voting Delegate to the House of Representatives. In 1973, home rule came to the District, giving local voters the right to elect a mayor and a city council. Though the District's non-voting Delegate was permitted to vote in the House Committee of the Whole in 1993, this right was terminated in 1995 and has remained as such to the present.

While DC's Delegate to the House of Representatives has no vote in Congressional affairs, Congress has forced its opinion on the District's affairs, often through the power of the purse. Measures supported by DC voters—for example, funding for reproductive rights, health care benefits for cohabiting couples, and implementing a syringe exchange program—have been restricted by riders to the DC budget. A rider to the District's budget was added to spend hundreds of thousands of dollars to change signage and maps through the Metro system to read, "Ronald Reagan National Airport," rather than the former name, "National Airport." The most recent example was a rider to the District's budget, supported by an overwhelming majority of House members, to repeal a series of gun restriction laws passed by the City Council and strongly supported by the mayor, the police chief and the citizens of DC. Wisconsin Congressman David Obey, in response, proposed an amendment to the District's budget, forcing Members of Congress to draw their pay from DC funds, and cutting their salaries to that of DC Councilmembers: "If the people in this House want to act like your DC city councilman, then they can be paid like a DC councilman," he said. Action by the Senate is still to come as of July 2005.

DC's disenfranchisement is particularly poignant when one considers its population and economy. There are more people living in DC than in the entire state of Wyoming, and DC's population is close in size to seven other states. Additionally, the per-capita federal income tax burden borne by DC residents exceeds that of 49 of the 50 states. Moreover, the District suffered more casualties in the Vietnam War than ten states, and doubtless, similar over-representation is true in Iraq and Afghanistan. DC residents have always risked and given their lives to protect our country and to fight for democracy abroad, yet they return from war to disenfranchisement in their own home district.

Possible Remedies

A range of remedies have been proposed, most in legislation that will likely never pass: creating a 51st state; counting District votes toward election of Maryland's House and Senate members; retroceding most of the District, save the core federal properties, to Maryland, where residents would vote as state citizens.

The current (as of July 2005) remedial proposal is to increase the number of House members by 2 to 437, allotting one new member to DC and the other to Utah, which came closest in the 2000 Census to being awarded an additional House seat. Since Utah would assuredly elect a Republican, while DC just as assuredly would elect a Democrat, partisan considerations are muted. Following the 2010 Census, the House would revert to 435 members and DC would retain its seat for the 2012 election. This proposal, the DC Fairness in Representation Act of 2005 (H.R. 2043) introduced by Representative Tom Davis [R-VA], has a chance of success, as it has Republican and Democratic backing.

The issue of partisanship of course looms large, but so does race, as both an explanation for past disenfranchisement as well as resistance to enfranchisement. DC is a majority minority city, with about 60% African-American and 10-12% Latino and Asian residents. With full voting representation, DC would certainly elect two Democratic Senators and one Democratic House member. Given the nature of the city's population, all three members of Congress would likely be African-American and on the progressive end of the political spectrum.

What Lies in the Future?

Other city and state legislatures are being urged to pass resolutions supporting democracy for the nation's capital. As of July 2005, Chicago, Philadelphia, Baltimore, San Francisco, Los Angeles, Cleveland, Detroit, and the Illinois and Hawaii state legislatures have passed such measures. This helps to create nationwide pressure for DC's enfranchisement.

A similar attention-getting move was the DC City Council's creation of the first-in-the-nation Presidential primary for the 2004 election, again a move to raise public awareness.

The issue of DC voting rights is gaining greater recognition and support internationally. In February 2004, the Inter-American Commission on Human Rights of the Organization of American States (OAS) released a report finding the United States government in violation of Articles II and XX of the American Declaration of the Rights and Duties of Man because of the denial of voting representation in Congress for DC residents. In response to the report, a spokesperson for the US State Department stated that he didn't see a connection between the OAS findings and the Bush Administration's goal of promoting a fully representative government in Baghdad and Iraq.

In October 2004, Belarus' Ambassador to the Organization for Security and Cooperation in Europe (OSCE) blasted the United States government, charging that the US was violating OSCE democratic election standards—which it is obligated to observe—by denying District residents the right to vote for Congressional representatives. The US Mission to the OSCE responded by stating that the disenfranchisement of DC residents was imaginary—referring to DC residents' lack of equal Congressional voting rights as a "supposed disenfranchisement." The Republic of Belarus' condemnation of the United States marks the first time that a sovereign state and a member of the 55-nation OSCE has publicly condemned the United States for its policy of disenfranchising the nearly 600,000 residents of its capital city. In November 2004, the Permanent Mission of the Republic of Belarus to the United Nations introduced a draft resolution to the UN General Assembly on the "Situation of Democracy and Human Rights in the United States of America," which highlights the case of the denial of equal Congressional voting rights to the people of Washington, DC.

In April 2005, the OSCE released a report that cited the United States government's obligation to ensure "equal voter rights" for all US citizens, including the people of Washington, DC. The report marks the first time that the OSCE has formally addressed this issue. While the OSCE Election Observation Mission Final Report primarily focuses on US compliance with OSCE democratic election standards during the November 2004 Presidential elections, the report pointedly cites the United States government's unqualified obligation as a member of the OSCE to ensure "equal voter rights" for Washington's disenfranchised citizens.

The 1990 Copenhagen Document, which represents the human rights commitments of all OSCE member nations—including the United States—clearly states that the right "to take part in the governing of [one's] country, either directly or though representatives freely chosen," is a fundamental right, and further guarantees "universal and equal suffrage to adult citizens" in all OSCE member states. At the July 2005 OSCE Parliamentary Assembly meeting held in Washington and attended by more than 300 legislators from 55 countries, unanimous approval was given by the Parliamentary Assembly to a recommendation (not legally binding, unfortunately) for full Congressional representation for District residents. Of particular significance is that all members of the US delegation of six Republican and six Democratic Members of Congress (co-chaired by Senator Sam Brownback [R-KS] and Congressman Christopher Smith [R-NJ]) voted yea.

In January 2005, Iraqi citizens and expatriates around the world had the great privilege of exercising the most important democratic civil right— the right to vote for their representatives in the national parliament. The same government that facilitated voting for Iraqi expatriates in the DC metro area continues to deny voting representation for DC residents. As keen as George W. Bush's Administration is to ensure fundamental rights to Iraqis, it has not ensured liberty and freedom in its most basic form for the residents of Washington. While the current Administration has spent more than $150 billion in Afghanistan and Iraq—and plans to spend another $80 billion—DC residents are prohibited by Congress from spending a single penny of their collected taxes on lobbying for full Congressional voting representation.

Moreover, DC residents risked and lost their lives to ensure that elections in Iraq took place. To illustrate this point, DC Vote joined DC's Delegate to the House of Representatives, Eleanor Holmes Norton, and three Washingtonian veterans of the Iraq war at a Capitol Hill press conference. Specialist Marcus Gray, a DC resident and a recent returnee from the front line in Iraq, said: "We expect equal treatment, and the Army tries hard to see that all soldiers are treated equally....However, I want equal treatment at home as well. I want the same voting representation in the House and the Senate as other soldiers. This step would make me as proud as I will be to see the Iraqi people go to the polls."

Chapter 52

The Birth of the White Corporation

Jeffrey Kaplan

James Baldwin once compared white Americans' view of their own history to a factory within whose walls they have barricaded themselves. They remain trapped in that factory which "at an unbelievable human expense, produces unnamable objects." Those objects are unnamable because they exist deep within our world of shared cultural beliefs. But we do have names for their outward manifestations: environmental degradation, class oppression and racism, to name a few. Such a list must also include the legal fiction that the corporation is a person.

The primary engine of white United States history has been the use of property, the ownership of things, as a means of domination over people—and the use of people *as* property, for slavery was the original basis for wealth in white America. But there are other ways besides slavery in which notions of property and race have become fused. For example, W.E.B. DuBois noted that whiteness yields a "public and psychological wage" to all white workers, which is expressed in the freedom to mingle across social classes, preferential treatment by police, eligibility for government jobs and simply a greater sense of well-being than is true for blacks.

DuBois well understood that most of the wages of whiteness accrue not to poor whites, who receive only a pittance, but to the dominant classes. But what even he may not have been aware of is how, at the time of its birth, the modern corporation received as its patrimony the wealth and privileges accumulated during slavery. In 1883, the very same year the US Supreme Court heard arguments in favor of declaring that a corporation is a natural person, the Court also invalidated the enforcement of civil rights for African Americans. This was the first of a series of decisions that led to the Court's approval of racial segregation. The Court eventually held that both corporate personification and racial segregation were justifiable under the Fourteenth Amendment, which was passed with the explicit purpose of protecting the rights of former slaves after the Civil War. This connection is more than a mere oddity of US legal history. These Court decisions are part of a common social structure in which the exercise of social power through property rights continues to mask the concomitant disempowerment of people of color. In effect, what the Courts decided is that corporations are people while African Americans are not; and that, while property could no longer be held in the form of black skins, it could still be invested in white ones.

Whiteness as Property

In a long article in the June 1993 *Harvard Law Review* called "Whiteness as Property," African-American legal scholar Cheryl Harris provides an analytical framework we can use to clarify some of the ways in which white-skin privilege has been generally conjoined with property. Her paper "investigates the relationships between concepts of race and property and reflects on how rights in property are contingent on, intertwined with, and conflated with race. Through this entangled relationship between race and property, historical forms of domination have evolved to reproduce subordination in the present....Whiteness and property share a common premise—a conceptual nucleus—of the right to exclude." The essence of property in the Anglo-American legal tradition is that its owner can exclude others from using it. The essence of white skin in the US is that those who do not possess it are excluded from certain rights and privileges, including that of being treated as a full human being.

Property is not restricted to those things we can sell that are separable from ourselves. For example, a college degree has market value. The courts have held that in the event of a divorce, a spouse who supported her husband while he earned a medical or law degree has an interest in that degree and is entitled to compensation for her efforts in helping him earn it. In a sense, every Caucasian in the US is born with a "masters" degree.

The financial interest white people have in race was recognized by the Justices who legitimized racial segregation in *Plessy v. Ferguson* in 1896. The case was a carefully staged challenge to a Louisiana law requiring segregation on railroads. The lawyers challenging the law purposefully chose a well-educated African American who could pass as white. One of the arguments the lawyers then made was that by publicly labeling Plessy as "colored," the railroad had deprived him of the reputation of being white, "which has an actual pecuniary value." The Court conceded that if such a thing were done to a white man he would have grounds for a lawsuit, but evaded the issue in its decision to uphold the state law. As recently as 1957, a white person could sue for defamation if she was called "black," but a black person could not sue if she was called "white."

The Personification of the Corporation

The corporate person is a white person. It was given its invisible, but nonetheless valuable, color because of the conjoint exclusionary privileges of whiteness and property. The reasons why men of means saw fit to create such a legal fiction can only be understood in the context of the rise of large-scale capital in the period before the Civil War. That war was fought not because the majority of the citizens of the North found slavery to be repugnant, but to determine which group would be the senior partner in the capitalist state: the old power elite of the Southern slave-holders or their challengers, the Northern industrialists. The Emancipation Proclamation was issued during the war not simply to free the slaves of the Confederacy but in large part because the Northerners feared they might lose unless they found a new source of recruits for their army. They hoped the slaves would fight for their freedom, and some 180,000 of them did. This complicated the problem for Northern capitalists who were trying to figure out how to consolidate their victory over the Southern planters. The politics of race in the years after the Civil War presented the Northern capitalists with both a threat to their newly enhanced position and an opportunity to achieve that consolidation. They moved quickly to eliminate the threat and take full advantage of the opportunity.

The war had not broken the power of the Southern elite. They still owned the plantations and thus controlled the only source of employment for the overwhelming majority of the newly freed slaves. If the Southern states were simply re-admitted to the Union without any other changes, the planters could have easily resumed the control of Congress they had held before the war. Enfranchising the freed slaves with the vote seemed to be the way to break the power of the planters. But to be effective, enfranchising blacks would also require that they have the means to support themselves. There would have to be a massive redistribution of land, not only to blacks but also to poor whites. This was the program favored by the Radical Republicans who, as W.E.B. DuBois put it, wanted to "make the slaves free with land, education and the ballot, and then let the South return to its place."

The Northern capitalists saw this possibility as a threat to their interests, first because it would have broken down the racial split between blacks and Southern whites that the elites of both the North and the South had long exploited. This would have likely spilled over to the white Northern wage workers as well. Second, it would have destroyed the capital base of Southern agriculture and turned the South into a producer-controlled society of independent farmers. The Northerners didn't want to eliminate Southern capital; they wanted to dominate it. Finally, it would be enormously expensive, requiring the long-term presence of federal troops in the South and draining away resources the Northerners wished to devote to expanding the industrial system. For these reasons, their Congressional allies opposed the proposals of the Radical Republicans. For the Northern capitalists, the newly won human rights of former slaves were of interest only insofar as black voters served as a check on the political power of the old Southern planter elite. That check was needed as long as the Northerners had not yet established economic control over the states of the former Confederacy. As DuBois described it, the Northern capitalists' plan was to "guard property and industry; when their position is impregnable, let the South return; we will then hold it with black votes, until we capture it with white capital."

The capture was complete by 1877 when the capitalists brokered a deal over a contested Presidential election whereby the federal troops were withdrawn from the South in return for a promise by the Southerners to become junior partners to the Northern capitalists. This event marked the end of Reconstruction and the beginning of the post–Civil War oppression of African Americans in the South. The Supreme Court gave its approval to the new social order in 1883 when it declared the Reconstruction-era Civil Rights Act unconstitutional. Frederick Douglass declared that this decision by the Court "inflicted a heavy calamity upon seven millions of the people of this country, and left them naked and defenseless against the action of a malignant, vulgar, and pitiless prejudice." He yearned for "a Supreme Court of the United States which shall be as true to the claims of humanity as the Supreme Court formerly was to the demands of slavery!"

The Birth of the White Corporation

After consolidating its political power over the South, the industrialists were hampered by the fact that the US legal system was heavily oriented toward the rights of individuals and, as such, did not fully support the kind of organization that was needed for the consolidation of control over the rapidly emerging industrial system. The personification of the corporation was their solution to this problem.

The legal argument made before the Supreme Court on behalf of corporate personification began with a lie perpetrated in December of 1882 in the case of *San Mateo v. Southern Pacific Railroad.* The lawyer who lied was Roscoe Conkling, a former US Senator and one of the politicians DuBois identified as a principal architect of capital's strategy during Reconstruction. Conkling had served on the Congressional committee that drafted the Fourteenth Amendment. He claimed that, according to his copy of the committee journal, the original intention was that the amendment should apply to corporations as well as to human beings. The journal had not been published at the time the case was being heard, and the Justices did not question his account. Some decades later, the journal was published. It showed that Conkling's claim was, as Howard Graham, a modern authority on the history of the Fourteenth Amendment, put it, "a deliberate, brazen forgery."

The railroad's lawyers did not let their case rest on a simple lie. Their concluding argument, made in 1883 by Silas W. Sanderson, leaves no doubt that they also made a blatant appeal to white racial solidarity:

> It is very clear, if we look back over the history of the past twenty years, that this country has done a great deal for [members of] the negro race....It has made them free men...it has placed them on a par and equality with the white man. But that is none too much; we do not complain of that. We only say that something should now be done for the poor white man. We ask that he...be lifted up and put upon a level with the negro. We ask that this fourteenth amendment be so construed as to concede to the white man equal rights under the Constitution of the United States with the black man. Our claim is for universal equality before the law....[M]y friends upon the other side, by their construction of this amendment, would create a privileged class. They have demonstrated...that the negro race... stands higher upon the plane of legal rights than the white man; that whenever his rights are invaded he founds a shield and a protection in the fourteenth amendment...but whenever the white man's rights are invaded, whenever he is outraged by unjust State legislation, we are told...that there is no shield for him to be found in the fourteenth amendment; that the white man is without protection in cases where the black man is protected....I understand, then, that we may consider, for the purpose of this case...that there are not two Constitutions in this country—one for the black man and one for the white man—and that the white man is at last on an equality with the negro.

Clearly, the modern corporation was not to be just any kind of person; it was to be—it *had* to be—a white person, a white person created by the corporations, of the corporations and for the corporations in direct opposition to the aspirations of African Americans to live their lives as human beings. But not only did the corporation have to be a white person, Sanderson also said he was arguing on behalf of the "poor white man." Of course he was not working at the behest of struggling white farmers and workers. Sanderson's client was Colis Huntington, one of the most powerful railroad barons in the nation. Sanderson sought corporate personification by claiming that the state was violating the railroad's civil rights when it wrote tax laws that made a distinction between individual human beings and corporations. However, there was a place for the poor white man in the worldview of men such as Sanderson. It was described nicely by an Alabama journalist in 1886: "The white laboring classes here are separated from Negroes...by an innate consciousness of race superiority which excites a sentiment of sympathy and equality on their part with classes above them, and in this way becomes a wholesome social leaven."

The Court never issued an opinion in *San Mateo* because the parties settled out of court. But the railroad barons had already instigated another case, this one involving the neighboring county of Santa Clara. In 1886, in *Santa Clara County v. Southern Pacific Railroad*, the Court declared it would not hear any further arguments on whether the Fourteenth Amendment applies to "these corporations...We are all of the opinion that it does." Even at the time, it was considered extraordinary that the Court did not state its reasoning for such an important statement. But then they would have had to expose to public scrutiny a blatant legal fabrication.

The White Corporation Comes of Age

At the time of its birth, the white corporation was a child of the railroads, which had long been the only truly large-scale enterprises in the US. But within a few years industrial and manufacturing firms also began to form massive conglomerates. Their leaders realized that the white corporation would serve them well as they sought to extend their industrial empires. The years from 1895 to 1907 saw what has been termed the great Corporate Revolution, at the end of which entire industries were controlled by one or two large firms. Of the 100 largest corporations in existence 50 years later, 20 were created by consolidation during this period. Eight more were created a few years later when the courts ordered the split-up of Standard Oil.

This was also the period during which racial segregation and imperialism became accepted features of white America's national identity. Not only did the US Supreme Court approve of racial segregation during those years, blacks were attacked in race riots in cities all over the country: Atlanta; New Orleans; New York City; Akron, Ohio; and even Lincoln's hometown of Springfield, Illinois. In 1903, the African-American novelist Charles W. Chestnutt noted that "the rights of the Negroes are at a lower ebb than at any time during the thirty-five years of their freedom, and the race prejudice more intense and uncompromising." White America had replaced the system of slavery with one of caste.

Once the caste system was safely in place, the white corporations could concentrate on expanding the privileges that inhered in their invisible white skins. Until about 1960, the corporations' status as persons was used primarily to protect and expand corporate property rights against attempts by the states to impose economic controls. In 1938, Justice Hugo Black noted that of the cases in which the Supreme Court applied the Fourteenth Amendment during the first 50 years after *Santa Clara*, "less than one-half of one percent invoked it in protection of the Negro race, and more than 50 percent asked that its benefits be extended to corporations." As this statistic shows, the white corporation had usurped the rights of the people whom the Fourteenth Amendment was meant to protect. It was using those rights—which it had obtained through what amounts to a legally engineered fraud—to expand its own interests. At the same time,

African Americans were deprived of their legal voice and forced to suffer a violent oppression in silence. Thus, we can look at each one of those actions on behalf of corporations as a transfer of both economic and human rights from black people to those who control large-scale capital. In a sense, James Baldwin's unnamable objects found their physical expression in the innumerable products marketed by the giant corporations.

But the desire for freedom found its own expression in the Civil Rights Movement, the environmental movement and the demands by women for a full role in social life. All of these attempts by real human beings to assert their rights threatened the prerogatives of the corporations. Corporate lawyers responded by seeking to expand the standing of corporate persons to include a number of protections under the Bill of Rights that previously had been granted only to human beings. Since 1960, the Supreme Court has granted to corporate persons the right of free speech—especially political speech—under the First Amendment, protection against double jeopardy under the Fifth Amendment, the right to counsel under the Sixth Amendment, and the right to a jury trial under the Seventh Amendment. In other words, the Court has endorsed a counterattack by property against the assertion of human rights by the public in general, and people of color and women in particular.

Of course, the white skin possessed by real human beings of European descent is no guarantee of protection against the artificial white person. Recently, a well-to-do white community challenged a federal law that allows telecommunications companies to ignore local zoning ordinances when putting up microwave towers. The community lost when their corporate opponents cited a civil rights statute whose language originated in a Reconstruction-era attempt to protect the rights of African Americans against the Ku Klux Klan. Such an irony would not have been lost on Baldwin: "People who imagine that history flatters them (as it does, indeed, since they wrote it) are impaled on their history like a butterfly on a pin and become incapable of seeing or changing themselves, or the world."

Chapter 53

Democracy Quiz

Peter Kellman

Answers are on page 405.

The dominant history taught in the United States today reinforces the notion that from 1776 to the present, "We the People" have formed our own government and this government has operated to protect and promote the interests of most people most of the time. Slavery and the denial of the right to vote for women are pointed to as exceptions that have been rectified through Constitutional amendments. The problem, of course, is that from its inception, the United States government and economy has been run by and for the very wealthy.

1. In 1770, what percentage of the colonial population lived in slavery?

2. At the time of the War of Independence, what percentage of the people who made up the colonies of Pennsylvania, Maryland and Virginia were or had been indentured servants?

3. What percentage of "We the People" couldn't vote in 1776?

4. Who said, "The people who own the country ought to Govern it?"

5. The Fourteenth Amendment to the Constitution was passed in 1868 to extend due process and equal protection to African Americans. In the first 50

years after its adoption, what percentage of cases brought under it were on behalf of African Americans, and what percentage on behalf of corporations?

6. The Supreme Court ruled in 1872 that women do not have the right to vote under the Fourteenth Amendment. In what year did the Supreme Court rule, "Corporations are persons within the meaning of the Fourteenth Amendment to the Constitution of the United States."

7. How can five people amend the Constitution?

8. It is easy for citizens of the US to form a corporation but difficult to form a union. Name three countries where workers can form a union as easily as investors can form a corporation in the US.

Miscellaneous

Chapter 54

Race, Poverty and Hunger

Alison Leff and Alexandra Cawthorne

Hunger and the implications of hunger strike hard at the core of low-income and minority communities. Ending hunger will solve not only the problem of malnutrition, but it will take America one step closer to its promise of a nation "created equal." The problems associated with hunger are devastatingly widespread. In 2003, the US Department of Agriculture (USDA) reported that 11.2% of households were food insecure at some time during that year. These 12.6 million households were uncertain of having, or were unable to acquire, enough food to meet the needs of all of their members due to a lack of financial and other resources. During a typical month, 8 million adults and 4.5 million children access resources provided by food pantries, and more than 1 million people each month are served by emergency kitchens.

Low-income and minority persons are more likely to suffer from food insecurity. Food insecurity affects over a third of low-income households that fall below the federal poverty line. According to the USDA's Food and Nutrition Service, a household's chances of being hungry or food-insecure decrease as income rises. People of color feel the pains of hunger disproportionately. According to the USDA, African-American and Hispanic households face food insecurity and hunger rates three times as high as those of white households. And African-American and Hispanic children confront higher rates of chronic hunger (46% and 40%, respectively) than do white children (16%). The disproportionate number of people of color who suffer from food insecurity and hunger comes partially from the fact that race and poverty are inextricably linked.

According to a 2003 update of Census 2000 data, 44.3% of those living in poverty are white, 24.4% are African-American and 22.5% are Hispanic, while in the general population whites make up 75%, African Americans 12.3% and Hispanics 12.5% of the population.

There are two main responses to the blight of hunger in this nation of plenty. Government programs are the first nutrition safety net. The government's main defense against hunger is the Food Stamp program. There are over 23 million Food Stamp recipients, 41% of whom are white, 35% African-American and 18% Hispanic. The Women, Infants and Children (WIC) and the school feeding programs are additional federal efforts to combat the problem of hunger. In 2004, WIC provided nutritionally balanced foods and services for approximately 7.9 million pregnant low-income women and their infants and children each month. More than 28.4 million children each day got their lunch through the National School Lunch program, which operates in 96% of the nation's public and private schools. The more recent, and less widespread, School Breakfast program feeds 8.4 million children each school day. These school feeding programs are available at reduced rates for households with incomes below 185% of the federal poverty line and are free for families with incomes under 130% of the federal poverty level. Currently, 16 million of the 28+ million participating students receive their lunches free of charge or at a reduced rate.

The next layer is the emergency food network, meant to catch those who fall through the government nutrition safety nets. America's Second Harvest operates the country's largest network of charitable food providers, each year supplying 1.7 billion pounds of food to over 200 food banks and food rescue programs which in turn supply 50,000 soup kitchens, food pantries and shelters. According to their latest study, *Hunger in America 2001*, the 23.3 million people served by America's Second Harvest's emergency food network represented a 9% increase from 1997. A survey of America's Second Harvest affiliates completed in late 2001 and early 2002 found that 86% had seen an increase in food requests within the previous year. Forty-five percent of their clients are white, 35% are African-American and 17% are Hispanic. Other organizations provide emergency food to agencies on the local level, but none have the larger national scope of Second Harvest.

Diet Quality and Food Access

There are many dimensions of food intake. Food insecurity represents not just the lack of enough food, but also the presence of nutritionally inadequate food. Both socioeconomic status and race have been shown to affect the quality of household diets. A high-quality diet is essential for human development and well-being. Recent studies have provided evidence that in the US, some dietary patterns are associated with 4 of the 10 leading causes of death. The USDA created an index to measure the overall quality of an individual's diet and to measure changes in dietary patterns. Scores from its Healthy Eating Index (HEI) show that individuals' nutrient content knowledge and diet-health awareness increase with income. Additionally, HEI results are correlated with race: African Americans and Hispanics have lower HEI scores than whites. USDA research shows that Hispanics and African Americans are less likely than whites to meet the Recommended Daily Allowances of such nutrients as vitamins A, C and E, calcium and iron. People of color and people with low incomes have lower rates of fruit and vegetable consumption.

Families face socioeconomic barriers that limit their control over their nutrition. Working families can lack the time needed to shop for and cook a full meal; time is even harder to find for single-parent households. This scarcity of time can lead to quick trips to a nearby McDonalds. A study in the *International Journal of Obesity* showed that low-income individuals and people of color eat fast food more often than others, a dangerous trend, as fast food tends to have high fat and low fiber intakes. When households are faced with tight budgets, they have to stretch their dollar by purchasing less expensive but higher-calorie and higher-fat foods–essentially facilitating a trade-off between food quality and quantity. These households typically do not have enough income to allow them to take advantage of bulk purchasing. Nutritious fruits and vegetables are high-cost purchases; as one low-income shopper commented in a study of public housing tenants' access to quality food, "You can clip a coupon for a can, but you never see a coupon for fresh fruits and vegetables."

Environment plays an overtly important role in food access and choice. Not only are low-income households faced with economic barriers to quality food purchase and time constraints in the preparation of more nutritious food, but they also confront geographic challenges. In 2004, researchers in New Orleans examined the geographic distribution of fast food restaurants relative to neighborhood demographics. They found that fast food restaurants in Orleans Parish are geographically associated with predominantly African-American and low-income neighborhoods after controlling for commercial activity, the presence of highways, and median home values. Similar research in other parts of the country has found that wealthy and predominantly white neighborhoods have more supermarkets and fewer neighborhood grocery stores than poor and predominantly African-American neighborhoods–a significant finding because several studies indicate that supermarkets have more "heart-healthy" foods compared to convenience stores and neighborhood grocery stores.

Supermarkets characteristically offer cheaper prices and a larger variety of food options than do smaller food sellers. Low-income and minority neighborhoods are less likely to have supermarkets; their food demands are usually met by more expensive, poorer-quality corner stores and convenience marts. Independent central city grocery stores that do exist often charge more than suburban stores because of higher operating costs, less competition and patrons' lesser mobility, which limits their ability to price-shop. These markets often offer poorer-quality, older produce. A USDA study shows that, limited by the poorer-quality, older produce. A USDA study shows that, limited by the type and location of food stores, low-income and minority households are forced to purchase their groceries at inflated prices. Such access problems produce the paradox that poor Americans pay more for basic nourishment when compared with their wealthier counterparts.

The Impacts of Hunger and Food Insecurity

The lack of a healthy diet has serious impacts on a person's quality of life. The effects on children are well documented. Lower-income children consume more fats and sugars, play outside less and have more health problems. Thus, a complicated situation results whereby children are undernourished but can gain an unhealthy amount of weight. Approximately 9 million children over the age of six are now considered obese; furthermore, the amount of weight carried by the heaviest children is greater than it was 30 years ago. Populations of color have higher levels of overweight and obesity and have experienced greater increases in weight over the past decade than have white populations. Specifically, African-American and Hispanic children suffer from the highest rates of obesity, according to the American Obesity Association. Childhood hunger and obesity can limit children's growth, restrict brain development and reduce immune function (thereby increasing illness rates). Food-insecure children are more likely to be tardy or absent from school. The Food Research and Action Center (FRAC) reports that insufficient access to food negatively impacts a child's ability to interact with others and with his or her surroundings. This is especially damaging in schools, where hunger has a debilitating effect on children's learning, concentration and ability to perform basic tasks.

Hunger has serious impacts on adults as well. Workers are likely to experience a lack of concentration that can increase on-the-job injuries as well as decrease productivity. Those suffering from hunger and malnutrition also face increased probabilities of having chronic and acute diseases. Poor diet and physical inactivity are major causes of heart disease, cancer, strokes, high blood pressure and diabetes. These conditions can also speed the onset of degenerative diseases among the elderly. Emotional and psychological consequences of food insecurity can include family tension, anxiety, low self-esteem and hostility. A few recent studies have even suggested that irregular access to nutritious food can lead to a preoccupation with food, influencing the development of eating disorders.

Immediate Needs in the Fight Against Hunger and Food Insecurity

Broad measures must be taken to strengthen America's current responses to food insecurity. Government feeding programs should focus on expanding participation, specifically for households unconnected to the federal welfare program. Food Stamp caseloads increased by 26% within three years ending October 2003, but, according a recent report by The Urban Institute, increased participation rates were highest for families with some experience with the welfare program. At least 2 million more families received Food Stamp benefits in October 2003 than in October 2000. This increase represents a dramatic reversal of the 40% caseload decline that occurred between 1994 and 2000. However, many eligibles still do not enroll in the program. Food Stamp participation rates among families without welfare experience–the largest share of poor families with children–have not improved. To be eligible for the Food Stamp program, a household must have gross incomes below 130% of the federal poverty line and must meet a variety of asset requirements. Over 38% of Food Stamp households have gross incomes at or below half of the federal poverty line ($19,350 for a family of four in 2005).

Confusion over the tighter eligibility requirements imposed by the 1996 welfare reforms had led some people to mistakenly believe they were no longer eligible. However, Congress subsequently reversed those reforms in legislation enacted between 2000 and 2002, giving states new opportunities to expand Food Stamp access. Outreach to help explain the Food Stamp program's complicated rules and regulations must be expanded. States put more effort into informing welfare recipients that they could retain benefits after the 1996 reforms and explained new program regulations, but not enough effort was made to increase knowledge among non-participating families. This could be accomplished through intense outreach efforts in grocery stores, community centers and schools. For example, FoodChange, a nonprofit in New York City, developed a field outreach team comprised of Food Stamp specialists who provide information on eligibility and benefits, pre-screen potential applicants to assure eligibility, assist in the complicated application process, and, year-round, visit numerous locations where low-income New Yorkers can easily be reached.

School feeding programs are key tools for lowering childhood hunger and obesity. These programs help provide schoolchildren the recommended amounts of key nutrients while helping them develop healthy eating patterns. By the first day of the 2006-07 school year, every school district that participates in the National School Lunch program is required to enact a local school wellness policy, a new tool to address obesity and promote healthy eating and physical activity through changes in school environments. For many students, these feeding programs provide the most nutritious (and, for some, perhaps the only) food they receive during a day. Research shows that low-income children who participate in the School Breakfast program have higher standardized test scores and are tardy and absent less often than low-income students who do not eat breakfast at school. Making school feeding programs universal—offering meals at no charge to all children, regardless of income—would enable all children to receive the positive results of the program and relieve any stigma associated with participation (a factor that likely deters many students). Some schools have already enacted universal school breakfast programs, many of which provide breakfast in the classroom when school starts in the morning, rather than in the cafeteria before school starts, making it easier for children to participate. However, these schools are still in the minority, and have to seek local and state resources to cover any extra costs. Currently, the 16 million students who receive free or reduced-price meals are eligible to receive two meals a day during the summer months as well, through the Summer Food Service program. However, in the summer of 2004 the program, funded by USDA and operated by summer camps, churches and community centers, reached only 3 million youth. This greatly underutilized summer feeding program must be expanded by reaching out to youth-serving organizations to assist them in applying for available funds.

While Second Harvest's network is critical in offering emergency supplies to households in need, the food provided leaves much to be desired. Kitchens and pantries distribute what is donated to them by corporations (which receive a healthy tax break) and food drives, the "leftovers" of society. There is little, if any, fresh produce and a plethora of unhealthy snacks. An agricultural program created in Ohio and coordinated by the Ohio Association of Second Harvest Food Banks, brings agricultural surpluses into food banks, aiding Ohio farmers and bringing quality fruits and vegetables into soup kitchens and food pantries. The issue of improved access to nutrient-rich, healthy foods is of growing concern in some school districts as well. In support of their feeding programs, some school districts in California and Texas have phased out machine sales of soda and junk foods in order to encourage children to eat healthier. Other districts have stocked vending machines with water, 100% juices and sports drinks, and have eliminated low-nutrition food. Teachers and administrators in a few of these schools have reported positive changes in student behavior, noting increased focus in class and reductions in suspensions for violent behavior.

Long-Term Solutions to Hunger and Food Insecurity

Currently, America uses the Food Stamp program and the emergency food system to address the symptoms of food insecurity and hunger, not the root causes. Such band-aid solutions will never end hunger, only soften its blow. The eradication of hunger will come when all households have equal access to affordable, nutritious food and are educated as to what makes up a healthy diet.

Access to quality food in low-income and minority neighborhoods is a major challenge. The locations and pricing structures of supermarkets need to be closely monitored, and measures enacted that allow for more efficient spending patterns and wider consumption of nutritious food. WIC and WIC Farmers Markets have the potential to increase food access for vulnerable populations of women and children, helping mothers to feed their children right from the start. The WIC Farmers Market Nutrition program slowly is being expanded across the United States and needs to be promoted and spread more effectively. Local growers bring produce to central city farmers markets, where women can use their WIC benefits. This program, and other community-run markets, can go far in helping low-income and minority participants gain access to the fruits and vegetables they need as part of a balanced diet, at the same time aiding local growers. Some farmers markets are even initiating programs that encourage more patronage from Food Stamp recipients. Recent federal legislation has mandated that Food Stamp coupons be converted to an Electronic Benefit Transfer (EBT) system. The Crescent City Farmers Market in New Orleans has put resources into developing a farmer-friendly EBT system to prevent the loss of their valuable Food Stamp clientele.

Community education and outreach are important tools for improving the purchasing and consumption patterns of low-income and minority communities. Small classes taught by peers and educators, focusing on health, nutrition and cooking tips, taking into account tight budgets and children's tastes, are a great start. Share Our Strength, a national anti-hunger organization, conducts such a program: Operation Frontline. Local nutritionists, chefs and community leaders lead classes for children and families on cooking, nutrition and food budgeting skills. The classes have been shown to increase health awareness and budgeting abilities. They are taught on a local level so as to make them culturally appropriate. It is imperative that such successful programs that help address complicated food access and cultural competency issues be expanded.

These solutions address the food side of hunger, but it is important to address the economics of hunger as well. The main hunger problem is not a lack of food; it is the lack of money with which to buy food, the lack of a car to reach the supermarket, the lack of a home with adequate facilities in which to safely store and prepare food, the lack of time to cook a nutritious meal for a whole family.

Thirty-nine percent of households that access emergency food resources have one or more working adults, and yet are unable to earn enough to feed their families. Households will not be able to break the hold of hunger without a livable wage that allows them to earn enough money to purchase quality food. The widespread hunger and food insecurity in America is, in part, driven by the erosion of the value of the minimum wage. Livable wages will allow individuals to work more reasonable hours, leaving them the money with which to buy food, and the time to shop and cook healthy meals (instead of taking the nutritionally vacuous fast-food "quick fix"). Other supports for working families, such as child care subsidies and health care, need to be reinforced. Racial wage discrimination must be addressed to moderate the disproportionate burden of poverty on people of color. According to the National Committee on Pay Equity, African-American and Hispanic men earn 78% and 63%, respectively, of what white men make, and the numbers for women are even more discouraging. Policies that address such disparities will allow all individuals to work and save, essentially the best anti-hunger strategies out there.

Housing often accounts for 50% or more of the budget of a low-income household, at the expense of the budget for other needs, especially food. According to the National Low Income Housing Coalition, wages are falling further and further behind rapidly rising housing prices, making affordable housing hard to find. A vast increase in decent and safe, affordable housing would be a great boon to families struggling to keep food on their tables.

The end of hunger will come only when we feed the full range of physical, emotional and economic needs of those suffering from hunger and food insecurity. The burden of hunger falls disproportionately on the shoulders of those with limited incomes and people of color. In working towards a hunger-free America, and indeed, a hunger-free world (hunger problems in the US pale in comparison to those in developing economies: In southern Africa alone, some 14 million people are currently at risk of starvation), we must, as David Shields asserts in his 1995 book *The Color of Hunger*, "conceptualize malnutrition as a civil rights issue and racism as an issue of public health."

Chapter 55

Race, Poverty and Youth Development

Carla Roach, Hanh Cao Yu and Heather Lewis-Charp

The Positive Youth Development Framework

The process commonly referred to as "youth development" is one that most young people pass through on their way to adulthood. During adolescence, ideally, young people receive support from their peers, families, caring adults, schools and community institutions, thereby increasing the likelihood of "positive" youth development and improved life outcomes. Yet even under the most ideal circumstances, adolescence is often a time of turbulence. It is a stage of rapid development physically, psychologically and socially; young people are simultaneously confronted with issues of identity formation, self-worth and acquiring a broad set of skills needed to function as an adult.

For young people growing up in low-income communities, however, the challenges of adolescence are exacerbated by a range of factors, including a lack of economic opportunity for their parents, family instability, inadequate schools, prevalence of drugs, violence, social isolation and, in the case of ethnic and racial minorities, racism. Most low-income youth enter adolescence having already experienced many of these challenges. Consequently, adolescence often represents one of the last opportunities to intervene in the human development of young people and help them overcome the academic, health and social barriers associated with growing up in poverty. Moreover, adolescents can be more easily accessed at this stage in life as they assemble in groups through schools, community centers and peer groups. For society, adolescence represents the final chance to intervene in the lives of young people before welfare dependency, limited productivity and other social problems become life patterns that ultimately are more costly.

Since the 1950s, there has been a steady growth in social programs and policies aimed at helping low-income youth meet the additional burdens imposed by the confluence of adolescence and poverty. During the late 1980s, the focus of these efforts shifted away from the prevention of specific problem behaviors (such as pregnancy, school failure, unemployment) to the promotion of positive development and preparation for adulthood among low-income youth.

Undergirding this shift to positive youth development was the work of leaders such as Michele Cahill of the New York City Department of Education and Karen Pittman of the Forum for Youth Investment. As co-founders of the Center for Youth Development and Policy Research at the Academy for Educational Development, Cahill and Pittman set forth the positive youth development framework. They argued that the term "youth development" refers to the ongoing process in which all young people are engaged and invested—even in the absence of family supports and formal programs. All young people will seek ways to meet their basic physical and social needs; and to build the individual assets or competencies (knowledge, skills, relationships, values) they feel are needed to participate successfully in adolescence and adult life. In other words, youth development is an inevitable process and, depending on the influences young people are exposed to, their development can either be negative or positive.

Three guiding principles are now routinely used to develop programs and policies and to evaluate the outcomes of positive youth development. The first principle is that society has to articulate a vision for what it wants for its young people. The second principle underscores the fact that young people grow up in communities, not programs, and that efforts to promote positive development must be focused on the overall context in which that development occurs. The third principle holds that youth in partnership with adults have critical roles to play as stakeholders in all efforts to promote positive youth development.

The factors influencing positive youth development suggest a number of key inputs. Young people need a stable place which is theirs and where they feel safe; access to basic care and services that are appropriate, affordable and, if necessary, confidential; high-quality instruction and training; opportunities to develop social and strategic networks; opportunities to develop sustained, caring relationships; challenging experiences that are appropriate, diverse and sufficiently intense; and opportunities for real participation and involvement in the full range of community life.

In short, all young people, affluent or low-income, need a mix of services, supports and opportunities in order to stay engaged. Promotion of positive youth development requires that young people have stable places, services and instruction. But they also need supports—relationships and networks that provide nurturing, standards and guidance, as well as opportunities for trying new roles, mastering challenges and contributing to family and community.

Poverty, Race and Other Contextual Factors

While the paradigm shift from a deficit-based to a youth development perspective moves us closer to defining promising program practices and settings that nurture positive youth development outcomes, the field has yet to address two areas critical to expanding the reach and impact of youth development programming. The first relates to effectively serving vulnerable young people who are not involved in traditional youth development activities. Field leaders such as Karen Pittman have identified this as a key challenge, explaining, "The youth-serving organizations and efforts that have capitalized most on the 'youth development paradigm shift' have not consistently addressed the needs of young people who are dealing with or are most at risk for poverty, school failure, family crises and problem behaviors." The second area entails mobilizing youth-serving agencies to effectively address the cultural and social contexts that mediate the potentially negative societal influences (e.g., poverty, discrimination) on young people's healthy identity development.

The development of vulnerable young people is often profoundly impacted by poverty and discrimination. Related societal factors—such as a lack of economic and employment opportunities, sexism, homophobia, lack of access to high-quality health and education services, and stereotypical media portrayals of certain groups—all contribute negatively to a young person's sense of identity, connectedness, competency and control over his or her fate in life. Unfortunately, a good number of youth programs try to treat "all youth" in an undifferentiated manner so as to minimize such differences among youth; however, these differences often reveal the most about the challenges youth face as they draw upon the supports and opportunities that are available to them. Further, youth organizations have often not provided a safe and comfortable space for youth to explore their own identities and develop a critical understanding of the differences in opportunities and experiences they face in their daily lives. Creating such safe spaces is pivotal to engaging vulnerable youth populations, who must resist the internalization of negative societal messages about who they are and their capacities.

While youth development occurs in a limited manner in formalized programs or institutional settings, it tends to occur more fully within multiple, naturalistic contexts, such as family and communities, over a span of time. These overlapping and nested contexts can play a positive role in supporting youth's mediation of negative messages and experiences. The quality and structure of the relationships that youth have in these settings play a pivotal role in contributing to the development of healthy and productive coping behaviors regarding stresses in their lives. At the same time, however, family and community factors, such as poverty or inadequate schools, can inhibit growth and lead to the devel-opment of negative coping skills. Unfortunately, many programs tend to focus on a discrete set of activities or experiences, and in fact fail to take into account the reciprocal and dynamic interactions that take place between the individual and various contextual arenas. In doing so, they fail to support bridge-building between youth and key supports within their "multiple worlds," thus missing the opportunity to further assist them as they seek to navigate around the pitfalls of adolescence or beyond the debilitating conditions that arise from poverty and social injustices.

The failure of youth development practitioners to provide adolescents with the appropriate developmental opportunities to explore issues of identity, inde-pendence, equality and decision-making is no small matter. As a consequence, programs and organizations that seek the participation and involvement of "at-risk" youth frequently have a difficult time with recruitment and retention of adolescent participants. These critical gaps alienate young people and leave them searching for ways to define how they fit into society and how they can make meaningful contributions as vital participants in American civic life.

Civic Activism: Bridging the Gap?

Young people with a combination of passionate indignation, optimistic enthusi-asm and a willingness to take risks and challenge the status quo have long been associated with social movements for justice and equity. For example, young people's determination to bring about an end to the war in Vietnam and to ex-tend civil rights to ethnic and racial minorities, women, and gays and lesbians transformed the cultural environment of the United States in the 1960s and 1970s. While much of this struggle was contentious and controversial and not every outcome was positive, there can be no question that the youth movement of those years made beneficial contributions to society. And in the process the lives of the young people themselves were enhanced.

Civic activism is being rediscovered as a particularly relevant approach for positive youth development today. Its focus on social justice issues provides a pivotal ideological frame of reference for youth who are searching for meaning and a place in their social world. Youth cannot form healthy political or civic identities without understanding how their own values, belief systems, experi-ences and expectations connect them to larger ideological and social communi-ties. As Erik Erikson argues, "Adolescent development comprises a new set of identification processes, both with significant persons and with ideological forces, which give importance to individual life by relating it to a living com-munity and an ongoing history." Thus, civic activism acts as a pivotal forum for youth to connect to social-historical challenges facing them and their communi-ties and to see a role for themselves and others in co-constructing a new reality. Such connection forms the basis for developmental outcomes, such as an increased sense of efficacy and a strong civic identity. Moreover, the networks of support developed through such efforts lead to a renewed trust in adults and institutions.

Conceptually, civic activism holds considerable promise as a strategy for dealing with difficult topics, such as race, poverty, gender, sexual orientation and immigrant status among young people. This approach would seem to have major implications for the content and delivery of youth development programs. The reality however, is that practitioners from these two fields have not traditionally collaborated or shared strategies. Recognizing the need to bridge this gap, the Ford Foundation created the Youth Leadership for Development Initiative (YLDI), to support and foster learning about civic activism as a youth development strategy that targets the leadership and civic engagement of marginalized youth. YLDI directed much-needed attention to the intersection of civic activism and youth development.

A Case In Point: Highlights from the Youth Leadership for Development Initiative

The Foundation launched YLDI in 1999 as a three-year learning network of 12 community-based organizations. These organizations represented an array of youth constituencies, including African-American, Latino and Latina, Native American, Asian Pacific American, low-income white suburban, gay and lesbian, faith-involved, girl leaders, and low-income Asian immigrant women and children. The YLDI network was managed by the Innovation Center for Community and Youth Development, a national intermediary organization. By design, the intermediary role was a central feature of YLDI. In addition to providing general oversight for the initiative, the Innovation Center sought to strengthen and sustain the work of each YLDI organization through targeted capacity-building strategies. Over time, the initiative also aimed to cull valuable lessons about civic activism as an effective youth development approach.

A multi-level evaluation of YLDI, conducted by Social Policy Research Associates, concluded that civic activism is indeed a powerful approach for reaching youth who are often not reached by conventional youth development programs. The average age of YLDI youth was 16, and many of the program participants described struggles with negative public perception of their abilities, limited options for employment and support, pressures to engage in gangs and drugs, and premature adult responsibilities and financial pressures. The study identified three features that seem to draw these older, more challenged youth populations to civic activism organizations: They provide young people with a place to focus on their own cultures and backgrounds; they offer a forum for youth to reflect on and address the day-to-day challenges faced by their families and communities; and they create applied vocational and leadership opportunities.

The study further determined that YLDI organizations made a positive contribution to young people's development. YLDI organizations engaged youth in a combination of organizing and identity work. Youth organizing practices include political education, campaign development and direct action. They also prioritized the creation of safe spaces for youth to develop positive identities, such as those based in race, ethnicity, immigrant status, and/or sexual orientation. These civic activism practices provided support for young people at a rate comparable to or higher than traditional youth-serving organizations. For instance, 69% of YLDI youth reported consistently high-quality relationships with adults and youth within the organization. This figure is nearly twice that reported by youth within other youth-serving organizations. (The final YLDI evaluation report and executive summary are available at www.theinnovation-center.org.)

In many ways, YLDI marked a turning point in the youth development field. The pendulum has swung back a bit from a romanticized notion of programs for "all" youth, to a renewed recognition of the challenging contexts that confront many youth of different racial, ethnic, socioeconomic, sexual orientation and immigrant backgrounds. At the same time, civic activism organizations have raised and continue to raise the bar for what youth can do. Youth within these programs are seriously engaged in critical reflection about themselves and their society, uniting with their peers in positive collective action, and engaging community leaders to see uncommon and innovative alternatives to chronic problems in our society. Adult leaders of today can choose to let the number of disenfranchised youth increase daily or be open to creating, learning, replicating and supporting civic activism programs so that youth determine for themselves how to make our society a better and more just place to live.

Chapter 56

Race, Poverty and LGBT Youth

L. Michael Gipson

In a capitalist society that places a premium on young adulthood (read: economic productivity and opportunity), reproductive capacity and propensity, masculinity, European lineage and conformity to strict gender roles—in such a society, ageism, sexism, racial prejudice and discrimination, transphobia, homophobia, and heterosexism will flourish. In a society that has disdain for racial and ethnic complexity, gender variance and sexual diversity, intolerance is the likely experience and oppression the probable condition for people who belong to communities that defy simplistic categorization, resist the values and ideals of the majority community, and consistently engage in political protest against the political and cultural dominance of those belonging to the status quo. For people from these communities, outcomes often include an increased potential to experience poverty, disease, incarceration and violence. In the US, these communities are easily identified as the poor, youth, the elderly, racial and ethnic minorities, women and those identifying as lesbian, gay, bisexual and transgendered (LGBT). Members of an oppressed community have unique obstacles to overcome in order to fulfill their potential. For individuals like LGBT youth of color (YOC) whose identities cross the lines of age, racial or ethnic identity, sexual orientation, gender and/or non-conformist gender expression, and low socioeconomic status, the challenge of achieving resiliency, economic prosperity, a healthy existence and the privileges of full citizenship are markedly reduced. Consequently, LGBT YOC may be the most vulnerable of any other youth population in terms of negative health and developmental outcomes because of a lack of research determining the needs and addressing the health status of the population; a lack of support either from their cultural communities and their LGBT community; an over-representation in the child welfare and juvenile justice systems; and the likelihood they will experience prejudice and discrimination on multiple fronts on the basis of their individual and collective identities.

Who are LGBT YOC?

While research on LGBT youth in general is scarce, research on LGBT YOC is virtually non-existent. In a 2001 review of the professional literature and research needs of LGBT YOC commissioned by the National Youth Advocacy Coalition, researcher Caitlin Ryan discovered only 16 studies (14 articles and 2 book chapters) published during the last 30 years on LGBT YOC. Most of these were empirical studies, with small sample sizes, samples of convenience or snowball samples that lack diversity in terms of class, geographic area and level of acculturation.

LGBT YOC data are also unlikely to be extracted from national data sources. National or government-sponsored studies on youth behaviors like the Department of Health and Human Services Youth Risk Behavior Survey (YRBS) that routinely ask questions about heterosexual sexual risk-taking behaviors do not ask youth questions about same-sex behavior or desires for fear that states already hostile to the data collection process and the politically charged outcomes of the survey's behavioral findings will not implement the survey tools and collect the necessary data. Some states, like Massachusetts, and municipalities, like New York City, do ask a few questions about same sex behavior among youth on their amended versions of the YRBS, but these locales are the exception.

The lack of comprehensive research about LGBT YOC, and to a lesser extent LGBT youth generally, means that the knowledge professionals working with LGBT YOC have is anecdotal or qualitative in nature. For LGBT YOC advocates, the research gaps on LGBT YOC present a credibility challenge during attempts to raise the public's awareness of the obstacles confronting this vulnerable population. With a paucity in peer-reviewed data to understand the unique experience of LGBT YOC, one has to make certain assumptions about their challenges and experiences based on information about LGBT youth and data on general population YOC.

Poverty

There may be more LGBT-identified youth, and potentially LGBT YOC, living in poverty now than at any point in US history. There are an estimated 60-70 million young people in the US between ages 5 and 20, a youth population explosion not recorded in the US since the baby-boom generation. Of these youth, one in three is a member of a racial or ethnic minority. Social scientists generally estimate that 10% of youth are or will become lesbian, gay, bisexual or transgender. The 2000 Census reports that youth under 18 comprise the largest number of people living in poverty in the US, and youth 18 to 24 had a poverty rate of 14.4%. Employer discrimination against youth based on age (which contributes to low youth wages and the income disparities between old and young workers); youth unemployment that can be as high as 33% in some cities; and government-sanctioned employment discrimination in 40 states against self-identified LGBT populations ensure that LGBT youth and young adults are well represented among communities of poor and working-class people. LGBT YOC, particularly those of African-American, Native American or Latino descent, may be disproportionately represented among LGBT youth living in poverty, given the high poverty rates for those communities, the disproportionately low wages paid to these workers, and the potential for racial discrimination in hiring and job promotion.

Discriminatory Behavior of Socializing Agents

Beyond poverty, LGBT YOC face enormous developmental obstacles in achieving resiliency. At a point when youth are already struggling with the developmental and emotional challenges of adolescence, including the phase of sexual awakening and intense pressure to conform to peer norms, LGBT youth are additionally confronted with their same-sex attractions and/or non-conformist gender expression.

Homophobia and heterosexism from socializing agents like family, church and school compound LGBT youths' challenges by enforcing rigid gender roles, condemning gender non-conformity and homosexuality. Perceptions and/or confirmation of youths' LGBT identity in school can lead to verbal or physical assault, consequently making school unsafe for many LGBT young people. In response, LGBT advocates have developed youth-led gay-straight alliances (GSAs) in schools and adult-led safe school coalitions. Of the more than 800 GSAs and the 40 or so safe schools coalitions in the US, few are located in schools or school districts in urban communities or those dominated by YOC. Significant numbers of LGBT youth face rejection and abuse from their parents and relatives, and some 26% of youth are forced to leave home due to conflicts over sexual orientation. Small studies note that this statistic may be higher for YOC, given the stringent cultural expectations and beliefs of families of color. Fundamentalist teachings and understandings of religious doctrine in mainstream society further alienate LGBT youth by contributing to their social stigmatization and low self-esteem. The majority of African Americans strongly identify as Christian, and the majority of Latinos and Filipinos identify as devout Catholic, and both communities have historically leaned more toward fundamentalist interpretations of biblical teachings that traditionally condemn same-sex behavior. Few of the youths' socializing agents are contributing to positive physical or emotional health outcomes for LGBT YOC.

Research suggests that homophobia and heterosexism greatly contribute to higher rates of suicide, suicidal thoughts, violent victimization, truancy, sexual risk-taking behavior and substance abuse among LGBT youth, as compared to their heterosexual peers. Compared to other adolescents, self-reporting LGBT youth are twice as likely to use alcohol, three times more likely to use marijuana and eight times more likely to use cocaine/crack. Among YOC, African-American and Latino/a in particular, and among Asian Pacific Islander (API) and Native American youth residing in resource-deprived communities, the risk of becoming a victim of violence, engaging in sexual risk-taking, substance abusing or criminal behaviors is even greater.

Racial, Ethnic and Cultural Concerns Facing LGBT YOC

LGBT YOC who come out in their racial or ethnic communities risk separation from their cultural communities and the loss of support for their racial and ethnic identities. The individualism often espoused by the framers of a Westernized gay identity, which often is a consequence of that identity, is often considered by communities of color to be antithetical to the interdependent communal and family relationships traditionally promoted by those communities. Through these interdependent family and communal structures, cultural expectations and determinants of cultural "authenticity" are defined and reinforced. Cultural expectation of and adherence to strict gender roles are also developed within the contexts of this communal framework. Such expectations may include machismo and sexual prowess in Latino, African-American and Filipino males. In some Latino and API communities, these cultural markers often allow same-sex behavior by men as long as these men discreetly engage in these behaviors, adhere to strict gender roles, and meet their family's expectations of marriage and reproduction.

Affirmed expressions of gender variance and open sexual liberation often found in the politicized gay, lesbian and transgendered identities in the US are viewed by many communities of color as a threat to the patriarchal family structure and the interdependent nature of their communities. This view holds particularly true for newly immigrated people of color and others who exhibit low levels of acculturation and place a premium on males and masculine behavior. Religious beliefs, like Islam, that condemn homosexuality and further determine the cultural norms and mores of communities of color reinforce resistance to acknowledging and affirming LGBT identities.

Despite evidence to the contrary, members of communities of color often see LGBT identities as "white identities" and declarations of an LGBT identity as a rejection of communities of color values and traditions. Communities of color are in denial about ethnographic studies that document known and occasionally celebrated instances of homosexuality and transgendered behavior in their pre-colonization histories. For example, men in some pre-colonial African tribes engaged in homosexual acts as a norm during an adolescent male's rites of passage into adulthood, and some Native American and Filipino cultures believed in a "third sex," those whose behavior seemed to embody both the masculine and the feminine, and placed those who exhibited this gender variance in a high place of esteem. Rather than accept a range of human sexuality and gender expression within their communities' culture and histories, communities of color often ostracize LGBT YOC who disclose their orientation, refuse to adhere to a cultural code of silence on sexuality, and/or are unable to comfortably fit the gender roles. Since these communities often are the only affirming constructs of a youth's cultural, racial and/or religious identity, LGBT YOC often lack cultural support.

Public Health Concerns for LGBT YOC

Race and ethnicity in the US are risk markers that correlate with other fundamental determinants of health status, such as poverty, limited or no access to care, and fewer attempts to obtain medical treatment. HIV and other sexually transmitted disease (STDs) disproportionately affect disenfranchised youth, particularly youth in social networks in which high-risk sexual behavior is common and either access to care or health-seeking behavior is compromised. The social norm of sexual risk-taking behaviors and substance abuse among LGBT youth populations and the health disparities between communities of color and white populations almost ensure that the health risks for LGBT YOC are higher than for their white peers. Some evidence of this phenomenon already exists, particularly in the HIV rates of young gay and bisexual men of color. African-American and Latino men in recent years have constituted the majority of AIDS cases among men who have sex with men (MSM), with the majority of these reporting infection before age 25. One sample of young, urban MSM aged 15 to 22 found that 7% were HIV-infected, with the highest rates among African-American and Latino youth.

Young African-American and Latino gay men are not alone in their sexual risk-taking behaviors. Scientific evidence supports the theory that young lesbian and bisexual women are at high risk for STDs, such as Hepatitis V Virus and Human Papillo-mavirus, and unintended pregnancy. A University of Minnesota study on adolescent women found that lesbian and bisexual women reported a 12.3% rate of unintended pregnancy, compared to the 5.3% rate of their heterosexual counterparts. Young lesbian and bisexual women are also at high risk for HIV, since many young lesbian, bisexual and questioning women engage in high-risk sexual activities with multiple partners in an effort to deny their same-sex feelings. Some research demonstrates that a portion of young lesbians engage in unprotected sexual activities with young gay men.

Sexual abuse also increases young lesbian and bisexual women's potential for physical and mental health disorders. The Minnesota study found that 22.1% of the lesbian and bisexual young women studied reported that they had been sexually abused. Many young lesbians believe that their lesbian identity lowers their risk for HIV, STD and unintended pregnancy, despite growing evidence to the contrary. Among African-American and Latina women, rates of STD infection and unintended pregnancy over the last 20 years have been disproportionately high. For African-American and Latina lesbians or bisexual young women, rates of STD and unintended pregnancy may be even higher than for their heterosexual counterparts. Since risk for any population is heightened by a lack of accurate and culturally relevant health promotion and prevention information, and since communities of color and young lesbian and bisexual women are among the least targeted with culturally appropriate or gender-specific STD prevention materials, one can speculate that the STD and pregnancy risk for lesbian and bisexual young women of color, including API and Native American women, may be disturbingly higher than their heterosexual and white lesbian and bisexual peers.

To address the alarming trends in health disparities in low-income communities of color and in some adult LGBT communities, the US Department of Health and Human Services (DHHS) has incorporated cultural competency guidelines in its recommended protocols to state and local health departments and community-based health agencies serving diverse populations. DHHS intended their recommended cultural competency or relevancy policies and practices to reduce the pervasive reluctance of those in marginalized communities to seek health services; to increase the effectiveness of outreach programs in efforts to reach vulnerable populations; and to prevent overt instances of staff-initiated or organizationally-sponsored racism, sexism, classism and homophobia in any government-funded health settings.

Still, such protocols rarely speak to the challenges youth experience in seeking health services and are notably silent around the unique challenges LGBT youth experience in their attempts to access health services in their communities. For insular Native American and Asian Pacific Islander communities, lack of confidentiality and anonymity prevent LGBT API and Native American youth from seeking service options like HIV testing, HIV or STD treatment, sexuality education and disease prevention from agencies familiar with their racial and ethnic health concerns. LGBT YOC brave enough to attempt to access health services from gay-identified community based organizations (CBOs) generally find that such services are tailored to adults and may experience instances of racial discrimination or prejudice from these organizations' usually predominately white, gay staff. Most CBOs tailored to serve communities of color generally assume that the youth who access services are heterosexual and may exhibit ignorance about or hostility toward the health concerns of LGBT youth. In one instance reported to National Youth Advocacy Coalition, a CBO staff member informed an African-American young gay male who had tried to schedule an appointment to receive the Hepatitis B vaccine that he didn't need to worry about getting the vaccine since he wasn't at risk. This youth was denied services despite evidence that the sexual practices of many gay and bisexual men put that youth at increased risk for contracting Hepatitis B.

LGBT Youth in the Juvenile Justice and Child Welfare Systems

LGBT youth represent 40% of the homeless youth population. In urban centers known as gay meccas, LGBT youth may comprise more than half of the homeless youth population. As a population that is more likely to experience homelessness, LGBT are over-represented in populations that are more likely to be involved in the juvenile justice and child welfare systems. There are a multitude of reasons for the disproportionate number of LGBT youth in these systems. For instance, homelessness often requires youth to engage in criminal activity such as prostitution and theft in order to survive. Consequently, homeless youth are at a greater risk of arrest and involvement in the system.

According to a 2001 report on LGBT youth and the juvenile justice system released by the Lesbian and Gay Youth project of the Urban Justice Center, an estimated 4-10% of the juvenile delinquency population identify as LGBT. The report further states that LGBT feelings of isolation and fear often facilitate the use and abuse of illegal substances as a form of escape. Researchers estimate that some 60% of gay and bisexual young men are substance abusers. According to a 1999 Massachusetts State Youth Risk Behavior Survey, LGBT high school students are more than twice as likely to report having been in a fight at school, three times more likely to carry a weapon to school and six times more likely to skip school than heterosexual students. All of the above behaviors reported by LGBT youth are defined as either crimes or delinquency, thus increasing potential for LGBT youth to enter the juvenile justice system.

When LGBT youth attempt to seek support from their families, many become further victimized by familial rejection and violence. Parental assault or neglect of a young person occasionally prompts child services to place the abused LGBT youth in foster care or a group home. Attorneys have handled cases in which parents, in an effort to rid themselves of their LGBT youth, have filed a Persons In Need of Supervision (PINS) petition, asking the state to step in and assume some responsibility for the youth. Sometimes rebellious behavior by LGBT youth inspired by the youth's fear, isolation, violent victimization, truancy and substance abuse play a role in a parent's desire to file and be granted PINS petitions, especially since truancy and drug use constitute legal grounds. But often parents use symptoms of LGBT youth rebellion as a way of hiding their own disapproval and hostility toward their LGBT youth. One study that found 45% of parents were angry, sick and disgusted when first learning about their child's homosexuality. Given that 26% of parents remove their LGBT children from the home immediately or soon after disclosure, it is not improbable that other homophobic parents may seek more seemingly humane measures through the juvenile courts.

Judges in juvenile court have little education or training about the life experiences of LGBT youth placed in their care. In an attempt to safeguard LGBT youth, judges often place LGBT youth in more restrictive settings than their heterosexual peers, or isolate them in protective custody. There are few sentencing options available to judges who are sensitive to the experiences and challenges that brought LGBT youth into the juvenile justice setting. There are no federal or state-level juvenile justice and delinquency prevention agencies handling secure facilities specifically geared to LGBT juvenile offenders. For LGBT youth whose crimes warrant sentencing to a non-secure facility, there are only three or four LGBT youth-specific facilities nationwide that meet the standards of a non-secure facility. These LGBT youth-specific, non-secure facilities generally have a waiting list of two or three years and are primarily populated by LGBT YOC.

Foster Care, Group Homes and LGBT YOC

LGBT youth who are removed from abusive or neglectful home environments are placed in foster care and group homes for their care and well-being. As in juvenile detention facilities, foster care and group homes are disproportionately populated by African-American and Latino/a youth. Forty-three percent of all youth in foster care are African-American and 15% are Latino. Consequently, there is a high probability that those LGBT youth in foster care are largely represented by LGBT YOC. In 1994, a joint task force of New York City's Child Welfare Administration and the Council of Family and Child Caring Agencies published a report finding that "lesbian and gay adolescents have often been misunderstood, neglected and in some instances discriminated against by the child welfare system." In 2001, Lambda Legal Defense and Education Fund issued a report assessing 14 states on the challenges confronting LGBT youth in foster care. The report found that LGBT youth in foster care who are assumed to be LGBT, self-disclose their orientation or express non-conformist gender behavior are subject to disapproval by caseworkers, rejection by foster families, harassment and violence by foster care peers, and prejudice and neglect by group home staff. The report further found that LGBT youth who remain closeted in foster care suffer isolation, shame and a sense of peril from being privy to the homophobic slights directed at openly gay individuals. As is the case in juvenile detention placements, foster care staff generally punish or expel LGBT youth who are harassed or hurt by peers, rather than punishing or expelling the perpetrators. Child welfare agencies that acknowledge the existence of LGBT youth generally identify LGBT youth as their hard-to-place children, unwanted by sectarian and other placement agencies that disapprove of homosexuality, and subject to multiple and unstable placements because of negative reactions to their sexual orientation. Child welfare employees who are sensitive to LGBT youth find that they have little organizational or peer support, and that protocols for cultural competency and resources for referral are non-existent or difficult to access.

Conclusion

Despite LGBT YOC's membership in groups with an increased probability of risk for developing chronic and costly conditions, the current public health system is largely hostile to or uniformed about their needs. Without significant system-wide reform and a healthy dose of tolerance, LGBT YOC will continue to exhibit high rates of preventable disease and poor health outcomes.

Similarly, the range of child protective services frequently fail LGBT youth and LGBT YOC, with their propensity to engage in implicit denial of the challenges LGBT youth experience in foster care and group home settings and these services' explicit refusal to acknowledge the existence of these populations in their care. The cultural and social support structures for youth to meet their developmental needs are too often denied to LGBT YOC, and the few resources available to LGBT YOC too often demand that these young people compartmentalize and prioritize their multiple identities and oppressions. Society sets up LGBT YOC for failure through institutional, economic and cultural oppression rooted in heterosexism, homophobia and transphobia. This societal and institutional failure is compounded by the additional challenges LGBT YOC confront in being a racial or ethnic minority.

To improve the health and developmental outcomes for LGBT YOC, more research is needed to determine the needs and address the health status of this population; there need to be more gay-straight alliances and safe school coalitions working in schools and districts with a high concentration of racial and ethnic minorities; cultural competency education is needed for LGBT CBO's working with LGBT YOC; targeted sexuality education and tolerance initiatives that address the homophobia and heterosexism culturally rooted in minority communities need to be developed and implemented; LGBT youth sensitivity protocols for professionals working in the child welfare and juvenile justice systems must be created; and societal tolerance must be increased.

Until society is able to scrutinize the values, systems and practices that create the oppressive conditions and poor life outcomes experienced by those whose lives and being defy simplistic categorization, LGBT YOC will continue to be the most underserved and vulnerable population of any youth population in the United States.

Quiz Answers

Answers to Race Literacy Quiz

1. **A. None.** There is no characteristic, no trait, not even one gene that distinguishes all members of one so-called race from all members of another race.

2. **C. Language.** The word barbarian comes from the Greek word "*bar-bar,*" meaning "stutterer, or unintelligible, or one who does not speak Greek." The Greeks, like most ancient peoples, did not attribute much meaning to physical appearance, nor did they sort people into races. In ancient Greece, language and culture were the differences that mattered (along with property and gender) because they indicated who was not Greek. Some historians believe the first to be labeled barbarian were the Scythians of circa 500 B.C., who lived northeast of the Black Sea and were very fair-skinned. Ideas of "race" did not exist during antiquity.

3. **E. None of the above.** The A, B and O blood groups can be found in all the world's peoples (the percentage of Estonians and Papua New Guineans with A, B and O blood are almost exactly identical). Skin color tends to correlate with the earth's geographic latitude, not race; sub-Saharan Africans, the Dravidians and Tamils of southern Asia, and Melanesians from the Pacific all have very dark skin. Ancestry is difficult to trace; we all have two parents, four grandparents, etc. If you could trace your family back 30 generations, slightly more than 1,000 years, you'd find one billion ancestors.

4. **D. Geographic latitude.** Skin color tends to correspond with ultra-violet radiation from the sun, hence latitude. People with ancestors from the tropics typically have darker skin, while those from the higher latitudes have lighter

skin. Sub-Saharan Africans, Asian Indians, Aboriginal Australians and Melanesians all have dark skin. But skin color really is only skin deep. Most traits are inherited independently from one another. The genes influencing skin color have nothing to do with those influencing hair form, eye shape and blood type, let alone complex traits such as intelligence, musical ability or athletic ability. Genetic diseases are inherited through families, not race. Sickle cell, for example, confers resistance to malaria. It occurs in people whose ancestors came from where malaria was once common: the Mediterranean, Arabia, Turkey, southern Asia, and western and central Africa—but not southern Africa. The presence of sickle cell is not an indicator of race but of having an ancestor from a malarial region.

5. **D. Fruit flies.** Fruit flies have been around for a very long time, plus they have a short life span, so lots of genetic mutations have accumulated over many generations. In contrast, modern humans are one of the most genetically similar of all species. On average, only one of every 1,000 nucleotides (the "letters" that make up our DNA) differ from one individual to another. This is because we are a relatively young species (approximately 150,000-200,000 years old). We simply haven't been around long enough to accumulate much genetic variation. Also, humans have always moved, mixed and mated, further homogenizing our gene pool. Beneath the skin, we're all very similar.

6. **E. Saudi Arabians and Ethiopians.** Populations that live near each other geographically tend to be genetically more alike than populations that live far apart. That's because they are more likely to have intermixed in the recent past and therefore share more genes. So even though Senegalese and Kenyans or Italians and Swedes are traditionally placed in the same "races," they live farther apart from each other and have had less contact and intermixing than Saudis and Ethiopians.

7. **A. Within any local population.** Eighty-five percent, or almost all, human variation, can be found within any single local population, whether it is Malay, Irish, Zulu or Korean. There is *far* more variation within groups than between groups. This means that there may be as many—or more—genetic differences between two random Koreans as between a random Korean and a Zulu. On average, approximately 94% of all genetic variation can be found within any continental area.

8. **C. Africa.** We are all Africans. Modern humans *(Homo sapiens sapiens)* originated in Africa, and we spent most of our evolution as a species together there. Some modern humans first left Africa 50,000-70,000 years ago and spread out around the world. All the other populations of the world can be seen as a subset of Africans. Every human genetic trait found elsewhere can also be found

in Africa, with the exception of relatively few recent variations favored by the environment, genetic drift or sexual selection—such as light skin.

9. **D. They were deemed innately inferior.** Throughout much of history, societies have enslaved people, often as a result of conquest, war or even debt. But people were not enslaved because they were first deemed inferior. African slaves were well suited to labor in North America. Unlike the Indians, they were resistant to European diseases; they couldn't easily run away; they were not Christians (and hence unprotected by English law); and they were skilled semi-tropical farmers. Finally, in the late 17th Century, African slaves became available in large numbers just as the original labor force on Virginia's tobacco plantations—English indentured servants—began to rebel and immigration from England slowed. Over time, the degradation of slavery became identified with blackness, giving white Americans the idea that Africans were a fundamentally different kind of people.

Answers to Reverse Discrimination Quiz

1. **A.** Several large-scale studies have included this type of question and show that the perceived victimization rate among Whites is very low. The percentage of Whites who say they have experienced employment discrimination because of their race ranges from a low of 2% to a high of 13%. When the same question is asked of different racial groups, the percent of Blacks, Hispanics and Asians who say they were discriminated against on the job is higher than the percentage of Whites. In spite of the fact that few individual Whites allege being discriminated against, between two-thirds and three-fourths of Whites *believe* that Whites, as a group, are hurt by affirmative action.

2. **B.** There are about 10 times more Black complaints than White complaints. There are more complaints by men alleging sex discrimination than by Whites alleging race discrimination. The EEOC data are consistent with the view that traditional discrimination against Blacks, Hispanics, Asians, Native Americans and women is still the major problem.

3. **C.** The most common complaint involves allegations of being unfairly fired. This is followed, in descending order of frequency, by terms of employment, harassment and intimidation, sexual harassment and denial of promotion. Discrimination in hiring does not make the top 5. These data are inconsistent with the popularly held view that White men can't get jobs because of affirmative action.

4.   **D.**   Only 38% of the decisions involved allegations of illegal affirmative action policies. The rest involved allegations of arbitrary and capricious treatment by minority or female supervisors or co-workers. Most plaintiffs do not win. Only 10% of the cases resulted in clear victories for the plaintiff; another 21% resulted in a procedural victory that was remanded to the lower court for further legal action.

5.   **A.**   Forty-four percent of the plaintiffs were professionals or managers, and another 27% were police officers or firefighters.

6.   **A.**   State and local governments accounted for 52% of the plaintiffs, followed by for-profit corporations (27%) and the federal government (17%).

7.   **C.**   Having a quota where White men can't compete at all is generally illegal, since it "trammels" on the interests of the majority group. Only rarely can employers voluntarily adopt quotas. Certain government contractors have to make "good faith" efforts to achieve goals. Quotas generally result in stronger legal sanctions for non-compliance.

8.   **A.**   Unemployment rate differences between men and women are usually small, with women college graduates slightly more likely than men to be unemployed in 2001. When controlling for education, the unemployment rates of Blacks and Hispanics are generally higher than for Whites (Bureau of Labor Statistics, www.bls.gov/cps).

9.   **A.**   After controlling for education, White men make more than everyone else. White women make more than Black and Hispanic women, while Black and Hispanic men make more than White women (Bureau of Labor Statistics and Bureau of the Census, http://www.census.gov.)

10.   **C.**   Even with special set-aside programs for women and minorities, White men are significantly over-represented among federal contractors (Office of Advocacy, www.sba.gov).

Answers to Poverty Quiz

1.   **False.** According to the US Census Bureau, the number of poor people increased by 1.3 million from 2002 to 2003, from 34.6 million to 35.9 million. One out of every eight Americans is living in poverty.

2.   **False.** Most Americans living in poverty are too young, too old or physically incapable of working due to illness or disability. In fact, nearly two-thirds of all Americans living in poverty have to depend on someone else in the household to bring in money to live.

3.   **True.** The number of Asian Americans living in poverty rose the greatest among all groups, to 11.8% and 1.4 million people in 2003, an increase from 10.1% in 2002. For Hispanics, the poverty rate was 22.5 % in 2003, unchanged from 2001. For African Americans, the rate rose only slightly, to 24.4%, up from 24.1%. Still, nearly one out of four African Americans is living in poverty.

4.   **False.** The federal government puts the (2004) poverty threshold at $18,810 for a family of four. However, a 2000 poll revealed that a majority of Americans believe it takes at least $35,000 annually to provide adequately for a family of four.

5.   **True.** The working poor in America grew poorer during 2003, with incomes dipping farther below the poverty line than in any other year since 1975, the first year for which such data are available. The average amount by which people living in poverty fell below the federal "threshold" ($18,810 for a family of four) was $3,018 in 2003.

6.   **False.** In 2003, the number of people living in extreme poverty—that is, with incomes below half the poverty line—rose by 1.2 million, to 15.3 million. The number of Americans living in extreme poverty reached the highest level on record since data first became available in 1975.

7.   **True.** In fact, the US child poverty rate is two to three times higher than in other major industrialized nations. According to the latest comparative numbers, the child poverty rate in Sweden in recent years has been less than 4%; in the Czech Republic, less than 6%; in France, 7%; in Germany, 10%, in Australia and Japan, 12%; in Canada, 14%; while in the United States, the child poverty rate has remained over 16% for the past two years—with some sources estimating that more than 23% of all children in America live in poverty.

8.   **True.** But for a mother who works full time at minimum wage to support one small child, that translates to earnings of $10,712 a year—which is $1,303 below the 2003 poverty threshold for a family of two.

9.   **False.** The poverty rate for America's elderly population, people over 65, stands at one out of every ten seniors, while the child poverty rate is one out of every six children.

10. **False.** Nine out of ten Americans believe the federal government has a responsibility to alleviate poverty. A strong majority believes that government should do more, not less, to help people move from welfare to work by providing skills needed to be self-sufficient.

Answers to Housing Quiz

1. **E. 98%.** Beginning in the 1930s and 1940s, the federal government created programs that subsidized low-cost home loans, opening up homeownership to millions of Americans for the first time. At the same time, government underwriters introduced a national appraisal system that tied property value and loan eligibility to race, effectively locking nonwhites out of the housing market just as most middle-class white Americans were beginning to get in.

2. **D. Affirmative action quotas.** Federal affirmative action guidelines specifically prohibit quotas. Beginning in the 1930s, the Federal Housing Administration and related programs made it possible for millions of average white Americans to own a home for the first time, sparking the post-World War II suburban building boom. The government established a national neighborhood appraisal system, explicitly tying mortgage eligibility to race, a policy known today as "redlining." European "ethnics" blended together in all-white suburbs while people of color, denied home loans, were left behind in central cities. Another federal program, urban renewal, was supposed to make cities more livable, but 90% of all housing destroyed by urban renewal was not replaced. Two-thirds of these displaced were black or Latino. Government policies and practices helped create two legacies that are still with us today: segregated communities and a substantial wealth gap between whites and nonwhites, much of which can be traced to the differential value of their homes.

3. **B. Ten times as much.** Probably no one statistic better captures the cumulative disadvantage of past discrimination than wealth. Even at the same income levels, whites still have, on average, twice as much wealth as nonwhites. In fact, the wealth gap between blacks and whites has grown since the Civil Rights Era. Much of this disparity is due to different rates of homeownership and the comparative values of homes in white and black neighborhoods. But wealth is not only the end point, it's the starting line for the next generation—helping finance one's children's education, helping them through hard times, or helping with the downpayment of their own home. Economists estimate 50-80% of one's lifetime wealth accumulation can be traced to this head start. As wealth gets passed down from generation to generation, the legacy of past discrimination grows, giving whites and nonwhites vastly different life chances.

4.   **D. White net worth is more than two times greater.** See answer to Question #3 for explanation.

5.   **C. Less than 1%.** According to the 2000 Census, whites are more likely to be segregated than any other group. This is largely a result of past housing discrimination, but it is perpetuated today by unfair practices such as predatory lending, racial steering and a substantial wealth gap between black and white families. Today, 74% of whites own their own home, compared to 47% of African Americans. Black and Latino mortgage applicants are 60% more likely than whites to be turned down for loans, even after controlling for employment, financial and neighborhood characteristics. On average, nonwhites who are approved for mortgages still pay higher rates.

6.   **A. 1964 Civil Rights Act.** The Civil Rights Act made racial discrimination in public places illegal. The other programs are all examples of racial preferences—for white people. Over a 40-year period, the Homestead Act gave away, for free, 270 million acres of what had been Indian Territory, almost all of it to white people. The Naturalization Act allowed only "free white persons" to adopt citizenship, thus opening our doors to European immigrants, but barring Asians and other groups. Racial barriers to citizenship were not removed until 1952. The Federal Housing Administration made it possible for millions of average white Americans—but not others—to own a home for the first time (see Answer #2 above). And the original Social Security Act specifically exempted two occupations from coverage: farmworkers and domestics, both largely nonwhite.

Answers to Health Quiz I

1.   **True.** But rates of death from diseases of the heart were 29% higher among African-American adults than among white adults, and death rates from stroke were 40% higher.

2.   **False.** For the first time in 40 years, the infant mortality rate in the US has increased, with 7 out of every 1,000 children born in America dying within their first year of life, according to the annual report, "America's Health: State Health Rankings (2004)," published by the United Health Foundation, American Public Health Association and Partnership for Prevention.

3.   **C. 28th.** The US infant mortality rate is about double the rate found in Hong Kong and Japan, according to "America's Health: State Health Rankings (2004)" (see citation above).

4. **B. 68.2 years,** according to the APHA Fact Sheets on Racial/Ethnic Disparities.

5. **D. 25.4 %.** According to the CDC, Office of Communication, Fact Sheet, in 2001, the age-adjusted death rate for cancer was 243.1 per 100,000 population for African Americans, 193.9 for whites.

6. **D. Five times,** according to the National Center for Chronic Disease Prevention and Health Promotion.

7. **False.** Research has shown that doctors rated African American patients as less intelligent, less educated, more likely to abuse drugs and alcohol, and more likely to fail to comply with medical advice. ("Closing the Gap 2003: Racial and Ethnic Disparities in Health Care," Alliance for Health Reform, October 2004, www.allhealth.org)

8. **A. 7 times higher.** (www.healthypeople.gov)

9. **D. 13 times higher.** In 1999, the age-adjusted death rate for HIV was 32.7 per 100,000 Puerto Ricans living on the mainland US, higher than any other racial or ethnic group; the national average was 5.4 per 100,000 and 2.4 per 100,000 for non-Hispanic whites.

10. **True.** While African Americans, Hispanic Americans and American Indians represent more than 25% of the US population, less than 9% of nurses, 6% of physicians and 5% of dentists are from these populations. ("Missing Persons: Minorities in the Health Professions, A Report for the Sullivan Commission on Diversity in the Healthcare Workforce," The Sullivan Commission, 2004)

11. **D. 32.4%.** ("Closing the Gap 2003: Racial and Ethnic Disparities in Health Care," Alliance for Health Reform, October 2004, www.allhealth.org).

12. **A. American Indians/Alaska Natives.** According to CDC, the SIDS rate among this minority is more than double that of whites in 1999.

13. **False.** ("Closing the Gap 2003: Racial and Ethnic Disparities in Health Care," Alliance for Health Reform, October 2004, www.allhealth.org)

14. **B. Asian Americans/Pacific Islanders.** This group had a rate of 33 per 100,000 in 2001, compared to 14 per 100,000 for non-Hispanic blacks, 12 per 100,000 for Hispanic/Latinos, 11 per 100,000 for American Indians/Alaska Natives, and 2 per 100,000 for non-Hispanic whites. (CDC, Office of Communication, Fact Sheet, April 2004)

15. **A. Less than one cent,** according to Research!America. (www.research america.org/publications/ra-prevention.pdf)

Answers to Health Quiz II

1. **C. South:** This reflects the generally lower levels of residential and geographic segregation and the historical pattern of centrally clustering health facilities, as opposed to the Northeast and Midwest pattern of dispersion of hospitals into ethnically more homogenous neighborhoods and suburban communities. (See Smith, *Healthcare Divided*, University of Michigan Press)

2. **C. 28%:** 64 % of the white population under 65 is covered by private health insurance but only 36% of the African-American population. (National Center for Health Statistics, *Health, United States 2004*.)

3. **C. 21%:** Only 16% of Hispanics but 37% of non-Hispanic whites receive private health insurance through employment. (National Center for Health Statistics, *Health, United States 2004*.)

4. **B. 11%:** About 21.5% of African Americans under 65 are covered under the Medicaid program while only 9.5% of whites are. (National Center for Health Statistics, *Health, United States 2004)*

5. **D. Widened:** In 1980, the rate for black patients under age 65 was 72% higher than the rate for white patients; in 1998, the black rate was 131% higher. (L.J. Kozak et al. "Trends in avoidable hospitalizations, 1980-1998," *Health Affairs* March-April: 20[2] 2001).

6. **C. 60% as often.** (K.A. Schulman et al. "The effect of race and sex on physicians' recommendations for cardiac catheterization." *New England Journal of Medicine* 340[8] 1999).

7. **D. Somewhat higher**. (Agency for Healthcare Research and Quality, *2004 National Healthcare Disparities Report*.) Significant strides have been made in closing the gap in preventive and screening services.

8. **D. About 30% higher:** Age-adjusted death rate for blacks in the United States in 2002 was 1,083 per 100,000 population and 829 for whites. (National Center for Health Statistics, *Health, United States 2004*.)

Answers to Democracy Quiz

1. **20%**

2. **75%**

3. **75%**

4. **John Jay**, First President of the Continental Congress and First Chief Justice of the Supreme Court.

5. **African Americans:** ½ of 1%; corporations: more than 50%.

6. **1886.**

7. **By becoming US Supreme Court Justices.**

8. **Sweden, Germany, Italy, Japan, Ireland and more.**

Contributors

Dolores Acevedo-Garcia (dacevedo@hsph.harvard.edu) is an Assistant Professor in the Department of Society, Human Development and Health, at the Harvard School of Public Health.

Nikitra Bailey (nikitra.bailey@self-help.org) is the Vice-President of External Affairs at the Center Responsible for Lending. At the Center, she coordinates outreach and educational efforts to national and locally based organizations, and provides technical assistance to policymakers. Prior to joining the staff at the Center, she interned at the NAACP Legal Defense and Educational Fund.

Gary Bass (bassg@ombwatch.org) is the founder and Executive Director of OMB Watch (http://www.ombwatch.org), a nonprofit research and advocacy organization that promotes increased citizen participation in public policy and greater government accountability. Under his direction, OMB Watch leads the Americans for a Fair Estate Tax Coalition.

Calvin L. Beale (cbeale@ers.usda.gov) is Senior Demographer in the Economic Research Service of the US Department of Agriculture. His research has focused on trends and conditions in rural and small town populations. Prior to joining the Department in 1953, he was on the staff of the Bureau of the Census.

Jared Bernstein (jbernstein@epinet.org), a Senior Economist at the Economic Policy Institute, is co-author of *The State of Working America* (Economic Policy Institute). In 1995-96, he was deputy chief economist at the US Dept. of Labor.

Martin J. Blank (BlankM@iel.org) is the Director for Schools, Family and School Connections at the Institute for Educational Leadership. He also serves as the Staff Director for the Coalition for Community Schools.

407

Robert Brand (r.brand@solutoinsforprogress.com) is President of Solutions for Progress in Philadelphia, which is committed to using technology, data analysis and policy development tools to help clients bring about a society that values equality, broad civic participation and a recognition of human interdependence. He is former Deputy Commissioner of Health for Philadelphia and was on the staff of SEIU and the National Union of Hospital and Healthcare Employees.

Xavier de Souza Briggs (xbriggs@mit.edu), a member of PRRAC's Social Science Advisory Board, is Associate Professor of Sociology and Urban Planning at the Massachusetts Institute of Technology. He was Acting Assistant Secretary for Policy Development and Research at HUD, 1998-99, and has been a community planner in the South Bronx and other inner-city communities.

Mike Calhoun (mike@self-help.org) is General Counsel for Self-Help and the Center for Responsible Lending; he was a lead drafter of North Carolina's landmark predatory lending law.

California Newsreel is the nation's leading resource for films and videos on race, diversity, African-American life and history, and Africa. Since 1968, it has specialized in bringing cutting-edge social interest documentaries and films to universities, high schools, public libraries and community-based groups. For more information, visit www.newsreel.org.

Sheryll Cashin (cashins@law.georgetown.edu) is Professor of Law at Georgetown Univ. She clerked for Supreme Court Justice Thurgood Marshall and DC Circuit Court of Appeals Judge Abner Mikva, and worked as an advisor on urban and economic policy in the Clinton White House.

Catholic Campaign for Human Development (cchdpromo@usccb.org) is the Catholic Church's domestic anti-poverty program. It raises funds to support organized groups of white and minority poor to develop economic strength and political power. Its second purpose is to "educate People of God to a new knowledge of today's problems...that can lead to some new approaches that promote a greater sense of solidarity."

Alexandra Cawthorne (acawthorne@hungercenter.org) was a Bill Emerson Congressional Hunger Fellow with PRRAC in 2004. She is currently on the staff of Citizens' Commission on Civil Rights.

Catherine Paskoff Chang (cpaskoff@alumni.princeton.edu) worked as a budget policy analyst at OMB Watch from November 2000 until May 2003. She is now completing her law degree at Columbia Univ. School of Law.

Jeff Chapman (jchapman@epinet.org) is an economic analyst at the Economic Policy Institute, providing technical assistance to living-wage campaigns and other economic justice organizations.

Linda Christensen (lchrist@aol.com) is language arts coordinator for the Portland (OR) public school system and director of the Portland Writing Project. She was a co-editor of *Rethinking School Reform: Views from the Classroom* (Rethinking Schools).

Richard Daynard (r.daynard@neu.edu) serves on the faculty at Northeastern Univ. School of Law. He is a principal in the Public Health Advocacy Institute (www.phaionline.org).

DC Vote (www.dcvote.org) is a nonprofit educational and advocacy organization whose mission is to secure full voting representation in Congress for the residents of the District of Columbia. It focuses on community and student outreach, actions with coalition partners and pro-democracy groups, and media work. Present and former DC Vote staffers Zainab Akbar, Kevin Kiger, John See and Amy Whitcomb Slemmer provided the material, published in series of *Poverty & Race* articles, from which this consolidated report was drawn.

Eric Foner (Efl7@columbia.edu) is DeWitt Clinton Professor of History at Columbia Univ. During the 1990s, he served as president of both the Organization of American Historians and the American Historical Association. His publications have concentrated on the intersections of intellectual, political and social history, and the history of American race relations.

David M.P. Freund (davidf@princeton.edu) teaches in the Department of History at Rutgers Univ., Newark. His publications include *Colored Property: State Policy and White Racial Politics in the Modern American Suburb* (Univ. of Chicago Press, forthcoming) and "Marketing the Free Market: State Intervention and the Politics of Prosperity in Metropolitan America," in Kevin Kruse and Thomas Sugrue, eds., *The New Suburban History* (Univ. of Chicago Press).

George Galster (aa3571@wayne.edu) is the Clarence Hilberry Professor of Urban Affairs at Wayne State Univ. He is the author of over 100 scholarly articles, mostly related to race, poverty and inequality in urban America. His latest book (co-authored) is *Why NOT In My Back Yard? Neighborhood Impacts of Assisted Housing* (Rutgers Ctr. for Urban Policy Research).

H. Jack Geiger (jgeiger@igc.org) is Arthur C. Logan Professor Emeritus of Community Medicine at the City Univ. of New York Medical School and a past president of Physicians for Human Rights. He is the author of major studies of racial disparities in care for the Institute of Medicine, National Academy of Sciences, and for Physicians for Human Rights.

L. Michael Gipson (lmgconsultinginc@earthlink.net) is founder and principal of the organizational consulting firm, LMG Consulting, Inc. He has worked for numerous national advocacy organizations, including the Human Rights Campaign, Advocates For Youth, and the National Youth Advocacy Coalition. He is co-founder and Associate Director of the Beyond Identities Community Center, an Ohio-based comprehensive social service agency primarily serving sexual minority youth of color.

Heidi Goldsmith (heidi@residentialeducation.org) is founder and Executive Director of CORE: the Coalition for Residential Education, the Washington, DC-based nonprofit organization promoting boarding schools and children's homes for economically and socially disadvantaged children and youth. She has been a community organizer and manager of social and educational services for disadvantaged populations for 25 years, including six in Israel and Europe.

Ira Harkavy (harkavy@pobox.upenn.edu) is an Associate Vice-President of the Univ. of Pennsylvania and the director of its Center for Community Partnerships. He also serves as Chair of the Coalition for Community Schools.

Andrew Hartman (ae.hartman@verizon.net) is a Ph.D. candidate in history at George Washington Univ., working on a dissertation titled "Education as Cold War Experience: The Battle for the American School, 1945-1960."

Chester Hartman (chartman2@aol.com) is Director of Research for the Washington, DC-based Poverty & Race Research Action Council, for which he was founding Executive Director from 1990-2003. He is also founder of The Planners Network, a national organization of progressive urban planners. His most recent books are *City for Sale: The Transformation of San Francisco* (Univ. of Calif. Press), *Between Eminence & Notoriety: Four Decades of Radical Urban Planning* (Rutgers Ctr. for Urban Policy Research) and *A Right to Housing: Foundation for New Social Agenda* (Temple Univ. Press).

Health Policy Institute, a project of the Joint Center for Political and Economic Studies, is committed to igniting a 'Fair Health' movement that gives people of color the inalienable right to equal opportunity for healthy lives—including equal access to quality health care as well as freedom from social and environmental disparities that influence poor health outcomes.

Thomas J. Henderson (thenderson@sprengerlang.com), a PRRAC Board member, is a partner at the Washington, DC lawfirm Sprenger & Lang. He is former Chief Counsel/Senior Deputy Director of The Lawyers' Committee for Civil Rights Under Law.

Adam Hughes (ahughes@ombwatch.org) is a budget policy analyst at OMB Watch, where directs their budget and tax program, including coordinating the Americans for a Fair Estate Tax Coalition and working to encourage nonprofit groups around the country to become active in advocacy on the federal budget.

Derrick Z. Jackson (Jackson@globe.com) is a *Boston Globe* columnist. He was a finalist for the Pulitzer Prize in 2001, a two-time winner and three-time finalist in commentary from the Education Writers Association, and a five-time winner and ten-time finalist in political and sports commentary from the National Association of Black Journalists.

Jesse L. Jackson, Jr. has represented Illinois' Congressional District 2 (Chicago's South Side and the city's South suburbs) since 1995. He sits on the House Appropriations Committee and is author (with Frank Watkins) of the 2001 book, *A More Perfect Union: Advancing New American Rights* (Welcome Rain Publishers).

John H. Jackson (jjackson@naacpnet.org) is National Director of Education for the NAACP, Chairman of the National Equity Center, and Adjunct Professor of Race, Gender and Public Policy at the Georgetown Univ. School of Public Policy.

Paul Jargowsky (jargo@utdallas.edu) is Associate Professor of Political Economy at the Univ. of Texas at Dallas, where he directs The Bruton Center, a research center specializing in spatial aspects of social science research. His principal research interests are inequality, the geographic concentration of poverty, and residential segregation by race and class.

James H. Johnson, Jr. (Johnsonj@kenan-flagler.unc.edu) is William Rand Kenan, Jr. Distinguished Professor in the Kenan-Flagler Business School at the Univ. of North Carolina at Chapel Hill.

Sharon Johnston (Sjohnston@flvs.net) is in charge of overseeing curriculum development and validation for Florida Virtual School, where she also teaches AP literature and composition.

Ann Moss Joyner (ann@mcmoss.org) is President of the Grove Institute for Sustainable Communities in Mebane, North Carolina.

Krista Kafer (Krista555@msn.com) is an independent education writer and consultant in Denver, CO. Previously, she was a Senior Policy Analyst for The

Heritage Foundation, a Washington, DC-based think tank. She has written extensively on federal education policy and school choice.

Richard D. Kahlenberg (kahlenberg@tcf.org), a Senior Fellow at The Century Foundation, is author of *All Together Now: Creating Middle-Class Schools through Public School Choice* (Brookings) and *The Remedy: Class, Race, and Affirmative Action* (Basic). He is currently working on a biography of Albert Shanker for Columbia Univ. Press.

Jeffrey Kaplan (JeffKaplan@att.net) is a writer and researcher in Berkeley, California. He works with the San Francisco Bay Area chapter of ReclaimDemocracy.org, a nonprofit organization working to restore citizen authority over corporations.

Stan Karp (stankarp@gmail.com) has taught high school English in Paterson, NJ for more than 25 years. He is co-editor of the Milwaukee-based magazine *Rethinking Schools* (www.rethinkingschools.org), and was a co-editor of *Rethinking School Reform: Views from the Classroom* (Rethinking Schools).

Peter Kellman is President of the Southern Maine Labor Council, AFL-CIO and a member of the American Federation of Teachers. He is the author of *Building Unions: Past, Present and Future* (Apex Press), *Divided We Fall: The Story of the Paperworkers' Union and the Future of Labor* (Apex Press), and is presently working on *Back to the Future—Labor's New Day*.

Michelle Kinley (mkinley@flvs.net) is Minority Recruitment e-Learning Manager for Florida Virtual School.

Andrew T. Lamas (atlamas@sas.upenn.edu) is on the faculty of the Urban Studies Program at the Univ. of Pennsylvania, where he teaches courses on community development and economic democracy. For more than 25 years, he has consulted with employee-owned firms and community development financial institutions in the US and abroad.

Alison Leff (alisonleff@yahoo.com) was a Bill Emerson Congressional Hunger Fellow with PRRAC in 2002. Afterwards, she worked for *The American Prospect* magazine. She is attending the Ross School of Business at the Univ. of Michigan.

Greg LeRoy (goodjobs@goodjobsfirst.org) is Executive Director of Good Jobs First and author of the 2005 book *The Great American Jobs Scam: Corporate Tax Dodging and the Myth of Job Creation* (Berrett-Koehler).

Heather Lewis-Charp (Heather@spra.com) is a Social Scientist at Social Policy Research Associates, in Oakland, CA. Her research interests include multicultural and race studies, youth development and civic participation.

James D. Loewen (jloewen@zoo.uvm.edu) is the author of *Lies My Teacher Told Me: Everything Your American History Textbook Got Wrong* (Simon & Schuster) and *Lies Across America: What Our Historic Sites Get Wrong* (Simon & Schuster), and his just-released book, *Sundown Towns: A Hidden Dimension of American Racism* (New Press)—an important new tool for organizing around housing discrimination issues.

Marc Masurovsky (mmasurovsk@aol.com) is co-founder of the Holocaust Art Restitution Project, and has served as an historian for plaintiffs in class action lawsuits filed against three leading Swiss banks, and against the US government on behalf of Hungarian Jewish survivors for recovery of items lost on the so-called Gold Train.

S.M. Miller (FIVEGOOD@aol.com), a PRRAC Board member, is a Senior Fellow at the Commonwealth Institute in Cambridge, MA, and professor emeritus of sociology at Boston Univ. He is a Senior Advisor to United for a Fair Economy and an advisor to poverty programs in Ireland, the UK and France. His most recent book (with Anthony J. Savoie) is *Respect and Rights: Class, Race and Gender Today* (Rowman and Littlefield).

Gus Newport (gus@iceclt.org) is Executive Director of the Institute for Community Economics in Springfield, MA. He is a former two-term (1979-86) Mayor of Berkeley, CA, and Director of Boston's Dudley Street Neighborhood Initiative. He has served on the faculty of Univ. Calif.-Santa Cruz, Univ. Mass.-Boston, Yale and Portland St. Univ.

Pedro A. Noguera (pan6@nyu.edu) is a professor in the Steinhardt School of Education at New York Univ. and Director of its Center for Research on Urban Schools and Globalization. From 2000-03, he served as the Judith K. Dimon Professor of Communities and Schools at the Harvard Graduate School of Education; from 1990–2000 he was a Professor in Social and Cultural Studies at the Graduate School of Education and the Director of the Institute for the Study of Social Change at the Univ. of Calif.-Berkeley.

Gary Orfield (orfielga@gse.harvard.edu), a member of PRRAC's Social Science Advisory Board, is Professor of Education and Social Policy at Harvard Univ. and Director of The Harvard Civil Rights Project. Among his works are *Dismantling Desegregation* (New Press) and *Deepening Segregation in American Public Schools* (Harvard Project on School Desegregation).

Teresa L. Osypuk (tosypuk@hsph.harvard.edu) is a doctoral student in the Department of Society, Human Development and Health, at the Harvard School of Public Health.

Wendy E. Parmet (w.parmet@neu.edu) serves on the faculty of the Northeastern Univ. School of Law. She is a principal in the Public Health Advocacy Institute (www.phaionline.org)

Allan Parnell (mcmoss@mindspring.com) is Vice-President of the Grove Institute for Sustainable Communities in Mebane, North Carolina.

Libby Perl (eperl@comcast.net) is a housing policy analyst with the Congressional Research Service; she formerly served as a program officer at The Century Foundation and worked on housing issues as a Legal Aid attorney.

Dianne M. Piché (dpiche@cccr.org), a civil rights lawyer, is Executive Director of the Citizens' Commission on Civil Rights, where she was principal editor of CCCR's 2004 publication, *Choosing Better Schools: A Study of Student Transfers Under the No Child Left Behind Act,* and their 2002 report, *Rights at Risk: Equality in an Age of Terrorism.* She also teaches education law and policy at the Univ. of Maryland-College Park.

Fred L. Pincus (pincus@umbc.edu) is Professor in the Department of Sociology & Anthropology, Univ. of Maryland-Baltimore County. A fuller discussion of Questions 1-7 in his Reverse Discrimination Quiz appears in his book, *Reverse Discrimination: Dismantling A Myth* (Lynne Rienner Publishers). A fuller discussion of Questions 8-10 will be found in his just-published book *Understanding Diversity* (Lynne Rienner Publishers).

Alexander Polikoff (apolikoff@bpichicago.org) is staff attorney and former Executive Director of Business and Professional People for the Public Interest, a Chicago public interest law and policy center. He is also lead counsel in the Gautreaux litigation and the author of *Waiting for Gautreaux: A Story of Segregation, Housing and the Black Ghetto* (Northwestern Univ. Press).

john a. powell (powell.355@OSU.edu), a PRRAC board member, is Director of the Kirwan Institute for the Study of Race and Ethnicity and holder of the Williams Chair in Civil Rights & Civil Liberties at the Moritz School of Law, Ohio State Univ.

Wendy Puriefoy (wpuriefoy@publiceducation.org) is Executive Director of the Public Education Network in Washington, DC.

Vernellia R. Randall (Vernellia.Randall@notes.udayton.edu) is a professor at the Univ. of Dayton School of Law and is a nurse-practitioner. She teaches "American Health Care Law" and "Race and Racism in American Law." The author of a number of publications, her most recent is the forthcoming book, *Dying While Black: Using Reparation to Eliminate the Slave Health Deficit.* She is also the web editor of Race, Racism and the Law (http://academic.udayton. edu/race/).

Jamin Raskin (raskin@wcl.american.edu) is a professor of constitutional law at American University's Washington College of Law and Director of its Program on Law and Government. He is also the founder of the Marshall-Brennan Constitutional Literacy Project, which sends gifted law students into public high schools in Maryland and Washington, DC, to teach a course in "constitutional literacy." He chairs Maryland's State Labor Board and is the author of several books, including *We the Students* (CQ Press) and *Overruling Democracy* (Routledge).

Carla Roach (croach@stanford.edu) is a doctoral student at the Stanford Univ. School of Education.

Anthony Robbins (anthony.robbins@tufts.edu) is Professor of Public Health at the Tufts Univ. School of Medicine. He is a principal in the Public Health Advocacy Institute (www.phaionline).

Richard Rothstein (rr2159@columbia.edu) is a Research Associate at the Economic Policy Institute and a visiting professor at Teachers College, Columbia Univ. He is the author of *Class and Schools: Using Social, Economic, and Educational Reform to Close the Black-White Achievement Gap* (Teachers College Press) and *The Charter School Dust-Up: Examining the Evidence on Enrollment and Achievement* (with Martin Carnoy, Rebecca Jacobsen and Lawrence Mishel, Teachers College Press).

David Rusk (drusk@starpower.net) is the former mayor of Albuquerque and a New Mexico state legislator. He is author of *Inside Game/Outside Game* (Brookings Institution Press) and *Cities Without Suburbs* (Woodrow Wilson Center Press). He serves as a national strategic partner of the Gamaliel Foundation and is a founding member of the Innovative Housing Institute.

Tamar Ruth (tamar_ruth@fc.mcps.k12.md.us) is an award-winning elementary school teacher in Montgomery County, MD, a doctoral student in education policy and leadership at the Univ. of Maryland, and on the board of the Montgomery County Education Association (the NEA teachers union).

Lisbeth B. Schorr (Lisbeth_schorr@hms.harvard.edu) directs the Pathways Mapping Initiative of the Project on Effective Interventions at Harvard Univ. (http://www.pathwaystooutcomes.org).

Theodore M. Shaw (tshaw@naacpldf.org), a PRRAC Board member, is Director-Counsel and President of the NAACP Legal Defense & Educational Fund.

Hilary Silver (hilary_silver@brown.edu) is Associate Professor of Sociology and Urban Studies at Brown Univ. She is currently finishing a book on grassroots initiatives to combat social exclusion and unemployment in France and Germany, and is editing a book on "The New Yankee City: New Immigrants in Urban New England."

Mark Simon (sim@gwu.edu) is the Director of the Center for Teacher Leadership in Maryland. Formerly, he taught high school Social Studies in Montgomery County, MD, and served for 12 years as the elected president of NEA's 3rd largest affiliate, the Montgomery County Education Association.

David Barton Smith (dbsmith2@comcast.net) is Professor in the Healthcare Management Program in the Fox School of Business and Management at Temple Univ. His book *Healthcare Divided: Race and Healing a Nation* (Univ. of Michigan Press) was influential in shaping current efforts to address racial disparities in treatment.

Rosa Smith (rs@schottfoundation.org) is former Superintendent of the Columbus, OH public schools. She is the President of the Caroline and Sigmund Schott Foundation and the Schott Center for Public and Early Education, in Cambridge, MA. Both organizations focus on equity for all children in public education.

William E. Spriggs (wspriggs@howard.edu) is the newly appointed Chair of the Economics Department at Howard Univ., the only HBU that offers a Ph.D. in Economics. Immediately prior to that he was a Senior Fellow at the Economic Policy Institute and a consultant to the Center on Budget and Policy Priorities. Formerly, he was Executive Director of the National Urban League Institute for Opportunity and Equality.

Gregory D. Squires (squires@gwu.edu), a member of PRRAC's Social Science Advisory Board, is Chair of the Department of Sociology at George Washington Univ. His recent books include *Insurance Redlining* (Urban Institute Press), *Color and Money* (with Sally O'Connor, SUNY Press), *Urban Sprawl* (Urban Institute Press), *Organizing Access to Capital* (Temple Univ. Press) and *Why the Poor Pay More: How to Stop Predatory Lending* (Praeger).

Catherine Tactaquin (ctactaquin@nnirr.org), a PRRAC Board Member, is Executive Director of the National Network for Immigrant and Refugee Rights in Oakland, CA.

Ellen Taylor (alcaldeellen@msn.com) worked as a senior budget policy analyst for OMB Watch from May 1999 until September 2004, where she directed the budget and tax policy program as well as coordinated the Social Investment Initiative, a project aimed at engaging state and local nonprofits in federal budget issues and priorities. Today, she lives in New Mexico.

Philip Tegeler (ptegeler@prrac.org) is the Executive Director of the Poverty & Race Research Action Council. Prior to coming to PRRAC, he worked as a civil rights lawyer at the Connecticut ACLU, where he litigated school and housing desegregation cases. Among his recent writings is "The Persistence of Segregation in Government Housing Programs," in Xavier de Souza Briggs, ed., *The Geography of Opportunity: Race and Housing Choice in Metropolitan America* (Brookings Institution Press).

Makani Themba-Nixon (mthemba@thepraxisproject.org) is Executive Director of The Praxis Project, a Washington, DC-based nonprofit organization working to advance health justice. Among her recent books is *Making Policy, Making Change: How Communities Are Taking Law Into Their Own Hands* (Jossey-Bass).

Margery Austin Turner (maturner@ui.urban.org), a member of PRRAC's Social Science Advisory Board, directs The Urban Institute's Metropolitan Housing and Communities Policy Center. She served as HUD's Deputy Assistant Secretary for Research from 1993-96.

Sudhir Alladi Venkatesh (sv185@columbia.edu) is on the faculty in Sociology and African-American Studies at Columbia Univ., where he also is Director of the Center for Urban Research & Policy.

Jenice L. View (jenice@aol.com) uses popular education techniques in a variety of educational settings with adults and youth. She is a middle-school educator, the education and training director of a national economic and environmental justice organization, and co-editor of *Putting the Movement Back Into Civil Rights Teaching* (Teaching for Change/PRRAC).

Paul L. Wachtel (paul.wachtel@gmail.com) is CUNY Distinguished Professor at the City College of New York. He is the author, among other books, of *Therapeutic Communication* (Guilford), *The Poverty of Affluence* (Free Press) and *Race in the Mind of America: Breaking the Vicious Circle between Blacks and Whites* (Routledge).

Peter Wagner (pwagner@prisonpolicy.org), is an Open Society Institute Soros Justice Fellow at the Prison Policy Initiative, a widely-used Internet project providing accurate, timely research and policy reports on criminal justice, and the author of "Importing Constituents: Prisoners and Political Clout in New York." He also edits PrisonersoftheCensus.org, which discusses the national implications of prisoner miscounting.

Tamara Wilder is a Ph.D. Candidate in Politics and Education, Teachers College, Columbia University. She holds an M.A. in Quantitative Methods in the Social Sciences from Columbia University.

Tim Wise (timjwise@msn.com) is the author of *White Like Me: Reflections on Race from a Privileged Son* (Soft Skull Press) and *Affirmative Action: Racial Preference in Black and White* (Routledge).

Hanh Cao Yu (Hanh_Cao_Yu@spra.com) is a Senior Social Scientist at Social Policy Research Associates in Oakland, CA. Her specializations are youth development, intergroup relations, diversity and organizational change.

PRRAC Board of Directors and Social Science Advisory Board

Board Member; BM-E = Board Member Emeritus; SSAB = Social Science Advisory Board; SSAB-E = Social Science Advisory Board Emeritus.

The first-listed institutional identification is that at the time of the person's PRRAC appointment, the one listed second is the person's present or recent location.

Darrell Armstrong: Shiloh Baptist Church, Trenton, NJ
Richard Berk: UCLA Dept. of Sociology (SSAB-E)
Deepak Bhargava: Center for Community Change, Washington, DC (BM-E)
Angela Glover Blackwell: Urban Strategies Council; PolicyLink, Oakland (BM-E)
Maria Blanco: Lawyers Committee for Civil Rights of the San Francisco Bay Area
John Charles Boger: Univ. of North Carolina Law School, Chapel Hill
Frank Bonilla: Hunter College Center for Puerto Rican Studies (SSAB)
Gordon Bonnyman: Legal Services of Middle Tennessee; Tennessee Justice Center (BM-E)
Xavier de Souza Briggs: MIT Dept. of Urban Studies and Planning (SSAB)
Nancy Duff Campbell: National Women's Law Center, Washington, DC (BM-E)
Camille Charles: Univ. of Pennsylvania Dept. of Sociology (SSAB)
David Cohen: The Advocacy Institute, Washington, DC (BM-E)
Sheila Crowley: National Low Income Housing Coalition, Washington, DC
Linda Darling-Hammond: Columbia Univ. Teachers College; Stanford University (SSAB-E)
Gary Delgado: Applied Research Center, Oakland (BM-E)

Index

N.B. Race is of course a central theme of this book. And in the US, the primary group victimized by racism of all types is Blacks/African Americans. Since entering a page number for each place where these terms appear would have yielded a massive and unwieldy set of entries, we have opted to omit these two terms from the Index, and instead direct the reader to the specific entries (health, education, housing, etc.) where text relevant to Blacks/African Americans appears. Other racial groups in the US—Hispanics/Latinos, Native Americans/American Indians, Asian Americans, etc.—are mentioned in these pages less frequently and so are indexed.

Academy for Educational Development, 382
Acevedo-Garcia, Dolores, 168, 169, 171
ACORN, 88, 196, 353
Addison Middle School (Roanoke, Virginia), 226
Additional Child Tax Credit, 94
Adenauer, Konrad, 45
Adler, Mortimer, 100
Advanced Placement. *See* education, Advanced Placement
Advancement Project, 253
affirmative action, 3, 4, 6, 7, 8, 57, 62, 69, 83, 199, 203, 221, 237, 253, 266, 321
Afghanistan, 253, 358, 360
Africa, 49
Agency for Healthcare Research and Quality (AHRQ), US Department of

Health and Human Services, 305, 306
Agrarian Justice (Paine), 98
Agriculture, US Department of, 294, 373, 374, 375, 376
Akron, Ohio, 367
Alabama, 13; segregation in, 366; Senate representation of, 341; special education and, 274
Alaska, 74; high poverty areas in, 73; special education and, 274; tax increment financing, 114
Alaska Natives, 333
Alaska Permanent Fund (APF), 100, 101, 102
Alberta, Canada, 101
ALERTE, 59
Alexander v. Mineta, 346
Alexander v. Sandoval, 180
Alexandria, Virginia, 83
Algebra Project, 340

All Together Now: Creating Middle-Class Schools Through Public School Choice (Kahlenberg), 238
Allen, George, 101
Allen, James, 42
Allport, Gordon W., 231
Allstate (insurance company), 185
America's Second Harvest, 374
American Association of Medical Colleges, 325
American Declaration of the Rights and Duties of Man, Articles II and XX, 359
An American Dilemma (Myrdal), 150
American Dream (DeParle), 137, 140
American Enterprise Institute, 310
American Family Mutual Insurance Company, 185, 186
American Farm Bureau Federation, 108
American Honda, 284
American Immigration Law Foundation, 351
American Indians, 3, 5, 35, 333. *See also* Native Americans
American Insurance Association, 184
American Jewish Joint Distribution Committee (AJDC), 45
American Journal of Preventive Medicine, 124
American Nazi Party, 41. *See also* Nazis
American Obesity Association, 376
The American Prospect, 109, 345
American Samoa, 347
Americans with Disabilities Act, 68
Amsterdam Treaty, 60
Anderson, Elijah, 140
Anna, Illinois, 15, 16
annexation, 21–22
Annie E. Casey Foundation, 171
Anoka, Minnesota, 114, 115
Anti-Bilingual Education Initiative (1998) (Proposition 227), 32, 33
anti-Semitism, 45, 140
apologies, 38–42
Appleton, Wisconsin, 16
Arizona, 17, 352, 353
Arkansas, 76, 113, 274
Arlington, Virginia, 218

Arlington County, Virginia, 83
Asbury United Methodist Church (Washington, DC), 39
Asian American Legal Defense and Education Fund, 352
Asian Americans, 116, 333, 347
Asian Development Bank, 62
Asian Pacific Americans, 385
Asian Pacific Islanders, 74, 77, 304, 352, 392
Asians, xiii, 3, 18, 144, 169, 171, 172, 222
Association of American Colleges and Universities, 49, 199
Association of Boarding Schools, 283
asthma, 131, 206, 242, 243, 304, 312, 316, 323
ATD-Fourth World Movement, 59
Atkinson, Tony, 61, 63
Atlanta, Georgia, 239, 367
Augusta, Georgia, 42
Auschwitz, 46, 47
Austin, Minnesota, 16
Australia, 40
Austria, 39, 40, 44

Baby College, 206
Baby Steps, 206
Baker v. Carr, 340
Baldwin, James, 137, 181, 362, 368
Baltimore, Maryland, 125, 126, 135, 139, 181, 195, 236, 315, 359
banks, 113, 133, 184, 187, 194
Barbour, Haley, 13
Barrett, Tom, 187
Barton, Paul, 288
Beacon Schools, 290
Begin, Menachem, 45
Belarus, 359, 360
Belgium, 39
The Bell Curve (Herrnstein, Murray*),* 6, 34
Belsky, Eric, 187
Berkeley, California, 86
Berlin, Ira, 96
Bern, Switzerland, 47
Besharov, Douglas J., 310
Black Entertainment Television (BET), 103, 105, 106, 108, 109, 110

Black Wealth/White Wealth (Oliver, Shapiro), 98, 229
Black, Hugo, 367
Blackwell, Kenneth, 344
The Black-White Test Score Gap (Cook, Ludwig), 238
Blair, Anthony, 60, 63
Bond, Julian, xv, 42
Borough of Manhattan Community College, 355
Borsodi, Ralph, 190
Boston College, 108
Boston Globe, 296
Boston, Massachusetts, 83, 85, 125, 128, 135, 162, 170, 191, 218, 301
Boykin, William, 339
Bradley, Bill, xv
Brandeis University, 192
Brennan Center for Justice, 88
Brennan, William, 8
Bridges to Success (Indianapolis, Indiana), 290
Brookings Institution, 104
Brown University, 298
Brown v. Board of Education, xii, 8, 17, 18, 166, 167, 178–82, 203, 215, 218, 223, 234, 235, 239, 252, 256, 264; anniversary of, 301; enforcement of, 339
Brown, James, 298
Brown, John, 298
Brown, Ron, 298
Brownback, Sam, 360
Buck v. Bell, 40
Buck, Carrie, 40
Buffalo News, 113
Burbank, California, 16
Bush (George W.) Administration, 101, 115, 142, 148, 161, 193, 264, 267, 310, 360
Bush v. Gore, 343, 346
Bush, George W., 4, 5, 41, 91, 100, 149, 153, 184, 218, 339, 342, 343, 344, 354
Bush, Jeb, 348
Business and Professional People in the Public Interest, 163
busing. *See* desegregation
Byrd, Harry, 341

Cahill, Michele, 382
California, 16, 23, 32, 139, 162, 262, 352, 353, 354, 378
California Newsreel, 49, 199
Cambridge, Massachusetts, 220, 240
Camden, New Jersey, 345
Campaign for Community Schools (Chicago, Illinois), 290
capitalism, and language, 36–37
The Capitalist Manifesto (Kelso, Adler), 100
Carlson, Arne, 282
Carter, James Earl, 138
Carter, Robert, 229
Cashin, Sheryll, 165
Castel, Robert, 60
CDFI Fund, 98
Census, US, 25–28, 57, 302, 329, 341
Center for Community Change, 353
Center for Responsible Lending (CRL), 195, 196, 197
Center for Voting and Democracy, 350
Center for Youth Development and Policy Research, 382
Centers for Disease Control and Prevention (CDC), 131, 331
Central Intelligence Agency (CIA), 39
Chad, 101
Chaney, Ben, 12
Chaney, James, 9, 10, 11, 12, 13, 14, 38
Chappell, David, 182
charitable giving, 104
Charles Hamilton Houston Institute for Race and Justice (Harvard Law School), 204
Charles, Camille, 172
Charles, Ray, 42
Charlotte, North Carolina, 240
Charlotte-Mecklenburg, North Carolina, 218
Chase (bank), 47
Chavez, Linda, 34
Chestnutt, Charles W., 367
Chicago, Illinois, 27, 84, 112, 114, 121, 125, 126, 135, 144, 150, 153, 154, 160, 161, 180, 181, 222, 243, 297, 359
Child and Dependent Care Credit, 94

child care, 67, 68, 106, 122, 135, 140,
206, 207, 242, 249, 264, 322, 379
Child Care Subsidy, 95
Child Welfare Administration, New
York City, 394
children, 74, 79, 89–92, 93, 117, 127,
309, 310, 312, 313, 376
Children's Aid Society, 290
Children's Health Insurance Plan, 94
Chinese, 10, 31, 148
Chinese Americans, 15
CHIP Program, 314
Choctaw Indians, 10, 12
Chomsky, Noam, 33
The Chronicle of Higher Education, 8
Churchill, Winston, 30
Cincinnati, Ohio, 83
Citizens' Commission in Civil Rights,
262
City & Community, 170
The City of Richmond v. Crowson, 229
City Schools and the American Dream
(Noguera), 250
Civil Rights Act (1964), 17, 18, 175,
181, 200, 238, 252, 261, 266, 302,
328
Civil Rights Movement, 9, 13, 14, 17,
138, 148, 182, 303, 353, 355, 368,
384
Civil War, xvi, 16, 179, 228, 284, 298,
321, 325, 341, 363, 364, 365, 368
Civilian Conservation Corps, 16
Clark, Kenneth, 137, 150, 252
Class and Schools (Rothstein), 258,
259, 260, 265
Cleveland, Mississippi, 339
Cleveland, Ohio, 359
Clinton, William J., 62, 156
Coalition for Community Schools, 288,
291
Cobb, Charles, 339
Coleman Report, 218
Coleman, James, 259
The Color of Hunger, (Shields), 380
*Colored Property: State Policy and
White Racial Politics in the Modern
American Suburb* (Freund), 173
Columbia University, 7

Comeback Cities (Grogan, Proscio),
147
The Coming Race War in America
(Rowan), 141
Commission on Civil Rights, US, 112,
329
Commission on Excellence in Special
Education, 274
Communities in Schools, 290
Community Development Block Grants
(CDBG), 21, 195
community development corporations
(CDCs), 94, 147, 271, 289
Community Land Trust (CLT), 189–93
Community Learning Centers Initiative
(Lincoln, Nebraska), 291
Community Reinvestment Act (CRA),
98, 183, 187
*Community Youth Development
Journal*, 295
Condition of Education 1998 (US
Department of Education), 238
Conference on Jewish Material Claims
Against Germany (Claims
Conference), 43, 45, 46
Congo, 39
Congress, US, xii, xiv, 25, 105, 138,
142, 145, 156, 161, 164, 165, 195,
244, 305, 348, 377. *See also* House
of Representatives, US; Senate, US
Congressional Black Caucus, 350
Congressional Budget Office (CBO),
104
Congressional Research Service (CRS),
91
Conkling, Roscoe, 365, 366
Conley, Dalton, 107, 130
Connecticut, 181
Consortium on Chicago School
Research, 208
Constitution, US, xiii, 31, 228, 342,
344, 369; Bill of Rights of, xiv, 69,
350, 368; District Clause and, 357;
Equal Protection Clause of, 223,
228, 347; Fifteenth Amendment to,
xiii, 342; Fifth Amendment to, 368;
First Amendment to, 368;
Fourteenth Amendment to, xi, xiii,
349, 363, 365, 366, 367, 369, 370;

Nineteenth Amendment to, 342; non-citizen voting and, 355; right to vote and, 340, 345; Second Amendment to, xii; Seventeenth Amendment to, 342; Seventh Amendment to, 368; Sixth Amendment to, 368; Tenth Amendment to, xiv; Territorial Clause and, 347, 348; Thirteenth Amendment to, xiii, xiv; Twenty-Fourth Amendment to, 342; Twenty-Sixth Amendment to, 342; Twenty-Seventh Amendment to, xiii; Twenty-Third Amendment to, 342
Consumer Federation of America, 187
Convention on the Elimination of All Forms of Racial Discrimination (CERD), 181
Cook County, Illinois, 27
Cook, Philip, 238
CORE: The Coalition for Residential Education, 283, 285
Corporation for Enterprise Development, 102
corporations, 100, 362–68, 370, 378
Council of Family and Child Caring Agencies, 394
Courts of Appeals, US, 53
credit card debt, 4
Crescent City Farmers Market (New Orleans), 379
crime, 65, 67, 68, 122, 123, 127, 132, 139, 147, 158, 168, 192, 275. *See also* prisons; violence
criminal justice, xiii, 4, 25, 27, 393, 394, 395, 388

Dallas Housing Authority, 27, 143
Darien, Connecticut, 15, 18, 19
Dark Ghetto: Dilemmas of Social Power (Clark), 252
Davis, Tom, 359
DC Vote, 361
DC Voting Rights Constitutional amendment, 347
Dearborn, Michigan, 114
Declaration of Independence, 31

Defense, US Department of, 161, 272, 284, 339
DeLand, Illinois, 16
Delaware, 76, 348
Democratic Party, 69, 233, 341, 342, 352
Democrats, xii, xiii, xiv, 100, 157
Denton, Nancy, 150
Denver, Colorado, 162
DeParle, Jason, 137, 138, 140
desegregation, 11, 134, 216, 219, 220, 223, 233, 239, 262
Detroit, Michigan, 16, 114, 180, 359
Dewey, John, 148, 232
Diebold Corporation, 344
Digital Divide Council, 280
Dinh, Viet, 357
disabilities, 61, 67, 72, 89–90, 92
discrimination, 69, 124, 161, 234, 301–3; anti-discrimination laws, 140; "driving while black" (DWB), 17; in housing, 134, 140, 174, 175, 180, 216; immigration and, 65, 66; insurance and, 185; testing for, 302, 303, 329, 330, 335
Dismantling Desegregation (Orfield), 218
District of Columbia, 346, 357–61. *See also* Washington, DC
Dominican Republic (Santo Domingo), 40
Douglass, Frederick, 365
Downs, Anthony, 154
Dred Scott, 228
DuBois, W.E.B., 37, 137, 208, 362, 364, 365
Dudley Street Neighborhood Initiative (DSNI), 191, 192, 193
Duluth, Minnesota, 221

Earned Income Tax Credit (EITC), 59, 85, 94
Ebonics. *See* language
economic development, xv, 111–15
Edelman, Marian Wright, xv
Edina, Minnesota, 15, 17, 18, 19
Educable Mentally Handicapped (EMH) programs, 34

education, xiii, xiv, xv, 4, 64, 65, 68, 81, 107, 139, 216, 226, 258, 269–72, 275, 291; and academic achievement, 126, 130, 155, 168, 279, 311–19, 383; Advanced Placement (AP) courses, 5, 217, 263, 279; charter schools and, 278, 283, 296; choice of, 171, 220, 262; early childhood programs, 249, 251, 264, 267, 276; home schooling, 278; immigration and, 73, 269; language and, 29, 32, 33, 35, 344; poverty and, 75, 76, 97, 105, 158, 197, 211, 212, 247, 269, 270, 271, 322; privatization of, 256; quality of, 7, 13, 135, 140, 147, 168, 219, 384; race and, 106, 163, 170, 182, 204, 207, 208, 212, 215–40; school location and, 71, 180, 192, 246, 270, 288; schools, 68, 94, 114, 122, 123, 127, 178, 179, 219, 241–68, 381; teachers and, 207, 208, 217, 225, 247, 253, 259–60, 263, 265, 267, 272, 274, 276, 277, 279, 284, 286, 288; unions and, 264, 265; "zero tolerance," 264

The Education Trust, 251, 258, 259, 261, 262, 266

Education, US Department of, 217, 244, 271

Educational Leadership, 251

Educational Testing Service, 288

Educational, Scientific & Cultural Organization (United Nations), 40

Ehrenreich, Barbara, 97, 189

Eisenhower, Dwight D., 8, 166

elderly, 67, 74, 95, 99, 117, 163, 189, 195, 376

Electoral College. *See* voting rights, Electoral College

Electronic Benefit Transfer (EBT), 379

Elementary and Secondary Education Act, and Title I, 253

Ellen, Ingrid, 133, 134

Elmore, Andrew, 85, 86

Emancipation Proclamation, xiv, 364

eminent domain, 17, 23, 191

employee stock ownership plans (ESOPs), 100

employment, xiv, 4, 8, 61, 64, 72, 82, 84, 85, 87, 97, 117, 127, 133, 140, 174, 180, 203, 230, 232, 248, 266, 268, 324, 364, 379, 380, 383. *See also* jobs; living wage movement

English for the Children, 32

Enterprise Foundation, 163

enterprise zones, 113, 114

environment, xiii, 63, 65, 69, 228, 321, 323, 362, 368

Equal Employment Opportunity Commission (EEOC), 52, 112

Erikson, Erik, 384

estate tax. *See* taxes, estate

Europe, 44, 45, 49, 57–70, 254

European Commission, 58

European Union, 57–70

Eurostat (EU Statistical Office), 58

Evers, Medgar, 41

Executive Order 11063. *See* Kennedy, John F.

Facing the Hard Facts of Education Reform (Barton), 288

The Failures of Integration: How Race and Class Are Undermining the American Dream, (Cashin) 156

Fair Deal, 138

Fair Housing Act, 146, 166, 179

fair housing. *See* housing, fair

Fair Market Rents, 144, 159, 164

Fairfax County, Virginia, 162

Fanon, Franz, 35

Federal Bureau of Investigation (FBI), 10, 12

Federal Communications Commission (FCC), 106

Federal Financial Institutions Examination Council, 186, 301

Federal Home Loan Bank Board, 176

Federal Housing Administration (FHA), 3, 174, 175, 176, 200

Federal National Mortgage Association (FNMA), 174

Federal Reserve Bank of Boston, 301

Federation for American Immigration Reform (FAIR), 34

Ferencz, Benjamin, 45

Filipinos, 74, 389, 390

The Fire Next Time (Baldwin), 181
First National Conference on
    Residential Education for
    Disadvantaged Children and Youth,
    282
Fischer, Claude, 169
Florida, 73, 95, 278, 342, 348, 352, 353
Florida Education Fund, 280
    Florida Virtual School (FLVS), 278,
279, 280
food, xvii, 57, 69, 106, 189, 285, 377,
    378, 379; insecurity about, 132,
    373–80; National School Lunch
    Program, 95, 374, 377; nutrition
    and, 206, 242, 250, 256, 311, 315,
    375; School Breakfast Program, 95,
    374; Summer Food Service
    Program, 378. *See also* Food
    Stamps; obesity
Food and Nutrition Service, US
    Department of Agriculture, 373
Food Research and Action Center
    (FRAC), 376
Food Stamps, 59, 68, 95, 310, 374,
    377, 378, 379
FoodChange (New York City), 377
Ford Foundation, 385
Ford Motor Company, 47
Forum for Youth Investment, 382
Foundry United Methodist Church
    (Washington, DC), 39
Foxx, Jamie, 42
France, 47, 59, 60, 63, 68, 244
Frankfurt, Germany, 46
Franklin, Benjamin, 35
Frazier, George, 96
Freedom Schools, 9
Freedom Summer, 11, 14, 298
French Revolution, 31

Galbraith, John Kenneth, 58
Gale, William, 108
Galloway, Lowell, 31
Galster, George, 140, 150, 164
Gamaliel Foundation, 182, 353
Gates, Bill Sr., 105
Gautreaux Program, 121, 125, 126,
    127, 128, 137–67, 222

gays and lesbians, xiii, 383, 384, 385,
    387–95
gender, 69, 97, 186, 197, 212, 233, 275,
    341, 385, 387, 389. *See also* women
General Accounting Office, US (GAO),
    269
Gentleman's Agreement, 15
gentrification, 80, 189, 191, 193, 271
*The Geography of Opportunity: Race
    and Housing Choice in Metropolitan
    America* (Harvard Civil Rights
    Project), 168
Georgetown University, 357
Georgia, 42, 73, 114
Georgia on My Mind (song), 42
Germany, Federal Republic of, 45, 67,
    244
Geronimus, Arlene, 124
ghettos, 137, 139, 140, 141, 142, 143,
    144, 145, 146, 147, 148, 149, 150,
    151, 154, 157, 163, 164, 166, 167,
    168, 171, 179, 368
Gingrich, Newt, 30, 139, 140
Ginsburg, Ruth Bader, 7, 8
Girard College, 283
Girard, Stephen, 284
GIS, 20, 23
Glendale, California, 16
globalization, 8, 36, 57, 97
Goering, John, 170
Goldmann, Nahum, 45
Good Jobs First, 113
Goodheart, Adam, 41
Goodman, Andrew, 10, 11, 13, 14, 38
Gore, Albert, 342, 343, 344
Graham, Howard, 366
Grantmakers Concerned with
    Immigrants and Refugees, 356
Gray, Marcus, 361
Great Britain, 44, 60, 63, 68, 244. *See
    also* United Kingdom
Great Depression, 99, 138, 175
Great Society, 138, 260
Greensboro, North Carolina, 41, 42
Greensburg, Indiana, 16
Grogan, Paul, 147
Grutter v. Bollinger, 157, 203, 210
Guam, 347
Gulf region, xviii

Gutierrez, Luis, 187

Haiti (Santo Domingo), 40
Hakuta, Kenji, 33
Hamilton, Alexander, 104
Hamilton County, Texas, 17
Harlem, New York City, 206, 243
Harper's, 344
Harrington, Michael, 97
Harris, Cheryl, 363
Harris, Katherine, 344
Harrison, Arkansas, 16
Hart, Betty, 246, 247
Hartford, Connecticut, 86
Harvard Civil Rights Project, 5, 168,
    178, 215, 253, 275, 276
Harvard Joint Center for Housing
    Studies, 184, 187
Harvard Law Review, 363
Harvard University, 84, 204, 218, 221,
    259, 343
Havens, John, 108
Hayakawa, S.I., 34
Hayden, Tom, 40
Hayduk, Ronald, 355
Head Start, 195, 258, 260, 261, 266,
    267
health, xv, 64, 288, 376; education and,
    129, 309, 310, 379; gays and
    lesbians, 387, 391–93; housing and,
    75, 123, 127–28, 129, 132, 134–35;
    racial disparities and, 20, 130–36,
    210, 311–19, 321; reparations and,
    320–30; standards for, 140. *See also*
    asthma; disabilities; health care;
    HIV-AIDS; lead poisoning; obesity
Health and Human Services, US
    Department of (DHHS), 294, 304–6,
    328, 388, 392
health care, xiv, 8, 60, 62, 63, 93, 99,
    106, 112, 122, 147, 171, 189, 209,
    250, 251, 256, 257, 264, 266, 268,
    325, 340, 379. *See also* health
Health Care Anti-Discrimination Act,
    330
Healthy Eating Index, US Department
    of Agriculture, 375
Help America Vote Act of 2002
    (HAVA), 345

Henderson, Thomas, 238, 239, 240
Heritage Foundation, and education,
    217, 250, 258, 259, 266
Herrnstein, Richard J., 34
Hershey, Milton, 284
*The Hidden Cost of Being African
    American: How Wealth Perpetuates
    Inequality* (Shapiro), 192
Hill-Burton Act, 325
Hirsch, Arnold, 173
Hispanics, xiii, 18, 36, 54, 72–73, 76,
    77, 80, 127, 145, 169, 171, 172, 207,
    221, 275, 304, 314, 332, 345, 346,
    347, 373, 374, 375, 376, 380; *See
    also* Latinos; Mexican Americans
Hitler, Adolph, 39
HIV-AIDS, 304, 317, 318, 332, 391
Holmes, Oliver Wendell Jr., 40
Holocaust, 43, 45, 48
Home Mortgage Disclosure Act
    (HMDA), 183, 186, 187, 301
Home Ownership and Equity
    Protection Act (HOEPA), 195
Homeland Security, US Department of
    (DHS), 354
homelessness, 61, 65, 94, 269, 270,
    271, 272, 283
homeownership, 19, 131, 132, 133,
    134, 156, 159, 177, 183, 185, 187,
    188, 190, 192, 194, 195, 197, 199,
    209, 323
Homestead Act (1862), 200
Hood, Jim, 13
Hoover, J. Edgar, 10
Hope and Lifetime Learning Education
    Credits, 94
HOPE VI Program, 80, 125, 126, 135,
    271
Horton, Willie, 140
House of Representatives, US, 38, 42,
    148, 325, 341, 358. *See also*
    Congress, US; Senate, US
housing, xiv, xv, 4, 8, 65, 93, 122–24,
    135, 178, 243, 250, 264; affordable, 98,
    249, 380; class-based integration of,
    222; discrimination and, 3, 7, 134, 140,
    176, 180, 216, 221, 230, 236, 239, 240;
    displacement, 191, 193; estate tax and,
    106; exclusion, 68, 221; fair, 160, 173–

77, 178–82, 185, 187, 230; mobile homes, 23; mobility, 121–29, 143, 148, 161, 165, 166, 168–72; opportunity-based, 154, 161; racial disparities, 130–36, 232; reparations and, 157; revitalization, 146–48, 199. *See also* gentrification; Housing and Urban Development, US Department of; Moving to Opportunity; neighborhoods; public housing; Section 8

Housing and Home Finance Agency, US (HHFA), 173, 174, 175, 176

Housing and Urban Development, US Department of (HUD), 143, 144, 159, 163, 175, 176, 185, 196, 294. *See also* Moving to Opportunity; Section 8

Houston, Texas, 27

Howard University, 325

Huling, Tracy, 27

Human Rights Watch, 348

Humphrey, Hubert, 138

Hundred Black Men, 280

Hunger in America 2001 (America's Second Harvest), 374

Huntington, Colis, 366

Hutchinson, Earl Ofari, 41

IG Farben, 46, 47

Illinois, 15, 16, 17, 27, 28, 162, 187, 352, 354

Illinois Advisory Committee to the US Commission on Civil Rights, 112

Immigrant Voting Project, 356

Immigrant Worker Freedom Ride, 353
  immigration, xvii, 3, 4, 31, 32, 34, 36, 37, 61, 63, 65, 66, 68, 73, 76, 169, 172, 221, 262, 269, 327, 351–56, 385, 386

Immigration Act (1965), 29

Immigration Policy Center, 351

"Importing Constituents: Prisoners and Political Clout" (Wagner), 27

In Pursuit of a Dream Deferred: Linking Housing and Education Policy (powell, Kearney, Kay), 226

inclusionary zoning, 146, 161–64. *See also* zoning

income inequality, 58, 64, 97–98, 99, 100, 102, 103, 106. *See also* employment; jobs; wealth inequality

Independent Insurance Agents of America, 187

Indiana, 16, 17, 114, 274

Indiana Soldiers' and Sailors' Home, 284

industrial revenue bonds (IRBs), 112

Ingersoll, Richard, 263

Innovation Center for Community and Youth Development, 385

Inside Game/Outside Game (Rusk), 147

Institute for Community Economics, 191, 193

Institute of Jewish Affairs, 45

Institute of Medicine, 305

insurance, 91; disability, 68; discrimination and, 185, 186, 192; health, 82, 83, 205, 206, 243, 304, 314, 318, 324, 326, 333, 334, 335; homeowners, 183, 187; life, 90; mortgage, 175, 176; paired-testing, 185; redlining and, 184–86, 187–88; wealth accumulation and, 187

Intelligence Quotient (IQ), 49, 311; bias of, 273, 274, 275; misuse of, 276; neighborhoods and, 123

Inter-American Commission on Human Rights, 181, 359

Inter-American Development Bank, 62

Intergroup Relations Service (IRS), 173, 174

Interior, US Department of, Bureau of Indian Affairs, 284

International Co-operative Alliance, 102

International Covenant on Civil and Political Rights, 342

International Day for the Remembrance of the Slave Trade and Its Abolition, 40

International Journal of Obesity, 375

Internet, 65, 93, 251, 280

Iowa, 17, 29, 114, 274

Iraq, 100, 253, 358, 359, 360, 361

Iraqi Permanent Fund, 100, 101, 102

Israel, 45, 284

Italy, 47, 99, 146

Jackson, Mississippi, 13, 41
Jackson State University, 11, 12
Jackson-Evers International Airport, 41
Japan, 244, 254
Japanese-Americans, 43, 104, 145, 320
Jay, John, 104
Jefferson, Thomas, 31, 35, 341
Jencks, Christopher, 259
Jewish Agency for Palestine, 45
Jewish Restitution Successor
    Organization (JRSO), 45
Jews, 9, 13, 15, 18, 40, 43, 45, 46, 146,
    154
Jim Crow, 7, 38, 43, 144, 145, 302,
    321. *See also* racism
jobs, 7, 33, 36, 52, 60, 67, 68, 69, 71,
    74, 82, 83, 93, 106, 112, 113, 114,
    115, 116, 129, 147, 165, 170, 185,
    216, 217, 218, 248. *See also*
    employment
Johnson, Jack, 298
Johnson, Lyndon B., 10, 138, 253, 341
Johnson, Magic, 297
Johnson, Robert, 103, 110
Johnston, David Cay, 108
Jones Act, 347
Jones v. Mayer, 18
Jordan, Michael, 297
*Journal of Epidemiology and
    Community Health*, 123
Journal of Research and Development,
    270
JP Morgan (bank), 47
Judicature, 203
Justice Department, US, 22

Kagan, Saul, 46
Kahlenberg, Richard D., 222, 223, 224,
    225, 226, 227, 231, 233, 234, 235,
    236
Kalawao County, Hawaii, 74
Kansas, 17, 113, 254
Kansas City Star, 115
Kansas City, Missouri, 205
Kelso, Louis, 100
Kenilworth, Illinois, 18, 19
Kennedy, John F., 173, 174, 175

Kentucky, 72
Kerner Commission, 140, 149, 179
Kerry, John, 153
Keys v. School District #1, 179
Keyssar, Alexander, 343
Killen, Edgar Ray, 13, 38
King, Martin Luther Jr., 179, 231, 306
Kingsley, G. Thomas, 178
KIPP Academies, 260, 266
Klestil, Thomas, 40
Knowledge Works Foundation (Ohio),
    291
Kotlowitz, Alex, 137
Krashen, Stephen, 33
Ku Klux Klan, 9, 10, 13, 38, 41, 368
Kuwait, 101

La Crosse, Wisconsin, 219
La Jolla, California, 19
labor, xiii, 3, 37. *See also* unions
Labor, US Department of, 284
Lake Forest, Illinois, 114
Lambda Legal Defense and Education
    Fund, 394
Lampton, Dunn, 13
land reform, 190
language, 29–37, 49, 73, 94, 344
Language of Government Act, 30
Latin American Association of
    Insurance Agents, 187
Latinos, 4, 5, 23, 25, 26, 27, 32, 36,
    113, 144, 154, 195, 196, 220, 222,
    234, 261, 332, 344, 351, 352, 353,
    385, 389, 391, 394. *See also*
    Hispanics; Mexican Americans
Lawyers' Committee for Better
    Housing, 161
Lazarus, Emma, 68
lead poisoning, 131, 134, 206, 242,
    311, 315, 317, 323. *See also* health
*Learning Together: The developing
    field of school-community initiatives*
    (Melaville), 292
Leave No Child Behind, xiii
Lee, Chungmei, 178
Lemann, Nicholas, 137
Lenoir, René, 59
leprosy (Hansen's Disease), 74
Leschi, Chief, 41

Leval, Pierre, 347
Levittown, New York, 16
Lewis, John, xv
Lewis Mumford Center, 131, 132, 134
Lexis-Nexis, 97
Liberty (insurance company), 185
Liberty, Oregon, 16
Lincoln, Abraham, 99, 102, 340
Lipsitz, George, 230
living wage, 82–88, 97, 209, 321, 322–23, 379. *See also* employment; jobs
Local Investment Commission (Kansas City, Missouri), 290
Long Island, New York, 112
Long, Huey, 99–100
Long, Russell, 100
Los Angeles, California, 16, 85, 125, 126, 127, 135, 145, 170, 297, 359
Los Angeles County, California, 27
Los Angeles Lakers, 297
Los Angeles Times, 101
"Losing the Vote: The Impact of Felony Disenfranchisement" (Sentencing Project, Human Rights Watch), 348
Louis, Joe, 298
Louisiana, 72, 76, 99, 113, 363
Louisiana Purchase, 143
Loury, Glenn, 232
Low Income Housing Tax Credits, 163, 181
Lowell, Massachusetts, 221, 298
Low-Income Heating and Energy Assistance, 95
Ludwig, Jens, 238
Lumumba, Patrice, 39
Luxembourg Income Study, 58
lynching, 16, 38, 42, 298. *See also* racism

Madison, James, 104, 341
Madison, Wisconsin, 84
Maine, 26, 274, 342
Majestic, Ann, 219
Making the Difference: Research and Practice in Community Schools (Coalition for Community Schools), 291
Malign Neglect (Tonry), 139

Malveaux, Julianne, 106
Malvern, Arkansas, 17
Manifest Destiny, 3, 35
Marcus, Paul, 6
Marshall, Illinois, 17
Marshall Plan, 7
Marshall, Thurgood, 8
Maryland, 17, 76, 359, 369
Massachusetts, 274, 341, 354, 388
Massachusetts Comprehensive Assessment System (MCAS), 296
Massachusetts State Youth Risk Behavior Survey (1999), 393
Massey, Douglas, 133, 150
Matthew, Eugene, 39
Mauer, Marc, 275
McDonald, Laughlin, 345
McDonalds, 375
media, 9, 97–98, 168, 179
Medicaid, 68, 95, 98, 106, 266, 324, 326, 335
Medicare, 161, 162, 266, 302, 306, 324, 334
Meharry (medical school), 326
Melaville, Atelia, 292
Memmi, Albert, 30, 35
Menomenee Falls, Wisconsin, 115
Meridian, Mississippi, 9
Mexican Americans, 3, 15, 124, 309. *See also* Hispanics, Latinos
military, 8, 25, 142, 143, 164, 197, 346
Miller, S.M., 239
Milwaukee, Wisconsin, 84, 183, 297
Milwaukee County, Wisconsin, 115
Milwaukee Journal Sentinel, 115
Minneapolis, Minnesota, 15, 114
Minnesota, 15, 114
Minority Students in Special and Gifted Education (National Research Council), 273
Missing the Bus (Good Jobs First), 113
Mississippi, 9–14, 38, 42, 76, 95 114, 228, 339, 340, 345, 348, 349
Mississippi Burning, 10
Mississippi State University, 10
Missouri, 16, 17, 72, 73
Mobilize the Immigrant Vote (MIV), 353, 354, 356
Modesto, California, 23

Mohl, Raymond, 173
Molpus, Dick, 11, 13
Monroe, James, 341
Montana, 27
Montgomery County Housing
    Opportunities Commission
    (Maryland), 163
Montgomery County, Maryland, 162,
    218, 262
Moore, Amzie, 339
Morehouse College, 222
mortgages: foreclosures and, 271;
    insurance and, 175, 176; interest
    and, 19; predatory lending and, 98,
    194–98; redlining and, 183, 187,
    199. *See also* banks; real estate
    industry
Moses, Bob, 9, 339, 340, 349
Moving to Opportunity (MTO), 125,
    126, 127, 128, 129, 135, 143, 156,
    157, 160, 170, 236, 237. *See also*
    housing; Housing and Urban
    Development, US Department of
Moynihan, Daniel, 252
Mt. Laurel, 222
Mt. Zion Methodist Church (Neshoba
    County, Mississippi), 9, 10, 11, 12,
    14
municipal services. *See* public services
Murray, Charles, 34
Muslims, 354
Myakka City, Florida, 16
Myrdal, Gunnar, 140

NAACP, 12, 41, 42, 280, 339
NAACP Legal Defense and
    Educational Fund, 215
*NAACP v. American Family Mutual
    Insurance Company*, 183
The Nation, 7
National African American Insurance
    Association, 187
National Assessment of Educational
    Progress, 261, 266, 313
National Association of Insurance
    Commissioners, 185
National Association of Latino Elected
    and Appointed Officials Education
    Fund, 351, 352

National Center for Employee
    Ownership, 102
National Committee on Pay Equity,
    380
National Community Reinvestment
    Coalition, 183, 188
National Council of La Raza, 353
National Fair Housing Alliance, 185
National Institutes of Health, 305
National Insurance Task Force of the
    Neighborhood Reinvestment
    Corporation, 187
National Korean American Service and
    Education Consortium, 353
National Low Income Housing
    Coalition, 380
National Research Council, 58, 274
National Urban League Institute for
    Opportunity and Equality, 90
National Voting Rights Institute, 27
National Youth Advocacy Coalition,
    388, 393
Nationwide (insurance company), 185
Native Americans, 15, 18, 49, 72, 73–
    74, 77, 304, 327, 385, 389, 392. *See
    also* American Indians
Naturalization Act (1790), 3, 200
The Nature of Prejudice (Allport), 231
Navy, US, 10
Nazis, 39, 44, 45, 47, 148. *See also*
    American Nazi Party
Neal, Derek, 259
Nebraska, 17, 342
*Negro Family: The Case for National
    Action, The*, 252
neighborhoods, 122–24, 125, 127, 128,
    131, 132–33, 134, 135, 141, 144,
    152, 153, 156, 158, 159, 168–72,
    180, 185, 190, 191, 208, 209, 220,
    230, 262, 285, 314, 316. *See also*
    housing
Neshoba County, Mississippi, 9, 10,
    11, 12, 14
Netherlands, 67
Nevada, 352
New Americans Vote '04, 354
New Deal, 100, 138, 153, 176

A New Era: Revitalizing Special Education for Children and Their Families, 273

New Hampshire, 42, 274

New Jersey, 25, 181, 222, 229, 274, 352

New Market, Iowa, 17

New Mexico, 73, 352

New Orleans, Louisiana, 84, 124, 367, 375

New York City, 9, 15, 25, 26, 33, 125, 128, 135, 145, 170, 297, 315, 354, 367, 382, 388

New York Immigration Coalition (NYIC), 354

New York State, 25, 27, 28, 112, 113, 274, 341, 352, 354

New York Times, 33, 98, 103, 108, 145, 197, 233, 250, 310

New York University, 106

New York Yankees, 297

Newark, New Jersey, 345

Newhouse News Service, 25

Ney, Robert, 195

Nickel and Dimed in America (Ehrenreich), 97, 189

Nightingale, Florence, 130

NIMBY. *See* Not In My Back Yard

Nisqually Indians, 41

Nixon, Richard M., 11, 59, 138, 148

No Child Left Behind Act (NCLB), 211, 244, 256, 258, 260, 261, 264, 288

Noguera, Pedro, 266, 267, 268

North Carolina, 21, 22, 23, 72, 162, 195

North Carolina A&T State University, 197

North Dakota, 114

North Platte, Nebraska, 16

Northern California Citizenship Project (NCCP), 353, 354

Northwestern University, 125

Norton, Eleanor Holmes, 346, 347, 361

Norway, 101

Not In My Back Yard (NIMBY), 159, 285

O'Connor, Sandra Day, 8, 204, 210, 229

Oak Park, Illinois, 18

Oakland, California, 33, 84, 86

obesity, 124, 127, 128, 135, 242, 254, 307–10, 318, 376, 377. *See also* health

Obey, David, 358

Office for Civil Rights (OCR), US Department of Education, 253

Office of Equity and Access, 280

Ogletree, Charles J. Jr., 204

Ohio, 17, 95, 113, 114, 195

Oklahoma, 17, 72, 83

Okolona, Mississippi, 206

Oliver, Melvin, 98, 107, 229, 230

One Florida, 280

One Voice, One Vote, 354

Operation Frontline, 379

Opportunity-Based Housing, 154

Oregon City, Oregon, 16

Orfield, Gary, 178, 218, 223, 225, 237, 238, 239, 233

Organization for Security and Cooperation in Europe (OSCE), 359, 360

Organization of American States (OAS), 359

Orshansky, Mollie, 57

The Other America (Harrington), 97

overweight. *See* obesity

Oxford, Ohio, 9

Paine, Thomas, 98

Palast, Greg, 344

Palestine, 45

Palm Beach, Florida, 280, 344

Pana, Illinois, 16

Paral, Rob, 351

Paris Reparations Conference, 45

Partnership for Immigrant Leadership and Action (PILA), 353, 354

Passel, Jeffrey, 352

Paterson, New Jersey, 212

Paugam, Serge, 60

Pennsylvania, 95, 284, 341, 352, 369

Peterson, Paul, 259

Pettit, Kathryn, 178

Pew Hispanic Center, 195, 352

Philadelphia, Mississippi, 9–14, 38, 297

Philadelphia, Pennsylvania, 27, 359
Physicians for Human Rights, 305
Piché, Dianne M., 266, 267
Pinckneyville, Illinois, 16
Pinehurst, North Carolina, 23
Piney Woods, Mississippi, 283
Pioneer Fund, 34
Pittman, Karen, 382, 383
Plessy v. Ferguson, xii, 228, 235, 236, 263
Poland, 340
Policy Matters Ohio, 114
Polikoff, Alexander, 150, 151, 152, 153, 154, 155, 156, 157, 159, 160, 162, 168, 172
Political Science Quarterly, 343
Popkin, Susan, 170
Population Research and Policy Review, 170
Portland, Oregon, 212
Poverty & Race Research Action Council (PRRAC), xv, 173, 179
poverty, xv, 57, 61, 63, 64, 71–78, 79–81, 111–15, 117, 374, 389
Poverty & Race, xv, 38, 168, 265
poverty line, 57, 58, 67, 83, 106, 170, 219, 373, 374, 377
Powell, Colin, 101
powell, john, 161, 166, 167, 239, 240
Powell, Lewis, 228
"Power and Potential: The Growing Electoral Clout of New Citizens" (Paral), 351
predatory lending. *See* mortgages, predatory lending
President's Commission on Excellence in Special Education, 273
President's Commission to Strengthen Social Security, 91
Presidential Advisory Commission on Holocaust-Era Assets in the United States, 43
Price, Cecil, 10
Princeton University, 39
Prison Policy Initiative, 27
prisons, 17, 25–28, 36, 139, 149, 275, 276. *See also* crime
Prisoners of the Census project, 27

Project on Human Development in Chicago Neighborhoods, 133
Proposition 187 (California), 353
Proposition 200 (Arizona), 353
Proscio, Tony, 147
Public Agenda, 216, 219, 220
Public Housing Administration, US (PHA), 174, 175
public housing, 80, 125, 128, 134, 135, 154, 163, 173, 175, 176, 180, 195, 215, 236
public services, 21, 23, 66, 122, 147, 332
Puerto Rico, 332, 347, 348

Quakers, 16
Quillian, Lincoln, 170, 171

race, xv, 49–54; achievement and, 241–68; attitudes on, 169, 172, 204, 213; colorblindness and, 8, 224, 297; corporations and, 364; economic development and, 111–15; inequality and, 137–49; preferences and, 3, 203, 205; quotas, 53; riots and, 16, 39, 367; welfare and, 205; youth and, 381–86
Race in the Mind of America (Wachtel), 150, 151
RACE—The Power of an Illusion (California Newsreel), 49, 199
Race to Incarcerate (Mauer), 275
"Racial Inequality in Special Education" (Harvard Civil Rights Project), 275
racism, xv, xvi 15–19, 41, 148, 238, 248; eugenics and, 34; and white supremacy, 30, 34, 223–24, 227, 228, 229, 230, 232, 363; restrictive covenants and, 17. *See also* discrimination; ghettos; Jim Crow; Ku Klux Klan; lynching
Radical Equations (Moses, Cobb), 339
Radical Republicans, 364, 365
Raspberry, William, 206
Ravenna, Kentucky, 16
Rawlston, Valerie, 90, 91
Ray, 42
Reagan Democrats, 219

Reagan, Ronald, 11, 14, 34, 38, 138, 139, 140, 345
real estate industry, 175
Reconstruction. *See* Civil War
redlining. *See* mortgages, redlining; insurance, redlining
Rehnquist, William, 340
rents, regulation of, 271
reparations, 38–42, 43–48, 320–30
Republican National Committee, 345
Republican Party, 153, 233, 342, 343, 345, 346
Republicans, xii, 11, 16, 42, 100, 157, 161, 340
Residents Rights Act, 19
Responsible Wealth Project, 105
retirement plans, 4, 91
Retsinas, Nicholas, 187
revitalization. *See* housing, revitalization
Reynolds v. Sims, 340
Rhode Island, 298
Rice, Jennifer King, 263
Richardson v. Ramirez, 349
Risley, Todd, 246, 247
Roanoke, Virginia, 226
Roediger, David, 37
Rolling Stones, 297
Ronald Reagan National Airport, 358
Roosevelt, Franklin D., 69, 90, 138, 148
Rothstein, Richard, 250, 251, 252, 253, 254, 255, 256, 257, 258, 259, 260, 261, 262, 264
Rowan, Carl, 141
Rowntree, B. Seebohm, 57
rural areas, 71–78, 190, 195
Rusk, David, 147, 164
Russia, 101
Ruth, Tamar, 266, 267
Ryan, Caitlin, 388

safety net, 109, 265
Sager, Alan, 325
Salem, Oregon, 16
San Diego, California, 285
San Francisco, California, 84, 240, 297, 323, 354, 359

San Mateo v. Southern Pacific Railroad, 365–66, 367
San Pasqual Academy, 285
Sanders, William, 263
Sanderson, Silas W., 366
Santa Clara County v. Southern Pacific Railroad, 367
Santa Fe, New Mexico, 84
SAT, 5
Sauve v. Canada, 348, 349
Savannah, Georgia, 96
Scalia, Antonin, 218, 232, 342
Schervish, Paul, 108
Schools Uniting Neighborhoods (Portland/Multnomah County, Oregon), 291
Schwarzenegger, Arnold, 34
Schwerner, Michael, 9, 10, 11, 13, 14, 38
Scotland School for Veterans' Children (Pennsylvania), 284
Second Harvest, 378
Section 8, 8, 80, 126, 127, 134, 135, 159, 170, 222, 268. *See also* housing; Housing and Urban Development, US Department of; public housing
segregation: residential, 20, 133, 134; "separate but equal," 235; schools and, 173; United Nations and, 181; zoning and, 180
Sen, Amartya, 229
Senate, US, 38, 42, 181. *See also* Congress, US; House of Representatives, US
Senge, Peter, 295
Sentencing Project, 348
sexual orientation, 385, 386. *See also* gays and lesbians
Shapiro, Thomas, 98, 107, 192, 229, 230
Share Our Strength, 379
Shaw, Theodore, 238
Shelby, Richard, 30
Sheridan, Arkansas, 17
Sherman, William Tecumseh, 96
Shields, David, 380
Shimmelman, Wendy, 355
Simon, Mark, 268

slave labor, 46, 47, 48
slavery, xiv, 3, 7, 34, 36, 38, 39, 41, 43,
    44, 49, 96, 109, 142, 144, 145, 157,
    165, 203, 204, 235, 296, 297, 320,
    321, 325, 327, 330, 341, 364, 365,
    369
Slemrod, Joel, 108
Small Business Administration, US, 54,
    112
Smith, Christopher, 360
Snow, Catherine, 32, 33
social exclusion, 57–70, 62
Social Policy Research Associates, 385
Social Security, xiv, 89–92, 161, 162
Socialism and Democracy, 29
Soros, George, 153
South Africa, 42, 324, 340, 342
South America, 49
South Bronx, New York City, 147
South Carolina, 113, 341
Southern strategy, 11
Soviet Union, 148, 181
Spain, 99
Springfield, Illinois, 367
Spruce Pine, North Carolina, 16
St. Genevieve, Missouri, 16
St. Louis, Missouri, 262
Standard Oil, 367
Stanfield, John, 222
Stanford University, 33
Stanton, Edwin M., 96
Staples, Brent, 145, 146
State Farm (insurance company), 185
State, US Department of, 359
states' rights, 11, 38
Statistics on Income and Living
    Conditions (SILC), 58
*A Stone of Hope: Prophetic Religion
    and the Death of Jim Crow*
    (Chappell), 182
Straying from Good Intentions (Good
    Jobs First), 113
suburbs, 16, 18, 19, 80, 113, 114, 115,
    134, 143, 146, 147, 176, 180, 182,
    190, 200, 221, 222, 224, 228, 239,
    266, 276, 385
Sun Reporter, 106
sundown towns, 11, 15–19

Supplemental Security
    Income/Disability Income, 95
Supreme Court, Canada, 348, 349
Supreme Court, Connecticut, 239
Supreme Court, Florida, 343, 345
Supreme Court, New Jersey, 229, 230
Supreme Court, US, xi, 4, 5, 7, 8, 11,
    40, 145, 157, 178, 179, 180, 182,
    203, 215, 218, 222, 230, 231, 235,
    237, 340, 343, 345, 346, 350, 362,
    363, 365, 366, 367, 368
Supreme Court, Washington State, 41
Swann, Bob, 190
Swiss Bank Corporation (SBC), 47

Takoma Park, Maryland, 354
Taney, Roger, 228
Tanton, John, 34
tax increment financing (TIF), 113
Tax Policy Center, 108
taxes: estate, 103–10; income, 94, 99;
    income enhancement programs and,
    94; poverty line and, 58;
    progressive, xiv, 99; property, 19,
    114; redistribution of wealth and,
    97; state, 94; tax increment
    financing and, 114
Taylor, John, 188
Temporary Assistance for Needy
    Families (TANF), 68, 69, 89
Tennessee, 17, 42
Texaco, 248
Texas, 27, 42, 72, 76, 343, 348, 352,
    378
Themba-Nixon, Makani, 238, 239
Third Reich, 39, 44
Thomas B. Fordham Foundation, 211
Thomas, Clarence, 218, 231
Thompson, Tommy, 305, 306
Thurmond, Strom, 341
Till, Emmett, 13
Title I, 261, 262, 263, 264, 266, 294
Tocqueville, Alexis de, 137, 141, 149,
    153
Tokyo, Japan, 297
Tonry, Michael, 139
Torres, Gerald, 154
Tougaloo College, 11, 12

transportation, 23, 67, 68, 71, 105, 112, 113, 115, 122, 171, 223, 246, 270, 271, 322
Treasury, US Department of the, 196
Trenton, New Jersey, 345
Truman, Harry, 138, 148
Tulane University, 12
Tulsa, Oklahoma, 39
Turner, Margery, 168, 169, 171

unemployment, 53, 54, 59, 63, 65, 68, 74, 77, 79, 80, 113, 197, 288, 382. *See also* employment; jobs
unions, 16, 36, 62, 83, 84, 86, 87, 94,, 264, 265, 266. *See also* labor
Unitarians, 16
United for a Fair Economy, 105
United Kingdom, 63. *See also* Great Britain
United Nations, 62, 181, 348
United Way, 292
University of California-Los Angeles, 221
University of Illinois, 325
University of Kansas, 246, 247
University of Michigan, 4, 5, 6, 7, 8, 157
University of Minnesota, 391, 392
University of North Carolina, 90
University of Pennsylvania, 290
Unz, Ron, 32, 33
Urban Institute, 125, 126, 135, 178, 352
Urban Justice Center, 393
Urban Renewal Administration, US (URA), 174
US English (organization), 34–35
Utah, 114, 359

Venkatesh, Sudhir, 165, 166, 169
Vermont, 26
Veterans Administration, US,, 176
Veterans Affairs, US Department of, 95
Vienna, Austria, 39
Vienna, Illinois, 16
Vietnam War, 42, 358
violence, 123, 124, 126, 170, 381, 392, 393
Virgin Islands, US, 347

Virginia, 40, 76, 114, 348, 369
Volker, Dale, 25, 26
voter registration, 9, 12, 95, 339, 353, 354
voting, annexation and, 21; anti-immigrant legislation and, 353; Census and, 26; disenfranchisement and, 27, 340, 344; districts and, 28; Electoral College and, 341, 342, 343, 344; gender and, 341; gerrymandering and, 343; language and, 29; non-citizen and, 354, 355; wealth and, 341
Voting Rights Act (1965), xii, 19, 22, 340, 342
voting rights, 65, 340, 342; disenfranchisement and, 345, 346, 348, 349, 357, 358, 359; District of Columbia and, 347, 359; Electoral College and, 358; Equal Protection Clause and, 347; immigrants and, 351–56; non-citizens and, 349; one person-one vote, 349; race and, 228, 276; registration lists and, 344
Voting Technology Project (CalTech and MIT), 345
vouchers, 80, 125, 127, 128, 134, 141, 142, 143, 144, 145, 148, 154, 156, 157, 158, 159, 160, 164, 165, 171, 216, 219, 222, 239, 259

Wachtel, Paul, 166, 167, 172
Wake County (Raleigh), North Carolina, 218, 219
Wall Street Journal, 233
Wallace, George, 19, 148, 341
WalMart, 86
War on Drugs, 139
War on Poverty, 251, 253
Warren, Earl, 340
Warren, Michigan, 16, 86
Washington College (Chestertown, MD), 41
Washington Post, 103
Washington State, 41, 73, 352
Washington v. Davis, 179
Washington Wizards, 297

Washington, DC, 12, 27, 95, 132, 139, 161, 162, 239, 274, 297, 315. *See also* District of Columbia
Washington, George, 341
Watkins, Frank, xvi
Wausau, Wisconsin, 221, 239
wealth, 96–102, 183, 185, 190, 195, 197; disparities in, 97, 103, 104, 105, 243, 254, 255, 257; education and, 105, 280; homeownership and, 195–96; inherited, 107, 192, 193; race and, 131, 192–93, 194, 195, 199; slavery and, 362, transportation and, 105; voting and, 228, 341. *See also* income inequality
Weaver, Robert, 173, 174, 175, 176, 177
Wehrum, Pennsylvania, 16
welfare, 67, 114, 139, 140, 163, 260, 271, 272, 282, 285, 286, 382, 388, 393–94, 395
West Philadelphia Improvement Corps, 290
West Virginia, 72
whites, 3, 4, 5, 6, 8, 9, 10, 12, 16, 17, 19, 23, 35, 52, 53, 222; attitudes of, 30, 151, 152, 154, 166, 176, 204, 218, 223–24; corporations and, 362–68; education and, 207, 216, 274, 275; employment and, 37, 52, 53, 54, 107; health and, 123, 309, 375; housing and, 22, 131, 144, 165, 177, 199; insurance and, 186; IQ tests and, 274; language and, 37; non-Hispanic, 77, 78; poverty and, 72, 74, 76, 106, 170, 374; prisons and, 26, 27, 275; privilege and, 226, 227, 230; reparations and, 321; vouchers and, 142; wealth and, 109, 195, 196

Why NOT In My Back Yard (Galster), 159
Williams, David, 130
Wilson, "Squab," 17
Wilson, William Julius, 146, 150, 204
Winston, Judith, 181
Wisconsin, 16, 17, 162, 187, 297
Without Sanctuary: Lynching Photography in America (Allen), 42
Wogaman, J. Philip, 39
Wolfensohn, James, 62
Wolff, Edward, 107, 109
women, 4, 52, 53, 63, 72, 75, 112, 124, 165, 170, 196, 254, 309, 312, 329, 332, 368, 369, 370, 380, 384, 391, 392. *See also* gender
Women, Infants and Children (WIC) Program, 374, 379
Woodstock Institute, 112
Work Force Innovation Boards, 280
Workforce Improvement Act, 69
World Jewish Congress (WJC), 45, 46
World War I, 44, 298, 355
World War II, 9, 36, 43, 44, 47, 62, 138, 145, 297, 298
Wresinski, Joseph, 59
Wright, Bruce M., 39
Wyoming, 42, 348

Yamamoto, Eric, 320
Yes In My Backyard (Huling), 27
Youth Leadership for Development Initiative (YLDI), 385–86
Ypsilanti, Michigan, 86

Zanesville, Ohio, 23
zoning, 17, 20, 22–23, 62, 134, 140, 179, 180, 191, 221, 368. *See also* inclusionary zoning